D0499143

SPIRITUAL AND
ANABAPTIST WRITERS

THE LIBRARY OF CHRISTIAN CLASSICS

ICHTHUS EDITION

SPIRITUAL AND ANABAPTIST WRITERS

Documents Illustrative of the Radical Reformation

Edited by
GEORGE HUNTSTON WILLIAMS., A.B., B.D., Th.D., D.D.
Winn Professor of Ecclesiastical History
The Divinity School, Harvard University
Cambridge, Massachusetts

and

Evangelical Catholicism as represented by Juan de Valdés

Edited by
ANGEL M. MERGAL, A.B., B.D., Th.D.
Professor of Theology, Evangelical Seminary of Puerto Rico
Rio Piedras, Puerto Rico

PHILADELPHIA
THE WESTMINSTER PRESS

Published simultaneously in Great Britain and the United States of America
by the S.C.M. Press, Ltd., London, and The Westminster Press, Philadelphia.

First published MCMLVII

Library of Congress Catalog Card No. : 57-5003

9 8 7 6 5 4 3 2 1

Typeset in Great Britain
Printed in the United States of America

GENERAL EDITORS' PREFACE

The Christian Church possesses in its literature an abundant and incomparable treasure. But it is an inheritance that must be reclaimed by each generation. THE LIBRARY OF CHRISTIAN CLASSICS is designed to present in the English language, and in twenty-six volumes of convenient size, a selection of the most indispensable Christian treatises written prior to the end of the sixteenth century.

The practice of giving circulation to writings selected for superior worth or special interest was adopted at the beginning of Christian history. The canonical Scriptures were themselves a selection from a much wider literature. In the Patristic era there began to appear a class of works of compilation (often designed for ready reference in controversy) of the opinions of well-reputed predecessors, and in the Middle Ages many such works were produced. These medieval anthologies actually preserve some noteworthy materials from works otherwise lost.

In modern times, with the increasing inability even of those trained in universities and theological colleges to read Latin and Greek texts with ease and familiarity, the translation of selected portions of earlier Christian literature into modern languages has become more necessary than ever; while the wide range of distinguished books written in vernaculars such as English makes selection there also needful. The efforts that have been made to meet this need are too numerous to be noted here, but none of these collections serves the purpose of the reader who desires a library of representative treatises spanning the Christian centuries as a whole. Most of them embrace only the age of the Church Fathers, and some of them have long been out of print. A fresh translation of a work already

9

translated may shed much new light upon its meaning. This is true even of Bible translations despite the work of many experts through the centuries. In some instances old translations have been adopted in this series, but wherever necessary or desirable, new ones have been made. Notes have been supplied where these were needed to explain the author's meaning. The introductions provided for the several treatises and extracts will, we believe, furnish welcome guidance.

JOHN BAILLIE
JOHN T. McNEILL
HENRY P. VAN DUSEN

CONTENTS

* The first part translated by Selina Gerhard Schultz.
† Translated by Christiaan Theodoor Lievestro.

PART TWO

EVANGELICAL CATHOLICISM AS REPRESENTED BY JUAN DE VALDÉS

ABBREVIATIONS

MQR . *Mennonite Quarterly Review*
BRN . *Bibliotheca Reformatoria Neerlandica*
WA . Weimar Ausgabe, Luther's works
CS . *Corpus Schwenckfeldianorum*
PL . *Patrologia Latina*
GQR . *Goshen College Quarterly Record*

PREFACE

This volume comprises a group of sixteenth-century writings once cherished and influential in fairly wide circles and intrinsically of no slight importance, but little known to modern readers. The editors of THE LIBRARY OF CHRISTIAN CLASSICS are confident that in both parts of the volume the selection has been carefully made and that the texts significantly represent the far more extensive body of material by Spiritual and Anabaptist writers from which they are drawn.

We are glad to have been able to enlist the scholarly services of Professor Williams and Professor Mergal, the former to explore the literature of the Radical Reformation in Northern Europe, and the latter to present an impressive selection from the work of the most important among the Spanish "reformers" of this period, Juan de Valdés. A considerable number of the documents included by Dr. Williams, revealing and arresting as they are, have hitherto been read in the English-speaking world by only a handful of scholars and have escaped notice even in the more copious histories of the Reformation. We believe that the presentation of these texts to the many readers of this Library not only will help materially to give a sound understanding of what has often been called "the left wing of the Reformation," but also will produce fresh insights into the meaning of Christianity itself.

JOHN T. McNEILL
HENRY P. VAN DUSEN

PART ONE

DOCUMENTS ILLUSTRATIVE OF THE RADICAL REFORMATION

Introduction

FROM ALL SIDES WE ARE COMING TO RECOGNIZE in the Radical Reformation a major expression of the religious movement of the sixteenth century. It is one that is as distinctive as Lutheranism, Calvinism, and Anglicanism, and is perhaps comparably significant in the rise of modern Christianity.

In assembling a collection of documents representative of this "Fourth" Reformation, the present editor had to decide, in the allotment of space, between the temptation to prepare the audience with an ample introduction and the claims of the dissidents to be heard directly. The only fully satisfactory intro-duction would be a fresh account of the history of that aspect of the Reformation Era into which the sometimes obscure and disparate figures selected for this volume would plausibly fit.[1]

1 The best general histories in English of the whole or of important segments of the Radical Reformation are the following: For the Anabaptists: Albert H. Newman, *A History of Anti-Pedobaptism to A.D. 1609* (Philadelphia, 1897); C. H. Smith, *The Story of the Mennonites*, re-edited by Cornelius Krahn (3d ed., Newton, Kans., 1950); John Horsch, *The Mennonites in Europe* (rev. ed., Scottdale, Pa., 1950); Franklin Littell's stress on one aspect of the movement is so comprehensive that it may serve as an intro-duction, *The Anabaptist View of the Church* (2d ed., Boston, Mass., 1956). Geographically circumscribed but still general are H. S. Burrage, *History of the Anabaptists in Switzerland* (Philadelphia, 1881); H. E. Dosker, *The Dutch Anabaptists* (Philadelphia, 1921); and for Moravian Anabaptism, John Horsch, *The Hutterian Brethren, 1528–1931* (Goshen, Ind., 1931). For the Spiritualists there is no comprehensive survey. The nearest to it is Rufus Jones, *Spiritual Reformers in the Sixteenth and Seventeenth Centuries* (London and New York, 1914), some Anabaptists as well as Spiritualists included. For the Evangelical Rationalists or Anti-Trinitarians: Earl M. Wilbur, *Socinianism and Its Antecedents* (Cambridge, Mass., 1945).

19

But that would be too extensive an undertaking. In its place is a sketch of the scholarly effort to evaluate and classify the diverse radical groupings of the Continental sixteenth century and to justify their inclusion in the same volume.

Common to all participants in the Radical Reformation were disappointment in the moral aspects of territorial Protestantism, as articulated by Luther and Zwingli, and forthright disavowal of several of its doctrines and institutions. Among the dissidents in the Radical Reformation there are three main groupings: the Anabaptists proper, the Spiritualists, and the Evangelical Rationalists.

Three communities among today's denominations can claim direct or indirect descent from them. The first community, made up of the Mennonites, the Amish, and the communitarian Hutterites (and quite indirectly the Baptists), goes back to the Anabaptists. The Schwenckfelder Church, with headquarters in Pennsylvania, stems directly from the Silesian followers of Caspar Schwenckfeld, perhaps the most original Spiritualist and certainly the most prolific in literary endeavor. A third community, the Unitarians, may lay claim in part to the heritage of the Evangelical Rationalists.

The vast theological distances which often separate members of these denominations today should alert the reader to expect great diversity of viewpoints in the following pages. In the upheaval of the sixteenth century, however, these currents had only begun to diverge. Their ultimate tendencies could not be so readily detected by the participants themselves as by us who look back upon their age.

For all three groupings of dissidents, John T. McNeill and Roland Bainton, among others, have given currency to the comprehensive designation "the left wing of the Reformation."[2] Inchoately, the left wing was a veritable banyan tree, to use the vivid image of Rufus Jones. Roots and branches, parent stock and offshoots, are difficult to distinguish. Certain Anabaptists, for example, were anti-Trinitarian in theology (Louis Haetzer, Adam Pastor). The Polish Brethren, the historic core of the later anti-Trinitarian Socinians, held to adult baptism; yet

---

2 See, for example, McNeill's subdivision "Left-Wing Religious Movements" in his contribution to *A Short History of Christianity*, ed. by Archibald G. Baker (Chicago, 1940), p. 127, and Bainton's "The Left Wing of the Reformation," *Journal of Religion*, XXI (1941), 127. Recent efforts to classify the left wing are reviewed by Robert Friedmann, *Church History*, XXIV (1955), pp. 132–151.

many of the earliest leaders and converts among the Anabaptists, like John Denck and John Bünderlin, came to have more in common with the universalism of the *later* Socinians than with the particularism of the Anabaptists.[3] Further, between Anabaptists and Spiritualists there was a good deal of common ground and mutual interaction before the positions had become fully clarified, for both experienced the driving of the Spirit.

Common to certain writers in all three groupings were a distinctive Christology (the celestial flesh of Christ) and a correspondingly mystical-physical view of the Lord's Supper. This position was taken, for example, by the "anti-Trinitarian" Michael Servetus, the Spiritualist Caspar Schwenckfeld, and the Anabaptist Dietrich Philips. Also common to all of the left wing was their espousal of the freedom of the will in the striving for sanctification.

But most characteristic was their common resistance to the linking together of church and state, a relationship which the Reformation espoused in principle and the Counter Reformation acquiesced in for reasons of expediency. It is pre-eminently the opposition of the dissenters to the *magisterial* Reformation of Protestantism and, in due course, the *papal* Counter Reformation, which has earned for these often disparate groups the designation "left wing." They would not tolerate the trespassing of pope, town council, prince, or king upon the rights of the loyal subjects of the King of Kings.

Although it is obviously useful to have an over-all term, the phrase "left wing" is not wholly felicitous. It gives prominence, to be sure, to the religio-political principle shared by almost all. Nevertheless, the term is dependent upon the political parlance of recent parliamentary history, during which the separation of the church from the state has been a "leftist" impulse only in contrast to "rightist" clericalism. Actually, the concern to separate the realms of church and state could be considered

---

[3] On the differentiation between Anabaptists and Rationalists, see Robert Friedmann, "The Encounter of Anabaptists and Mennonites with Anti-Trinitarianism" (a critique of Wilbur's thesis), *MQR*, XXII (1948), pp. 139 ff., and Robert Kreider, "Anabaptism and Humanism," *ibid.*, XXVI (1952), pp. 123 ff. H. Richard Niebuhr makes an important contribution to the typology of the left wing in distinguishing a "unitarianism" of the Father, a unitarianism of the Son (Christomonism; possibly Schwenckfeld, certainly Swedenborg), and the unitarianism of the Spirit. "The Doctrine of the Trinity and the Unity of the Church," *Theology Today*, III (1946), 371.

with equal propriety "conservative" or "legitimist," since, for nearly three hundred years of its most crucial development, the church was in conflict with the Roman Empire. Moreover, within the so-called left wing not all parties and persons held to a strict separation of the church from temporal concerns. Balthasar Hubmaier, for example, rejoiced in the protection accorded his group by the princes of Moravia, while among the fully communistic Anabaptists of Moravia (the Hutterites) the church and the community were in effect indistinguishable as the godly *Gemeinde*. Further, the goal of the Spiritualist revolution of Thomas Müntzer and the revolutionary theocracy of the Münsterite Anabaptists was a Biblical commonwealth in which a regenerated church and godly state were effectually one.

As an alternative over-all designation for the three subsidiary groupings of dissent in the sixteenth century, I have preferred "the Radical Reformation." Though Anabaptists, Spiritualists, and Evangelical Rationalists differed among themselves as to what constituted the root of faith and order and the ultimate source of divine authority among them (the New Testament, the Spirit, reason), all three groupings within the Radical Reformation agreed in cutting back to that root and in freeing church and creed of what they regarded as the suffocating growth of ecclesiastical tradition and magisterial prerogative. Precisely this makes theirs a "Radical Reformation."

It is useful to observe that the established and protected churches, both Protestant and Catholic, were, so to speak, churches of the exigent *present*, and therefore disposed to compromise and accommodation out of a basically conservative social concern to prevent any radical dissociation of citizenship (in civil society) and membership (in the church of the masses). The proponents of the Radical Reformation, having been inspired by the Protestant Reformers to look back to the church of the apostolic past, yearned to restore it unambiguously in their midst. Accordingly, most of them early abandoned any hope of a fully Christian society coterminous with political boundaries, except it be the Church of the End of Time coterminous with the frontiers of the Kingdom established on earth.

Within this Radical Reformation there were, nevertheless, two subsidiary impulses which help to mark off the Anabaptists from the Spiritualists. The former looked steadily into the *past*, finding their own image and ecclesiastical blueprints in the Bible and the martyr church of antiquity. The Spiritualists gazed mostly into the *future*. Convinced that the true church was not yet re-established in their midst, either they sought revolutionary relief in their impatience or, suspending all human effort, they solaced themselves with the fellowship of the invisible church of the Spirit, while quiescently awaiting God's action.

Thus the Anabaptists organized disciplined communities of believers, stressing at once individual faith and witness (adult baptism) and corporate discipline (the ban); and they adhered pacifistically to the authority of Holy Scripture, pre-eminently the New Testament. Only the turbulent Anabaptists of Münster, combining the plans of the Old Testament Jerusalem with the blueprints of the heavenly Jerusalem of the book of Revelation, resorted to force in setting up their polygamous theocracy. The Spiritualists, in contrast both to the Evangelical Anabaptists and to the revolutionary Münsterites, were utterly individualistic and quietistic except in one instance. The exception was the quite distinctive revolutionary Spiritualism of the Müntzerites in their totalitarian egalitarian zeal. (Like the Münsterites they drew upon both the New and the Old Testament for inspiration.)

The third subdivision of the Radical Reformation, the Evangelical Rationalists, represents the spirit of reform as it first found expression pre-eminently in Romance lands. Many of them remained within the church of their fathers. Evangelical Catholics,[4] like Erasmus and particularly Lefèvres and Juan de Valdés (to whom a third of this volume is devoted), nevertheless had much in common with that small band of free spirits who broke from the Roman Church on principle, namely, Michael Servetus, Bernardino Ochino, Sebastian Castellio, George Biandrata, and Faustus Socinus. Common to almost all of these, whether they remained within the Catholic Church as did the Evangelical Catholics or withdrew from both the papal and the Protestant territorial churches to form separatist conventicles, was the general recognition of the place of natural piety and of both intuitive and speculative reason alongside

---

[4] Eva Maria Jung, "Evangelismo," *Enciclopedia Cattolica*, V (Vatican City, 1950), col. 886. Gerhard Ritter reflects tentatively on the relationship of the Catholic Evangelicals and the Anti-Trinitarians in "Wegbahner eines 'aufgeklärten' Christentums in 16. Jh.," *Archiv für Reformationsgeschichte*, XXXVII (1940), 268–89; and for the medieval scholastic antecedents of Anti-Trinitarianism, see the important contribution of Roland Bainton in *Autour de Michel Servet*, ed. by B. Becker (Haarlem, 1953).

that of Scriptures. Where this emphasis found full theological and institutional expression outside of Catholicism, as in the Unitarianism of Transylvania and the Socinianism of Poland, it may be said to constitute a distinct subtype of the Radical Reformation. These Evangelical Rationalists, who broke with both the Protestant and Catholic Churches, for the most part shared with the Anabaptists the urge to create disciplined congregations on the New Testament pattern; at the same time they shared with some of the Spiritualists the urge to carry through the Reformation impulse in the realm of theology as well as in polity and the sacraments; and eventually the programmatic abandonment of the doctrine of the Trinity became their distinguishing mark. Subsequent church historians group them together as anti-Trinitarian, from Servetus to Socinus. A representative collection of documents illustrative of this whole movement is a desideratum.[5]

Evangelical Rationalism, which is not represented in this volume (except for Juan de Valdés), has been touched upon in the foregoing paragraph merely by way of defining the two other radical groupings whose writings constitute two thirds of our volume, the Anabaptists and the Spiritualists.

The Radical Reformation (Evangelical Rationalist, Spiritualist, and Anabaptist) was ruthlessly suppressed alike by Protestant and Catholic magistrates. It is an anomaly of Western history in modern times that the lands in which dissent first found heroic expression muzzled it so swiftly and brutally that only its echo was to be heard thereafter in the interiorized and socially often quite conservative form of Pietism.

In England, in contrast, where two phases of the religious Reformation were, so to speak, spaced a century apart—the national Reformation in the sixteenth century and the socio-constitutional re-formation in the seventeenth—the voices of dissent were able to make a permanent contribution to the pluralistic character of society. Perhaps this was because unlike the freewill Anabaptists of the Continental Reformation, the Regular (Calvinistic) Baptists and the other parties of the left in the English seventeenth-century turmoil (Civil War, Commonwealth, Restoration, and Revolution) never abandoned an interest in the state. Though they fought for the principle of the separation of church and state, they were nevertheless articulately concerned for the strengthening of the latter

[5] The anti-Trinitarian Evangelical Rationalists are, however, represented in the bibliography below.

no less than for the purification of the former. And they were thus able to participate directly in the formation of our modern open, responsible democracy in a way which was never vouchsafed to the still more heroic and ethically resolute Anabaptists of sixteenth-century Germany.

From the point of view of classical Protestantism and its modern restatements the Radical Reformation (particularly Anabaptism) has seemed theologically and culturally impoverished. But the whole Western world, not only the direct descendants of the Continental Anabaptists, not alone even the larger Protestant community, but all who cherish Western institutions and freedoms, must acknowledge their indebtedness to the valor and the vision of the Anabaptists who glimpsed afresh the disparities between the church and the world, even when the latter construed itself as Christian.

The Radical Reformation broke on principle with the Catholic–Protestant *corpus christianum* and stressed the *corpus Christi* of committed believers. Moreover, in looking both to the apostolic past and the apocalyptic future, the Radical Reformation induced currents in history and the interpretation thereof which pulsate today in diverse conceptions of history ranging from explicitly Christian theologies of history, through democratic progressivism, to Marxism.

The problem of God's controversy with his ongoing Israel and the recurrent re-formation of righteous remnants thereof is being raised anew in our time. Our once-packed white-steepled meetinghouses in rural New England and the once-thronged cathedrals in old England are but remnants among the cherished monuments of a Christendom or *corpus christianum* now fragmented by the inexorable forces of modern history. Thus many may be prompted or inspired in perusing the acts and accounts which survive from the heroic period of self-disciplined conventicles and pilgrim fellowships under the headship of Christ, to participate in some neo-radical reformation in the area of ethics and social practice and perhaps also in the area of the theology of history and the theological undergirding of democratic political pluralism. In this way the recovery of some of the ethical impulses of the Radical Reformation may serve to supplement the neo-orthodox repossession of the theological insights of classical Protestantism.

So much for the general significance of the Radical Reformation as a whole. Henceforth we shall be limited to the Anabaptists and the Spiritualists.

It will be useful at this point to trace the main stages by which contemporary scholarship has come to agree on the distinction between the Anabaptists and the Spiritualists. Then we can go on to characterize the main types in each grouping in reference to the illustrative documents selected for this volume.

Certainly the Anabaptists are no longer regarded as the step-children of the Reformation[6] by those who are informed on the most recent revisions of sixteenth-century history. Indeed, many Christians outside the two historic churches stemming directly from sixteenth-century Anabaptism (the Mennonites and Hutterites) have come to recognize in the Anabaptist tractarians and martyrs their own spiritual ancestors or at least distant kin, who fought for principles which most Protestants today, especially in the English-speaking world, consider distinctively "Protestant." Yet the major Protestant Reformers and their associates were the bitterest foes and persecutors of the Anabaptists; and Protestant scholars and polemicists, beginning with Martin Luther, Ulrich Zwingli, Philip Melanchthon, John Calvin, and Henry Bullinger, drew and redrew a composite portrait of them as fanatics and revolutionaries. Except for Mennonite circles, the consequence was that up until the nineteenth century "Anabaptist" was synonymous with "Münsterite" or "Müntzerite," i.e., seditious, polygamous, licentious, tyrannical.

An important step in the re-evaluation of the Anabaptists was the work of the Catholic scholar C. A. Cornelius. He assembled and reworked the surviving documents bearing on the history of the Münsterite theocracy.[7] Thereupon the Münster archivist and director of the Comenius Society, Ludwig Keller, sought to give further historical documentation to the claim, which had grown up within the Mennonite community itself and been fostered by the influential seventeenth-century compilation known as the *Martyrs' Mirror*, that a remnant of faithful Christians had continuously survived down through the Middle Ages of whom the sixteenth-century Anabaptists were the heirs.[8] Keller took from the *Mirror* the designation "Old Evangelical" and sought to establish a succession from the Waldensians, the Hussites, and the artisans of the masonic sodalities to the Anabaptists. He found in Luther's teacher,

---

6 The term is that of J. Lindeboom, *Stiefkinderen van het Christendom* (The Hague, 1929).
7 *Die Geschichte des Münsterischen Aufruhrs* (Münster, 1855).
8 *Die Reformation und die älteren Reformparteien* (Leipzig, 1885).

Staupitz, a connecting link between the free spirits of the Middle Ages and modern times. Albrecht Ritschl similarly sought to establish a continuity between the pietists of the late Middle Ages and those of the modern era, stressing the Spiritual Franciscans as forerunners of the Anabaptists.[9] Presently the Tübingen church historian, Alfred Hegler, made a major contribution by singling out the seeker Sebastian Franck as a representative "Spiritualist" distinct from the Sectarians.[10] Shortly thereafter, Sectarianism was sociologically defined by the economist Max Weber in an article on his impressions of organized religion in the United States in 1909.[11] For the first time a distinction was drawn between a sect and a church in terms of the voluntarist and moral criteria of the American scene as distinguished from the religio-political criteria by which the state church was distinguished from the sect in Europe.

With the fresh understanding of the inner nature of a true sect derived from Weber and with Hegler's clarification of the difference between a Sectarian and a Spiritualist (or "mystic"), the Heidelberg sociologist of religion, Ernst Troeltsch, worked out his tripartite scheme in which the Spiritualists are a third distinct type, co-ordinate with the sect type (our Anabaptists) and the church type.[12] In his rehabilitation of the Sectarians, Troeltsch went so far as to regard them as the forerunners of the modern world; and upon his socioreligious typology he based his influential periodization of history, in which the Reformation Era with its lingering sense of a *corpus christianum* is considered much closer to the medieval than to the modern era.[13] Troeltsch placed the beginnings of Anabaptism in Zurich.

Against Troeltsch, both Karl Holl and Heinrich Boehmer and their students revised and vigorously restated the Old Protestant thesis, linking Anabaptism with the fanaticism of Thomas

[9] *Geschichte des Pietismus* (Bonn, 1880), I, 22–36.
[10] *Geist und Schrift bei Sebastian Franck: Eine Studie zur Geschichte des Spiritualismus in der Reformationszeit* (Freiburg i.B., 1892) and posthumously *Beiträge zur Geschichte der Mystik in der Reformationszeit* (Berlin, 1906).
[11] "'Kirchen' und 'Sekten' in Nord Amerika," *Die Christliche Welt*, XX (1906), coll. 558; 578; reprinted in *Gesammelte Aßsätze*, I (Tübingen, 1922).
[12] First enunciated in "Protestantisches Christentum und Kirche in der Neuzeit," *Kultur der Gegenwart*, I, iv (1906), pp. 253–458, and elaborated in *Die Soziallehren der christlichen Kirchen und Gruppen* (Tübingen, 1912); English translation (New York, 1931), I, esp. p. 378.
[13] *Die Bedeutung des Protestantismus für die Entstehung der modernen Welt* (Munich/Berlin, 1911).

Müntzer and the Zwickau prophets.[14] But the work of Troeltsch was already encouraging a new generation of Mennonite and other scholars to "excavate" extensively in the environs of Zurich. By locating the origin of Evangelical Anabaptism in the Zwinglian reformation, they sought to vindicate the fully Protestant and Biblically *pacifist* character of their movement. Around John Horsch[15] and his son-in-law, Harold Bender, has grown up a whole generation of younger American Mennonite scholars whom they have trained and encouraged. Among most of them there is a tendency in their scholarly revision of the history of the Radical Reformation to dissociate Evangelical Anabaptism from the other movements at a point earlier in the development than the sixteenth-century Anabaptists themselves were able to do.

The most recent literature and the earlier but specialized studies will be cited at appropriate places in the notes on the selections.

It is to a classification and further characterization of the subtypes of Anabaptism and of Spiritualism that we now turn.

The yeasty ferment of dissent leavened a great mass of diverse sorts and conditions of men before it was separated, worked, and molded into different forms. The editor of the Selections from the writings of the Anabaptists and the Spiritualists has found it useful to distinguish within Anabaptism itself three main subdivisions and within Spiritualism three roughly corresponding variants.

Besides the *evangelical* Anabaptists, who of late have received the most attention especially from Mennonite scholars, there are

14 The literature is discussed in connection with Thomas Müntzer, Selection II, note 1.

15 John Horsch, *The Mennonites*; see also the memorial and bibliography, *MQR*, XXI (1947), 131–232; Harold Bender, *Conrad Grebel: The Founder of the Swiss Brethren* (Goshen, Ind., 1950), also his detailed refutation of the Old Protestant view in "The Zwickau Prophets, Thomas Müntzer, and the Anabaptists," *MQR*, XXVII (1953), 3. A mediating position between Zurich and Wittenberg is taken by two non-Mennonite Swiss scholars, Walther Köhler and Leonhard von Muralt. See, for example, Köhler's "Die Züricher Täufer," *Gedenkschrift zum 400 jährigen Jubiläum der Taufgesinnten oder Mennoniten* (1525–1925), edited by Christian Neff (Karlsruhe, 1925), and von Muralt's "Zum Problem: Reformation und Täufertum," *Zwingliana*, VI (1924), 65 ff., wherein he is at pains to correct what he regards as the one-sidedness of Horsch's position; and see also his theologically discerning *Glaube und Lehre der Schweizerischen Wiedertäufer* (Zurich, 1938).

the *revolutionary* and the *contemplative* Anabaptists. And just as the Spiritualists and the Anabaptists as a whole have certain traits in common with the whole of the Radical Reformation (including the Evangelical Rationalists) and are yet profoundly different, so within Anabaptism itself the three foregoing groupings have much in common but they also display several major differences. We shall first characterize the three variants of Anabaptism with special reference to representatives whose writings are included in this volume.

Revolutionary Anabaptists. All Anabaptists stressed the recovery or restoration of the church of the past (as the Spiritualists tended to stress the church of the future), but the Revolutionary Anabaptists regarded the Old Testament as well as the New Testament church as normative for the theology and especially the constitution of that church. In fact, they had gone so far in conceiving the church as God's Israel that when they came to extend the sway of the New Commonwealth (*Gemeinde*) in Münster, Amsterdam, and elsewhere, they found themselves drawing more and more upon the Old Testament in the regulation of their fierce and eventually polygamous theocracy. In this volume they are not directly represented. Instead, an observer from the Netherlands, Obbe Philips, describes them (Selection X). At the time he wrote his piece Obbe Philips had completely dissociated himself from Dutch and North German Anabaptism, including its first prophet, Melchior Hofmann. The latter, a seminal spirit in the transfer of Anabaptism from the Upper to the Lower Rhine, is represented by an excited tractate on baptism (Selection IX). Hofmann interprets the Old Testament, including its apocrypha, as containing the types of the institutions of the New Covenantal Church of the Spirit. But when his thinking was applied in Münster, his allegorization of the law thickened once again into the law of a regenerated and regulated remnant engaged in the rebuilding of a Jerusalem in Westphalia. The Revolutionary Anabaptists of Münster and Amsterdam might also be called "charismatic" (Rudolf Sohm) Anabaptists in that Spirit possession made up the visible credentials of their leaders, beginning with Hofmann. Hofmann himself was not an overt revolutionary. They have also been called "chiliastic" or "Maccabean" (Franklin Littell) Anabaptists in allusion to their "utopian" (Karl Mannheim) pretensions to forcing the establishment of the millennial Kingdom.

Contemplative Anabaptists. Farthest removed from the Revolutionary Anabaptists and closest to some of the Spiritualists were the Contemplative Anabaptists, represented in this volume by John Denck (Selection IV). Louis Haetzer and Adam Pastor, not included in the collection, might also be classified here. John Denck had contacts with all trends within the Radical Reformation. Although he could be regarded from within and from without Anabaptism as one of its major spokesmen and leaders, it is clear from a close examination of all his writings and the conduct of his life that he had essentially another spirit from that of the main body of Evangelical Anabaptists over whom he presided for a season in South Germany. While he followed the example of the historic Jesus in submitting to (re)baptism as an adult, administered the rite to fresh converts, and accepted Jesus' instructions concerning the ban, he felt most deeply the claim of the inner Christ. He identified this inward Christ with the inner Word common to all mankind wherever, as though a spark blown upon by the Spirit, it bursts into the flame of conscience.

Evangelical Anabaptists. Certain traits noted in the Revolutionary Anabaptists are found also among the Evangelical Anabaptists. This is much less the case among the Swiss Brethren than among the Obbenites, who were the immediate forerunners of the Dutch and Low German Mennonites. The distinguishing marks, however, of the Evangelicals among the Anabaptists were the following: For them, only the New Testament was normative for doctrine, ethics, and polity. The Old Testament and its apocrypha were interpreted allegorically or typically. Consequently they held that, for them, the ban had replaced the sword. Their great stress on the ban and on shunning (spiritual avoidance of the banned) distinguished them not only from the Spiritualists but also from the more contemplative and humanistic Anabaptists (above). They were or soon became distrustful of Spirit possession and the vagaries of prophecy. The historic Jesus—his specific instructions, his life, and his crucifixion—was for them normative. They understood that the imitation of Christ, from hazardous rebaptism at some Germanic Jordan to a martyr's pyre, represented the fullness of the Christian Way. As Christ began his public ministry at baptism, so many Evangelical Anabaptists felt compelled to imitate him in an *itinerant* ministry of proclaiming the gospel of repentance. They understood that faith in Christ meant the fulfilling of his express commandments in every particular, that Christian faith meant the progressive sanctification of every aspect of a simplified life, and that love of God meant love of the brethren not only at the Supper but also in every human relationship. Among the Hutterite Anabaptists of Moravia this communitarian impulse developed into a highly disciplined communism of production as well as of consumption. Church and community became one. The gospel became a new law. Conjoined with a discipleship which could easily harden into legalism was their indisposition to fall into the intellectualism of producing systematic theologies.

Ulrich Stadler (Selection XIII) has been selected to speak in this volume for the Hutterite form of Evangelical Anabaptism. Balthasar Hubmaier (supplying for our collection a treatise on free will, Selection V) represents a connecting link between Swiss and Moravian Anabaptism. Of all the Evangelical Anabaptists, he happens to come closest to the spokesmen of magisterial Protestantism in his recognition of the validity of the sword for Christians. George Blaurock (Selection I) and Conrad Grebel (Selection III) speak in the collection for Swiss Evangelical Anabaptism. In the trial and martyrdom of Michael Sattler (Selection VI) we overhear the voice of an Anabaptist in whom the Swiss and South German movements are joined, for he was the formulator of the seven famous Schleitheim articles of faith of 1527. These articles more succinctly than any other document sum up the distinctive convictions of Evangelical Anabaptism. The Dutch and Lower German movement is represented in the collection by Dietrich Philips (Selection XI) and Menno Simons (Selection XII). From the latter, of course, the main body of the direct descendants of sixteenth-century Evangelical Anabaptists today take their name as Mennonites, be they in Holland, Germany, Switzerland, or America.

We turn now to the three roughly analogous variants of Spiritualism represented in this volume, namely, the *revolutionary*, the *evangelical*, and the *rational* Spiritualists. For all of them spirit was central in their life and thought, as the driving spirit, as the enlightening spirit, or as the rational spirit. These Spiritualists, like Christians generally, knew that the spirits had to be tested, but they were always confident that the source of their particular authority was none other than the Holy Spirit. Moreover, they felt that the Holy Spirit as the inspiration of Holy Scripture, of the prophets of old, and of the present day, and also as the cohesive power of the Christian fellowship, was superior to any historic record of the work of the Holy

Spirit, be it the Bible (or any part thereof, like the New
Testament) or the church (or any institution thereof, like the
clergy).

Revolutionary Spiritualism. In Revolutionary, or charismatic,
Spiritualism, the Spirit is experienced as a driving power. The
Zwickau prophets (Luther's *"Schwärmer"*), Andreas Bodenstein
von Carlstadt and Thomas Müntzer, were Spiritualists of this
type. They drew upon the prophets (especially Daniel) and the
book of Revelation. Among them the Spirit defined the Word,
rather than the Eternal Word as recorded in Scripture (or
tradition) defining and interpreting the Spirit, as in their
contemporaries, the Protestant Reformers.

It is still undetermined whether or not genetically Thomas
Müntzer (Selection II) stands at the point where the two major
trends in the Radical Reformation (Spiritualism and Anabaptism) become differentiated. He was not technically an
"Anabaptist," for he repudiated infant baptism as meaningless
without moving on to adult baptism. And this is because he was
a Spiritualist, holding to the primacy of inward baptism in the
specialized sense of meaningful suffering. Yet this theology of
suffering, of the cross, of the "bitter Christ," connects him very
closely with Evangelical Anabaptists, whom on this point he
doubtless influenced. But the prophetic and apocalyptic sources
of his inspiration brought him in the end to identify the Kingdom of God with a theocratic order to be established after the
defeat of the "ungodly"; and this trait surely brings him closer
to the Revolutionary Anabaptists of Münster. Yet again,
literalist though he could be as at once a prophetic forthteller
and a foreteller in his always socially relevant exegesis of the Old
Testament, he construed the Bible not as the source of faith but
only as the guide to and the confirmation of the personal
experience of the compulsive Spirit. In this he was close to the
position of the Contemplative Anabaptists, like John Denck,
whom he indeed avowedly influenced. Moreover, like such an
Evangelical Spiritualist as Caspar Schwenckfeld, Müntzer
virtually assimilated one to the other: the Spirit which speaks to
man through a living prophet, the inner Christ, the pre-
existent Christ, the Word of God, the gospel of Christ, the
Scriptures and even the law. Unlike the Evangelical Anabaptists of Swiss origin, Thomas Müntzer clearly displays
medieval dependencies, notably in his appeal to the mystics
(Tauler, Suso, *Theologia Germanica*), to the Taborites (Hussites),
and to Pseudo-Joachim of Flora. Although Thomas Müntzer

was a convert to Lutheranism for a season and tried to maintain contact with Luther as long as possible (to be sure, with the hope of inducing the Wittenbergers to follow his more radical lead), in the end he enunciated a system of redemption which replaced Luther's doctrine of *sola fide* with a doctrine of the experienced cross, "the bitter Christ." If Luther, Zwingli, and Calvin were "twice-born" Christians in their experience of justification on the boundary between the law of the Creator and the love of the Redeemer, Thomas Müntzer and his kind were in a sense thrice-born Christians in moving to the "sanctification" of society under the sway of the third Person of the Trinity (identified, however, with the pre-existent Christ of the Old Testament). Significantly, Müntzer's Spiritualism, with its concern to sanctify, assigned an important role to a vernacular liturgy.

Rational Spiritualism. Rational or speculative Spiritualism, grounded more in the *spiritus* of man than in the *Spiritus sanctus*, emphasizes the universal aspects of Christianity and may go on to a contemplation of the order of nature. For example, in Paracelsus (1493–1541), the physician, alchemist, and natural theologian, and in Valentine Weigel (1533–1588), the Lutheran pastor of Zschopau who confided his deepest musings to works published only after his death, this speculative Spiritualism allegorizes the Bible into a cosmic philosophy, mystically contemplates the celestial flesh of Christ, and delights in the correspondences between the microcosm and the macrocosm. In Sebastian Franck, Rational Spiritualism stresses the seminal reason or Logos common to all mankind as revealed in history and in contemporary societies, which he studied comparatively. Rational Spiritualism tends to dissolve ecclesiastical institutions from within and allegorizes the doctrines and even the practices of apostolic Christianity, since the true church of the Rational Spiritualists is a fellowship of kindred spirits in all ages who, like them, have come to hold that behind the changing nomenclature of theology is a common piety and a common vision of the divine.

Sebastian Franck has been chosen to represent them in this volume. Selection VII is one of the earliest and best-rounded accounts of the radical Spiritualist conception of the church in the Reformation Era, and is therefore important for the present-day effort to work out an ecclesiological typology.

The Rational Spiritualists of the sixteenth century are the kin, though of course not the spiritual ancestors, of the nineteenth-century New England Transcendentalists. Being a philosophy of religion more than a way of life, and a way of life far more than an organization of it, Rational Spiritualism has, on its own, no community-creating impulse, and passes from *church* history into general intellectual history the moment its position is completely clarified.

Evangelical Spiritualism. Evangelical Spiritualism is a recurrent phenomenon, nurtured Biblically by the Johannine Gospel and Epistles. At times it comes very close to Rational Spiritualism, but it is more mystical than speculative. It is based on grace as understood in the Bible and has the strength to create fellowships, even if not disciplined sects or massive churches. It is not primarily an intellectual movement; it stresses piety.[16] From the point of view of the contemporary church, Evangelical Spiritualism is the most important of the three kinds of Spiritualism we have distinguished. Of it, in our period, Caspar Schwenckfeld (Selection VIII) and the former Hutterite Gabriel Ascherham may be taken as the most adequate spokesmen.

Schwenckfeld came to regard his position as at once the Middle Way between Catholicism and Lutheranism; and, within Protestantism, especially on the doctrine and practice of the Lord's Supper, he thought of himself as one working out a middle way between Lutheranism and Zwinglianism, and he even sought to be heard on this matter at the Marburg Colloquy. But he also stood at a point midway between the Anabaptists and the Spiritualists. Like the Evangelical Anabaptists he was a New Testament Christian, although he was Johannine rather than Matthaean. He consorted with the Anabaptists and debated with them. He (like Weigel) shared with them the doctrine of the celestial flesh of Christ, a teaching which not only supplied the ultimate theological basis for their doctrine of the sanctity of the self-disciplined church as the body of Christ but also undergirded their theory of the Lord's Supper.

Schwenckfeld's formative religious experience was conceived in the terms and imagery of the sacrament of the altar, just as Luther's saving experience of justification by faith was a transfiguration of the language and categories of the sacrament of penance, and just as the redemptive experience of the Anabaptists was, at its core, a reappropriation of the sacrament of baptism through adult conversion and witness (and, as such, a

16 In the late seventeenth and the eighteenth centuries the impulse is known as Pietism. This term could have served as the generic designation but for its specialized meaning.

fresh and more meaningful equivalent of the long-abused sacrament of penance). Schwenckfeld's doctrine of the Lord's Supper was much more Catholic, at least in being partly Augustinian, than that of the Anabaptists; and unlike Luther he would not admit to "the bread of the Lord" those who had not experienced "the bread which is the Lord."

Evangelical Spiritualism is clearly based upon the Holy Spirit as experienced and defined in patristic and medieval Christianity. Here the Holy Spirit is felt more as a "fluid" and force than as person. A physico-realist sense of deification through the restorative and healing ministry of the Spirit is characteristic. Sanctification in the sense of perfectionism is the goal and achievement of the Christian life according to the Evangelical Spiritualists, who nevertheless acknowledge the divine initiative in the process.

In a word, Evangelical Spiritualism is by nature individual-istic, while the establishment of a holy commonwealth is often the goal of Revolutionary Spiritualism, which draws upon the visions of corporate salvation of the prophets (especially David) and the Seer of Revelation. An irenic philosophy of religion, the ordering of the disparate elements of religion in an intellectual pattern, is the goal and achievement of Rational Spiritualism. Rational and Evangelical Spiritualism are tolerant and accommodative by reason of their individualism, whereas Revolutionary Spiritualism is righteously indignant in its collectivist intolerance as it pushes forward to a disciplined, theocratic community.

The following Selections are arranged roughly in chrono-logical order, but the sequence of ideas has also entered into the arrangement. It is therefore possible to read consecutively and, with the help of the two-page special introductions, to gain a comprehensive picture of the Radical Reformation.

One of the features of this collection is the bibliography of all the primary works of the Radical Reformation available in English translation. Since much of the sixteenth-century source material is difficult to read even for those who use the modern German and Dutch freely, and is in any case difficult to get at in rare imprints or scholarly serials, the bibliography will be of some use to all students of the Reformation Era. It was with this bibliography in mind as an integral part of this volume that the documents have been selected for inclusion. In general, while seeking to print representative works illustrative of the whole range of Anabaptism and Spiritualism, duplication of the more readily procurable works already translated has been avoided.

This principle of selection will go far to explain what at first sight might appear to be a defect in this volume, namely, the fact that several leaders after whom the remnants of the Radical Reformation are today named are either absent from or poorly represented in the volume: Faustus Socinus, Caspar Schwenckfeld, Menno Simons, and Jacob Hutter. But, of course, we have already indicated that to the Socinians as indeed to the whole company of non-Catholic Evangelical Rationalists a separate anthology should be devoted. Schwenckfeld, who gives his name to the Schwenckfelder Church, is represented by only three portions of a single incidental work against Luther. It is to be regretted that of the sixteen large volumes of the *Corpus Schwenckfeldianorum*, by far the greater part of which is the work of Caspar Schwenckfeld himself, only this sample is offered. But the reader will be pleased to find in the bibliography a rather extensive listing of his works separately available in English. Menno Simons is represented only by an excerpt on the ban. In contrast, Dietrich Philips, a secondary leader of Dutch Mennonitism, is allowed to speak more fully. As it happens, the complete works of each are available in English translation, though difficult to procure. In the decision to favor Dietrich the primary consideration was the expectation that Menno's works would be presently appearing from the Mennonite Publishing House in a new translation by Dr. Leonard Verduin. It remains to explain the absence of Jacob Hutter, whose name is borne by the communitarian Hutterites. The Hutterite epistles are currently being critically edited by Robert Friedmann, and it seemed wise to await the publication of this partly new source material and to allow an avowedly lesser spokesman (Ulrich Stadler), writing exclusively on the doctrine and practice for which they are renowned, to represent the Hutterite community. (Students confined to English will find the recently translated comprehensive *Account* [1565; London, 1950] of Peter Riedemann the best introduction to Hutterite Anabaptist thought and practice as a whole.)

The collection, translation, and interpretation of the following Selections would not have been possible except for the encouragement and direct aid of many friends and new acquaintances.

First I wish to acknowledge my great indebtedness to Dr. Franklin Littell, who put his extensive library of *Anabaptistica* and related documents at my disposal before he left Boston University to take up his duties in Bad Godesberg. Dean Harold Bender of Goshen College has been an adviser from the beginning of this enterprise, and although he may have some reservations about my final selections, I wish publicly to salute him as a mentor, scholar, and churchman. It was a moving experience to sit in the library in Goshen, presided over by Mr. Nelson P. Springer, to see around me volumes and pamphlets, some of them scarred by the same persecutions that made martyrs and confessors of their authors and former owners, and to behold them reassembled after the centuries, side by side, in the best collection of early *Anabaptistica* in the New World, a monument of the scholarship of John Horsch and Harold Bender.

Similarly, I am indebted to Mrs. Selina Gerhard Schultz, an editor of the *Corpus Schwenckfeldianorum* and author of a major biography of Caspar Schwenckfeld, for the counsel she has given me. She has been an indefatigable translator and interpreter of the great Silesian Spiritualist. The first part of Selection VIII is her translation.

To Mr. Christiaan Theodoor Lievestro, Harvard candidate for the Ph.D. in Dutch political and social thought, the volume as a whole owes much for his translation of Selection X, which supplies the collection with its principal narrative material.

I wish also to thank the following, in some cases for their sage counsel in the field, in other cases for specialized assistance in the translation, in other cases for the loan of volumes, microfilms, and MSS.: Professor Roland Bainton of Yale Divinity School; Dr. Leonard Verduin of Ann Arbor, Michigan; Dr. Cornelius Krahn of the Bethel College Historical Library of North Newton, Kansas; Professor Roger Nicole of Gordon Theological School, Beverly Farms, Massachusetts; the late Dr. Earl Morse Wilbur of the Pacific Unitarian School for the Ministry, Berkeley, California; Mrs. Charlotte Blaschke of George School, Pennsylvania; Dr. Leon T. Crismon, Librarian of the Southern Baptist Theological Seminary, Louisville, Kentucky; Dr. Theodore Trost, Librarian of the Colgate Rochester Divinity School, Rochester, New York, for the extended use of the Vedder transcripts of the Hubmaier writings; Dr. Edward C. Starr, Curator of the Colgate Baptist Historical Library, Rochester, New York, for the use of that valuable collection including the Hosek transcripts; Dr. Frederic Weis of Peterborough, New Hampshire; Mrs. Marion Doyle and Holley M. Shepherd of the Andover-Harvard Library; Dr. Arnold Weinberger of Houghton Library; Pastor Walter Fellmann of Kreis Heidelberg for a critical text of John Denck; the Reverend Gerald Studer of Smithfield, Ohio; my colleagues John Dillenberger and Ralph Lazzaro of Harvard; and, again, and especially my closest collaborators, Mrs. Schultz, Mr. Lievestro, and my two loyal Teaching Fellows, James Vendettuoli, Jr., and the Rev. Rudolph Nemser of Harvard Divinity School. At two important places in the galleys I benefited much from the counsel and resources of Professor James Luther Adams now of Harvard Divinity School, Dr. Walter Grossmann of Widener Library, and Professor Robert B. Hannen of the Sandford Fleming Library of the Berkeley Baptist Divinity School. I wish also to thank the editors of the *Mennonite Encyclopedia* for the privilege of consulting the galleys and typescripts of the forthcoming volumes of this massive and scholarly project.

I

The Beginnings of the Anabaptist Reformation
Reminiscences of George Blaurock

AN EXCERPT FROM THE HUTTERITE
CHRONICLE
1525

INTRODUCTION

THE FOLLOWING DOCUMENT IS AN EXCERPT FROM the Hutterite *Chronicle* begun by Caspar Braitmichel. Looking back upon the heroic age of Anabaptism, the Hutterite Chronicler of Moravia was disposed to conceive of this renewal of the Apostolic Church as an episode in the long history of God's recurrent sifting of a righteous remnant. The search for continuities and a spiritual lineage had begun, in contrast to the temper of most of the restorationists themselves in the first phase of the radical reform.[1] The *Chronicle* briefly traces the history of the people of God through the Old Testament and as a righteous remnant within or alongside of the ancient and medieval church. It mentions, among others, Wyclif, Hus, and a number of Hussites, and then Luther's challenge of 1517 and Zwingli's of 1519. The *Chronicle* then proceeds to give what must be a transcript of George Blaurock's reminiscences of the first years of radical evangelicalism in Zurich and environs. The excerpt, though short, is worthy of inclusion (*a*) because it mirrors the Anabaptist view of church history as a whole and, as such, serves as a counterpart of the Spiritualist image of church history given elsewhere in this volume (that of Sebastian Franck, Selection VII, and that of Obbe Philips, Selection X); (*b*) because it gives a brief account of several of the persons prominent in this volume and clearly indicates the interrelatedness of the Swiss Brethren, as the originators, and of the Mennonites in Holland and of the Hutterites in Moravia, as their successors, in the unfolding of a pan-Germanic movement of radical dissent; (*c*) because it

[1] The most recent study of the Anabaptist view of church history is that of Frank J. Wray, Yale Ph.D. dissertation under Roland Bainton, 1954.

preserves an account of the first rebaptism (Blaurock's) and the first martyrdom of a "Protestant" (Felix Mantz) at the hands of Protestants; and (d) because it samples a major document of the Reformation Era which has been uniquely preserved in manuscript on American soil among the Hutterite community of the Dakotas and Western Canada. It should be added that this particular sample has not the fullness of detail that we find in the later narratives and transcripts of letters embodied in the more distinctively Hutterite portion of the *Chronicle*. The selection at this point is not, indeed, so yielding in facts as the *Martyrs' Mirror*, the comparable work produced by the Dutch Mennonites and from which we have taken Selection VI (the martyrdom of Michael Sattler), an episode common to both narratives. Nevertheless, it represents the pertinent section of the oldest Anabaptist history of the beginnings of the Radical Reformation.

The Beginnings of the Anabaptist Reformation
Reminiscences of George Blaurock[2]

AN EXCERPT FROM THE HUTTERITE CHRONICLE[3] 1525

THE TEXT

... Luther, with his following, teaches and holds that the body of the Lord Jesus Christ is essentially in the bread of the Supper [which] therewith is also a [means] of forgiving sins. Zwingli and his, however, taught and held that it [the Supper] is a recollection and a commemoration of the salvation and grace of Christ and not a sacrifice for sin, since Christ accomplished that on the cross. But both of them were pedobaptists and let go of the true baptism of Christ, who most certainly brings the cross with him, followed instead the pope with infant baptism, retained of him also the old leaven, the ferment, and cause of all evil, in fact the access and portal into a false Christianity, however much they otherwise eliminated him. But the pope did not derive infant baptism from Holy Scripture

---

[2] George Blaurock (d. 1529) was the first Anabaptist, having been the first of the Swiss Brethren to submit to rebaptism. As Anabaptist missionary and martyr in the Tyrol, he is, with Balthasar Hubmaier, a major link in the chain that connects Swiss Evangelical Anabaptism and Hutterite communitarian Anabaptism in Moravia.

[3] The *Chronicle* was begun by the *Vorsteher* of the Hutterite community, Caspar Braitmichel, who carried it up to 1542. Others added to it. Often cited in Hutterite literature, it had long been thought lost. It was recovered for scholarship among the most cherished possessions of the Hutterite colony at Bon Homme in South Dakota. It was thereupon published under their auspices by Rudolf Wolkan (Macleod, Alberta and Vienna, 1923). A philologically orientated, diplomatic edition with glossary was published by A. J. F. Ziegelschmid, *Die älteste Chronik der Hutterischen Brüder* (Philadelphia: Carl Schurz Memorial Foundation, 1943). It was from this text that the present translation was made, and the numbers bracketed in the translation refer to the pagination in this edition.

any more than purgatory, the Mass, prayer to the saints, letters of indulgence, and all the rest.

Luther and Zwingli defended with the sword this false teaching [pedobaptism] which [readiness] they really learned from the father and head of Antichrist, well knowing that the weapons of the Christian knight are not carnal but are nevertheless mighty before God in withstanding all human blows. Faith is not like that, a matter of coercion, but rather a gift of God. And Christ speaks to his disciples [Matt. 16:24]: If anyone will follow me—notice, if anyone wishes or has a desire—let him deny himself and take his cross upon him. He does not say the sword, for this has no place beside the cross. They stand together like Christ and Pilate; they are to be compared to each other as a wolf and a sheep in the same fold.

[45] BUT BECAUSE GOD WISHED TO HAVE HIS OWN PEOPLE,[4] separated from all peoples, he willed for this purpose to bring in the right true morning star of his truth to shine in fullness in the final age of this world, especially in the German nation and lands, the same to strike home with his Word and to reveal the ground of divine truth. In order that his holy work might be made known and revealed before everyman, there developed first in Switzerland an extraordinary awakening and preparation by God as follows:

It came to pass that Ulrich Zwingli and Conrad Grebel,[5] one of the aristocracy, and Felix Mantz,[6]—all three much experienced and men learned in the German, Latin, Greek, and also the Hebrew, languages—came together and began to talk through matters of belief among themselves and recognized that infant baptism is unnecessary and recognized further that it is in fact no baptism. Two, however, Conrad and Felix, recognized in the Lord [46] and believed [further] that one must and should be correctly baptized according to the Christian ordinance and institution of the Lord, since Christ himself says that whoever *believes* and is baptized will be saved. Ulrich

---

4 Here begins a major section in this *Chronicle* of the church of God. The preceding section ending with the failure of the Zwinglian and Lutheran Reformation had begun with the birth of Christ. The *Chronicle* before Christ is similar to that of Dietrich Philips in *The Church of God* (Selection XI).

5 On Grebel, see further, p. 71.

6 Felix Mantz was the son of a canon of the Zurich minster. Well trained in Hebrew, he had been marked out by Zwingli for teacher of Hebrew in the projected evangelical academy. Mantz addressed to the Zurich magistracy his eloquent *Petition of Protest and Defense* in December, 1524.

Zwingli, who shuddered before Christ's cross, shame, and persecution, did not wish this and asserted that an uprising would break out.[7] The other two, however, Conrad and Felix, declared that God's clear commandment and institution could not for that reason be allowed to lapse.

At this point it came to pass that a person from Chur came to them, namely, a cleric named George of the House of Jacob,[8] commonly called "Bluecoat" (*Blaurock*) because one time when they were having a discussion of matters of belief in a meeting this George Cajacob presented his view also. Then someone asked who it was who had just spoken. Thereupon someone answered: The person in the blue coat spoke. Thus thereafter he got the name of Blaurock. . . . This George came, moreover, with the unusual zeal which he had, a straightforward, simple parson. As such he was held by everyone. But in matters of faith and in divine zeal, which had been given him out of God's grace, he acted wonderfully and valiantly in the cause of truth. He first came to Zwingli and discussed matters of belief with him at length, but accomplished nothing. Then he was told that there were other men more zealous than Zwingli. These men he inquired for diligently and found them, namely, Conrad Grebel and Felix Mantz. With them he spoke and talked through matters of faith. They came to one mind in these things, and in the pure fear of God they recognized that a person must learn from the divine Word and preaching a true faith which manifests itself in love, and receive [47] the true Christian baptism on the basis of the recognized and confessed faith, in the union with God of a good conscience, [prepared] henceforth to serve God in a holy Christian life with all godliness, also to be steadfast to the end in tribulation. And it came to pass that they were together[9] until fear (*angst*) began to come over them, yea, they were pressed (*gedrungen*) in their

---

[7] Zwingli did, indeed, in his earlier phase entertain the view here ascribed to him. For his later arguments against the position, see, for example, his *Vom Touff*, translated in part by G. W. Bromiley, The Library of Christian Classics, XXIV, 129 ff.

[8] George Cajacob is well documented in the Zurich archives.

[9] Bible discussion groups or "schools" were the forerunners of the Anabaptist conventicles or house churches. This particular meeting was in the home of Mantz, on the night of January 21, 1525. Such is the reconstruction of Fritz Blanke, "Ort und Zeit der ersten Wiedertaufe," *Theologische Zeitschrift*, VIII (1952), 74. For a vivid reconstruction of the gathering of the first Anabaptist conventicle, see, by the same scholar, "The First Anabaptist Congregation," *MQR*, XXVII (1953), 17.

hearts. Thereupon, they began to bow their knees to the Most High God in heaven and called upon him as the Knower of hearts, implored him to enable them to do his divine will and to manifest his mercy toward them. For flesh and blood and human forwardness did not drive them, since they well knew what they would have to bear and suffer on account of it. After the prayer, George Cajacob arose and asked Conrad to baptize him, for the sake of God, with the true Christian baptism upon his faith and knowledge.[10] And when he knelt down with that request and desire, Conrad baptized him, since at that time there was no ordained deacon (*diener*)[11] to perform such work. After that was done the others similarly desired George to baptize them, which he also did upon their request. Thus they together gave themselves to the name of the Lord in the high fear of God. Each confirmed (*bestätet*) the other in the service of the gospel, and they began to teach and keep the faith.[12] Therewith began the separation from the world and its evil works.

Soon thereafter several others made their way to them, for example, Balthasar Hubmaier of Friedberg,[13] Louis Haetzer,[14] and still others [48], men well instructed in the German, Latin, Greek, and Hebrew languages, very well versed in

10 Another account of this first rebaptism is preserved in the Zurich archives. The Anabaptist material has been most recently edited and calendared by Leonhard von Muralt and W. Schmid, *Quellen zur Geschichte der Täufer in der Schweiz* (Zurich, 1952), Nos. 29–33. Here the date of the meeting is made either January 30 or February 7. January 25 had been commonly accepted hitherto.

11 The word could, of course, be translated "minister." But it is useful to bring out the fact that among the several New Testament ministries it was that of deacon or servant which was most characteristically given prominence by the Anabaptists.

12 Rebaptism in the first days of the movement was almost equivalent to ordination or commission on the analogy of Jesus whose public ministry began with his baptism at the hands of John. The apostolic succession in Anabaptism was originally a baptismal succession in water and the Spirit. Only gradually were such usages as election or recognition (*Bestätigung*) and the laying on of hands developed in a distinctive act of ordination. Significantly, within Anabaptism in contrast to the Lutheran and Zwinglian Reforms, the clerical status of recruits from the older order was never recognized; and the new commission or reordination was, in effect, the baptismal rite.

13 See below, Selection V, introduction, and Selection X at n. 4.

14 Haetzer (d. 1529) was an anti-Trinitarian Hebraist and close associate of John Denck in the Worms translation of the prophets. The most recent study is that of Gerhard Goeters, *MQR*, XX, IX (1955), 251.

Scripture, some preachers and other persons, who were soon to have testified with their blood.

The above-mentioned Felix Mantz they drowned at Zurich[15] because of this true belief and true baptism, who thus witnessed steadfastly with his body and life to this truth.

Afterward Wolfgang Ullmann,[16] whom they burned with fire and put to death in Waltzra, also in Switzerland, himself the eleventh, his brethren and associates witnessing in a valorous and knightly manner with their bodies and their lives unto death that their faith and baptism was grounded in the divine truth. . . .

Thus did it [the movement] spread through persecution and much tribulation. The church (gmain) increased daily, and the Lord's people grew in numbers. This the enemy of the divine truth could not endure. He used Zwingli as an instrument, who thereupon began to write diligently and to preach from the pulpit that the baptism of believers and adults was not right and should not be tolerated—contrary to his own confession which he had previously written and taught [49], namely, that infant baptism cannot be demonstrated or proved with a single clear word from God. But now, since he wished rather to please men than God, he contended against the true Christian baptism. He also stirred up the magistracy to act on imperial authorization and behead as Anabaptists those who had properly given themselves to God, and with a good understanding had made covenant of a good conscience with God.

Finally[17] it reached the point that over twenty men, widows, pregnant wives, and maidens were cast miserably into dark towers, sentenced never again to see either sun or moon as long as they lived, to end their days on bread and water, and thus in the dark towers to remain together, the living and the dead, until none remained alive—there to die, to stink, and to

15 He was drowned with a stick thrust between his roped, doubled-up legs and arms, the first "Protestant" martyr at the hands of Protestants, January 25, 1527.
16 Ullmann had been a fellow monk with Blaurock and Veit in Chur. After his baptism at the hands of Grebel he became a "reader" of the advanced evangelical group in St. Gall. He went to Moravia and returned to lead other Swiss brethren to this Anabaptist asylum. On their way thither he and ten other brethren were apprehended in Swabia and beheaded, their womenfolk drowned.
17 This paragraph is taken verbatim from Balthasar Hubmaier's Gesprech with Zwingli (Nicolsburg, 1526). The same paragraph is quoted in the Martyrs' Mirror. There is another record in the Zurich archives, von Muralt, op. cit., No. 170A, dated March 7, 1526.

rot. Some among them did not eat a mouthful of bread in three days, just so that others might have to eat.

Soon also there was issued a stern mandate[18] at the instigation of Zwingli that if any more people in the canton of Zurich should be rebaptized, they should immediately, without further trial, hearing, or sentence, be cast into the water and drowned. Herein one sees which spirit's child Zwingli was, and those of his party still are.

However, since the work fostered by God cannot be changed and God's counsel lies in the power of no man, the aforementioned men went forth, through divine prompting, to proclaim and preach the evangelical word and the ground of truth. George Cajacob or Blaurock went into the county of Tyrol. In the meantime Balthasar Hubmaier came to Nicolsburg in Moravia, began to teach and preach. The people, however, accepted the teaching and many people were baptized in a short time.

[18] Actually the same date, March 7, von Muralt, *op. cit.*, No. 172.

The Justinianic law against rebaptism as a capital offense was soon to be formally revived by the Emperor Charles V at the Diet of Spires in 1529 and confirmed at the Diet of Augsburg in 1530 at a moment in Reformation history when under the leadership of Melanchthon it seemed p.udent to demonstrate as far as possible the orderliness and orthodoxy of territorial Protestantism. The capital laws against Anabaptism have been recently edited by Gustav Bossert, *Quellen zur Geschichte der Wiedertäufer*, I, Herzogtum Württenberg (Leipzig, 1930), Nos. 1–10. Although the laws were not to be directly operative in Switzerland, they were to have their effect whenever the Brethren fled from the Confederated Cantons into imperial territory.

II

Sermon Before the Princes
By Thomas Müntzer [1]

AN EXPOSITION OF THE SECOND
CHAPTER OF DANIEL
ALLSTEDT, JULY 13, 1524

INTRODUCTION

THE FOLLOWING IS ONE OF THE MOST REMARKABLE
sermons of the Reformation Era. It represents the high-
water mark of torrential Revolutionary Spiritualist
counterreformation directed against Luther. It was delivered
in the presence of Duke John (brother of Frederick the Wise,
protector of Luther), the Duke's son, and selected town and
electoral officials. Ducal father and son were divided on the
proper role of the Christian magistrate. The son sided with
Luther and the conservative interpretation of the Reform.
But the father stood under the influence of such radicals as the
preacher of the ducal residence in Weimar, Wolfgang Stein, of
Jacob Strauss of Eisenach, and of Carlstadt, soon to be identified
with radical changes in Orlamünde. All these radical preachers
were loyal to their prince but held fiercely to the view that with
the overturn of papal authority Mosaic law should obtain in

---

1 There is no adequate life of Müntzer in English. Modern scholarship is
especially indebted to Heinrich Boehmer, Karl Holl, Annemarie Lohmann,
and Carl Hinrichs. Boehmer's works are *Studien zu Thomas Müntzer* (1922);
"Thomas Müntzer und das jüngste Deutschland," 1923, reprinted in
Gesammelte Aufsätze (1927), 187–222; and with Paul Kirn as continuator
after his death, *Thomas Müntzer's Briefwechsel auf Grund der Handschriften
und ältesten Vorlagen* (1930). Holl's contribution is a clear delineation of
Schwärmertum on the basis of a careful analysis of Schwenckfeld, Franck,
and Müntzer in "Luther und die Schwärmer," *Gesammelte Aufsätze*,
I (1927), 420–67. Lohmann's contribution is her demarcation of the
distinct religious phases through which Müntzer passed to emerge as an
independent Reformer. Her *Zur geistigen Entwicklung Thomas Müntzers*
(Leipzig/Berlin, 1931) contains a brief survey of Müntzer scholarship to
date (pp. 1–3) and a bibliography (69–71). Otto H. Brandt, in *Thomas
Müntzer: Leben und Schriften* (Jena, 1933), is indebted to all three of these
interpreters for his succinct biographical and theological introduction to a

evangelical lands. Earnest about getting to the heart of the problem, curious about how things were going in Allstedt, the Duke consented to hear Müntzer in his Allstedt castle. Müntzer had had more than a week to prepare for the momentous occasion. In his sermon he clearly enunciates his conception of faith in contrast to that of Luther. Herein he declares with passion that revelation has not been stopped, that it is instead the authentic sign of the last days. He recognizes, to be sure, that there are spurious visions and false prophets. Therefore he waves before the godly princes in the congregation his credentials as a true prophet and as the priest needed by them to go before their armies. In slaying the enemies of Christ, they are permitted by God to help bring to an end the fifth monarchy, that abominable feudal intermixture of clerical and princely power which is feudalism, foreseen by Daniel in the feet and toes of the colossus to be overturned by the Stone (Christ and his saints). Here is a bold theology of history, a vigorous repudiation of Luther's radical "debiblicizing" the office of the magistrate. Here is an impassioned plea to root out the mockery of separating the sweetness from the sternness of Christ, an impulse (found, he would say, in both the Lutherans and the Evangelical Anabaptists) which renders ineffectual and unworldly the commands of Christ!

Since Müntzer had contacts with the Evangelical Anabaptists (Selection III) and had often been classed with the Revolutionary Anabaptists of Münster (described disparagingly in Selection X), it has seemed desirable to let Müntzer speak for himself at that very moment when his movement was passing over into its violent phase.

modernized edition of Müntzer's writings and allied documents, which admirably supplement Boehmer-Kirn's critical edition of the letters. Hinrichs edited the political works *Thomas Müntzer: Politische Schriften mit Kommentar*, Hallesche Monographien, 17 (Halle, 1950). He enlarged his fascinating commentary into a comparative study, *Luther und Müntzer: Ihre Auseinandersetzung über Obrigkeit und Widerstandsrecht*, Arbeiten zur Kirchengeschichte, 29 (Berlin, 1952). Two of the more important recent Marxist studies produced in East Germany are M. M. Smirin, *Die Volksreformation des Thomas Müntzer und der grosse Bauernkrieg*, translated from the Russian by Hans Nichtweiss (Berlin, 1952), and Alfred Meusel, *Thomas Müntzer und seine Zeit mit einer Auswahl der Dokumente des grossen deutschen Bauernkrieges* (Berlin, 1952). The Müntzer documents in the latter are taken from Brandt's work. Neither of these writers is prepared to give much attention to the specifically theological in Thomas Müntzer. In some cases their sociopolitical observations help round out our picture. Meusel's work is largely based on secondary studies. See also Karl Mannheim, *Ideology and Utopia* (New York, 1954), pp. 190–197.

Sermon Before the Princes
By Thomas Müntzer

AN EXPOSITION OF THE SECOND CHAPTER OF DANIEL
ALLSTEDT, JULY 13, 1524[2]

THE TEXT

Firstly. The text of the aforementioned chapter of prophecy of the prophet Daniel will be recounted[3] and translated and thereupon the whole sermon will be set forth in harmony with the text, as follows.

It is known that poor, ailing, disintegrating Christendom can be neither counseled nor aided unless the diligent, untroubled servants of God daily work through the Scriptures, singing, reading, and preaching. But therewith the head of many a pampered priest will continuously have to suffer great blows or [he will] miss out in his handiwork. But how ought one otherwise to deal with him at a time when Christendom is being so wretchedly devastated by ravenous wolves, as it is written in Isaiah (ch. 5:1–23) and in Ps. 80 (vs. 9–14)[4] concerning the vineyard of God? And Saint Paul teaches how one should exercise oneself in singing divine praises (Eph. 5:19). For just as in the times of the beloved prophets Isaiah, Jeremiah, Ezekiel, and the others, the whole congregation of the elect of God had become so utterly implicated in the way of idolatry that even God could not help them but had to let them be led away captive and punish them in the midst of the heathen to the point where they once again recognized his holy name, as it stands written (Isa. 29:17–24; Jer. 15:11; Ezek. 36:8–12; Ps.

---

[2] The full title is: *Exposition of the second chapter of Daniel the prophet preached at the Castle of Allstedt before the active and amiable dukes and administrators of Saxony by Thomas Müntzer, minister of the Word of God.*

The critical text is edited by Hinrichs, *Politische Schriften*, 1–28. From this text the present translation has been made. A modernized German version is printed by Brandt, *op cit.*, pp. 148–163.

[3] Verse by verse in the Vulgate.   [4] Ps. 79 in the Vulgate.

89: 31–38⁵) so, no less is it true in the time of our fathers and our time, that poor Christendom is even more deeply obdurate and the more so for having the unspeakable semblance of the divine name with which the devil and his servants adorn themselves (Luke 21:5; II Tim. 3:5; II Cor. 11:13–15).

[6]⁶ Yea, so nicely that the real friends of God are thereby misled; and even with the diligence of the most intense application, they are scarcely able to detect their error, as Matthew (ch. 24:24) clearly shows. This is what the simulated sanctity and the flattering absolution of the godless enemies of God accomplish. For they say the Christian church cannot err,⁷ even though, in order to protect against error, it should be continuously edified by the Word of God and held free of error.⁸ Surely [the true church] should also acknowledge sin through ignorance (Lev. 4:13 f.; Hos. 4:6; Mal. 2:1–7; Isa. 1:10–17). But that is indeed true. Christ the Son of God and his apostles and indeed, before him, his holy prophets began a real pure Christianity, having sown pure wheat in the field, that is, [they] planted the precious Word of God in the hearts of the elect as Matthew (ch. 12:24–30), Mark (ch. 4:26–29), and Luke (ch. 8:5–15) have written, and Ezekiel (ch. 36:29). But the lazy, neglectful ministers of this same church have not wished to accomplish this and maintain it by dint of diligent watchfulness; but rather they have sought their own [ends], not what was Jesus Christ's (Phil. 2:4, 21). For this reason they have allowed the harmfulness of the godless vigorously to take over, that is, the weeds (Ps. 80:9–14).⁹ For the cornerstone, here [Dan. 2:34 f., 44 f.] indicated, was still small. Of this Isaiah (ch. 28:16) [also] speaks. To be sure, it has not yet come to fill the whole world, but it will soon fill it and make it full, very full. Therefore the prepared cornerstone was in the beginning of the new Christianity rejected by the builders, that is, the rulers (Ps. 118:22 f.¹⁰ and Luke 20:17 b.). Thus I say [7] the church since its beginning has become in all places dilapidated, up to

---

5 Ps. 88 in the Vulgate.
6 The bracketed numbers refer to the pagination of Hinrichs' edition.
7 A reference to Gregory VII's *Dictatus Papae*: it held that the Roman Church cannot err.
8 Here Müntzer sets over against the authoritarian view of the historic church his own conviction as to the Gathered Church of the elect saints, ever renewed and corrected by the living Spirit and Word.
9 Ps. 79 in the Vulgate. The reference is to the weeds choking the [true] vine of Israel (= the church).
10 Ps. 117 in the Vulgate.

the present time of the "divided"[11] world (Luke 21:10; Dan. 2:35; I Esdras 4:45). For Hegesippus[12] (and Eusebius) in [*Ecclesiastical History*] IV, 22, concerning the [early] Christian church, declares that the Christian congregation did not remain a virgin any longer than up to the time of the death of the disciples of the apostles and soon thereafter became an adulteress, as had indeed already been prophesied by the beloved apostles (II Peter 2:12–15). And in the Acts of the Apostles (ch. 20:28–31a) Saint Paul said to the shepherds of the sheep in clear, translucent words: Take heed therefore unto yourselves, and to all the flock, over which the Holy Ghost hath made you overseers, to feed the church of God, which he hath purchased with his own blood. For I know this, that after my departing shall ravenous wolves enter in among you, not sparing the flock. Also of your own selves shall men arise, speaking perverse things, to draw away disciples after them. Therefore watch. . . .

The same is to be found in the general letter of the apostle Jude (vs. 4–19). Revelation (ch. 16:13) points to the same. Therefore our Lord Christ warns us to be on guard against false prophets (Matt. 7:15). Now it is as clear as day that nothing is esteemed so bad and unimportant—before God be it said in sorrow—as the Spirit of Christ, and yet none may be saved unless the selfsame Holy Spirit have previously assured one of salvation, as is written (Rom. 8:9; Luke 12:8; John 6:63; 17:2 f.). But how do we miserable little worms expect to come to this, as long as we hold the prestige of the godless in such respect that Christ, the gentle Son of God, unfortunately appears in contrast to the great titles and names of this world like a hempen hobgoblin to scare the birds or a painted doll of a man? And yet he is the very Stone,[13] which will be thrown from the mountain into the sea (Ps. 46:2 ff.),[14] away from the splendorous luxury of this world. He is the Rock which was made without human hands and cut out of the great mountain, his name is Jesus Christ (I Cor. 10:4), who was born precisely when that greatest of all bondage [slavery] prevailed (Luke

---

[11] The reference is to the feudal age in which power is divided between lords temporal and lords spiritual, symbolized by the feet of the multimetallic statue.

[12] Church historian Hegesippus lived in Rome in the third quarter of the second century. His five books of memoirs of the church in the form of historical polemic against Gnosticism are preserved only in fragments in the larger History of Eusebius of Caesarea.

[13] Dan. 2:45. [14] Ps. 45:3 ff. in the Vulgate.

1:52; 2:1–3) in the times of [8] Octavian, when the whole world was in motion and was taxed. Then it was that one powerless in the Spirit, a miserable dung sack,[15] wanted to have the whole world, which was of no use to him, however, except for splendor and arrogance. Indeed he let himself imagine that he alone was great. O how very small was that cornerstone Jesus Christ then in the eyes of men! He was assigned to the cow stall like an outcast of men (Ps. 22:6).[16] Accordingly the scribes refused him (Ps. 118:22;[17] Matt. 21:44–46; Mark 12:10–12; Luke 20:17–19), as they are still accustomed to do today. Verily in fact they have been re-enacting the Passion with him, ever since the pupils of the apostles died. They have taken the Spirit of Christ for laughing-stock and do indeed as it is written in Ps. 69 (11 f.).[18] They have quite openly stolen him like the thieves and murderers (John 10:1). They have robbed Christ's sheep of the true voice and have made the true crucified Christ into an utterly fantastic idol. How has this happened? Answer: They have rejected the pure handiwork of God[19] and set in his place a pretty little golden statue of deity, before which the poor peasants slobber, as Hosea has clearly said (ch. 4:8–10) and [again] Jeremiah in Lamentations (ch. 4:5): They that did eat fine spiced food have now received in its place dirt and filth. O woe to the abomination of desolation of which Christ himself says (Matt. 24:15) that he will be so wretchedly mocked with the devilish holding of Mass, with superstitious preaching, ceremonies, and manner of life! And yet all the time there is nothing there but a mere wooden statue of deity—yea, a superstitious wooden priest, and a gross, boorish, coarse people [9] who are unable to conceive of God in the slightest. Is that not a great pity, a sin, and a scandal? Yes, I maintain, the beasts of the belly (Phil. 3:19) and the swine (of which it is written in Matt. 7:6, II Peter 2:22) have completely trampled the precious Stone Jesus Christ with their feet, as far as they could. For he has become for the whole world like a rag to wipe off one's boots. For this reason all the unbelieving Turks, pagans, and Jews have very cheaply ridiculed us and held us for fools, as one should hold senseless men who do not want to

---

15 Octavian.   16 Ps. 21:7 in the Vulgate.
17 Ps. 117 in the Vulgate.   18 Ps. 68 in the Vulgate.
19 This expression derives from German mysticism. It denotes the mystical way of salvation and the experienced Word in self-conscious rejection of Luther's stress upon doctrine.

hear the [true] Spirit of their faith [even] mentioned. For this reason the suffering of Christ is nothing other than such a fairing at the hands of the desperate knaves as no lansquenet ever had [to give at Calvary] and as Ps. 69:2[20] says. Therefore, you dear brothers, we ought to arise from this filth and become God's real pupils, instructed of God (John, ch. 6; Matt., ch. 23). Thus it will be necessary for us that a great mighty power, which will be vouchsafed us from above, should punish and reduce to nothingness such unspeakable wickedness. This is the most clear knowledge of God (Prov. 9:10) which alone springs from the pure unsimulated fear of God. The same must alone arm us with a mighty hand for the avenging of the enemies of God with utmost zeal for God, as is written (Prov. 5:12; John 2:17; Ps. 69:9[21]). For there is absolutely no excusing [of the enemies of God] by means of human or rational expedients, since outward appearance of the godless is above all measure pretty and deceptive like the pretty [10] poppy among the golden ears of wheat (Eccl. 8:10).[22] But the wisdom of God discerns this deception.

Secondly. We must examine further and well that abomination which despises this Stone. If we are, however, to recognize the rightfulness of him,[23] we must be daily conscious of the [fresh] revelation of God. Oh that is become quite precious and rare in this wicked world, for the wily expedients of the captiously clever would overwhelm us every moment and hold us much more strongly from the pure Handiwork of God (Prov. 4:16–19; Ps. 37:12–15, 32 f.[24]). Such a person one must stave off in the fear of the Lord. If only the same [the fear] would be assured in us, then surely holy Christendom could come easily again to the spirit of wisdom and revelation of divine will. This is all comprehended in Scripture (Ps. 145:18 f.;[25] Ps. 111:5, 10;[26] Prov. 1:7). But the fear of God must be pure without any fear of men or creatures (Ps. 19:10;[27] Isa. 66:2; Luke 12:4 f.). O how highly necessary fear is for us! For as little as one can happily

---

20 Ps. 68 in the Vulgate. At the cross the soldiers gave no prettified present (like a gift from the fair) but rather gall and vinegar.
21 Ps. 68 in the Vulgate.
22 It is the Vulgate rendering that is here alone meaningful: I saw the wicked buried: who also when they were yet living were in the holy place, and were praised in the city as men of just works: but this also is vanity.
23 In the daily revelation of God we can ascertain whether the Stone, the Spirit of Christ, is the true Spirit.
24 Ps. 36 in the Vulgate.   25 Ps. 144 in the Vulgate.
26 Ps. 110 in the Vulgate.   27 Ps. 18 in the Vulgate.

serve two masters (Matt. 6:24), so little can one happily reverence both God and his creatures. Nor can God have mercy upon us (as the Mother of Christ our Lord says [Luke 1:50]), unless we fear him with our whole heart. Therefore God says (Mal. 1:6): If I be your Father, where is my honor? If I be your Lord, where then is my fear? Thus, ye amiable princes, it is necessary that we apply utmost diligence in these parlous days (I Tim., ch. 4), as all the dear fathers have delineated in the Bible from the beginning of the world, in order to cope with this insidious evil. For the age is dangerous and the days are wicked (II Tim. 3:1; Eph. 5:15 f.). Why? Simply [11] because the noble power of God is so wretchedly disgraced and dishonored that the poor common people are misled by the ungodly divines all with such rigmarole, as the prophet Micah (ch. 3:5–37) says of it: This is now the character of almost all divines with mighty few exceptions. They teach and say that God no longer reveals his divine mysteries to his beloved friends by means of valid visions or his audible Word, etc. Thus they stick with their inexperienced way (cf. Ecclesiasticus 34:9) and make into the butt of sarcasm those persons who go around in possession of revelation, as the godless did to Jeremiah (ch. 20:7 f.):[28] Hark! Has God just recently spoken to thee? Or hast thou recently asked at the mouth of God and taken counsel with him: Hast thou the Spirit of the Christ? This is what they do with scorn and mockery. Was that not a big [thing] that took place in the time of Jeremiah? Jeremiah warned the poor blind people about the [impending] punishment of captivity to Babylon (just as did the pious Lot the husbands of his daughters, Gen. 19:14). But it seemed [to them][29] quite foolish. They said to the beloved prophet: Oh, yes, oh, yes, God would indeed warn men in this fatherly way![30] What then actually happened to the scornful crowd in the Babylonian Captivity? Nothing less than that they were brought to shame by the heathen king Nebuchadnezzar.[31] Examine the text [of Dan. 2:47]: He accepted the declaration of God and was nevertheless a bloodthirsty tyrant and a rod for the people of the elect who had offended against God. But out of the blindness and stubbornness of the people of God the

---

28 Müntzer is paraphrasing the text for dramatic effect.
29 The blind people of Jerusalem.
30 This is the sarcastic retort of the rabble who doubted the validity of direct revelation.
31 This may be a reference to the threat of Turkish power.

goodness of the Most High had to be made plain to the world, as Saint Paul says (Rom. 11:25) and Ezekiel (ch. 23:22–35). Thus for your instruction I say here that God the Almighty showed forth to the heathen king not solely the things that were many years in the future, to the unspeakable shame of the stiff-necked among the people of God who did not want to believe any prophet. It is the same way also with the unproven people[32] of our own times. They are not conscious of the [imminent] punishment of God, even when they see the same right before their eyes. What then shall God the Almighty have to do with us? For this reason[33] he must withdraw his goodness from us. Now follows the text [Dan. 2:1–13]: The king Nebuchadnezzar had a dream which is gone from him, etc.

What now should we say to this? It is an unspeakable, indeed uncom[12]mon, and odious matter to discuss the dreams of others. The reason is that the whole world has been from the beginning deceived by the interpreters of dreams, as it is written (Deut. 13:2–4; Ecclesiasticus 34:7). Therefore it is shown in this chapter (II) that the king did not wish to believe the clever soothsayers and interpreters of dreams, for he said [vs. 5 ff.]:[34] Tell me my dream, then the interpretation, otherwise you will be telling me nothing but deception and lies! Then what? They were unable and could not tell him the dream and said: O beloved king, there is not a man upon the earth that can tell thee the dream except the gods who have no fellowship with human beings on the earth.[35] Of course, according to their understanding, they were speaking in a finite rational way. But they had no faith in God; they were, rather, godless hypocrites and flatterers, who there spoke what their masters gladly hear, just as the learned divines now do in our time, who very much like to eat the choice morsels at court. But what is written there in Jeremiah (chs. 5:13; 31 and 8:8 f.) is against them. What else is [written] there! The text [of Daniel] says it would have to be men who would have fellowship in heaven![36] Oh, that is a bitter medicine for the clever! And yet Saint Paul will take it in the same sense in

32 Christians without the experience of the Spirit or mediation of fresh revelation.
33 The want of responsiveness to his current revelation.
34 Again Müntzer paraphrases for dramatic effect.
35 Müntzer makes the astrologers talk like the Lutherans in utterly separating the divine from the human in respect to ongoing revelation.
36 That is direct communication with heaven as he has.

Philippians (ch. 3:20 [—our citizenship in heaven]). Nevertheless such wise men would like to explicate the mystery of God right off. Oh, of such rascals the world has enough, who openly arrogate this to themselves! And of these Isaiah says (ch. 58:2): They wish to know My ways, as [though they were] a nation that had accomplished My righteousness. Such learned divines are the soothsayers who then publicly repudiate the revelation of God and thus attack the Holy Spirit at his handiwork. [They][37] wish to instruct the whole world and what is not according to their inexperienced understanding must right off be for them from the devil. And yet [they] are not even assured of their own salvation, which surely ought to be required (Rom., ch. 8). They can prattle prettily of faith and brew up a drunken faith for the poor confused consciences of men. This makes all the inexperienced judgment and the abomination which they have for the contemptible deception of the wholly damnable, poisonous vagaries of the monks.[38] Through them the devil effected all his purposes and has illicitly deceived indeed also many of the pious elect, when they, without any instruction [from the Spirit or inner Word], straightway yielded themselves up to visions and dreams with their crazy belief. [13] And thus their talk and licentious black magic[39] is written by means of the revelation of the devil, against which the Colossians were vigorously warned by Saint Paul (ch. 2:4, 8). But the damnable monastic ecstatics[40] have not known how they ought to await the power of God. Over it they have become hardened into a contrary mind and are become for the whole world nothing but a mass of sin and shame like sluggish wastrels. Also they are blind in their folly. Nothing else has misled them and nothing else misleads them farther in the present day than this wrong belief. For without any experience of the arrival of the Holy Spirit, the overcomer[41] of the fear of God, they fail to separate (in their disdain for divine wisdom) the good from the bad which is camouflaged under the appearance of good. Over such as these God cries out through Isaiah (ch. 5:20): Woe to you who call good bad

---

[37] The Lutherans.
[38] Müntzer is here thinking of the mystical excesses of monastic self-discipline.
[39] The word is *pockfintzerey*, its meaning uncertain. The first constituent of the compound is the he-goat which figured in the rituals of black magic. The word may not, however, convey this degree of explicitness and would mean something then like mere "superstition."
[40] Literally, "monk dreamers."   [41] Literally, "master."

and bad good. Therefore it is not the habit of pious people to reject the good with the bad, since Saint Paul says to the Thessalonians (I, ch. 5:20–22): Despise not prophesyings. Prove all things; hold fast that which is good, etc.

Thirdly. You ought to know the view that God is so utterly well disposed toward his elect that if even in very minor matters he could warn them (Deut. 1:42–44; 32:29; Matt. 23:37), he would surely do it if they could but receive the same in the immensity of unbelief. For our text in Daniel agrees here with Saint Paul in I Corinthians (ch. 2:9 f.) which is taken from the holy Isaiah (ch. 64:4), saying that: Eye hath not seen, nor ear heard, neither have entered into the heart of man, the things which God hath prepared for them that love him. But God hath revealed them unto us by his Spirit: for the Spirit searcheth all things, yea, the deep things of God. Therefore in short it is one's earnest conviction that we must *know*—and not merely be up in the air in our belief—whether what is given us be from God or from the devil [14] or from nature. For if our natural understanding of the same [—what comes from God and what not—] ought to be captured for the service of faith (II Cor. 10:5), it must arrive at the final degree in [its capacity for] judgment as is shown in Romans (ch. 1:18–23) and Baruch (ch. 3:12–37). Of these judgments one is incapable of proving any in good conscience without God's revelation. For man will clearly discover that he cannot run with his head through heaven[42] but rather that he must first become wholly and utterly a fool (Isa. 29:13 f.; 33:18; Obad. 1:8; I Cor. 1:18). O what a rare wind that is indeed then for the clever, fleshly, sensual world! Thereupon follow at once the pains like [those of] a woman in travail (Ps. 48:6;[43] John 16:21). Therefore Daniel (ch. 2:17 f.), and every single pious person along with him, finds that for him in all circumstances, exactly as for other ordinary people, it is impossible to search out all the things from God. This is what the wise man [the Preacher] means when he says (Eccl. 3:11):[44] He who wishes to search out the majesty of God will be overwhelmed by his splendor. For the more nature[45] gropes after God [to lay hold upon him], the further the operation of the Holy Spirit withdraws itself there-

---

[42] That is, cannot be saved by reason.

[43] Ps. 47 in the Vulgate. Here Müntzer stresses not only the epistemological significance of rebirth but also quite characteristically the anguish thereof.

[44] A paraphrase.   [45] The natural man.

from, as Ps. 139:6[46] clearly shows. Indeed if man were only aware of the presumption of the natural light [of reason], without doubt he would not seek improvised help with pilfered [passages of] Scripture,[47] as the learned do with one or two little scraps (Isa. 28:10; Jer. 8:8), [15] but rather he would soon feel the operation of the divine Word spring out of his own heart (John 4:14). Yea, he need not put up with the stagnant water in the well (Jer. 2:13), as our learned men now do. They mix up nature and grace without any distinction.[48] They impede the progress of the Word (Ps. 119:11b),[49] which comes forth from the deeps[50] of the soul, as Moses says (Deut. 30:14):[51] The word is not far from thee, behold, it is in thy heart, etc. Now you may ask, How does it then come into the heart? Answer: It comes down from God above in exalted and terrifying astonishment,[52] which I shall let stand as it is [to be discussed] another time. And this astonishment as to whether it be God's word or not, commences when a child is six or seven years old [16] as is signified in Num., ch. 19.[53] Therefore Saint Paul cites Moses (Deut. 30:14) and Isaiah (ch. 65:1) in Rom. 10:8 and 20 and speaks there of the inner Word to be heard in the deeps of the soul through the revelation of God. And what person has not become aware of and receptive to this [Word] through the living testimony of God (Rom. 8:9). He [who has not the Spirit] does not know how to say anything deeply about God, even if he had eaten through a hundred Bibles! From that anybody can well judge how far the world really is from Christian faith. But no one wants to see or hear. If man would now become aware of the Word so that he become receptive thereto, God must take from him his fleshly lusts. And when the motion of God comes in his heart, so that he wishes to slay all the desires of the flesh, [it is necessary] that the [man]

46 Ps. 138 in the Vulgate.
47 Passages which they have intellectually appropriated without spiritual experience.
48 The reference is not only to the Catholic view that grace perfects nature but also to the Lutheran view of justification, according to which, so Müntzer holds, the work of God in the form of suffering is not allowed to operate to the point where the natural man is completely eliminated.
49 Ps. 118 in the Vulgate.   50 The text reads *abgrund.*
51 Slightly different from Vulgate and English versions.
52 The text: *in eyner hochen verwunderung,* but the last word preserves its original sense.
53 Ch. 19 deals with the regulations concerning uncleanness (the red heifer's ashes used in sprinkling at the third day after contracting ritual uncleanness) and the ritual recovery of cleanness on the seventh day.

give way to Him, in order that he may get the benefit of His
operation. For the man of animal nature does not perceive
what God speaks in the soul (I Cor. 2:14), but rather he must
be adverted by the Holy Spirit to the serious consideration of
the plain pure meaning of the law (Ps. 19:7 f.),[54] otherwise he is
blind in his heart and fashions for himself a wooden Christ and
misleads himself. Look therefore in this respect how distasteful
it became for blessed Daniel to interpret the vision to the king,
and how diligently he sought out God in this matter and prayed.
Thus, also, for the self-disclosure of God man must separate
himself from all diversion (II Cor. 6:17) and have a heart
resolute for the truth and must through the exercise of such
truth distinguish the undeceptive vision from the false one. For
this reason the beloved Daniel speaks in ch. 10:1 [that like
Daniel himself] a man may very well have understanding of
[certain] visions [and] therefore they are not all to be rejected,
etc.

Fourthly. You ought to know that the elect person who wishes
to know which vision or dream is from God, nature, or the
devil must with his mind[55] and heart and also his natural
understanding take leave of all temporal consolation of the
flesh; and it must happen to him as to beloved Joseph in
Egypt (Gen., ch. 39) and with Daniel here in this very chapter.
For no sensual person will accept it [the Word] (Luke 7:25),
since the thistles and thorns—these are the pleasures of this
world, as the Lord says (Mark 4:18 f.)—stifle [17] the whole
working of the Word, which God speaks in the soul. Therefore
when God has already spoken his holy Word in the soul, man
cannot hear it, if he is unpracticed [Ps. 49:20],[56] for he does
not turn in upon himself or look inwardly upon himself and the
deeps of his soul. Man will not crucify his life with its vices and
desires, as Paul the holy apostle teaches (Gal. 5:24). Therefore
the field of the Word of God remains full of thistles and thorns
and full of big bushes, all of which must be gotten out of the
way for this work of God, in order that a person not be found
neglectful or slothful (Prov. 24:3 f.). Accordingly, if a man has
regard for the fruitfulness of the field and the rich growth at the
end, then will such a person become aware for the first time
that he is the dwelling place of God and the Holy Spirit for
the duration of his days, yea, that he has been created truly for
the one purpose that he might search out the testimonies of

---

54 Ps. 18 in the Vulgate.   55 *Gemüth.*
56 Ps. 48:21 in the Vulgate.

God in his own life (Ps. 93 and 119:95).[57] Of this he will come to know in part, now in a figurative way,[58] then also in perfection in the deeps of his heart (I Cor. 13:10–12).[59] In the second place he must notice well that such figurative comparisons[60] in the visions or dreams with all their attendant phenomena are [to be] tested in the Holy Bible, in order that the devil may not intrude and spoil the unction of the Holy Spirit and its sweetness, as the wise man [the Preacher] says of the flies which die from it (Eccl. 10:1). In the third place, the elect person must take note of the working of the vision, that it not flow out by means of human improvisation, but rather that it flow simply [18] according to God's immovable will; and [he] must look out quite carefully that not one little bit be lost of what he has beheld, for it [the vision] will positively come true. But when the devil wants to accomplish something, his rotten ugly brood betrays him, and in the end his lies peer out despite all, for he is a liar (John 8:44). This is clearly shown forth in this chapter concerning Nebuchadnezzar and after that is borne out by the facts in the third. For he [the king] speedily forgot the warning of God. This without doubt was caused by his fleshly desires, which he directed toward lust and creaturely things. For so it must always go, when a person wants to cultivate continuously for himself a high degree of pleasure and deal [only] with the works of God and does not want to be in tribulation.[61] The power of the Word of God cannot [in this state] overshadow him (Luke, ch. 8).[62] God the Almighty directs the valid visions and dreams to his beloved friends most frequently in their deepest tribulation, as he did pious Abraham (Gen. 15:1–6; 17:1–3). For the Lord appeared to him there when he shuddered in fear. So also with beloved Jacob. When in great tribulation he fled before his brother Esau, a vision came unto him wherein he saw a ladder raised

57 Ps. 92 and 118 in the Vulgate.
58 In the figures and allusions of vision and dream.
59 It will be noted that where Paul saw the perfection of holy vision as eschatological fulfillment, Müntzer saw it as a stage in the mystical experience here and now.
60 The exact construction at this point is obscure: *solche figurn gleichnis*.
61 Note that Müntzer is not contrasting sensuality with probity but goes beyond a middle course to laud the state of spiritual turmoil and suffering as a token of divine approbation.
62 Müntzer refers here at once to the seminal power of God in Luke 1:35 and the failure of the divine seed on the different kinds of unproductive ground of Luke 8:13, 14. A suffering or saddened heart is receptive, he is saying.

up toward heaven and the angels of God going up and down (Gen. 28:12). After that, when he turned homeward again, he was afraid of his brother Esau beyond measure. Then the Lord appeared to him in the vision in which he crushed him in the hip and wrestled with him (Gen. 32:25 f.). Or again, pious Joseph was hated by his brothers, and in this tribulation he had two visions of exigency (Gen. 37:5–11). And thereafter in his heartfelt tribulation in Egypt in prison he was so highly illumined by God that he could interpret all visions and dreams (Gen. 39:20; chs. 40; 41). Above all this, that other holy Joseph (Matt. 1:20–23 and 2:13 ff.) is to be held up in front of the [spiritually] inexperienced, sensual swine, who think they are clever. He had four dreams (for he was turmoiled in his tribulation) and was reassured by the dreams, as the Wise Men were also instructed during sleep by the angel not to return to Herod (Matt. 2:12). Again the beloved apostles had to be diligently attentive to [the meaning of] visions, as it is clearly written in their Acts. Indeed, it is a [mark of the] truly apostolic, patriarchal, and prophetic spirit to attend upon visions and to attain unto the same in painful tribulation. Therefore it is no wonder that Brother Fattened Swine and Brother Soft Life[63] rejects them (Job 28:12 f.).[64] If [19], however, a person has not hearkened to the clear Word of God in the soul, he must have visions,[65] as when Saint Peter in the Acts of the Apostles failed to understand the law (Lev., ch. 11). He had doubts as to [the ritual cleanness] of food and as to whether to have [table] fellowship with pagans (Acts 10:10 ff.). Thereupon God gave him a vision in a flush of emotion. There he saw a linen sheet with four corners let down from heaven to the earth, filled with four-footed animals, and heard a voice from heaven, saying: Kill and eat. Devout Cornelius had something of the same when he did not know how he [as a God fearer] should act (Acts 10:1 ff.). Also when Paul came down to Troas, a vision appeared to him in the night. There was a man from Macedonia who stood and besought him, saying: Come over into Macedonia and help us. And after he had seen the vision, immediately we endeavored (says the text: Acts 16:8 ff.) to journey toward Macedonia, for we were certain that the Lord had called us

---

63 The reference is to Martin Luther.
64 It is only in the Vulgate text that the allusion to Job is pertinent: Neither is it [wisdom] found in the land of them that live in delights.
65 Müntzer stresses as above, p. 55, the secondary character of visions over against the clarity and certainty of the inner Word.

thither. Again, when Paul was afraid to preach in Corinth (Acts 18:9 f.), the Lord said to him in the night by a vision: Be not afraid, etc. No man shall set on thee to hurt thee, for I have many people in this city, etc. And what need is there to bring forward much testimony from Scripture? It would never be at all possible in these far-flung dangerous matters which rightful preachers, dukes, and princes have [to deal with] that they would on all sides take heed to act securely and blamelessly, if they did not live within the revelation of God, as Aaron heard from Moses [Ex. 4:15], and David from Nathan and Gad [II Chron. 29:25]. For the same reason the beloved apostles were quite accustomed to visions, as the passage in Acts [ch. 12:7–9] demonstrates. When the angel came to Peter and led him out of the prison of Herod, and it seemed to him he was having a vision, he did not know that the angel was carrying out the work of salvation in him. Now if Peter had not been accustomed to visions, how did it happen then that he recognized he was having one? From this now I infer that whoever wishes, by reason of his fleshly judgment, to be utterly hostile about visions [and dreams] without any experience of them, rejecting them all, or [again, whoever] wishes to take them all in without any distinction (because the false dream interpreters have done so much harm to the world through those who think only of their own renown or pleasure)—that surely [either extremist] will [20] have a poor run of it and will hurl himself against the Holy Spirit [of these Last Days (Joel 2:28)]. For God speaks clearly, like this text of Daniel, about the [eschatalogical] transformation of the world. He will prepare it in the Last Days in order that his name may be rightly praised. He will free it of its shame, and will pour out his Holy Spirit over all flesh and our sons and daughters shall prophesy and shall have dreams and visions, etc. For if Christendom is not to become apostolic (Acts 2:16 ff.)[66] in the way anticipated in Joel, why should one preach at all? To what purpose then the Bible with [its] visions?

It is true, and [I] know it to be true, that the Spirit of God is revealing to many elect, pious persons a decisive, inevitable, imminent reformation [accompanied] by great anguish, and it must be carried out to completion. Defend oneself against it as one may, the prophesy of Daniel remains unweakened, even if no one believes it, as also Paul says to the Romans (ch. 3:3).

66 Mistakenly Acts, ch. 27, in Müntzer's text.

This passage of Daniel is thus as clear as the sun, and the process of ending the fifth monarchy of the world is in full swing.

The first [kingdom] is set forth by the golden knop.[67] That was the kingdom of Babylon. The second [was represented] by the silver breast and arms. That was the kingdom of the Medes and Persians. The third was the kingdom of the Greeks, which, resounding with its science, was symbolized by the [sounding] brass. The fourth [was] the Roman Empire, which was won by the sword and a kingdom of coercion. But the fifth [symbolized by the iron and clay feet] is this which we have before our eyes, which is also of iron and would like to coerce. But it is [21] matted together with mud,[68] as we see before [our] discerning eyes—vain, pretentious schemes of hypocrisy which writhe and wriggle over the whole earth. For whoever cannot [detect] the ruses[69] must be indeed an imbecile. One sees nicely now how the eels and the vipers all in a heap abandon themselves to obscenities. The priests and all the wicked clerics are the vipers, as John the baptizer of Christ calls them (Matt. 3:7), and the temporal lords and princes are the eels, as is figuratively represented in Leviticus (ch. 11:10–12) by the fishes, etc. For the kingdoms of the devil have smeared themselves with clay. O beloved lords, how handsomely the Lord will go smashing among the old pots with his rod of iron (Ps. 2:9). Therefore, you much beloved and esteemed princes, learn your judgments directly from the mouth of God and do not let yourselves be misled by your hypocritical parsons nor be restrained by false consideration and indulgence.[70] For the Stone [made] without hands, cut from the mountain [which will crush the fifth kingdom, Dan. 2:34], has become great. The poor laity [of the towns] and the peasants see it much more clearly than you. Yea, God be praised, it has become so great [that] already, if other lords or neighbors should wish to

---

[67] A disparaging reference to the head.

[68] Müntzer further debases the clay by calling it "mud," the German for which has also the secondary meaning of "ordure."

[69] The text has an obscure word, *plaststueckenn*, which must be "deceive," but the sense of the section requires the insertion of the bracketed word. A word may indeed have dropped from the text, though neither Hinrichs nor Brandt seems to feel the need for emendation. The copulation of lamprey eels and vipers may go back to a passage in Saint Basil.

[70] Literally, by a fabricated patience and goodness. Müntzer's impatience with political reformation of a Christian society is clearly different from the "false forbearance" of the radical Evangelical Anabaptists whose impatience was directly against ecclesiastical leaders for insufficient purification of the Christian conventicle.

persecute you for the gospel's sake, they would be driven back by their own people! That I know for a certainty. Yea, the Stone is great. Before It the dim-witted world had long been afraid; It fell upon It when It was still small.[71] What should we then do now when it has become so great and mighty and when It has so powerfully, imminently struck against the great Statue and smashed it right down to the old pots?[72] Therefore, you esteemed princes of Saxony, step boldly on the Cornerstone as Saint Peter [22] did (Matt. 16:18)[73] and seek the perseverance [imparted] by the divine will. He will surely establish you upon the Rock (Ps. 40:2).[74] Your ways will be right. Seek only straightway the righteousness of God and take up courageously the cause of the gospel! For God stands so close to you that you wouldn't believe it! Why do you want then to shudder before the specter of a man (Ps. 118:6)?[75] Look at our text well [Dan. 2:13]. King Nebuchadnezzar wanted to kill the wise men because they could not interpret the dream for him. That was a deserved reward, for they wished to rule his whole kingdom with their cleverness and yet could not even do that for which they had been installed. Such is also the case of our clerics now, and I say this to you for a truth. If you could only as clearly recognize the harm being [done] to Christendom and rightly consider it, you would acquire just the same zeal as Jehu the king (II Kings, chs. 9 and 10); and the same as that which the whole book of Revelation proclaims. And I know for a certainty that you would thereupon hold yourselves back only with great effort from [letting] the sword exert its power. For the pitiable corruption of holy Christendom has become so great that at the present time no tongue can tell it all. Therefore a new Daniel must arise and interpret for you your vision[76] and this [prophet], as Moses teaches (Deut. 20:2), must go in front of the army.[77] He must reconcile the anger of the princes and

71 The allusion is to Christ's first appearance of which only the small number of elect within the mighty Roman Empire, the fourth monarchy, took cognizance.

72 Here Müntzer lets the clay vessels, signifying the princes and prelates, stand for the iron and clay feet which together represent the whole of the Holy Roman Empire in the process of crumbling.

73 Müntzer makes Christ, rather than Peter, the Rock in this pre-eminently papal passage.

74 Ps. 39 in the Vulgate. The text is particularly apt: He brought me up . . . out of the miry clay and set my feet upon a rock.

75 Ps. 117 in the Vulgate. The same psalm contains the rejected cornerstone reference in v. 22.

76 Literally, revelation.   77 This is the Vulgate reading.

the enraged people. For if you will rightly experience the
corruption of Christendom and the deception of the false
clerics and the vicious reprobates,[78] you will become so enraged
at them that no one can think it through. Without doubt it
will vex you and go right to your heart that you have been so
kindly after they, with the very sweetest words, misled you into
the most shameful conceptions (Prov. 6:1 ff.) against all
established truth. For they have made fools of you so that
everyone swears by the saints that [23] the princes are in
respect to their office a pagan people. They are said to be able to
maintain nothing other than a civil unity. O beloved, yea, the
great Stone there is about to fall and strike these schemes of
[mere] reason and dash them to the ground, for he says
(Matt. 10:34): I am not come to send peace but a sword.
What should be done, however, with the same?[79] Nothing
different from [what is done with] the wicked who hinder the
gospel: Get them out of the way and eliminate them, unless
you want to be ministers of the devil rather than of God, as
Paul calls you (Rom. 13:4). You need not doubt it. God will
strike to pieces all your adversaries who undertake to persecute
you, for his hand is by no means shortened, as Isaiah (ch.
59:1) says. Therefore he can still help you and wishes to, as he
supported the elect King Josiah and others who defended the
name of God. Thus you are angels, when you wish to do justly,
as Peter says (II, ch. 1:4). Christ commanded in deep gravity,
saying (Luke 19:27): Take mine enemies and strangle them
before mine eyes. Why? Ah! because they ruin Christ's government for him and in addition want to defend their rascality
under the guise of Christian faith and ruin the whole world
with their insidious subterfuge.[80] Therefore Christ our Lord
says (Matt. 18:6): Whosoever shall offend one of these little
ones, it is better for him that a millstone be hung about his
neck and that he be thrown in the depth of the sea. You can
gloss over here and there as much as you like—these are the
words of Christ. Now if Christ can say, Whosoever offends *one*

---

[78] The reference is primarily to the Lutheran divines.

[79] The text reads, *mit demselbigen* and may refer specifically to Luther.

[80] Here and at n. 82 Müntzer is reinterpreting the politically conservative
text of Rom. ch. 13, into a revolutionary document. By reversing the
sequence of ch. 13:1–4 and construing vs. 1 f. as the sequel of vs. 3 f., he
would make the Ernestine princes, by hortatory anticipation, the execu-
tors of God's wrath against the godless and the protectors of the revolutionary saints. But he warns them that if they fail to identify themselves
with the covenantal people, the sword will revert to the people.

of the little ones, what should one say then if somebody offends a great multitude in their faith? That is what the archvillains do, who vex the whole world and make it forsake the true Christian faith and say: No one may know the mystery of God. Everyone should behave himself according to their words and not according to their works (cf. Matt. 23:3). They say that it is not necessary for faith to be tried like gold [24] in the fire (I Peter 1:7; Ps. 140:10).[81] But in this way Christian faith would be worse than a dog's faith where he hopes to get a piece of bread because the table is being set. This is the kind of faith the false divines juggle before the blind world. This is not remarkable after all, for they preach only for the stomach's sake (Phil. 3:19). They cannot say anything further from [the experiences of] their heart (Matt. 12:34). Now if you want to be true governors, you must begin government at the roots, and, as Christ commanded, drive his enemies from the elect. For you are the means to this end.[82] Beloved, don't give us any old jokes about how the power of God should do it without your application of the sword. Otherwise may it rust away for you in its scabbard! May God grant it, whatever any divine may say to you! Christ says it sufficiently (Matt. 7:19; John 15:2, 6): Every tree that bringeth not forth good fruit is rooted out and cast into the fire. If you do away with the mask of the world, you will soon recognize it with a righteous judgment (John 7:24). Perform a righteous judgment at God's command! You have help enough for the purpose (Wisdom of Solomon, ch. 6), for Christ is your Master (Matt. 23:8). Therefore let not the evildoers live longer who make us turn away from God (Deut. 13:5). For the godless person has no right to live when he is in the way of the pious. In Ex. 22:18 God says: Thou shalt not suffer evildoers[83] to live. Saint Paul also means this where he says of the sword of rulers that it is bestowed upon them for the retribution of the wicked as protection for the pious (Rom. 13:4). God is your protection and will teach you to fight against his foes (Ps. 18:34).[84] He will make your hands skilled in fighting and will also sustain you. But you will have to suffer for that reason a great cross and temptation in order that the fear of

81 Ps. 139:11 in the Vulgate. The allusion is not clear.
82 The princes possess the sword whereby the decision against the ungodly can be made.
83 The Vulgate has *maleficos* for the modern rendering "witch" or "sorceress."
84 Ps. 17:35 in the Vulgate.

God may be declared unto you. That cannot happen without suffering, but it costs you no [25] more than the danger of having risked all for God's sake and the useless prattle of your adversaries. For though even pious David was drawn from his castle by Absalom, he finally came again into ascendancy when Absalom got hung up and was stabbed.[85] Therefore, you cherished fathers of Saxony, you must hazard all for the sake of the gospel. But God will chasten you out of love as his most beloved sons (cf. Deut. 1:31) when he in his momentary anger is enraged. Blessed at that time are all who trust in God. Free in the Spirit of Christ, say only (Ps. 3:6): I will not be afraid of a hundred thousand though they have set themselves against me round about. I suppose at this point our learned divines will bring out the goodness of Christ, which they in their hypocrisy apply by force. But over against this [goodness] they ought also to take note of the sternness of Christ (John 2:15–17; Ps. 69:9),[86] when he turned over the roots of idolatry. As Paul says in Col. 3:5–7, because of these the wrath of God cannot be done away with in the congregation. If he, according to our view, tore down the lesser,[87] surely without doubt he would not have spared the idols and images if there had been any. For he himself commanded the same through Moses (Deut. 7:5 f.) where he says: Ye are a holy people. Ye ought not to have pity on account of the superstitious. Break down their altars, smash up their images and burn them up, that I be not angry with you. These words Christ has not abrogated, but rather he wishes to fulfill them for us (Matt. 5:17). There are [of course] all those figures interpreted by the prophets, but these [in Matthew] are bright clear words which must stand forever (Isa. 40:8). God cannot say yes today and tomorrow no, but rather he is unchangeable in his Word (Mal. 3:6; I Sam. 15:10–22; Num., ch. 22). [In reply to the argument] that the apostles of the Gentiles did not disturb the idols, I answer thus. Saint Peter was a timid man (Gal. 2:11–13). If he dissembled with the Gentiles, he was a symbol of all the apostles, so that Christ said of him (John 21:15–19) that he mightily feared death. And, because of this [fear, it] is easy enough to understand [that he] gave no occasion [to arouse the pagans] by such [action] [26]. But Saint Paul spoke out quite sternly against idolatry. If he had been able to push his teaching to its conclusion among the

85 II Sam. 18:10, 14 f.
86 Ps. 68 in the Vulgate.
87 Namely, the tables of the money-changers.

Athenians (Acts 17:16–31), he would without any doubt have cast it down, as God through Moses has commanded, and as it also happened many times thereafter through [the action of] the martyrs in trustworthy histories. Therefore no justification is given us in the inadequacy and the negligence of the saints to let the godless have their way. Since they with us confess God's name they ought to choose between two alternatives: either to repudiate the Christian faith completely or put idolatry out of the way (Matt. 18:7–9). That our learned divines, however, should come along and, in their godless prevaricating manner, say in reference to Daniel (2:34) that the Antichrist ought to be destroyed without [human] hands is as much as to say he [Antichrist] is already inwardly collapsed, as was' the [Canaanite] people when the Chosen were bent on entering the Promised Land, as Joshua (ch. 5:1) writes. He [Joshua] notwithstanding did not spare them [the Canaanites] the sharpness of the sword. Look at Ps. 44:5[88] and I Chron. 14:11. There you will find the solution in this way. They did not conquer the land by the sword but rather through the power of God. But the sword was the means, as eating and drinking is for us a means of living. In just this way the sword is necessary to wipe out the godless (Rom. 13:4). That this might now take place, however, in an orderly and proper fashion, our cherished fathers, the princes, should do it, who with us confess Christ. If, however, they do not do it, the sword will be taken from them (Dan. 7:26 f.). For they confess him all right with words and deny him with the deed (Titus 1:16). They [the princes], accordingly, should proffer peace to the enemies (Deut. 2:26–30). If the latter wish to be spiritual [in the outmoded sense] and do not give testimony of the knowledge (*kunst*) of God (cf. I Peter 3:9, 12), they should be gotten out of the way (I Cor. 5:13). But I pray for them with the devout David where they are not against God's revelation. Where, however, they pursue the opposition, may they be slain without any mercy as Hezekiah (II Kings 18:22), Josiah (ch. 23:5), Cyrus (cf. II Chron. 36:22 f.), Daniel (ch. 6:27), Elijah (I Kings 18:40) destroyed the priests of Baal, otherwise the Christian church (*kirche*) cannot come back again to its origin. The weeds must be plucked out of the vineyard of God in the time of harvest. Then [27] the beautiful red wheat will acquire substantial rootage and come up properly (Matt. 13:24–30). The

[88] Ps. 43 in the Vulgate.

angels [v. 39], however, who sharpen their sickles for this purpose are the serious servants of God who execute the wrath of the divine wisdom (Mal. 3:1-6).

Nebuchadnezzar (Dan. 2:46) perceived the divine wisdom in Daniel. He fell down before him after the mighty truth had overcome him. But he was moved like a reed before the wind, as ch. 3 (vs. 5 ff.) proves. Of the same character are many people now, by far the greater number, who accept the gospel with great joy as long as everything is going fine and friendly (Luke 8:13). But when God wishes to put such people to the test or to the trial by fire (I Peter 1:7), oh, how they take offense at the smallest weed, as Christ in Mark (ch. 4:17) prophesied. Without doubt inexperienced people will to such an extent anger themselves over this little book[89] for the reason that I say with Christ (Luke 19:27; Matt. 18:6) and with Paul (I Cor. 5:7, 13) and with the instruction of the whole divine law that the godless rulers should be killed, especially the priests and monks who revile the gospel as heresy for us and wish to be considered at the same time as the best Christians. When hypocritical, spurious (getichte) goodness becomes engaged and embittered beyond the average, it then wishes to defend the godless and says Christ killed no one, etc. And since the friends of God thus quite ineffectually command the wind, the prophecy of Paul (II Tim. 3:5) is fulfilled. In the last days the lovers of pleasures will indeed have the form of godliness (Göttickeit), but they will denounce its power. Nothing on earth has a better form and mask than spurious goodness. For this reason all corners are full of nothing but hypocrites, among whom not a one is so bold as to be able to say the real truth. Therefore in order that the truth may be rightly brought to the light, you rulers—it makes no difference whether you want to or not—must conduct yourselves according to the conclusion of this chapter (ch. 2:48 f.), namely, that Nebuchadnezzar made the holy Daniel an officer in order that he might execute good, righteous decisions, as the Holy Spirit says (Ps. 58:10 f.).[90] For the godless have no right to live except as the elect wish to grant it to them, as it is written in Ex. 23:29-33. Rejoice, you true friends of God, that for the enemies of the cross their heart has fallen into their breeches. They [28] must do right even though they have never dreamed it. If we now fear God, why

---

89 How many other changes were made in converting the sermon into a printed booklet is difficult to ascertain.
90 Ps. 57:11 f. in the Vulgate.

do we want to enrage ourselves before slack defenseless people (Num. 14:8 f.; Josh. 11:6)? Be but daring! He who wishes to have rule himself, to him all power on earth and heaven is given (Matt. 28:18). May He preserve you, most beloved, forever. Amen.

III

Letters to Thomas Müntzer
By Conrad Grebel[1] and Friends

ZURICH, SEPTEMBER 5, 1524

INTRODUCTION

THE FOLLOWING TWO LETTERS FROM THE spokesman of the radical evangelicalism of Switzerland to the leader of Revolutionary Spiritualism in Saxony constitute an invaluable document from the very beginnings of Evangelical Anabaptism. They make clear in a few pages both the widespread sense of camaraderie among the dissenters from the territorial or magisterial Reformation of Luther and Zwingli and the early differentiation of positions within the Radical Reformation itself.

As an expression of left-wing solidarity it has been called the manifesto of a "new program," the third in a series of five acts in which, on a diminutive scale, the whole drama of the Radical Reformation was enacted in the circle of Conrad Grebel in and about Zurich.[2] The first act had been the disillusion of Grebel, humanist turned Biblicist, with the temporizing of his friend and former teacher Zwingli. The second act had been the design which failed, a fleeting proposal for the election of a truly Christian, i.e., radical evangelical, magistracy which would implement at once the reform as preached by Zwingli. Failing in this, Grebel and his associates then turned to establish contact with Müntzer and Carlstadt as supposedly kindred spirits in a comparable opposition to the way the Reform was proceeding in Wittenberg. In the letters before us the Swiss Brethren give evidence both of their esteem

---

[1] The best biography is that by Harold Bender, *Conrad Grebel* (Goshen, Ind., 1950).

[2] Delineated with characteristic clarity, precision, and economy of phrase by Fritz Blanke, "La Préhistoire de l'Anabaptisme à Zurich," *Mélanges historiques offerts à M. Jean Meyhoffer* (Lausanne, 1952), 17–29.

for Müntzer and their uneasiness about him, especially in three matters soon to be of pre-eminent importance to them. In making these three points these letters provide us with our earliest documentation in the Reformation Era of a concern for believer's baptism, an insistence on the separation of the church from both the support of and control by the state, and a programmatic renunciation of war.

When the Swiss Brethren received no response to their overture—and it is clear that the preacher of the Sermon Before the Princes (Selection II) had a different spirit from theirs—Grebel opened the fourth act in making one last effort to dissuade Zwingli and the magistracy from pedobaptism in a public debate. Baptism was then felt, much more than is evident in our Letters, to be the key to the full imitation of Christ, who was circumcized as a child of Israel but baptized in Jordan as the head of the New Israel. Antagonizing instead of converting the magistracy, the Brethren turned to the final act, rebaptism and rupture with magisterial Protestantism. This fifth act, Grebel's rebaptism of Blaurock, is recorded in Selection I.

Letters to Thomas Müntzer [3]
By Conrad Grebel and Friends

ZURICH, SEPTEMBER 5, 1524

THE TEXT

To the sincere and true proclaimer of the gospel, Thomas Müntzer at Allstedt in the Hartz, our true and beloved brother with us in Christ: May peace, grace, and mercy from God, our Father, and Jesus Christ, our Lord, be with us all. Amen. [4]

Dear Brother Thomas:

For God's sake do not marvel that we address thee without

[3] The present translation is a revision of that published by Walter Rauschen-busch in *The American Journal of Theology*, IX (1905), pp. 91–99. This was, based upon the text as first published by C. A. Cornelius, *Geschichte des Münsterischen Aufruhrs*, II (Leipzig, 1860), pp. 240–247. The Letters were republished in modernized German (but not always accurately) by Christian Neff in *Gedenkschrift zum 400 jährigen Jubiläum der Mennoniten oder Taufgesinnten* (Ludwigshafen, 1925), pp. 91–102. The critical text of the Letters was edited by Heinrich Böhmer and Paul Kirn, *Thomas Müntzers Briefwechsel* (Leipzig/Berlin, 1931), pp. 92–101, which was reproduced by Leonhard von Muralt and Walter Schmid, *Quellen zur Geschichte der Täufer in der Schweiz* (Zurich, 1952), pp. 13–21. The original is in the Stadtsbibliothek, St. Gall, Band XI, 97, and Band II, 204, of the Vadian Corpus. It is from the critical text that the Rauschenbusch translation has been reworked and supplied with notes and completed Biblical references. A portion of the original Rauschenbusch translation was republished by Bender, *Grebel* (Ind.), pp. 282–287; the background and purport of the Letters are fully discussed, *ibid.*, pp. 171–183.

The Letters are not only a documentation of Evangelical Anabaptism. They also constitute a *pièce justificative* on both sides of the contemporary scholarly controversy as to whether Anabaptism took its rise in Saxony in opposition to Luther and was hence *primitively* revolutionary (Müntzer and Münster), as the Leipzig Luther scholars Heinrich Böhmer and Karl Holl and their schools have held, or whether it rose in Switzerland in opposition to Zwingli and was hence consistently pacifistic as the American Mennonite scholar Harold Bender and his associates maintain.

[4] The phrasing evokes the memory of the introductory verses of the Epistle to Titus and the two to Timothy.

73

title, and request thee like a brother to communicate with us by writing, and that we have ventured, unasked and unknown to thee, to open communications between us. God's Son, Jesus Christ, who offers himself as the one master and head of all who would be saved, and bids us be brethren by the one common word given to all brethren and believers, has moved us and compelled us to make friendship and brotherhood and to bring the following points to thy attention. Thy writing of two tracts on fictitious faith[5] has further prompted us. Therefore we ask that thou wilt take it kindly for the sake of Christ our Saviour. If God wills, it shall serve and work to our good. Amen.

Just as our forebears fell away from the true God and from the one true, common, divine Word, from the divine institutions, from Christian love and life, and lived without God's law and gospel in human, useless, unchristian customs and ceremonies, and expected to attain salvation therein, yet fell far short of it, as the evangelical preachers have declared, and to some extent are still declaring, so today too every man wants to be saved by superficial faith, without fruits of faith, without baptism of trial and probation, without love and hope, without right Christian practices, and wants to persist in all the old manner of personal vices, and in the common ritualistic and anti-Christian customs of baptism and of the Lord's Supper, in disrespect for the divine Word and in respect for the word of the pope and of the antipapal preachers, which yet is not equal to the divine Word nor in harmony with it. In respecting persons and in manifold seduction there is grosser and more pernicious error now than ever has been since the beginning of the world. In the same error we too lingered as long as we heard and read only the evangelical preachers who are to blame for all this, in punishment for our sins. But after we took Scripture in hand too, and consulted it on many points, we have been instructed somewhat and have discovered the great and harmful error of the shepherds, of ours too, namely, that we do not daily beseech God earnestly with constant groaning to be brought out of this destruction of all godly life and out of human abominations, to attain to the true faith and divine practice. The cause of all this is false forbearance, the hiding of the divine Word, and the mixing of it with the human. Aye, we say it harms all and

---

[5] *Von dem getichten glawben* (1524) and *Protestation odder Empietung vnnd tzum anfang von dem rechten Christenglawben vnnd der tawffe* (1524).

frustrates all things divine. There is no need of specifying and reciting.

While we were marking and deploring these facts, thy book against false faith and baptism[6] was brought to us, and we were more fully informed and confirmed, and it rejoiced us wonderfully that we found one who was of the same Christian mind with us and dared to show the evangelical preachers their lack, how that in all the chief points they falsely forbear and act and set their own opinions, and even those of Antichrist, above God and against God, as befits not the ambassadors of God to act and preach. Therefore we beg and admonish thee as a brother by the name, the power, the word, the spirit, and the salvation, which has come to all Christians through Jesus Christ our Master and Saviour (*seligmacher*), that thou wilt take earnest heed to preach only the divine Word without fear, to set up and guard only divine institutions, to esteem as good and right only what may be found in pure and clear Scripture, to reject, hate, and curse all devices, words, customs, and opinions of men, including thy own.

(1.) We understand and have seen that thou hast translated the Mass into German and hast introduced new German hymns.[7] That cannot be for the good, since we find nothing taught in the New Testament about singing, no example of it. Paul scolds the learned among the Corinthians more than he praises them, because they mumbled in meeting as if they sang,[8] just as the Jews and the Italians chant their words song-fashion. (2.) Since singing in Latin grew up without divine instruction and apostolic example and custom, without producing good or edifying, it will still less edify in German and will create a faith of outward appearance only. (3.) Paul very clearly forbids singing in Eph. 5:19 and Col. 3:16 since he says and teaches that they are to speak to one another and teach one another with psalms and spiritual songs, and if anyone would sing, he should sing and give thanks in his heart. (4.) Whatever we are not taught by clear passages or examples must be regarded as forbidden, just as if it were written: "This do not; sing not." (5.) Christ in the Old and especially in the New Testament bids his messengers (*botten*)[9] simply proclaim the word. Paul too

---

6 *Protestation.*

7 Grebel may have seen Müntzer's three liturgical works. The twenty-five items here numbered in parens appear partly in written, partly in numeral form and Nos. 8 and 12 are not indicated.

8 Cf. I Cor. 14:9, 16.

9 In the translations in this volume *Boten* appears as "emissaries" wherever it is combined as *Sendboten* (and the Dutch equivalent).

says that the word of Christ profits us, not the song. Whoever sings poorly gets vexation by it; whoever can sing well gets conceit. (6.) We must not follow our notions; we must add nothing to the word and take nothing from it. (7.) If thou wilt abolish the Mass, it cannot be accomplished with German chants, which is thy suggestion perhaps, or comes from Luther. [8.] It must be rooted up by the word and command of Christ. (9.) For it is not planted by God. (10.) The Supper of fellowship Christ did institute and plant. (11.) The words found in Matt., ch. 26, Mark, ch. 14, Luke, ch. 22, and I Cor., ch. 11, alone are to be used, no more, no less. [12.] The server from out of the congregation should pronounce them from one of the Evangelists or from Paul. (13.) They are the words of the instituted meal of fellowship, not words of consecration. (14.) Ordinary bread ought to be used, without idols and additions. (15.) For [the latter] creates an external reverence and veneration of the bread, and a turning away from the inward. An ordinary drinking vessel too ought to be used. (16.) This would do away with the adoration and bring true understanding and appreciation of the Supper, since the bread is nought but bread. In faith, it is the body of Christ and the incorporation with Christ and the brethren. But one must eat and drink in the Spirit and love, as John shows in ch. 6 and the other passages, Paul in I Cor., chs. 10 and 11, and as is clearly learned in Acts, ch. 2. (17.) Although it is simply bread, yet if faith and brotherly love precede it, it is to be received with joy, since, when it is used in the church, it is to show us that we are truly one bread and one body, and that we are and wish to be true brethren with one another, etc. (18.) But if one is found who will not live the brotherly life, he eats unto condemnation, since he eats it without discerning, like any other meal, and dishonors love, which is the inner bond, and the bread, which is the outer bond. (19.) For also it does not call to his mind Christ's body and blood, the covenant of the cross, nor that he should be willing to live and suffer for the sake of Christ and the brethren, of the head and the members. (20.) Also it ought not to be administered by thee.[10] That was the beginning of the Mass that only a few would partake, for the Supper is an expression of fellowship,

---

10 The objection here appears to be against the perpetration of the priestly conception of administering the elements. To avoid any suggestion of a sacerdotal act, Müntzer, ordained to the old priesthood, should relinquish to a server from out of the congregation the distribution of the elements. Cf. article 24 below. Besides the informality, note the inwardness and stress on John, ch. 6; cf. Caspar Schwenckfeld, Sel. VIII, pp. 166 ff.

not a Mass and sacrament. Therefore none is to receive it alone, neither on his deathbed nor otherwise. Neither is the bread to be locked away, etc., for the use of a single person, since no one should take for himself alone the bread of those in unity, unless he is not one with himself—which no one is, etc. (21.) Neither is it to be used in "temples" according to all Scripture and example, since that creates a false reverence. (22.) It should be used much and often. (23.) It should not be used without the rule of Christ in Matt. 18:15–18, otherwise it is not the Lord's Supper, for without that rule every man will run after the externals. The inner matter, love, is passed by, if brethren and false brethren approach or eat it [together].[11] (24.) If ever thou desirest to serve it, we should wish that it would be done without priestly garment and vestment of the Mass, without singing, without addition. (25.) As for the time, we know that Christ gave it to the apostles at supper and that the Corinthians had the same usage. We fix no definite time with us, etc.

Let this suffice, since thou art much better instructed about the Lord's Supper, and we only state things as we understand them. If we are not in the right, teach us better. And do thou drop singing and the Mass, and act in all things only according to the Word, and bring forth and establish by the Word the usages of the apostles. If that cannot be done, it would be better to leave all things in Latin and unaltered and mediated [by a priest]. If the right cannot be established, do not then administer according to thy own or the priestly usage of Antichrist. And at least teach how it ought to be, as Christ does in John, ch. 6, and teaches how we must eat and drink his flesh and blood, and takes no heed of backsliding and anti-Christian caution,[12] of which the most learned and foremost evangelical preachers have made a veritable idol and propagated it in all the world. It is much better that a few be rightly taught through the Word of God, believing and walking aright in virtues and practices, than that many believe falsely and deceitfully through adulterated doctrine. Though we admonish and beseech thee, we hope that thou wilt do it of thy own accord; and we

---

[11] Cf. more completely below, p. 80, and Menno Simons on the ban and shunning, Selection XII.

[12] False forbearance. The same phrasing is prominent in Caspar Schwenckfeld, Selection VIII, i.e., p. 170. For a violent denunciation of false caution, see Müntzer, Selection II, p. 63.

admonish the more willingly, because thou hast so kindly listened to our brother[13] and confessed that thou too hast yielded too much, and because thou and Carlstadt[14] are esteemed by us the purest proclaimers and preachers of the purest Word of God. And if ye two rebuke, and justly, those who mingle the words and customs of men with those of God, ye must by rights cut yourselves loose and be completely purged of popery, benefices, and all new and ancient customs, and of your own and ancient notions. If your benefices, as with us,[15] are supported by interest and tithes, which are both true usury, and it is not the whole congregation which supports you, we beg that ye free yourselves of your benefices. Ye know well how a shepherd should be sustained.

We have good hopes of Jacob Strauss[16] and a few others, who are little esteemed by the slothful scholars and doctors at Wittenberg. We too are thus rejected by our learned shepherds. All men follow them, because they preach a sinful sweet

---

[13] This is undoubtedly Hans Hujuff, mentioned again below (n. 23), and a signatory of the second letter to Müntzer, where he signs himself as "thy countryman of Halle." In the second letter reference is also made to his having been "recently" with Müntzer. Two scholars have concluded from these references that Hujuff must have had personal contact with Müntzer. See here Otto Schiff, "Thomas Müntzer als Prediger in Halle," *Archiv für Reformationsgeschichte*, XXIII (1926), esp. p. 291, and Karl Simon, "Die Züricher Täufer und der Hofgoldschmied Kardinal Albrechts," *Zwingliana*, VI (1938), 50–54. Harold Bender discusses the arguments of both men and goes on to argue that "there are grave doubts as to the authenticity of the supposed conversation" (*op. cit.*, 257, n. 56). To me the contact seems more than plausible, but surely not detrimental to Grebel's originality.

Schiff identified Hujuff as court goldsmith of Albert of Brandenburg (later cardinal). Simon advances additional fact and argument to make it probable that Anabaptist Hujuff was son of court artist Hujuff, both of them goldsmiths. Our Hujuff is known to have received from his brother in Saxony a copy of Luther's polemical tract against Müntzer. See second letter to Müntzer below.

[14] Andreas Bodenstein von Carlstadt, originally an ally of Luther in Wittenberg, subsequently an opponent on the issues of the Supper and Scripture. He died, a professor in Basel, in 1541.

[15] I.e., in Zwingli's Zurich.

[16] Dr. Jacob Strauss, born in Basel, was active as a Lutheran preacher in Tyrol, then in Wertheim and Eisenach. He was conspicuously opposed to usury in his espousal of the cause of the peasants who listed him third (next to Luther and Melanchthon) in the South German Peasant Constitution of Memmingen, February, 1524. See Bender, *Grebel*, pp. 312–315, where the literature is cited. See also Gustav Bossert, *Realencyclopädie für protestantische Theologie und Kirche*, 3d ed., XIX, 92 ff.

Christ,[17] and they lack clear discernment, as thou hast set forth in thy tracts, which have taught and strengthened beyond measure us who are poor in spirit. And so we are in harmony in all points, except that we have learned with sorrow that thou hast set up tablets,[18] for which we find no text or example in the New Testament. In the Old it [the law] was to be written outwardly, but now in the New it is to be written on the fleshly tablets of the heart, as the comparison of both Testaments proves, as we are taught by Paul, II Cor. 3:3; Jer. 31:33; Heb. 8:10; Ezek. 36:26. Unless we are mistaken, which we do not think and believe, do thou abolish the tablets again. The matter has grown out of thy own notions, a futile expense, which will increase and become quite idolatrous, and spread into all the world, just as happened with the idolatrous images. It would also create the idea that something external always had to stand and be set up in place of the idols, whereby the unlearned might learn—even if it be only the external word which is so used, as is declared to us, according to all example and commandment of Scripture, especially I Cor. 14:16 and Col. 3:16. This kind of learning from this word only[19] might in time become insidious,[20] and even if it would never do any harm, yet I would never want to invent and set up anything new and to follow and imitate the slothful and misleading scholars with their false forbearance, and from my own opinion invent, teach, and establish a single thing.

Go forward with the Word and establish a Christian church with the help of Christ and his rule, as we find it instituted in Matt. 18:15–18 and applied in the Epistles. Use determination and common prayer and decision according to faith and love, without command or compulsion. Then God will help thee and thy little sheep to all sincerity, and the singing and the tablets will cease. There is more than enough of wisdom and counsel in the Scripture, how all classes and all men may be taught, governed, instructed, and turned to piety. Whoever will not amend and believe, but resists the Word and action of God and thus persists, such a man, after Christ and his Word and rule have been declared to him and he has been admonished

---

17 The "bitter" as opposed to the "sweet" Christ is pointed up by Müntzer in *von dem getichten glawben*, G. Brandt, *op. cit.*, p. 129. It is also found in John Denck, Selection IV, at n. 12.
18 Two tablets bearing the Ten Commandments.
19 From *dem einigen wort*, i.e., the displayed tablets.
20 Rauschenbusch renders *hinderstellig werden* as "to lag," but acknowledges that "the connection is not clear."

in the presence of the three witnesses and the church,[21] such a man, we say, taught by God's Word, shall not be killed,[22] but regarded as a heathen and publican and let alone.

Moreover, the gospel and its adherents are not to be protected by the sword, nor are they thus to protect themselves, which, as we learn from our brother,[23] is thy opinion and practice. True Christian believers are sheep among wolves, sheep for the slaughter; they must be baptized in anguish and affliction, tribulation, persecution, suffering, and death; they must be tried with fire, and must reach the fatherland of eternal rest, not by killing their bodily, but by mortifying their spiritual, enemies. Neither do they use worldly sword or war, since all killing has ceased with them—unless, indeed, we would still be of the old law. And even there [in the Old Testament], so far as we recall, war was a misfortune after they had once conquered the Promised Land. No more of this.

On the matter of baptism thy book pleases us well, and we desire to be further instructed by thee. We understand that even an adult is not to be baptized without Christ's rule[24] of binding and loosing. The Scripture describes baptism for us thus, that it signifies that, by faith and the blood of Christ, sins have been washed away for him who is baptized, changes his mind, and believes before and after; that it signifies that a man is dead and ought to be dead to sin and walks in newness of life and spirit, and that he shall certainly be saved if, according to this meaning, by inner baptism he lives his faith; so that the water does not confirm or increase faith, as the scholars at Wittenberg say, and [does not] give very great comfort [nor] is it the final refuge on the deathbed. Also baptism does not save, as Augustine, Tertullian, Theophylact,[25] and Cyprian

21 Matt. 18:15–17. See item 22 above.
22 Grebel is thinking here of the Inquisitorial punishment of heretics and Paul's excommunication of the Corinthian sinner in I Cor. 5:5, wherein the phrase "destruction of the flesh" could be and had been often interpreted as legitimizing capital punishment for heresy or immorality. Of I Cor. 5:5 there is an interesting parallel in the Dead Sea Manual of Discipline.
23 Hans Hujuff. See above, n. 13. Herein, of course, Grebel is deceived. See Selection II, esp. p. 64.
24 That is, without submitting to the rule of Matt. 18:15–17.
25 Theophylact (c. 1038–c. 1118), archbishop of Achreda, wrote commentaries on the New Testament widely esteemed. Cf. Cornelius, *Geschichte des Münsterischen Aufruhrs*, I, 226, 236, 238. Hubmaier, in contrast to Grebel, mistakenly thought Theophylact wrote A.D. 189 and cited him approvingly as a witness to apostolic usage. C. Sachsse, *Hubmaier*, p. 34.

have taught, dishonoring faith and the suffering of Christ in the case of the old and adult, and dishonoring the suffering of Christ in the case of the unbaptized infants. We hold (according to the following passages: Gen. 8:21; Deut. 1:39; 30:6; 31:13; and I Cor. 14:20; Wisdom of Solomon 12:19; I Peter 2:2; Rom., chs. 1; 2; 7; 10 [allusions uncertain]; Matt. 18:1–6; 19:13–15; Mark 9:33–47; 10:13–16; Luke 18:15–17; etc.) that all children who have not yet come to the discernment of the knowledge of good and evil, and have not yet eaten of the tree of knowledge, that they are surely saved by the suffering of Christ, the new Adam, who has restored their vitiated life, because they would have been subject to death and condemnation only if Christ had not suffered; but they're not yet grown up to the infirmity of our broken nature—unless, indeed, it can be proved that Christ did not suffer for children. But as to the objection that faith is demanded of all who are to be saved, we exclude children from this and hold that they are saved without faith, and we do not believe from the above passages [that children must be baptized], and we conclude from the description of baptism and from the accounts of it (according to which no child was baptized), also from the above passages (which alone apply to the question of children, and all other scriptures do not refer to children), that infant baptism is a senseless, blasphemous abomination, contrary to all Scripture, contrary even to the papacy; since we find, from Cyprian and Augustine, that for many years after apostolic times believers and unbelievers[25a] were baptized together for six hundred years, etc. Since thou knowest this ten times better and hast published thy protests against infant baptism, we hope that thou art not acting against the eternal word, wisdom, and commandment of God, according to which only believers are to be baptized, and art not baptizing children. If thou or Carlstadt will not write sufficiently against infant baptism with all that applies, as to how and why we should baptize, etc., I (Conrad Grebel) will try my hand, and I have already begun to reply[26] to all who have hitherto (excepting thyself) misleadingly, and knowingly, written on baptism and have

---

25a Grebel means that adults from believing homes, like Augustine, and converts from among the unbelieving pagans were alike baptized on confession of faith.

26 This is the *Taufbüchlein* of the spring of 1526, destined to be refuted by Zwingli in his *In Catabaptistarum Strophas Elenchus* (July, 1527). For the English translation see bibliography.

deceived concerning the senseless, blasphemous form of baptism, as for instance Luther, Leo,[27] Osiander,[28] and the men at Strassburg,[29] and some have done even more shamefully. Unless God avert it, I and we all are and shall be surer of persecution on the part of the scholars, etc., than of other people. We pray thee not to use nor to receive the old customs of the Antichrists, such as sacrament, Mass, signs, etc., but to hold to and rule by the word alone, as becomes all ambassadors (*gesanten*), and especially thee and Carlstadt, and ye do more than all the preachers of all nations.

Regard us as thy brethren and take this letter as an expression of great joy and hope toward you through God, and admonish, comfort, and strengthen us as thou art well able. Pray to God the Lord for us that he may come to the aid of our faith, since we desire to believe. And if God will grant us also to pray, we too will pray for thee and all, that we all may walk according to our calling and estate. May God grant it through Jesus Christ our Saviour. Amen. Greet all brethren, the shepherds and the sheep, who receive the word of faith and salvation with desire and hunger, etc.

One point more. We desire an answer, and if thou dost publish anything, that thou wilt send it to us by this messenger and others. We also desire to be informed if thou and Carlstadt are of one mind. We hope and believe it. We commend this messenger to thee, who has also carried letters from us to our brother Carlstadt. And if thou couldst visit Carlstadt, so that ye could reply jointly, it would be a sincere joy to us. The messenger is to return to us; what is lacking in his pay shall be made up when he returns.

God be with us.

Whatever we have not understood correctly, inform and instruct us.

Given at Zurich on the fifth day of September in the year 1524.

Conrad Grebel, Andrew Castelberg, Felix Mantz,[30] John Ockenfuss, Bartholomew Pur, Henry Aberli, and other

---

[27] Leo Judae (d. 1541), Zwingli's close associate in Zurich.
[28] Andreas Osiander (d. 1552), Lutheran reformer of Nuremberg, who developed special views on justification which led to the Osiander controversy.
[29] Particularly Martin Bucer and Capito.
[30] Referred to in Selection I at n. 6.

brethren of thine in Christ, if God will, who have written this
to thee, wish for thee and us all and all thy flock till further
message and true word of God, true faith, love, and hope with
all peace and grace from God through Jesus Christ. Amen.

I, C. Grebel, meant to write to Luther in the name of all of
us, and to exhort him to cease from his [policy of] caution,[31]
which he uses without [authority of] Scripture and which he
established in the world, and others after him. But my affliction
and time would not permit. Do it according to your duty, etc.

POSTSCRIPT OR SECOND LETTER

Dearly beloved Brother Thomas:

When I had subscribed all our names in a hurry and had
thought this messenger would not wait until we wrote to Luther
too, he had to bide and wait on account of rain. So I wrote to
Luther[32] too, on behalf of my brethren and thine, and have
exhorted him to cease from the false sparing[33] of the weak, who
are [really] themselves. Andrew Castelberg has written to
Carlstadt. Meanwhile there has come here to Hans Hujuff[34] of
Halle, our fellow citizen and brother, who recently visited thee,
a letter and shameful tract[35] by Luther, which no man ought
to write who wants to be first fruits like the apostles. Paul
teaches differently: *porro servum Domini*, etc.[36] I see that he
wants to have thee outlawed and deliver thee to the prince[37] to
whom he has tied his gospel, even as Aaron had to hold Moses
as a god. As for thy tracts and protestations I find thee without
guilt, unless thou dost reject baptism entirely, which I do not
gather from them, but that thou dost condemn infant baptism
and the misunderstanding of baptism. What "water" means in
John 3:5 we shall examine carefully in thy book[38] and the
Scripture. The brother of Hujuff writes that thou hast preached

---

31 The false forbearance.
32 Grebel never received a direct reply from Luther, but from Erhard
  Hegenwalt, January 1, 1525.
33 The false forbearance.   34 See above, n. 13.
35 *The Letter to the Princes of Saxony Concerning the Tumultous Spirit*, 1524,
  directed against Müntzer and Carlstadt. See John S. Oyer, "The Writings
  of Luther Against the Anabaptists," *MQR*, XXVII (1953), pp. 100 ff.
36 The allusion may be to II Tim. 2:24.
37 Elector Frederick the Wise of Saxony.
38 This is another reference to the *Protestation*, article 6; Brandt, *op. cit.*,
  p. 135.

against the princes, that they are to be attacked with the fist.[39]
Is it true? If thou art willing to defend war, the tablets, singing,
or other things which thou dost not find in express words of
Scripture, as thou dost not find the points mentioned, then I
admonish thee by the common salvation of us all that thou wilt
cease therefrom and from all notions of thy own now and
hereafter. Then wilt thou be completely pure, who in other
points pleasest us better than anyone in this German and other
countries. If thou fallest into the hands of Luther or the Duke,[40]
drop the points mentioned, and stand by the others like a hero
and champion of God. Be strong. Thou hast the Bible (of which
Luther has made bible, blare,[41] babble[42]) for defense against
the idolatrous caution[43] of Luther, which he and the learned
shepherds in our parts have propagated in all the world;
against the deceitful, weak-kneed faith, against their preaching
in which they do not teach Christ as they should, although they
have just opened the gospel for all the world so people might or
should read for themselves. But not many do it, for everybody
follows their authority. With us there are not twenty who
believe the word of God; they trust persons: Zwingli, Leo
[Judae], and others, who elsewhere are esteemed learned. And
if thou must suffer for it, thou knowest well that it cannot be
otherwise. Christ must suffer still more in his members. But he
will strengthen and keep them steadfast to the end. May God
give grace to thee and us. For our shepherds also are so wroth
and furious against us, rail at us as knaves from the pulpit in
public, and call us *Satanas in angelos lucis conversos.*[44] We too

---

[39] *The Sermon Before the Princes of Saxony,* July 13, 1524; see above, esp.
pp. 64, 68 f.

[40] George of Saxony.

[41] *Bubel,* which then meant "drum," hence "blare," or "wanton mis-
conduct."

[42] Babel, which can refer to the presumptuous Tower or to babbling. The
alliterative phrase was originally Müntzer's and was apparently recounted
to Luther by Agricola, a former associate of Müntzer. (The phrase was
later printed by Agricola in his Exposition of Psalm XI[x]. See Gustav
Kawerau, *Johann Agricola* [Berlin, 1881], p. 48.) Luther thereupon
repeated the phrase when he placed it on the lips of all "fanatics" in
summarizing their view of Scripture in the aforementioned Letter to the
Saxon Princes, *Werke* (Weimer), XV, p. 211. Grebel did not fully
understand Luther's point. Luther, arguing against the spiritual use of
the Bible, desired to show how, on the testimony of Müntzer himself,
the Bible in the hands of the radicals had led to *Bubel* (license) and *Babel*
(babbling divisiveness).

[43] False forbearance.

[44] Satans changed into angels of light. Cf. II Cor. 11:14.

shall in time see persecution come upon us through them. Therefore pray to God for us. Once more we admonish thee, and we do so because we love and honor thee so heartily for the clearness of thy word and hence dare write thee trustfully. Do not act, teach, or establish anything according to human opinion, your own or that of others, and abolish again what has been so established; but establish and teach only the clear word and practices of God, with the rule of Christ,[45] unadulterated baptism and unadulterated Supper, as we have touched upon, in the first letter, and upon which thou art better informed than a hundred of us. If thou and Carlstadt, Jacob Strauss and Michael Stiefel[46] do not give sincere diligence to it (as I and my brethren hope that you will do), it will be a sorry gospel that has come into the world. But ye are far purer than our men here and those at Wittenberg, who flounder from one perversion of Scripture into the next, and daily from one blindness into another and greater. I think and believe that they propose to become true papists and popes. Now no more. God, our Captain, with his Son Jesus Christ, our Saviour, and with his· spirit and word be with thee and us all.

Conrad Grebel, Andrew Castelberg, Felix Mantz, Henry Aberli, Johannes Pannicellus,[47] John Ockenfuss, John Hujuff, thy countryman of Halle, thy brethren, and seven new young Müntzers against Luther. . . .

[45] Matt., ch. 18, on church discipline.
[46] A Lutheran who on mathematical apocalyptic grounds set the date for the end of the world, October 19, 1533. The booklet by Stiefel which Grebel may have known was *Das Evangelium von dem verlorenen Sohn*, 1524. A former Augustinian friar, he became a professor of mathematics in Jena (d. 1567).
[47] Hans Broedli from the Grisons became preacher in Zollikon, early identified himself with radical reform, was driven from Zurich after the Disputation of January 17, 1525, was active in Stallan (Schaffhausen), and was burned 1528.

IV

Whether God Is the Cause of Evil
By John Denck [1]

AUGSBURG, 1526

INTRODUCTION

PREDESTINATION AND THE BONDAGE OF THE WILL in the realm of saving faith constituted the theological center of Lutheranism. Anabaptism stressed the freedom of the will and the morally and religiously responsible adult's decision for or against Christ. And in further contrast to Lutheranism it stressed progressive sanctification in imitation of Christ over against the forensic justification through faith in the redemptive work of the historic Christ.

[1] The principal interpretations of Denck in English are as follows: Rufus Jones, *Spiritual Reformers* (1914), Ch. XI; Frederick L. Weiss, *The Life, Teachings and Works of Hans Denck* (Strassburg, 1924), based upon the sources, all of which are listed and located in the Appendix; and Alfred Coutts, *Hans Denck, Humanist and Heretic* (Edinburgh, 1927), which was written without knowledge of Weiss's effort. Of these three works it may be said that in the first Denck appears as a Quaker, in the second as a Unitarian, and in the third as a humanist, thus reflecting the authors' sympathies. Neither Weiss nor Coutts was familiar with the Troeltschian typology. Coutts all too readily takes over the concept of Spiritual Reformer from Jones, unaware of the religio-sociological typology with which Jones was familiar, and uses the term of Denck as though he were spokesman of the whole of the "right wing" of Anabaptism in which Grebel and Blaurock would be reckoned lesser representatives over against the revolutionaries. The basic German biography upon which all three of these writers draw is that of Ludwig Keller, *Ein Apostel der Wiedertäufer* (Leipzig, 1882). It contains some of the writings of Denck *in extenso*. The most important later works in German are as follows: Otto Vittali, *Die Theologie des Wiedertäufers Hans Denck* (Freiburg, 1932) and Albrecht Hege, "Hans Denck, 1495–1527," an unpublished dissertation, Tübingen, c. 1939, a copy of which is available in the Mennonite Historical Library in Goshen, Indiana. This is by far the clearest delineation both of the life and the thought of Denck. Another German work contains profuse excerpts from Denck's writings: Adolf Schwindt, *Hans Denck: Ein Vorkämpfer undogmatischen Christentums* (Schlächtern/Habertshof, 1924).

Because of the importance of the voluntarist principle both in the soteriology and the ecclesiology of the Anabaptists, the editor has chosen two representatives, John Denck and Balthasar Hubmaier, to deal with the subject. In Denck's work, Augustinian Neoplatonism and medieval mysticism constitute a major strand. In Hubmaier's work late scholastic categories are prominent and they are regarded as valid argumentation with the Protestant divines. In effect the two treatments of free will are so differently oriented that the reader will not be wearied by any considerable duplication. In fact, Denck's treatise is a comprehensive treatment of the religious life as understood by one of the most beloved of the Anabaptist leaders.

By means of questions and answers Denck deals not only with predestination but also with many other themes, for example: the diverse manifestations of selffulness and its desirable opposite, *Gelassenheit* (cf. Selection XIII, introduction); the imitation of Christ, leading to divinization and inner lordship over all that is creaturely; the relation between the inner and outer Word, and the possibility of universal salvation on repentance. After exploring the bounds of enlightened conscience through the inner Word, Denck avers that salvation is *in* us but not *of* us and that the universal "truth of God" must be perceived in the historic and experienced "truth of Christ." Thus, though he holds much closer to the framework of traditional Christianity than, for example, Sebastian Franck (Selection VII), it is clear from this as from most of his other writings that Denck was, from the moment of his conversion to Anabaptism all the way to his qualified and despairing "retraction," at the interior of his being primarily a Contemplative Anabaptist.

Whether God Is the Cause of Evil[2]
By John Denck

AUGSBURG, 1526

THE TEXT

I, John Denck, freely confess before all God-fearing persons that I open my mouth against my own will and reluctantly speak before the world of God who nevertheless compels me so that I cannot be silent.[3] And in his name alone do I willingly and joyfully speak however difficult it may be for me. There are

---

[2] The full German title is *Was geredt sey das die Schrifft sagt Gott thue vnd mache guts vnd böses. Ob es auch billich das sich yemandt entschuldige der Sünden vnd sy Gott vberbinde* ([Augsburg], 1526). *What Does It Mean When the Scripture Says: God Does and Works Good and Evil? Also, Whether It Is Fair that Man Exculpate Himself for His Sins and Blame Them on God.* A copy is preserved in Munich in the Stadtsbiblicthek, Mor 136. The bracketed pagination in the present translation refers to this edition. This booklet along with several other works by Denck was reprinted in the German of a later period in *Geistliches Blumengärtlein* (Amsterdam, 1680). I am grateful to the Goshen College Library for presenting to the Andover-Harvard Library a microfilm of the *Blumengärtlein*. The title in the *Blumengärtlein* differs somewhat from that of the original edition. It echoes the secondary title of the original which appears in the table of contents as *Ob Gott eyn ursach sei des bösen* and which has been taken as the main title for the present translation.

The translation has been prepared with the galleys of the critically edited text prepared by Rev. Walter Fellmann, pp. 22–42, and made available through the great kindness of Dean Harold Bender of Goshen College. My whole translation has benefited from the examination of Fellmann's galleys and where I have used his footnote I indicate my explicit indebtedness with an asterisk.

[3]* The very first lines of the Foreword indicate that our tract is an early work. Denck must have written it shortly after being expelled from Nuremberg. Early in 1524, Andreas Bodenstein von Carlstadt had written in Orlamünde on whether God is the cause of the fall of the devil. On Quinquagesima Sunday, 1524, Diebold Schuster preached in Nuremberg on predestination. It is to the local repercussions of this sermon and to Luther's *De servo arbitrio* (late 1525) that Denck undoubtedly refers in the

a few brethren[4] who imagine that they have utterly explored the gospel, and whoever does not everywhere say yes to their talk must be a heretic of heretics. Should one wish to give an account of one's faith to those who desire it, then they say that one wants to cause discord and tumult among the people. If one lets bad words fall on the ears, then they say that one shrinks from the light. Very well, God has drawn me out of my corner. Whether it will do anyone any good, only God knows. For there are many who ask after the truth, but one sees few who like to hear it. If I speak the truth, may he hear it who wants to hear. Let him who ascribes to me lies, give testimony against me. O Lord my God! Let me be obedient unto thee and do me whatever thou wouldst through thy most beloved Son, Jesus Christ, through whose Spirit the world should and must be chastized. Amen.[5]

God speaks through the prophet [Isa. 45:5]: I am God and there is none else . . .; who makes the light and creates the darkness, who makes peace and creates evil. This some scribes interpret as though God were an originating causer of sin. Thus they say: Since God is in all creatures, he works in them all good and evil, that is, as they say: virtue and sin.

True indeed, if God had created nothing, sin would never have occurred. But that God himself therefore created it does not follow therefrom. For, since God is good, he cannot in truth create anything but the good. Therefore all creation has by God been made good, which in a certain sense is like God. What human beings do over and beyond this by sinning, that they do out of their own property and against God. For if God himself did it, he would be against himself, and his Kingdom would be destroyed and [then] man would be wronged by the punishment which he had not deserved. And even if God should take away the punishment, it would not be occasion for gratitude, so long as he himself brought it [sin] about.

You may say: If, then, God does not make sin but rather ordains it, what is there in the one different from the other? If he ordains it, his will must be therewith. If his will is present, what difference does it make whether one puts it that he does it

title. Hermann Barge, *Karlstadt* (Leipzig, 1905), II, 21; 32; 190 f.; 240. Carlstadt also wrote a work on *Gelassenheit* which later circulated under the name of Valentine Weigel.
[4] Diebold Schuster ("der Bauer von Wörhdt") and Luther among others.
[5] It is at this point following the Foreword that the longer title *Was geredt sey* appears in the edition of 1526.

himself or that he lets someone else do it? Is not the receiver as bad as the thief? If He has [merely] looked on and would actually have preferred to prevent it, is not the fault his? Answer: It is better that he had ordained sin than that he had prevented it, which he could not have done without having forced and driven men like a stone or a block. But then his name would not be recognized and praised by men. The reason: They would have presumed, since they would be aware of no sin [Aij], that they were just as righteous as God. Therefore it is infinitely better [to have] ordained than to have prevented sin. For sin is over against God to be reckoned as nothing; and however great it might be, God can, will, and indeed already has, overcome it for himself to his own eternal praise, without harm for any creatures. But God would not have been able to alter his own regulation, to maintain his creatures without sin, without disadvantage to his eternally abiding truth. For he could never with full praise have been praised, which was his first and only reason for having begun to create. And it would be for God and for all creatures forever detrimental if praise of him could not be [somewhere] in progress. Yea, if sin could not be wiped out, it would be better if God had not created than that he had ordained sin. Nevertheless if it were otherwise for him than it is for him, it would not be right for him. If he had not created, he would not be recognized except by himself, which would not be sufficient for his glory. If he had prevented sin, his mercy would not have been mercy, so long as it had had no object in which to exercise or which had need of it. But if sin could not be overcome, God would not be omnipotent and [he] would have to acknowledge an enemy standing eternally alongside and over against himself. Yea, his enemy would be as powerful as he.

You may say: Since God is in all creatures and effects everything in them, must it not follow that he also commits sin? Answer: God is in and works in all creatures truly. But that he also effects sin cannot be retorted so simply. The reason: Sin may be understood in two ways, namely, that it is, differently, good and bad. In the sense in which it is bad it is before God nothing, which is made without God, as John [ch. 1:3] says. In the sense in which sin, however, is a good, it *is* something and made by God as a punishment for one person or another.

You may say: If then sin is made as a good by God, is he not then the cause of the same? Answer: God, in so far as he doeth sin and all that one calls bad, he does it as punishment, as has been said. Now, if God does punish someone without cause and unfairly, it is true what the divines say that God would be outright a cause of sin. But who wishes to accuse God of such except him who knows Him not?

You may say: If then sin, as man commits it, is nothing before God, why does he then punish? Answer: For the same reason that a schoolmaster punishes his children for doing nothing. To do something is good. If we did *something*, to this extent we would have less need of punishment. But how sin [really] is nothing may be perceived by whoever gives himself over to God and becomes nothing, while at the same time he is created something by God. This each one will understand according to the measure of his resignation, as all the declarations of God must be heard. Whoever has ears to hear, let him read the example of the sons of Jacob, who sold Joseph their brother in Egypt, and after honest remorse, heard from Joseph [Gen. 50:20]: Not you (he says) but God has sent me hither. You thought evil against me, but God meant it for good about me and brought it to pass. Thus God always creates the best in the first place, namely, light and peace. The sooner man accepts them, the sooner he is united with God. However, when someone bars himself off and resists, there God, through his eternal wisdom (which nothing can exceed), takes exactly the opposite, namely, darkness and discord—just as long as we ourselves want to have them. And with these [he] contends against us, as vigorously as we have ever fought against him. Does God therefore commit a sin in that he punishes someone who himself wishes it not otherwise? Yea, punishment is not a sin but a good. For what father who loves his child does not also punish it until it is prepared to do what it should have done before the sin?

You may say further: If then God uses sin as a punishment, must it not then always be committed? For it surely would not be good [Aiij] that a punishment be withheld. If now it must always be committed, what can a man do about it? Answer: Whoever recognizes sin as a punishment in truth, for him it is no longer a sin but is for him rather a wonderful encouragement to acknowledge and to love the real good.

You may say: If sin is then good, what harm is it then for one to commit it? So may we not wish to sin much in order that we may be much advanced? Answer: To him who recognizes it for a punishment and does it no more sin is a good. Whoever does it again and again cannot say that he does the good as

God's will so long as God has displeasure in sin. And whoever defends sin resists the truth and the Holy Spirit who punishes the world because of sin. Again, whoever recognizes sin as darkness and discord which he has deserved is already in part in the light and peace to which God has led him. Since God has now brought him into the light as one who will never again rue the bestowal of his grace, he will never again lead him into sin. Those whom he lets fall again into sin are only those who are not satisfied with the light. These, however, who do not permit themselves to be satisfied with the light (Jesus Christ) are already in darkness. And also they hold the light for darkness. Therefore God punishes them and gives them over into the darkness until they become weary thereof. A parable: [Imagine] one who had long erred and been in misery and had at last come home and had been well and lovingly received by his father and brothers, and who yet would not acknowledge that this was his real homeland, father, and brothers, but desired to search further and did not want to give credence to the testimony of his brothers and father. He could not say with forthright truth that he had suffered much misery and want, even though such be the case. For if he actually recognized for misery what had befallen him, he would in contrast recognize his homeland and not desire to return to misery, since the father does not give him cause but rather instead reason to stay. Thus whoever will not find sufficiency in God, his Father, and yield himself to him and [who] senses nevertheless nothing unfair or unfriendly but only what is right and good—which is good for everyone in truth—he cannot plausibly say that he recognizes sin as a punishment decreed by God for him. The reason: He would recognize the punishment as good and thank the Father for it and henceforth remain with him, make himself subject to him, and do with him whatever pleases the Father himself. Sin, however, does not please him, otherwise he would not have forbidden it, and also he will not bring it about in any yielded (*gelassnen*) person. Therefore it is a fabrication when false Christians say that they can do nothing but what God works in them, for the mouth speaks otherwise than it is in the heart. The mouth speaks of its resignation while the heart makes use of all its own liberty. Such a person steals from God the will which he has created good and free and makes it thus his own against God's will. Yea, the mouth and the heart steal from God his highest and greatest honor that they can conceive and say: God has made a temple in which he does not wish to dwell. If, however, they say that he does dwell therein, how inconsistent they are, for they accuse God of that of which he has eternal abhorrence.

You may say: Say what you will, I can never do anything good. Answer: But can God do good? You will of course say yes. So let him do what he wills to do. He will not incur a punishment for you. If you, however, will not concede to him that he do it, you thereby prove that you have no contentment in him, which is an arrogance, which God has not created, as Scripture[6] says.

You may say: I [could] have contentment in him, but what can I do about it, that he will not work it in me? Answer: When you are contented in him, then you also believe that he has overcome sin. For if you did not believe this, you could not seek his help. If, however, you truly believed that he had overcome sin, then it would not be able to get you any more. Now you confess yourself, however, that you cannot do anything but sin. Yes, you have said just that, sin has overpowered you and continues to overpower you. If sin, however, has been able to overcome you, as you yourself say, God has not overcome it, according to your declaration, or slain it, for were it dead, it would not be able to get at you. Do you not see, you who hear the Word of God and do not heed it, that you neither believe this nor that, that you are neither thus nor otherwise spiritually content? Now as soon as you believe, you will be saved. If you believe in a fleshly salvation, then you will have also a fleshly felicity. In this sense Paul [in dealing] with the Jews used the words of Moses about the ways of the perverse, saying [Rom. 10:5]: The man who keeps the commandments shall live by them—as though Paul wished to say: You keep the commandments only outwardly, therefore also you lead no more than a superficial life. In like manner Moses spoke of the *true* life [Lev. 18:5], as also Christ, saying [Luke 10:28], This do and thou shalt live. Yes, truly you will live, in so far as you truly fulfill the commandments. Truly you will be saved in so far as you in truth believe and not hypocritically.

You may say: If, then, it is not at all for want of God's [intent] and if the difficulty is only in myself, then does it not also rest with me whether I am saved? And if so, then we have our salvation not from God through Christ but from ourselves. Answer: Salvation is *in* us but not *of* us, just as God is in all creatures but not for that reason from them, but rather they

6 Cf. Ecclesiasticus 10:21; Prov. 8:13; Isa. 13:11.

from him. For if God is in me, then in fact everything is in me that belongs to God—omnipotence, righteousness, mercy. If I do not believe this, I am a liar, for it is true what God has declared: he fills the heaven and the earth, that is, all creatures. You may say: If then salvation is in me, what do I lack further? Am I not already saved? Answer: No. Why? Because it is not enough that God be in you; you must also be in God. What purpose does it serve that you have God and yet do not honor him as God? What does it help that he created you in the beginning through his Word and has made you his child when you do not conduct yourself as a child? Can he not disinherit you although he has promised you equally along with other children the inheritance?

You may say: If I hear aught, does it not depend upon my obeying, doing, or running—against Paul [Rom. 9:16] and Scripture? Answer: It does not rest with my willing or running, but rather, as I have said, with the fact that one fails precisely, out of one's own strength, to run straight toward heaven and thereupon falls and runs thereafter toward the opposite. Where I, however, run in the truth, there not I but the Word of God runs in me, that is, I run in a suffering manner, in such a way that my running will not be in vain, as also Paul says of himself [Gal. 2:21].

You may say: Nevertheless I should very much like to know what in me prevents me from gladly wishing to accept the salvation as long as God wills to give it to me, as you say and as I can well say. Answer: Just this hinders you which has hindered all the elect, namely, that your will and God's will, although they appear to be one, are nevertheless not one. The reason: God seeks not himself in his willing, as you do. This he proves by the fact that he renounces his power and does not shatter the sinner at once, which he would have every right to do, but instead, in his patience, gives him occasion for remorse in order that he might bring him to himself in the very gentlest manner. This he would not do, were he seeking himself. That you, however, seek yourself and not God for his own sake, you demonstrate in your incomposure (*ungelassenheit*) in the fact that you are always looking for a hiding place from which you would like to escape the hand of God. For you are always anxious, so long as you [B] are a little blade of grass and he an immeasurably great stone, that he will crush you where you are holding still over against him. For so it appears to flesh and blood before man has yielded himself. Because he seeks salvation that [God in his power] seems [to him] damnation. That does not taste good to perverted nature. If man held himself still, that would be the time and place for the Spirit of the Lamb to give testimony and say that this is the only way to salvation, namely, to lose oneself. For, since God and all his action is the best, it must necessarily follow that his breaking of the will (*brechen*), which is surely contrary to our nature, is infinitely better than to do all things in heaven, on, and under the earth. Yea, since blood and flesh are thus obstinate toward God, so that before God our activity (*thun*) is passivity (*lassen*), our making before God a breaking, our something before God a nothing—we always ought to hear what the Spirit says to us: that God's breaking, as it appears to us, is the best making and that the nought of God—that which seems like nothing to us— is the highest and noblest something. This testimony is in all people and it preaches to every single one in particular, according to how one listens to him. Whoever wants to exhaust himself in talk [saying] he does not hear [the testimony] is a liar, for he has blinded himself, even though God has given him good vision. For this Lamb[7] has been from the beginning of the world and remains to the end a mediator between God and men. Which men? You and me alone? No, not at all, but rather all men, whom God has given him [the Lamb] as an inheritance. Has he not, however, given him all pagans and Jews? Why do you, then, close to them the way which you yourself do not want to follow? If he, then, is a mediator who promotes the cause of both, impeding none (which is indeed also true of him), then he must, without interruption, proclaim and announce again and again to everyone the will of the Other. Thus David says [Ps. 19:4]: Their line is gone out through all lands and their words to the ends of the world. Heaven, day and night and all the works of God proclaim his honor, yesterday, today, and tomorrow, so long as the world endures.

You may say: The heavens proclaim indeed according to their manner, but the Lamb himself does not, as you hold [proclaim]. Answer: Why do the creatures proclaim? Is the Lamb so lazy or imperious that it does not want to preach? No, it is not for that reason, but rather, since one does not want to hear it, he sends us creatures to mock us, but not to harm us. That the Lamb, however, proclaims, can be perceived there where a person has long been preached to from without and nevertheless is never able to receive it for himself unless he has previously

7 The inner Word.

received testimony from the Spirit of God in his heart, even
though covered over. What is creaturely, one may well be able
to bring to a place, where it had not been before. But where
God is not, thither he may never be brought. The Kingdom of
God is in you, says the Truth [Luke 17:21]. Whoever looks
toward and awaits it from outside himself, to him it will not
come. Whoever seeks God truly has him also truly, for without
God one can neither seek nor find God. But we do not really
want to hear him. Therefore we say, "He does not proclaim,"
so that we are enabled to excuse ourselves. But why do we not
want to hear? Because we do not wish to endure his work in us.
We should very much like to be saved without any means
whereby any hurt would occur. Therefore we reverse God's
will. Therefore also he reverses our will and gives us damnation
instead of the salvation we desire. For our own sensuality,
which we do not want to give up, [he gives us] trouble and
anxiety, which will also not leave us. The devil has always
gotten the upper hand by his lying testimony, wishing to make
it such a trifling thing to resist God and so impossible to heed
him, for the reason that it seems to him and to his kind to be a
troublesome thing to do and suffer God's will.

God wished to give the world testimony against their presumption, that thus, uncalculatingly, they would, without any
fear, wish to do his will which they had not at all experienced
or perceived as to how it would happen according to [his]
ordering. Therefore he also commanded [Bij] preaching and
punishment. Then the devil rushed up right away and thought
up a little contrivance whereby his power might not be circum-
vented, gave to the servants, whom God had called, the task of
preaching up and down the reverse, all with the appearance
and indication that this must be the right; yet all the time it is
displeasing to God. Thus men became—indeed, they were
already and remained as presumptuous and without reverence
for God in their passivity (*lassen*) as before in [their] activity
(*thun*). But you ought to know, you poisonous snake, that your
own cunning will fail you and must turn out to your harm! Or
did you not know that when someone is deceived by one of the
two highest opposites, he will ever thereafter be only that much
more cautious? Whosoever burns himself with the heat and is
frozen with the cold seeks the mean. All the elect already see
your deception in part. Therefore they also have no peace or
satisfaction therein, but rather seek a mean between your
former and your present lies, and they will also find it un-

hindered by you. The mean, however, existed before the outer extremes existed. Yea, the mean remains in eternity, even if the extremes may disappear and appear. The mean is the Word of Truth, which says thus: It is hard for the rich man (that is, all persons who are full of the creaturely, each one according to his measure) to enter into the Kingdom of Heaven; but not impossible [Matt. 19:23]. If it is not impossible, let each one leave off the creaturely, that is, take upon himself the yoke of Christ; and it will become wondrously easy. Now he can very well let the creatures go, since this is nothing impossible. If, however, he says, It is impossible, he lies according to habit and uncreated nature against God, for whom nothing is impossible and who is ever ready to do the best in so far as one will suffer it. Yea, it is impossible to retain the creaturely, as the false Christians do, and at the same time to receive salvation. The reason: God is jealous and gives his honor to none other. Whoever then will be a Christian and nevertheless has such love for the creaturely that he will not let them go (lassen) deceives himself, and God cannot hold him in his presence but rather spews him out in abomination because he is lukewarm, because such a one wants to be the bride of God and nevertheless wantons with the creaturely world.

You may ask: Why does not God take away the creaturely and make us as he himself would have us? Answer: If he already takes away the creaturely, as often happens for many, then he gives man absolute free choice, as he gave in the beginning, in such a way that man might grasp either the good or the bad, as Scripture testifies [Gen. 2:16 f.; Ecclesiasticus 15:14; Deut. 30:19; Jer. 21:5]. The reason has been given above, namely, that God does not wish to compel, so that his mercy might be recognized and not despised. Otherwise he need not have poured a soul into man at creation. He would have received his satisfaction if he had [simply] made man blessed [to begin with]. Thus Christ also says (when several broke away from him) to his disciples [John 6:67]: Do you also wish to go away?—as though he wished to say, You should be unconstrained. Scripture speaks of a tranquillity (gelassenhait), which is the means of coming to God, that is, Christ himself, not to be regarded physically, but rather spiritually, as he himself also proclaimed before he came in the flesh. This is the way those who are cunning in Scripture speak, who are not instructed for the Kingdom of Heaven, about a stark blindness, and [they] give the world testimony of their boldness. This [blindness], according to them, is also without any distinction wrought by God, as though the godless also stood tranquil in God and [as though] not they but rather God sinned in them (as one [quite] rightly says of the elect that in them not they but rather God works the good). Say it, somebody. How could the devil have better messengers?

Out of all this it is clearly understandable that Moses, the faithful servant of God, says to the whole people of Israel without exception—for they were an uncommonly stubborn and faithless people and there were few orthodox believers among them—says verily to them all with utter truth [Deut. 30:14]: The commandment, which I command you today, is not too high or distant but rather [Biij] it is in your mouth and heart to do it. And Paul says [Rom. 10:8] that is the word which he preaches.

You may say: The word and the preaching of Paul is Christ crucified and raised from the dead. How was this or how can this word have been in the heart of Jews? Answer: The Spirit of God has given them testimony that God alone is to be loved because he alone is good. Furthermore, if one is to love him, one must hate and lose all [else] which hinders this, namely, oneself and all that is creaturely. Again, since God is also good, he cannot, because of his benignity, allow harm to come to anyone, but rather he would make it up for everyone who gets lost from his ways—a hundredfold, yea, infinitely. What is now this word other than that which both Moses and Paul preached, although with a difference? But this difference is alone in exteriors, which is not the Truth itself, but rather only a testimony of the Truth. Therefore, whoever holds the testimony higher than the Truth itself inverts the order, all of which is an abomination in the sight of God. This is what all perverse Jews do and have done, who denied the law which God has written with his finger on their hearts and sought it [instead] in the book written by human hands, out of which they would learn and would like to maintain what they had previously determined among themselves they would not and could not do. This same thing all perverse Christians do today who deny Christ preaching in their hearts. Yet this Word is a work powerful in proving to every single one in particular the glory of the Father in the [inward] killing and resurrection. For they [the Lutherans] do not wish for Christ from above, but rather they seek him only in the [historic] flesh all in the expectation that it is enough that the work of God be manifested in him, it not being necessary that it be manifested in all. Otherwise there couldn't ever be a Christian, they say; yea, one would rather be damned before he learned where and how he should seek Christ. They wish to know Christ by themselves and not wait until he gives himself to them to be known. To these Paul speaks bluntly, as it is fitting, to give a fool answer according to his question [Rom. 9:16]: It is not, he says, of him who willeth nor of him who runneth but of God who showeth mercy.

The Word which is in the heart one should not deny, but rather [one should] listen diligently and earnestly to what God would declare in us. At the same time [one should] not arbitrarily throw out all external testimony, but rather hear and test all and make, in fear of the Spirit, comparisons. Thus the understanding (*verstand*) could, day to day, become ever more pure the longer we wait, until we would hear God in uttermost forthrightness speak with us, and we would become certain of his will: which is to leave off all of selffulness (*aigenschafft*) and to yield oneself to the freedom which is God. For man imitates God, takes on the traits of the divine generation, as one who is the son of God and coheir with Christ. Therefore such a one also lives, according to his measure, just as Christ lived. Yea, he himself does not live alone but Christ in him. He does not consider it robbery that he is in some sense equal to God [Phil. 2:6], but rather, even though he is a lord of all creatures, he submits himself to all creatures most humbly, not in order that they serve him, but rather that he, according to his measure, might serve them, fulfilling the will of his Father.

You may say: In a sense, then, do you not make all Christians the equal of Christ? That sounds exactly as though they would have no need of Christ. Answer: All Christians are in some sense like Christ, for, as he offered himself up to the Father, so they are ready to offer themselves. Not, I say, that they are so perfect, as Christ was, but rather that they seek exactly the perfection which Christ never lost. In like manner the earthly (*irdisch*) and elementary (*elementisch*) fires are also equal and one with warming, drying, burning, and lighting; and yet the elementary is in an ineffable way more subtle than the earthly fire. Thus Christ calls himself a light of the world and calls also his disciples, that is, all Christians, a light of the world. Again, he is come to kindle a fire [Luke 12:49] which also Jeremiah [ch. 5:14] lighted, as the Holy Spirit says to him: Behold! I will make my words in thy mouth fire, and this people wood, and it shall devour them. And of the same there is much. In sum, all

Christians, that is, they who have received the Holy Spirit, are in God, like unto Christ and equal to him, in such a way that what refers to the one refers also to the other. As Christ does, so do they also. And thus they have Christ as a Lord and Master, for the reason that he is the most perfect mirror of his Father [Wisdom of Solomon 7:26], than which he could not be more perfect unless he had not become man [at all]. And if he could have become more perfect even by a shade[8] and did not, he would not have been the true Saviour; we would have had to seek another. Far be that! That he was, in fact, the most perfect he proved in that he, on his own, offered up his life, without complaint, without acclaim, through the power of the Father and received it back. And in all this he never wavered a moment but rather finished all for the best in due season, neither too early nor too late. This none has ever done. And in so far as anyone has done this he has merely taken from Him, that is, righteousness out of grace. But he received it from none except from the Father, that is, grace out of righteousness.

That we need him, however, and would not want to be without him may be demonstrated and perceived from the following. Since God does not wish to have forced anyone and [wishes] to have everyone in his service of one's own free will and [since] we have nevertheless, without his fault, completely rejected him in such a way that we, as far as in us lay, were utterly without God and lay in darkness and could not even stand up any more (for we had withdrawn ourselves from God and all good and all capacities which we had from God)— accordingly, it did not behoove God merely to set us up again without means—the more so for the reason that we didn't ever want to have him, and [that] he does not wish to hold up anybody against the person's will. Still the good pleasure of his will remained unabated such as he has determined it from all eternity, namely, that he desires the salvation of all men. Accordingly, he sets forth a means, which had been prepared from eternity, [and] in which men would be saved just as they had been created therein; that is, his Word. In this Word is hidden alike the mercy and the righteousness of God. And the operation which was impossible has become through the omnipotence of God again possible also through the Word. For man could not accept grace without grace, so also God could not impart his righteousness to unrighteousness without this means. Now, however, this means is so near to all persons

8 Literally, by a straw.

(however much they have wanted to reject God) that they can easily receive it in [simply] returning to God. Not that they themselves are able to do anything, but rather because the Word is always in them trying to unite them with the Father, and they will not have it. And nevertheless, as said, God wishes to have forced no one; the fault is theirs who do not wish to do what they very well could by means of the Word. And they are liars and God remains nonetheless sincere and true, as Paul says to the Romans [ch. 3:4] and as has been asserted above.

You may say: Maybe there is a voice in me, but I do not hear it, because I am deaf by reason of sin. Maybe a light does shine in me, but I do not see it, because I am blind. Answer: This is a false excuse, as are they all [which are designed to] put themselves in a good light and to blame and condemn God. For the Word of God surely addresses everyone clearly: the dumb, the deaf, the blind; yea, unreasoning animals, indeed, leaf and grass, stone and wood, heaven and earth, and all that is therein, in order that they might hear and do his will. Only man, who does not [C] wish to be nothing and yet is even more than nothing, strives against him. O what a perverse way! Has then God promised eternal life to the unreasoning animals and not much more to human beings? But only continue to do what you do so long as nothing else appeals to you. If you knew, however, what was still to come over you, you would be eager enough! For sometimes you would give yourselves up gladly to suffer all if he would only, with a single little word, comfort you.

You may say: If, then, the Word is thus in all people, what need had it of the humanity of Jesus of Nazareth? Could not the Word, in some other way, carry out the will of the Father? Answer: The Word was in human beings for this purpose that it might divinize them, as happens to all the elect. And the Scripture [John 10:34] calls them therefore also gods, and they are not therefore many gods or idols who point away and turn one away from the one God, but they [who are] many are all one in the one true God. Nevertheless whoever honors them apart from God makes them, without their fault, into idols, which they were not and never would be. The Word, however, had to become man in Jesus for this reason that people both in spirit and in the flesh, from within and without, behind and before, and in all places might have testimony. Both [would thus have testimony], the elect for their furtherance and salvation, the others for the reason that they then could not say: God leaves a person free to lay hold of whatever he will to the end that he actually sin and die, which would [,accordingly,] be God's secret pleasure, however much he might give the appearance of its not pleasing him. Thus argue the perverse even in this day, and this argument is so common that many elect also agree with them, though not yet with the same satisfaction as the perverse. May this lie, however, be understood as punished and stigmatized [precisely] by the *humanity* of Jesus, since God has created all persons equal to himself, but none has so remained except one, who is Jesus, who has so loved all the others, that he offered up to the Father his life for their death, which he must surely have learned from the Father, since he was completely equal to the Father and heeded him in all things. Thus God has always had this love from eternity which Jesus displayed under Pilate. He had always loved his Son like the apple of his eye. Yet he found heart-deep satisfaction in his death, which he would have preferred to suffer himself had such a thing not been against order and had men been able to perceive the spiritual, for he is a Spirit, which no fleshly eyes or ears can see or hear.

You may say: Yes, he died indeed out of love, but not for all; rather, only for a few. Answer: Since love in him was perfect and [since] love hates or is envious of none, but includes everyone, even though we were all his enemies, surely he would not wish to exclude anyone. And if he had excluded anyone, then love would have been squint-eyed and a respecter of persons. And that, [love] is not! Why should it, however, be strange that we should reject the Son as before we rejected the Father? Should it therefore be not true that he died for all, just because all are not saved? Should it therefore be not true that the Father created all men good just because they have not remained good? Far from it! Indeed, Christ was so extremely resigned (*gelassen*) that, although he loves all men without measure, if it had pleased the Father, he would also have willed to suffer even in vain. Therefore this sacrifice was accordingly pleasing to the Father. If there had been even a thousand times as many worlds, it would nevertheless have satisfied him for the guilt of all. That Scripture does say [Matt. 20:28; Mark 10:45] that he died for *many*, and yet again [I John 2:2] for *all* is not contradictory but rather written to this end that not all have received the light, although it has illumined all [John 1:9] and though many deny the Lord, who has nevertheless ransomed them all, as Scripture abundantly testifies.

[Cij] You may say: These your arguments sound just as

though God did not himself know the moment of a man's conversion and [as though] the foreknowledge and providence of God were uncertain. Answer: God has indeed known from the beginning how he would relate himself to creatures and the creatures to him, namely, how he would always offer the best and they would always desire the worst, and he would also give it to them occasionally, but nevertheless always for the best. And although he did not wish the death and destruction of the sinner (and knew nevertheless that his will would be effected) since it did not become him to draw by force into his service, he continued to use death in such a way that it [became] the eternal praise of his holiness, as we [have misused] his grace to our disgrace and ridicule. Therefore he, marvelous to relate, found satisfaction in the death, not for its own sake but rather for the sake of the trophy, namely, that the uncreated[9] death should be swallowed up in the created death. This is the great secret, which the great and the wise of this world do not perceive, while the angels marvel thereat and praise the Lord, who reigns in eternity and forever. Amen.

He who ordains evil and [yet] can compensate with greater gain than [the loss he cannot] prevent is not to be blamed for the evil. As an example: If there were a child with a propensity to steal and the father put a penny before him in order to find out whether he would steal it and thereupon to punish him and to get rid of the naughtiness, would the father now be guilty of this sin for the reason that he had deposited the penny, even though he had previously often forbidden and enjoined the child not to steal? No one could say this. In like manner, the Father in heaven warned his child Israel from its youth up by means of the law not to steal, that is, to take possession of the creaturely instead of himself, and nevertheless he laid before him so much thereof that he surely had occasion to steal something. Now the boy did not leave it, and the father regarded him for a little while in order that he would have reason to punish the child with success, which before the sin he would not have found suitable. Also it would not have been for the boy's improvement. If he, however, wishes now to discipline him, the boy remonstrates with the father and says: "Why did you put the money in my way, if you didn't want me to steal it? Didn't you very well know? Didn't you have some satisfaction in it, otherwise why didn't you prevent it?" Say now,

---

[9] That is, the originally unintended death of Adam in contrast to the purposeful death of the Second Adam.

all you who hear and behold this. Is it now fair that the child should speak this way? Is not this very talk even more punishable than the thieving which took place? Truly, if the boy will not leave off his complaint, the father will lead him to the judges at the gate to deal with him according to the law of Moses [Deut. 21:18–21] as with a disobedient child, to the end that he be covered with stones, if he will not take switches for his improvement.

Therefore, although the Lord of all things knew reason enough to indicate why it would have pleased him to disregard our sin, nevertheless it is not seemly for us to question it, but rather, if he wishes to punish us, to attend to it that we hold still for him without any retort since we know we are guilty. For all the arguments that children improvise after they have sinned, they do only to excuse themselves, and thus only the more so do they accuse themselves. It does not help us, dearest brothers, our questioning and disputing about [God's] foreknowledge (*fürsehung*) whether it be before or after our sin. It serves no other purpose than to excuse ourselves, which is the worst of all poisons. Yea, Adam our father also sought a similar idle alibi; but it would not help him, even though he was not so impious that he would have ascribed the fault to God, as we do so completely; although also here again, the excuses of Adam and of all people are of such sort that they do not leave God unjustified. People make out as though they feared they could do something against God's foreknowledge, or God would err and [they] make him into a liar, when they, studious of his command and law, think to themselves that all is carried out when they with ardent mouth above a cold heart say: [Ciij] We are poor sinners. They would like thus in their mind to leave to God all honor even though in the eyes of all pagans he has nothing from us but shame and outrage. How gross this rogue[10] is to look at, however subtle and facile he is! For if someone burdens himself to do something against God, why does he not take heed of His commandments, which He has given for the purpose that they be obeyed, rather than of foreknowledge about which absolutely nothing has been ordered or revealed? If he does not will sin and nevertheless knows that it takes place, we should not in this case bother ourselves about him. He will not become disparate in himself, as do we. His foreknowledge, which is unknown to us, will surely, without our prying spirit, accord with his will, which even the perverse know in part. But

10 Luther.

the [theologically] clever thus have to become fools who yearn to know God's mystery and [yet] despise the commonly recognized (erkanten) intention (willen) of his commandments.

You may say: We do not need [the doctrine of] foreknowledge, as you say, except as a comfort for all the elect that they might know that their help and salvation lie in the hand of God and that there is no power so mighty which will or could wrest it from him. Answer: This comfort you can give to none and also none can take it from you. For whoever has yielded himself to the chastisement of the Father [and who] has in a measure tasted the sweetness of the bitter cross,[11] to him the Father has revealed himself through his Spirit in defiance before that person's enemies, but [he is] not the less to fear God because of it nor to despise anyone. For whom God has received in faith, he can and wills to reject again in case the person does not remain in faith, since he did not even spare the angels for the reason that they were so certain of the matter[12] that they thereby developed satisfaction in themselves and forgot God. Therefore also the elect instrument of God, Paul, says not in vain [I Cor. 10:12]: Let him that thinketh he standeth take heed lest he fall. If God gave his Spirit to King Saul and took it away again and it is nevertheless true that he never rues his gifts, what blame should there be in him if he should wish to take back from us the talent which he had given us, so that we have nothing—that is [from those of us for] whom grace also means nothing—and yet remain [in our sight] sincere and just? Is it not mishandling providence (fürsehung) to wish to be certain of the reward of the Lord, however we may serve him? In brief we'd be saying: God has provided (fürsehen) for the salvation of his own regardless of their works. Thus we would be saying further: Regardless also of faith. Therewith Christ would be completely thrust from the middle.[13] For if works are in this manner, without distinction, to be rejected, why then does Paul say so earnestly [I Cor. 6:9 f.]: No fornicator, no adulterer, no miser, no drunkard, no idolater will inherit the Kingdom of God. And Christ says [Matt. 10:39] that whoever does not lose himself is not worthy of him. And we [who] wish to be so highly worthy of him with

---

11 Cf. the bitter-sweet Christ in Thomas Müntzer; see also above, Conrad Grebel, Selection III at n. 17.
12 Salvation.
13 Mittel suggests, as the English does not, Christ's mediatorial role, as Mittler.

our own loquacious faith have not left off in the slightest from creaturely things for his sake, to say nothing of ourselves, which we therefore suppose to be impossible also for God to do. Therefore, the whole of nominal Christendom (*Christenheit*) is full of adulterers, misers, drunkards, and more of the same.

Clearly, all who truly fear God must renounce the world. And in the measure that they have to use the world out of necessity, they ought always to be prepared for struggle and ready for adversity as sojourners upon the earth. Whoever lives in security and happiness in the world should take care lest he be overtaken with her, and the ignominy of his fornication become publicly exposed and rebuked. For the Lord cometh. He will come at night, when none will take note of him, like a thief, to take off what he commended to us as shepherds, to serve him therewith, and which like thieves we have appropriated for ourselves in order to rule. Then it will help no one to cry: Lord, I have preached the gospel! Lord, I have heard it [preached]. For he will answer [Matt. 25:12]: I do not know you. Or, do we suppose he will not with full right make use of this answer? Or ought he only to get rid of pagans in this fashion? How so, when the same will have as good a case before him as we? O dear brethren! He will not need a long reckoning with us: The words which he declared from the beginning and which we have heard will convict us. He always says [Luke 11:28]: Blessed is he who heareth the Word of God and keepeth it; [Matt. 7:26]: Whoever heareth it and doeth it not is like unto a fool; [John 10:3]: He is a sheep of Christ who hears his voice and obeys. For they who hear the law of God and do not fulfill it in practice are not righteous before God. If now someone wishes to come before God without the righteousness which holds before God, he kicks out of the way the Means, which is what the whole world does. Woe, woe, and again woe to the perverse, who know the will of their Lord and do it not, and yet want to be regarded as justified. How much more unbearable it will be for them than for them for whom it has been in part hidden! Is it not disgrace upon disgrace that we should want to learn to know Christ and yet none the less retain our old godless nature? And we excuse ourselves accordingly with the saying of Paul [I Cor. 7:20] which has it that every single one seould abide in his calling wherein he was called. [And we take it] in the sense that if the Lord called someone in adultery, he should remain therein! Why then did not Matthew remain in the customs house? Verily, the fishermen, according to our

view, did wrong in leaving their work! This is the way it works
out for us when we sort out Scripture in fragments and mend
the old garment with new patches. What Paul [I Cor., ch. 7]
spoke of the married and single, we would like to apply also to
our profligate handiwork, bargaining, usury, and offices. Not
so, but rather—to be brief—whoever is not ready with Zacchaeus
[Luke 19:8] to make fourfold restitution, if anyone should have
ought against him, is not worthy of Christ and will not hear the
voice of the Bridegroom. Yea, if he hears it in his mind, it
becomes plain poison for him and damnation. We should
bring empty hearts to Christ which should be ready to renounce
themselves—all that we have—if we could but be receptive to
his mystery. For really we are bringing only crowded (*volle*)
hearts and presume to accomplish only *our* purpose with
Christ, however it may be. In this manner laborers seek for
good days with Christ, the poor for wealth, and the servants for
rule. Likewise the idle wish to enrich themselves, and the masters
do not wish to give themselves over to lose anything but rather
through him to retain everything. Nevertheless they all ought
to lose themselves in him if they hearken otherwise to his voice
and don't want to be children of the world.

You may say: We come therefore and seek Christ in order
to find and learn all this in his presence, but you have it [that]
one ought already to have this [attitude]. How does this all
fit together? Answer: The Word of God is already with you
before you seek it; gives to you before you ask; opens up for
you before you knock. No one comes of himself to Christ except
the Father draw him, which he truly does of course according
to his goodness. Whoever on his own initiative, however,
undrawn, wishes to come on his own, presumes to give God
something which he has not received from him. He wishes to be
deserving from God in order that he need not thank him for his
grace. Abraham [John 8:56] rejoiced in the day of Christ
before he had seen it. Cornelius [Acts 10:2] was a spiritual and
God-fearing man long before he acknowledged Christ. Paul
[Phil. 3:6] had a righteous and godly zeal for the law before
the revelation of Christ. The disciples of Christ [Matt. 19:27]
left at once house and home, wife and child for Christ's sake
and did not yet know who he was. All the elect seek and rejoice
and do not themselves know for what and why, all of which is
without disadvantage to the gospel of Christ. For such a work
has not gone forth from human beings but rather from God,
from whom comes all, that in truth may [D] be called some-

thing, as also the gospel testifies. Therefore, no one can vaunt himself before God for his works or his faith, for whoever glorifies within himself has in himself sufficient satisfaction and is one of the rich whom God sends empty away. The poisoned selffulness of the flesh which man has taken on himself against God and without God ought and must be mortified. Where this has begun in a person and he ascribes it to himself, such a one steals from God his honor and slurps up the poison and the devil's milk and, more than that, all on his own wishes to be something over against God—which he is not. But whoever does not want to endure this work of mortification but prefers to practice the works of darkness will not be able to excuse himself before any creature and much less before God. For whoever wishes to excuse himself before God ascribes to God what He has not done and never at all will do, and God must be to him what He had not been before. For if God were in truth that which such a one accuses him of being, he could and would not punish anybody (since he is righteous and punishes none without guilt), unless all creatures were repentant, which is not ever the case, but rather one must first come at it through some Means. But this Means is Christ, whom none may truly know unless he follow after him with his life. And no one can follow after him except in so far as one previously knows (*erkennet*) him. Whoever does not know him has him not and cannot without him come to the Father. But whoever knows him and does not testify thereto by his manner of life, God will judge along with others who are perverse, regardless of the fact that the person had been previously called and received in the fellowship of the gospel. With this he cannot comfort himself otherwise than in repudiating himself.

You may say: Now do I rightly take it from you that the foreknowledge of God is variable? Answer: God is and remains sincere in all things and his decree will not be reversed. But to whom has he revealed it that one may rely upon it and not fail? The Truth and the Word of God is in itself constant. We, however, are inconstant and vacillate therein. Blessed is the man in whom the Word is true as it is true in God and remains true in eternity for all eternity. Therefore, those whose hearts God hardens so that they cannot believe, he has not rejected in the sense that he does not want to have them but rather that he might beforehand show them their unbelief, all to the end that they might recognize the pity of it and bewail it and be comforted. Just so, a father goes about it with a naughty child. He may punish or disown it as vehemently as he wants; if the child should come back and pray for mercy, he would receive it back, and if he had in wrath strangled the child, so that it could never come back, he would nevertheless hope for improvement in the child; and could he but make it alive again, he would do it gladly. This even men who are wicked do. Will not God wish the same and be able to accomplish it, he whose wealth and bounty none can sufficiently imagine or declare? O blessed is the man who recognizes the mercy of God in fear and pain and, contrariwise, is fearful in grace! For this reason the Lord shows all tribulation to all people and IS THAT HE IS which is his name alone (which may be given to no creature), as he called himself and wherewith he indicated to his servant Moses [Ex. 3:14] he should be recognized. When and by whom it would be acknowledged, where and for how long he would be resisted, has never been concealed to him. He forbade that Nineveh be destroyed and because of its penitence took it back again. He accepted Saul the king and bestowed upon him his Spirit, but because of disobedience rejected him again. He redeemed Israel out of Egypt, but in Babylon he exiled [them] and then took them back and again rejected them. Yet in all this nothing alien or unexpected is encountered in him. Yea, verily! He is still the God who wills to save the whole of Israel, as Paul [Rom. 11:26] says. [Dij] For he wills not the death of the sinner but that the sinner may be converted and live. Therefore one can never in truth ascribe to him the guilt, for he has no joy or pleasure in the vessels of wrath, but rather with great patience he has drawn them forth from obscurity. For these he postpones punishment so long that he is prepared to take all of them back on repentance.

Of this truth I speak freely in the Lord who makes [us] dead and quick. Whoever wishes to offer himself in the depths of his soul and in truth to the Lord, that is, whoever wishes to leave off his own will and to seek the will of God and has respect for the work of God, him the merciful Father will receive with great joy and take back regardless of how he had conducted himself hitherto, however despicably he had used up his inheritance, yea, regardless of whatever the Father himself might have decided against him. O that the whole world would come in this manner! The Lord would surely be wonderfully ready to favor them. He bids all people be called and proffers his mercy to everyone in cordial earnestness and yearning in order to fulfill all that he has promised in truth. Is it not therefore malicious when our divines say that he bids someone be invited to the Supper but that it is not his will that this person come? The good Spirit of God has surely not bidden them to say this and the like—he who does sincerely all that he does. Surely he does not say, Come hither, and intend or wish secretly that this person remain where he is. Surely he does not give someone grace and secretly wish to withdraw it again. Surely he does not work up repentance in us for our sins and secretly adjudge us guilty of hell. For he is ever constant and sincere in all his gifts. And when he has considered us to be inconstant (which comes from our guilt alone and the sin in us and is not in him), he is nevertheless ever anew ready to entertain [the possibility] that he perchance has changed, indeed that we ourselves have changed. But you can sing and say to us, call and shout at us, whatever you want, the world does not wish to hear. And even those children of the world who do hear would like to be observed in this respect and thus conceal their wickedness. They say yes to the command of the Father but do not carry it out. O these are extremely bad children! Therefore also the Lord has already, not unfairly, blinded some and will blind, harden, and punish them still more, simply for the reason that they do not accept the Lord in truth, that is, they wish to come to the Father without the Son, wish to rule with God and not to be ruled with Christ. They wish to find their souls and not lose them, to do God's will and not leave off their own. They speak of spiritual freedom and remain in fleshly thralldom and imprisonment. But I testify and [I] beseech you, by the Advent of Christ our Lord, all [of you] who in the foregoing manner behold, or otherwise perceive the truth *of God*, that you will to accept it in the truth *of Christ*— that is, according to the manner, way, and form which Christ taught and himself demonstrated, that is, by denying and losing himself—in order that you may stand before his Judgment Seat blameless and confident; otherwise the Truth is and will be for you the greatest lie, because of your perverse manner. And if you do not return while the Lord gives you opportunity and time, then you will have part with him who from the beginning bore forth the lie out of his own substance [John 8:44]. This inheritance is the gnawing worm that none can kill and the eternal fire that none can quench [Mark 9:44].

He for whom these words go to the heart ought and will have satisfaction in the fact that we get covered over with scorn and shame because of sin, and [yet he] does not alienate

himself [from us], even when we are persecuted by all creatures.
For one may still and indeed ought to beseech God, merciful
and sincere, that he take the shame from us in his good time
and according to his very best will, not for our sakes, but rather
in order that his name might be praised among all pagans and
nations, all of which he promised us [Diij] through his servants,
the holy prophets and his Son Jesus the Anointed, whom he has
for this reason established as King over all kings and Lord over
all lords [Rev. 19:16]. Before him the whole world is afraid
and yet it does not believe but will in truth soon experience
[him] on the Day to which all the saints look forward in joy.
Amen.

V

On Free Will
By Balthasar Hubmaier[1]

NICOLSBURG, 1527

INTRODUCTION

IN THE FOREGOING TREATISE ON THE FREEDOM OF
the will by John Denck evil was, in a Neoplatonic sense,
understood to be either (1) the absence of or the failure to
understand good or (2) the consequence of the will of a good
God so to create that he might elicit praise *freely* offered from
man. Denck's discussion did not deal with the Fall and with
original sin. This problem, in contrast, is a major theme of
Hubmaier's treatise. Here we have a boldly speculative anthro-
pology based upon an allegedly Biblical and pre-eminently
Pauline distinction between the flesh, soul, and spirit, each of
which has its own separate will. Only the flesh (Eve) and the
soul (Adam) were implicated in the Fall. The soul, following
the leading of the flesh, willed to know more than was necessary
to do God's will and in tasting of the fruit of the tree of the

[1] The best life in English is that of Henry C. Vedder, *Balthasar Hubmaier*
(New York, 1905). It is based in part on the researches of J. Loserth,
BH und die Anfänge der Wiedertaufe in Mähren (Brünn, 1893), but it is an
independent study with a clear delineation of thought and character.
Vedder had visited the places in which Hubmaier was active and incor-
porated the insights of German scholarship to date, making clear distinc-
tions within the left wing and fully rehabilitating the Evangelical
Anabaptists by locating their origin in Zurich rather than in Wittenberg.
Two German titles subsequent to Loserth's should be mentioned: Wilhelm
Mau, *BH* (Berlin/Leipzig, 1912), and Carl Sachsse, *D. BH als Theologe*
(Berlin, 1914). Mau discusses life and works concurrently and discerningly.
Sachsse, who did not know of Mau's work until the very end of his own
research, begins with a careful classification and analysis of all the works
attributed to Hubmaier, going considerably farther than Loserth (and
Vedder). In the school of Böhmer, Sachsse regards Hubmaier as dependent
upon the Zwickau prophets no less than upon the Zurich radical evangelicals (cf. p. 158).

knowledge of good and evil man actually lost his pristine capacity for such a distinction, or, as Hubmaier vividly puts it, his taste for what God regards as good and evil. To rectify this, God sent Christ, the Samaritan, the Eternal Physician, to administer the wine of the law which enables the fallen soul to know what is righteous in God's sight and the oil of the gospel to enable it to do the right. Born again in faith, man becomes a member of the church by believers' baptism. In this church the conditions of paradise are restored. Outside it the will is in bondage to worldly flesh and there is no salvation.

In a final section excerpted from Hubmaier's second treatise on the freedom of the will and here incorporated, God's will or power is seen under two aspects, as *potestas absoluta* and as *potestas ordinata*. Hubmaier's use of scholastic categories and his appeal to several of the Fathers sets his work apart from the Biblicism of most of the Anabaptist treatises. Hubmaier also comes near the Spiritualists in this treatise by holding that the spirit of man, which was not implicated in the Fall, enjoys an unobtrusive sovereignty over creation, once it is kindled by the Holy Spirit; for the spiritual man judges all things and is judged by none and, when thus strengthened, can enlist the renovated soul so that they together can will to "make the flesh go into the fire for the sake of the name of Christ."

On Free Will[2]
By Balthasar Hubmaier

NICOLSBURG, 1527

THE TEXT

FOREWORD

To the serene, noble prince and lord, Lord George[3] Margrave of Brandenburg, Duke in Pomerania and Stettin, and of the Kashubes and the Wends, Burgrave of Nuremberg, and prince of Rügen, my very gracious lord, grace, joy, and peace in God.

Most serene Prince, most gracious Lord. Though for some years now great zeal and diligence have been expended to make known the gospel to all creatures, yet I find several people who, alas, have up to now really learned and grasped only two articles from all the preaching. The first is, as they say: "We believe; faith saves us." The other: "We cannot do anything good, God works in us the willing and doing, we have no free will." Now such assertions, however, are only half-truths, from which also one can gain nothing more than half a judgment. Therefore, whoever makes up a complete evaluation from these and does not lay on the scale the opposing passages of Scripture, for him the half-truth is far more harmful than an outright lie, when the half-truth is believed and sold by its appearance for a whole truth. Hence come all sects, quarrels, and heresies,

2 The German title is as follows: *Von der Freyhait des Willens, Die Gott durch sein gesendet wort anbeüt allen menschen, und jnen dar jn gwalt gibt seine Khinder ze werden, auch die waal guttes ze wöllen und ze thon . . .* (Nicolsburg, 1527).

The translation is based upon the transcript procured by Henry C. Vedder for his book on Hubmaier and deposited in the library of the Colgate Rochester Theological School, which has generously placed at the editor's disposal the whole collection of Vedder manuscripts. This one, assigned by Vedder and Sachsse the number 22, was not translated. The translation has been checked against a second transcript controlled by F.-X. Hosek; made in Brno, 1872, and preserved in the Samuel Colgate Baptist Historical Collection housed in the Colgate Rochester Theological School.

3 Duke George I (1493-1531).

when one makes patchwork of the Scriptures, not putting together the opposing Scriptures and uniting them both in a final conclusion. He who thus cannot divide judgment on the Scriptures eats of the unclean beasts which divide not the hoof (Lev., ch. 2).[4] It is under just the cloak of these aforementioned half-truths that all sorts of wickedness, unfaithfulness, and unrighteousness have completely gotten the upper hand.

Now every frivolity and brashness has been swept into fashion. There unfaithfulness and falsehood sit in their splendid seat, rule, and triumph grandly in all things. Christian work no longer shines with men. There brotherly love is extinguished in all hearts, and it is as the prophet says (Isa. 59:14): Truth has fallen in the streets, and equity can nowhere enter in. Wisdom calls aloud and no one will hear her (cf. Prov. 1:20 ff.). For as all histories demonstrate, the world is worse now (to God be our lament) than it was a thousand years ago. All this takes place, sad to say, under the appearance of the gospel. For as soon as one says to them it is written (Ps. 37:27): Depart from evil, and do good—immediately they answer: "We cannot do any thing good; all things occur by the determination of God and of necessity"—meaning thereby that it is allowed them to sin. If one says further: It is written (John 5:29; 15:6; Matt. 25:41) that they who do evil go into eternal fire, immediately they find a girdle of fig leaves to cover their crimes and say: "Faith alone saves us and not our works." Indeed, I have heard from many people that for a long time they have not prayed, nor fasted, nor given alms because their priests tell how their works are of no avail before God and therefore they at once let them go.

Just these are the half-truths under which we, as though under angelic form cover over all license of the flesh and lay all our sin and guilt on God, as Adam did on his Eve, and Eve on the serpent (Gen., ch. 3). Yea, God is the cause of all our crimes, which is the greatest blasphemy on earth. To root out such tares, most gracious Sir, I have composed a little book, dedicated to your princely Grace; and in it I have shown how and what man in and outside of God's grace is and what he can do. I wish as quickly as possible to add another in which I will unanswerably and even more powerfully prove by divine writ the freedom of man [to choose] good or evil, and also thoroughly explain the opposing passages of Scriptures concerning Pharaoh, Esau, Jacob, the potter, and the like. I humbly beg your princely Grace graciously to accept this little

4 See below, n. 14

book. Herewith may your princely Grace be commended to
God.
Given at Nicolsburg, April 1, 1527.

Your Grace's servant,
Balthasar Hubmaier of Friedberg

[PART I]

Man is a corporal and rational creature, made up by God of
body, spirit, and soul. These three things are found to be
essential and distinct in every man, as the Scriptures plainly
demonstrate. When the Lord God made man of the dust of the
earth, he breathed into him the breath of life, and thus man
became a living soul. Here Moses (Gen. 2:7) points out three
things with distinct names. First, the flesh or body, made of
earth. This clod or lump of earth is called in Hebrew *aphar*
and *erets*; in our language, dust, ashes, or dirt from the earth.
Secondly, there was then the breath of life, in Hebrew, *neshamah*;
in our language, blowing, breathing, or spirit. Thirdly, the
soul, which animates the body, is expressed separately, and
called *nephesh*. Saint Paul plainly named these three essential
substances by special, distinct Greek names when he wrote
to the Thessalonians (I, ch. 5:23) about *pneuma*, *psyche*, and
soma; in Latin: *spiritus*, *anima*, *corpus*; in our language: spirit,
soul, body. He said: May he, the God of peace, sanctify you
wholly; and your spirit, soul, and body must be preserved
blameless unto the coming of our Lord Jesus Christ.

Likewise we read in Hebrews (ch. 4:12) of a distinction
between the soul and the spirit. Thus the Word of God is
quick and active and sharper than a two-edged sword, piercing
so that it separates soul and spirit, joints and marrow, and is a
discerner of the thoughts and intents of the heart. Mary, the
pure chaste virgin, indicated the distinction when she said to
Elizabeth (Luke 1:46 ff.): My soul magnifies the Lord and my
spirit rejoices in God, my Saviour; for he has looked upon the
misery of his servant. Here stand expressly: soul, spirit, and
misery—which refers to the flesh. For *tapeinosis* in Greek is
misery or lowliness in a person. *Tapeinophrosynē* is humility of
mind. Christ expressed this distinction more than superficially
when he said to his disciples on the Mount of Olives (Matt.
26:38 f., 41): My soul is exceeding sorrowful, even unto death.
The spirit indeed is willing, but the flesh is weak. Because of

this the saddened soul of Christ cried out at the bidding of the
flesh: My Father, if it be possible, let this cup pass from me.
But the soul adds, at the bidding of the spirit: Nevertheless not
as I will, but as thou wilt. Here, Christian reader, you see
clearly these three separate and distinct substances: soul,
spirit, and body, in every man, made and united after the image
of the Holy Trinity.

Now since no one, by dint of Scripture, can deny these three
essential things, *substantiae* or *ousiai*, it follows that three kinds of
will must be recognized in man, namely, the will of the flesh
the will of the soul, and the will of the spirit. In order that I
may prove by Scripture the distinctions of these three wills, see
that the Spirit of God says in John (cf. ch. 1:13): the will of the
flesh which does not want to suffer; the will of the soul is willing
to suffer, and yet, on account of the flesh, is also unwilling; the
will of the spirit is glad to suffer. But in order that I may bring
in further evidence concerning the distinct separation of these
three wills, the Spirit of God speaks by the mouth of that
disciple whom Christ especially loved (John 1:9 ff.) the
following words about the true eternal light, which was made
man and came to his own, and his own received him not. But
as many as received him, to them gave he the power to become
the children of God; to them who believe on his name, not by
blood, nor by "the will of the flesh," nor by " the will of man"
(so is the soul called in the passage: ch. 1:13), but those who
are born of God. Now we were born once in original sin and
wrath, as Paul laments to the Romans (ch. 5:12) and Ephesians
(ch. 2:3); as also David (Ps. 51:5), Job (ch. 3:3), and Jeremiah
(ch. 20:14 f.). But afterward, we must be born again, or we
cannot see the Kingdom of God, nor enter into it (John 3:4).
We must be born of water and of the spirit, that is, through the
Word of God, which is a water for all who thirst for salvation
(John 4:14), made alive in us through the Spirit of God.
Without his working, it [the Word] is a letter that killeth
(II Cor. 3:6; Rom. 8:2). He helps our spirits, witnesses to
them, strengthens them to fight and strive against the flesh, sin,
the world, death, the devil, and hell. Therewith every word that
proceeds from the mouth of God (Deut. 8:3) helps so that the
flesh with its evil will and lusts cannot flee, hide, or conceal
itself anywhere. It finds no rest or peace outside of the preached
Word of God, whose sound is gone out through all the earth
(Ps. 19:4; Mark 16:15; Acts 1:8; Rom. 10:18); nor inwardly
in the spirit; for everywhere it is convicted, while all testimony

is proved by the mouth of two or three witnesses. Then comes conscience and the gnawing worm into the heart of man (Rom. 2:15).

That is the real rebirth of which Christ speaks in John, ch. 3, whereby our Adam, who through the Fall had become a woman and an Eve, becomes a man again; and the soul, which had become flesh, becomes again spirit. Saint Peter (I, ch. 1:22 ff.) speaks quite straightforwardly of this rebirth, saying: Make your souls pure, through obedience to the truth, in the Spirit unto unfeigned brotherly love, and have fervent affection for one another, out of pure hearts, being born again not of corruptible but of incorruptible seed, namely, the living Word of God which liveth forever. For all flesh is as grass, and all the glory of man as the flower of grass. The grass withereth, the flower fadeth, but the Word of the Lord endureth forever (Isa. 40:8). Observe, pious Christian, how the soul, made flesh by the disobedience of Adam, must be born anew by the Spirit of God and by his living Word, as a spirit and become spirit, for what is born of the Spirit is spirit (John 3:6). I shall pass over now why Peter makes mention only of the soul here, saying: Make your souls pure, without adding: your spirit and flesh. However, he knows very well that the spirit ever since its divine creation has been whole and is in need of no rebirth. So he said: through obedience to the truth in the spirit. Thus rebirth does not help the flesh since on it sentence has already been passed and put in force by God that it must wither as the grass and become ashes, otherwise it cannot possess the Kingdom of God (I Cor. 15:50; Matt. 16:17).

PART II

It is to be noted that man must be considered in three states or forms: first, as he was before the Fall of Adam; then as he became after the Fall; thirdly, as he should be when restored.

(1) *How Man Was Before the Fall of Adam*

Before Adam's transgression, all three substances in man—flesh, soul, and spirit—were good. When God looked at all of the things which he had made, they were found good, especially man made in the image of God (Gen. 1:26). The three substances in him were entirely free to choose good or evil, life or death, heaven or hell. They were originally made by God good and free in the recognition, in the choice, and the doing of good and of evil, as Scripture testifies, saying (Ecclesiasticus 15:14 ff.): God made man from the beginning and left him free in the power of his own counsel. He gave him commandments and the law, saying: If thou wilt keep the commandments (God says: If thou, O man, *wilt*; it is enjoined upon thee to keep the commandments), they will also preserve thee. He has set water and fire before thee (notice the "thee"); stretch forth thy hand unto whatever thou wilt. Before man is life and death, good and evil; that which pleases him (yes: "him") shall be given him.

Here the Scripture shows us plainly and evidently that man was originally, in body, soul, and spirit, capable of carrying to completion a free choice of good or evil. But after the Fall of Adam, it was different.

(2) *How Man Became After the Fall of Adam*

Concerning the Flesh

After our first father, Adam, through disobedience, had transgressed the command of God, he lost this freedom for himself and all of his descendants. As when a nobleman receives a fief from a king and then acts against the king, the latter takes the fief away from the nobleman and from all of his heirs, for they all must bear the guilt of their forefather, so the flesh, by the Fall of Adam, lost its goodness and freedom irrevocably, and became utterly nought and helpless, even unto death. It can do nothing except sin, strive against God, and hate his commands. From this comes the grievous complaint that Paul makes to the Romans (ch. 7:5 ff.) against his wretched and accursed flesh. That is why it must return, according to the curse of God to earth, whence it came, or it cannot inherit the Kingdom of Heaven. So also it is with the blood, for the two are of one will (Gal. 5:13 ff.; Gen., ch. 3; I Cor. 11:27), as Paul writes (I Cor. 15:50): Flesh and blood cannot inherit the Kingdom of God. And Christ says to Peter (Matt. 16:17): Simon Bar-Jonah, flesh and blood have not revealed it unto thee. When Eve, who is a figure of our flesh, wished to eat, and did eat the forbidden fruit, she thereupon *lost* the knowledge of good and evil, yea, she lost the power of even wishing and doing good and had to pay for this loss by death; as soon as man is conceived and born, he is conceived and born in sin (Ps. 51:5). He is in sin from the first moment of his life, right up to his ears in sin, and when he has completed his earthly course, he must die and become dust.

As God said (Gen. 2:17): On the day that thou eatest of the tree of the knowledge of good and evil, thou shalt die. That is why Job (ch. 3:1 f.) and Jeremiah (ch. 20:14 f.) cursed the day of their birth. Likewise King David (Ps. 51:5) bitterly laments the day of his conception and birth and cries out to God that he was conceived in sin, that his mother bore him in sin, as we have already indicated. And Paul says (I Cor. 15:22), in few words, that we all die in Adam, and God himself calls it becoming dust and ashes.

Concerning the Spirit

But the spirit of man has remained utterly upright and intact before, during and after the Fall, for it took part, neither by counsel nor by action, yea, it did not in any way consent to or approve of the eating of the forbidden fruit by the flesh. But it was forced, against its will, as a prisoner in the body, to participate in the eating. But the sin was not its own, but rather that of the flesh and of the soul, for the latter had also become flesh. Saint Paul demonstrates this integrity and uprightness of the spirit especially in writing to the Thessalonians (I, ch. 5:23): May your whole spirit and soul and body be preserved blameless unto the coming of our Lord Jesus Christ. He says: Your *whole spirit*,[5] not your whole soul nor your whole body; for anything that has once fallen and been broken is no longer whole. King David also laments concerning the Fall and cries to God (Ps. 31:12): I have become as a broken vessel, etc.; and Paul (I Cor. 5:5) delivers the fornicator to the devil, for the mortification of his flesh, in the strength of our Lord Jesus Christ, that is, in the strength of the keys which Christ has entrusted to his bride, the Christian church, commanding inclusion and exclusion on earth, that the spirit be saved. It is as if he were to say: Let the flesh be mortified, let it fall to the devil. We give it up to him. But may the spirit be whole and safe in the day of judgment. Then let God deal with him according to his good pleasure. We need know no more now.

Concerning the Soul

The soul, the third part of man, through the disobedience of

---

[5] As Vedder has pointed out, Hubmaier improperly construes the *integer* of the Vulgate text of I Thess. 5:23 to apply only to *spiritus*. Valentine Weigel, perhaps dependent on Hubmaier, also divides man in three parts on the basis of this text.

Adam was so maimed in will and wounded even unto death that it can of itself not even choose good or reject evil, for it has lost the knowledge of good and evil, and nothing is left to it but to sin and to die. As for doing good, it has become powerless and impotent (Rom. 7:18 ff.). This comes from the flesh, without which the soul can do no outward act, for the flesh is its implement. Now when the implement has become worthless, how can anything good be done with it, although the soul wished to do good, and made every possible effort? Nevertheless this fall of the soul is remediable through the Word of God (Ps. 19:7), which teaches us anew to will or not to will what is good and what is evil, and to live accordingly through the resurrection of the flesh. This will thereafter become a celestial, indestructible, glorified, and spiritual body for action and fulfillment (I Cor., ch. 15). These will be the bodies of men who were born of water and of the spirit, since the first man, Adam, was made for the earthly life, the last Adam for spiritual life. The first man was of the earth, earthy; the other man was from heaven and heavenly.

The reason that the fall of the soul is partly reparable, however, and not fatal, even here on earth, but the fall of the flesh is to a certain extent irreparable and deadly, is that Adam, as a type of the soul (as is Eve, of the flesh), would have preferred not to eat of the forbidden tree. He was also not deceived by the serpent, but Eve was (I Tim. 2:14). Adam knew very well that the words of the serpent were contrary to the words of God. Yet he willed to eat the fruit against his own conscience, so as not to vex or anger his rib, his flesh, Eve. He would have preferred not to do it. But when he was more obedient to his Eve than to God, he lost the knowledge of good and evil, so that he could not wish nor choose anything good (Ps. 14:1; 33:13; 53:1). Neither could he reject or flee from anything evil, for he no longer knows what is good or bad in the sight of God. Everything has lost its savor for him, except what is savory and pleasing to his Eve, that is, his flesh. He has lost the real sense of taste.

A comparison: A wounded or feverish man cannot or will not eat or drink anything wholesome. Only cold water and harmful food appeal to him. That is because his sound nature and healthy constitution has been deranged by illness, for he has lost the right, sound taste of knowledge. He has a bitter tongue. He judges to be good what is harmful to him and deems as evil what is good for him. So is it with our soul since the defection of Adam. As soon as he had eaten of the tree of the knowledge of good and evil, from that very hour he lost the taste to recognize good and evil and can thus no longer know or judge what is good or evil in the sight of God, what deeds of piety are pleasing to God, or what works God will bless, although according to his spirit, he would like to do right. That wish exists today in all men, in Jews and pagans, as Paul writes to the Romans (ch. 2:14). If a man be blind, he would like to see. If he be lame, he would like to be straight. If he is fallen among murderers and has been left half dead, he would like to be healed. But as to the right way and means of arriving at this health of the soul, all are confused, save those who are instructed by the Word of God. From this now flow also all aberration, marginal teaching (*nebenleer*), error, idolatry, and heresies. Not included under the above words are all men who have sinned against the Holy Ghost (Matt. 12:31; Luke 12:10). In them, the will, the desire, everything is perverted (Rom. 1:21 ff.). They are scourged with the wrath of God on account of their stubborn, criminal, persistent evil, with which they fight against the knowable and recognized truth. Indeed, they turn their backs on God, and then say he will not let himself be seen. They stop up their ears, lest they should hear his voice. For if they heard his voice, so they believe, they would have to die, when really one should and must thereby, become alive. They also turn their eyes away from God and complain that he will not know them. They close their hearts and hide themselves, complaining that God will not knock at the door nor seek them. And when he knocks for them, they will not open; when he seeks them, they will not let themselves be found. What they have, they deny. Therefore God gives them what they do not want. So it happens to all those who deny the freedom of will in newborn men. There comes, however, the time when they will seek God but will not be able to find him. Also as they now flee from him, so will they then fall into his hands. And as they have treated God, so will he encounter them, and act according to their lack of faith. Therefore their sins can be forgiven neither here nor in the world to come, since the Spirit of God has been withdrawn from them, without which our spirit is utterly helpless. Therefore it is necessary, with David (Ps. 51:11), to pray earnestly that God will not take his Holy Spirit from us.

On the other hand, God will receive all men who hunger and thirst after piety and very much wish to do what is right (Matt. 5:6); desire and pray for the same from the God that made heaven and earth, whose invisible essence they perceive, namely, his eternal power and divinity (Rom. 1:20). If they are aware of him through his works since the creation of the world, he will not send them away empty without instruction but will fill them with good things (Luke 1:53) and send them messengers and letters missive to lead them on the straight road of truth. So he did with the treasurer of Queen Candace, in Egypt, through Philip (Acts 8:27 ff.); so he did with Cornelius through Peter (Acts 10:3 ff.). Yea, and before God would desert such who hungered for the Spirit, all angels would have to come down from heaven and, through them, announce and declare the praises of God (which he would have from us in the highest) and true peace on earth and good will toward men, as to the shepherds in the field at Christmas night (Luke 2:8 ff.). That is why God commonly referred to his word in Scripture as bread, water, drink, flesh, or blood (John 4:6, 7), for he will feed and give drink to all who accordingly hunger and thirst and will let no one suffer. Now, as to whether such a power of wishing what is right and good is in us, surely it is not in us as though out of us, for it is originally from God and from his image in which he first created us (Gen. 1:27; II Cor. 3:18). The old serpent (Gen. 3:1 ff.) has indeed almost obscured it and blacked it out through sin, but nevertheless he could never entirely extinguish God's breath in us, nor would he ever be able to do it, since God suffers no one to be tempted above what he can bear (I Cor. 10:13). But God himself can extinguish it as a punishment, so that man may have eyes, ears, and a heart, and yet not see, hear, or comprehend (Matt. 13:43).

Here one can see really how the flesh, after the Fall (Rom. 7:5), was absolutely nought (Gal. 5:17; Gen. 6:3), useless for good, and dead, as to all its powers, impotent for good and powerless (I John 2:16 f.), an enemy of the law, to which it is absolutely unwilling to be subjected even into the grave; as King David (Ps. 38:3) very bitterly complains, crying out that there is no soundness in his flesh. And so speaks Paul (Rom. 7:18; 8:26): Truly I know that in me, that is, in my flesh, dwelleth no good thing. The Spirit would gladly will and do, but it is imprisoned—it can accomplish nothing except that he give inward testimony to godliness against sin, and cries out to God, without ceasing, like a prisoner in unspeakable groaning. Thus the soul is also fallen in among murderers, and sorely wounded by them and lies half dead (Luke 10:30 ff.), no longer having any taste or perception of either good or evil. And as Paul says in this regard (I Cor. 2:14 f.): The psychic man (*seelisch*) does not receive the things of the Spirit of God, for they are foolishness unto him and he can not understand them, because they must be spiritually discerned. But one who is spiritually minded judges all things, and is judged of none. Observe, pious Christian, the wholeness of spirit in man, which judges all things aright; and the wounds of soul, which in the judgment has nothing to say on its own. Both flesh and soul are devastated and sorely wounded. Only the spirit has maintained its inherited righteousness, in which it was first created; only it, among the three substances in men, has the same form before and after the Fall of Adam, our forefather, whatever proud thinkers may say about the higher and lower faculties (*Portionen*) of man. Aristotle the heathen misled them, who was aware of and postulated in man nothing except soul and body. For him, spirit was too heavenly. With his natural and heathen understanding he could not comprehend this breath of the living God.

(3) *How Man Is After He Is Restored*[6]

When man is looked at as restored through Christ, we find that the flesh is still worthless and good for nought, as all Scripture laments. But the spirit is happy, willing, ready for all good. The soul, sad and anxious, standing between the spirit and the flesh, knows not what to do, is blind and uncomprehending as to heavenly things, in its natural powers. But because it has been awakened by the Word of God—jolted, warned, and led by the Heavenly Father through his comforting word, his threatening word, his promise, his benefits, his punishments, and all other means; made whole through his dear Son; also enlightened through the Holy Spirit (as the three principal articles of our Christian faith referring to God the Father, and Son, and the Holy Spirit show) thereby the soul now again comes to know what is good and what is evil. It has recovered its lost freedom. It can now freely and willingly be obedient to the spirit and can will and choose the good, just as well as though it were in paradise. And it can reject and flee from evil. Such effects the sent Word of God produces in it, as David declares (Ps. 107:20): He sent his Word, and made them whole (*gsund*), and Christ says (John 8:31): If you continue in my Word, then are ye my disciples, indeed and ye shall know the truth, and

6 The German here and elsewhere below is *nach dem widerbrachten fall*.

the truth shall make you free. When the Son makes you free, you are truly free. Let him who has ears hear and observe that we are freed again by the sent Word and truth of God, through his only begotten Son, Jesus Christ. So there must be genuine soundness (*gsundhayt*) and freedom in man, after restoration, when God works his will in us (Phil. 2:13), both to will and to do according to the good intention of his mind. Although the flesh in its will does not will accordingly, nevertheless it must, against its own will, do what the soul wants which is now united with the spirit. David cries to God (Ps. 119:25): My soul cleaveth unto ashes (that is, the flesh): but quicken thou me, according to thy Word. And for this reason there must be true soundness and freedom in man, after restoration, or these Scriptures must collapse—which God forbid! Therefore Christ (Matt. 19:17) and Paul (Rom. 8:4) bring this home to men, and say: If thou wilt enter into life, keep the commandments; if ye want to live according to the flesh, ye will die; if ye will walk according to the spirit, ye shall live. Hence arose the proverb of the ancients: Man, help thyself, and then I will help thee. God speaks forth and gives strength through his Word. Now through the power of the Word man can help himself—or can willfully neglect to do so—and this is brought home to him. Therefore it is said God created you without your aid, but he will not save you without your aid. Since God first created the light, whoever will receive it may do so according to God's promise. Whoever despises it, falls, by God's just judgment, into darkness (John 1:5 ff.; 3:19). The talent that one would not use, but hides in a napkin, is justly taken from him (Matt. 25:24 ff.).

Now all the while the soul stands between the spirit and the flesh, as Adam stood between God, who said to him that he should not eat of the tree of the knowledge of good and evil, and his Eve, who said to him that he should eat of the tree (Gen. 2:3).

Now the soul is free and can follow either the spirit or the flesh. If it follows Eve, that is, the flesh, it becomes an Eve and carnal. But if it is obedient to the Spirit, it becomes a spirit. But let the soul take heed not to linger too long at this oak tree of human choice, and ponder whether it shall follow the flesh or the spirit. It might be left, like Absalom (II Sam. 18:9),[7]

---

[7] This is a characteristic image of Hubmaier. He used it, for example, in *Reason and Cause* (1527) in reference to repudiators of infant baptism who hesitated to submit to rebaptism. Cf. also Thomas Müntzer, *Sermon Before the Princes*, above, p. 67.

hanging between heaven and earth. It might be pierced by the servant of sin, that is, the flesh, with three wounds: in will, in word, in deed. Therefore David says (Ps. 119:60): Lord, I have made haste, and not delayed to keep thy commandments. And in another place (Ps. 95:7): If ye hear the voice of the Lord *today*, ye shall not stop your ears. *Today* he says, not *Cras, cras* (tomorrow, tomorrow), as the ravens cry.

So now, the soul, after restoration, is whole, through the sent Word, and is truly made free. Now it can choose and do good, as much as is required of it, since it can command the flesh, tame it, dominate it, to such an extent that it must make it go against its own nature even into the fire[8] with the spirit and the soul, for the sake of the name of Christ. And although an imperfection, infirmity, and lack always accompanies it in all its action and resignation (*lassen*), whereby we are all unprofitable servants, these are not fatal or destructive to the soul, but to the flesh, which is a poor implement—a worthless tool.

A comparison: A cabinet maker wants to construct a clean and smooth table. But his plane is crooked and full of gaps. It is impossible for the worker to attain his purpose, although it is not he but his plane that is at fault. And likewise such failings are not damnable for the soul, since it is grieved by them, and recognizes its weakness before God. But to the flesh they are destructive; it must pay its penalty, must suffer a return to earth. But the soul is so free, after restoration, that it also can will evil and accomplish the same, because for wickedness it has an effective, convenient tool in the flesh. The flesh is quick and inclined by nature to follow any evil. Whence comes the saying: Sin is a matter of the will; if it were not voluntary, it could not be sin. To this self-will apply all the Scriptural passages where God reproves us for not being willing to hear, know, and accept the good. As when Christ says (Matt. 23:37): Jerusalem, Jerusalem, how often would I have gathered thee, as a hen gathers her chickens under her wings, and ye would not. Also he said it to the young man who asked him what good thing he should do to have eternal life; he answered him (Matt. 19:17 ff.): If thou wilt enter into life, keep the commandments. Therefore willing and keeping must have always been in the power of the young man who answered: I have kept them, from my youth up. Beyond a doubt he spoke the truth, for Jesus looked upon him and loved him, and Jesus loves not liars. Yet Christ points out to him his innate imperfection, such

[8] The reference is clearly to the stake of martyrdom.

as lurks in every man, and bids him sell all that he has and give
to the poor people; at that, the young man was moved with
sorrow. But this would not harm him, were he filled with
Christ, who is the Alpha and Omega (Rev. 1:8), the beginning
and the end of the fulfillment of the divine commandments
(Col. 1:19). For our perfection is in him. When the commands
of God are fulfilled, says Augustine, even if they are not fulfilled by us, we are forgiven. John wrote (I John, ch. 1) in
even a more than cheerful tone of this power, saying that God
bestowed upon us and brought home to us the power to become
children of God.

Christian reader, you see plainly how in us to whom the
Word has been sent there is a good will adhering, but its
perfection we do not find in ourselves because of our miserable
body, in which nothing but sin dwells (Rom. 7:20). In short,
the spirit is intact also after restoration; the flesh is good for
nought; but the soul may sin or not sin. However, the soul that
sins shall die (Ezek. 18:4, 20). It may well say: *propter me orta
est haec tempestas*: it has to do with me. The flesh has already
received its judgment. The spirit preserves its integrity. If I
will, I can be saved, by the grace of God. If I will not, I shall
be damned—and that by my own fault, from obstinacy and self-
will. So speaks the Spirit of God through Hosea (ch. 13:9):
Destruction is thine, O Israel; in me alone is thy salvation.

It is easy to deduce from this how the law was given with
distinguishable purposes: to the *flesh* for the recognition of its
sins; to the *spirit* as an aid and testimony against sin, to the
soul as a light whereby to discover and learn the path of piety
and to flee from sin and wickedness. Accordingly, when the
flesh hears the law, it is frightened and its hair stands on end
with terror. The spirit leaps up with joy. The believing soul
thanks God and praises him for the lamp and light for its feet
(Ps. 119:105). As the devil neither will nor can do anything
good, but is set in his evil, so also is our flesh, for it has sinned
presumptuously when it saw that the forbidden fruit was good
to eat, beautiful to the eyes, and a thing to be desired (Gen.,
ch. 3). But the soul did not sin out of willfulness, but from the
obtuseness and the presumption of the flesh. Adam did not wish
to vex his Eve, which was the flesh, as he tried to excuse himself,
saying (Gen. 3:17): The woman whom thou gavest me for my
companion gave me of the tree, and I ate of it. The spirit alone
remained upright in the Fall. Therefore it will return unto the
Lord who gave it (Eccl. 12:7).

In brief, you see here, reader, how God created man so free that it was originally possible for him, without new grace, to continue in his pristine innocence and purity unto eternal life. But he could also forfeit this grace by disobedience, as actually happened when, through the Fall, grace and freedom were to such a degree obscured and lost that, without an especial and new grace of God, man could not know what was good or evil. How could he, then, choose good and eschew evil, when one can will nothing but what he has previously known? But after the restoration man acquired such grace, health (*gsundheit*), and freedom through the merits of Jesus Christ our Lord that he is able again to will and to accomplish the good, even against the nature and will of his flesh, in which there is nothing good.

Part III

Since free will in man is nothing but a force, power, strength, ability of soul to will or not to will something, to choose it or to flee from it, to accept or reject good or evil, according to the will of God, or according to the will of the flesh (and this will or potency of the flesh could be called more properly weakness rather than force or power), the soul, through the eating of the forbidden fruit, lost its perception of good and evil in the sight of God. This knowledge it had possessed before the Fall in so far as it was necessary and sufficient for creaturely mankind. Therefore the tree was called the tree of the knowledge of good and evil, and God had forbidden Adam to eat of it, that is, to wish to learn and experience *more* than was necessary for man. Since Eve wanted to know *everything* that God knows, as the crafty serpent promised her (Gen. 3:5): On the day that ye eat thereof, then your eyes shall be opened, and ye shall be as gods, knowing good and evil—they were, accordingly, fairly dispossessed and bereft by God of this knowledge of good and evil and were become like a horse or a mule in which there is no understanding (Ps. 32:9). For man who does not receive thankfully the gift of God, or will not accept it, is rightly deprived of that which he has (Matt. 13:12). And so it happened in this case. Man can *now* no longer elect good nor flee from evil unless he knows what is good and what is evil in the sight of God. Therefore, this knowledge and power of knowing, willing, and working must be effected and acquired from a new grace and calling of the Heavenly Father, who now, through the merit of Jesus Christ our Lord, looks upon man anew, blesses him, and draws him by his life-giving Word. This Word he preaches into the heart of man. This drawing and bidding is compared to an invitation to a wedding or a dinner. God gives power and capacity to all men in so far as they themselves desire it (John 1:12; Jer. 21:8; Deut. 30:19). Free choice is restored to them to come, and a new birth, a new beginning of the creaturely, as man had been originally in paradise, save for the flesh. They have become the children of God (James 1:18; John 1:13).

But whatever man will not, like Jerusalem (Matt. 23:37) —and they who buy oxen and villages, and marry wives, and will not come—these he will leave outside, as unworthy of his supper (Luke 14:16). He wants guests and dispensers that are uncompelled, willing, and joyful. These he cherishes, for God compels no one, save by the sending and the summoning of his Word (II Cor. 9:5), just as the two disciples at Emmaus did not compel Christ to stay with them, save by petition and good words (Luke 21:13 ff.). Likewise the two angels did not compel Lot to leave Sodom (Gen. 19:15), for God's Word is so mighty, powerful, and strong (that is, in believers) that man (but not a godless man) can will and achieve all that he is bidden to will and to do in that Word. For the gospel is the power of God unto salvation for all believers (Rom. 1:16). When the man who had lain sick thirty-eight years among the derelicts at the pool of Bethesda heard the word of Jesus saying (John 5:8): Arise, take up thy bed and walk, in the power of this word of God, he got up freely, took up his bed, and departed. He might not have been able to do it and could have said to the Lord in unbelief: It is impossible; or: I'd rather lie here— as Christ did not work many miracles in his own native country because of their unbelief (Matt. 13:58). But when this sick man heard the Word, and believed it, he was saved, stood up, and walked. And as soon as Christ says to a man (Matt. 19:17): Keep my commandments; leave evil and do good—from that very hour the man receives through faith the power and strength to will and to do the same. Yea, all things are possible to a believer, by him who strengthens him, namely, Christ Jesus (Phil 4:13). We could adduce here all Scriptures (Rom., ch. 1; Heb., ch. 4; Isa, chs. 46; 55; Jer., chs. 6; 7; 23; Jonah, ch. 3; Amos, ch. 8) in which the power and working of God's Word is shown. So we know of a surety that God originally made all things good, and especially man, in spirit, soul, and body. But by Adam's disobedience this goodness in us was in respect to the soul wounded; in respect to the spirit, it was impeded and obscured by the darkness of the body; and, as for the flesh, it was completely ruined. If we are to be free again in respect to the spirit and healed in respect to the soul, if the fall of the flesh is to be harmless, this *must, must, must* take place through a rebirth, as Christ himself says (John 3:3), otherwise we shall never enter the Kingdom of God. God now of his own will begets us, as James (ch. 1:18) says, by the Word of his power, that we should be anew the first fruits of his creatures. In this Word, which Peter (I, ch. 1:23) calls uncorruptible seed, we become anew free again and sound (*gsund*), so that absolutely nothing corruptible is left in us (Rom. 8:2). Thus Christ says (John 8:32): The truth shall make you truly free. And David says (Ps. 107:20): He sent his word and healed me; and in another place (Ps. 119:107): Quicken me, O Lord, according to thy word. Now it follows indubitably that from the power of the divine Word in believers must come real freedom, real health (*Gsundhait*), and real life. Else we must disregard half the Bible. Far be that from us!

From the foregoing things it is plainly and surely to be seen that man received two wounds in the Fall of Adam: an inner one, that is, ignorance of good and evil, because Adam was more obedient to the voice of his Eve than to the voice of God; the other wound outward, in deed and action in such a way that man cannot perfectly execute or obey the commandments of God, because of the innate depravity of his flesh, but rather in all his doings is an unprofitable servant (Luke 17:10). And this fault or lack originates from the fact that Adam did not rightly master his rib, Eve, according to the command of God, but, contrary thereto, ate of the tree forbidden to him under penalty of death.

The first wound is healed by the wine poured on it by the Samaritan Christ (Luke, ch. 10), that is, by the law, through which man is taught anew, by new grace, what is really good or bad in the sight of God. The second wound is healed by the oil, that is, the gospel which thus deprives these sins or faults of their venomous destructive power, unless we presumptuously pursue them. Therefore Christ, the true Physician, mingled in the New Covenant both wine and oil, that is, law and gospel, and made of them a wholesome plaster for our souls, which he wanted to make righteous and well again.

Here one can take hold with both hands of how Christ

made the Fall of Adam for us no longer damaging or damning. He, through the woman's seed, crushed the head of the old serpent, took out the fang, and made its poison harmless to her (Rom. 16:20; I Cor. 15:30 f.). So now no one can any longer complain about Adam and Eve, nor try to excuse or palliate his sin by Adam's Fall, since everything has been adequately restored, healed, made whole, which has been lost and wounded and had died in Adam. For Christ, through his Spirit, has won for our spirit from God his Heavenly Father that its prison should no longer be harmful to our spirit; and through his soul he recovered for our soul the capacity to be taught and illuminated again by his divine Word, as to what is good or evil. Yea, through his flesh, he has earned for our flesh that after it has moldered to ashes, it will be resurrected in honor and immortal (I Cor. 15:35 ff.). Henceforth, each soul that sins must bear its own sin. It is guilty—not Adam, nor Eve, nor the flesh, nor sin, nor death, nor the devil. For all these, by the power of God, have been captured, bound, overcome.

Let us say with Paul: Praise, honor, and thanksgiving to him, through all eternity.

[Part IV]

Lastly, it is clear and evident what rubbish all they have introduced into Christendom who deny the freedom of will in man, saying that this freedom is a vain and empty designation and nothing in itself. . . .[9]

After my opponents come thus daily to me, bringing many writings by which they would fain wipe out entirely human free

[9] The remainder of Part IV on the moral dangers in the failure of Lutheran and Zwinglian preachers to distinguish for their people God's *praedestinatio* and his *praescientia* has been omitted to make room for a corresponding but theologically richer section from Hubmaier's second treatise. The German title thereof is *Das ander Biechlen von der Freywilligkait des menschens* . . . (Nicolsburg, 1527).

For inclusion here, only Part III, Arguments I and II, have been selected, beginning on folio *Di verso* in the original imprint and on p. 664 in the bound volume of photographed imprints collected by W. O Lewis.

These portions constitute the most interesting arguments supplementary to those of the first treatise and furthermore reveal the extent to which Hubmaier, virtually alone among the Anabaptists, was willing to use scholastic categories. He also quotes approvingly in the untranslated portions the vigorous anti-Pelagian Fulgentius of Ruspe, *Ad Monimum, lib.* i., and Augustine, *Contra Julianum,* iii, 8. He also quotes from or paraphrases John Denck's *Was geredt sey,* Selection IV.

will, exigency compels one to remove such stumblingblocks and countertricks from the way, and to hew them down with the sword of the divine Word (Eph. 6:17), so that no one will fall on them or be hurt. Now follow their arguments, one after the other.

[ARGUMENT I]

God has mercy on whom he will; whom he will he hardens (Rom. 9:18).

Here my dear friends cry out against me, as did the friends of Job against him. They say: Behold how it is all with God, and not in our power. What God wills, shall and must take place. Answer: That is a reference to the omnipotent and hidden will of God, who owes nothing to anyone. Therefore he may, without injustice, have mercy on whom he will, or harden the same; save or damn him. This power or will the Schools have called a plenary power or will of God (*voluntas absoluta*).[10] As Paul says [Rom. 9:19] no one can resist it. God indeed has full right and power to do with us whatever he will. He can make us vessels of honor or dishonor, just as a potter has power over his clay. And we cannot justly say: Why dost thou this?

But we find also a revealed will of God [*voluntas revelata*], by which he makes all men to be saved, and to come to the knowledge of truth. Christ showed us this very plainly when he said (John 3:16): God so loved the world that he gave his only begotten Son, that whosoever believeth on him should not perish, but have eternal life. He suffered for our sins, not for ours alone, but for the sins of the entire world (I John 2:2). He gave himself a ransom for all men (I Tim. 2:6). He is the true Light that lighteth all men who come into this world (John 1:9). To all who receive him, he gives power to become the children of God. That is why he bade the gospel to be preached to all creatures (Mark 16:15), so that all who receive it, believe on it, and are baptized shall be saved. Hence we can easily infer that God according to his preached and revealed Word absolutely does not want to harden, to blind, to damn anyone, save those who of their own evil and by their own choice wish to be hardened, blinded, and damned. Such are men who, when Christ comes to his own, receive him not (John 1:11). They do not acknowledge the time of their visitation (Luke 19:44). When he knocks, they will not let him in. Scripture does not refer to this revealed will of God when it says: No one can

10 Marginal reference in Latin.

resist his will, but rather it speaks of the hidden will. Now if you try to equivocate and confuse the two wills [*equivocatio*],[11] there arise marked misunderstanding, error, and confusion of the Scriptural passages. Therefore one should wisely split (*spaltenn*) the sentences (*vrtayl*) in Scripture, and really ruminate[12] in order to know which passages refer to the secret will of God, and which to the preached will.

This revealed power or will of God the Schools call the ordinary will (*voluntas ordinata*), not that the other will is extraordinary, but because all that God wills and does is orderly and good. He is subject to no rules; his will itself is the rule of all things. But therefore they call that will ordinary because it happens according to the preached Word of Holy Scripture, in which he has revealed his will to us. Hence the distinction between the hidden and the revealed will of God. Not that there are two wills in God, but rather the Scripture speaks in a way adapted to our human understanding. So we know that although God is omnipotent, and can do all things, yet he will not act toward us poor human beings according to his omnipotence, but according to his mercy, as he amply proved to us by his most beloved Son, and through all [the passages] which in the Old and the New Testament refer to him.

Paul spoke clearly and plainly of this distinction of the two wills when he said (I Cor. 2:16): Who hath known the mind of the Lord? But we have the mind of Christ. When Paul writes: Who has known the mind of the Lord? he refers to the hidden will of God, just as Isaiah (ch. 45:15) calls our God a hidden God. When Paul says: We have Christ's mind, he refers to the revealed and preached will of God, who was God himself, and became man, and we have seen his glory, a glory as of an only begotten Son of the Father (John 1:14), full of grace and truth.

Very well. We shall treat by way of an illustration the distinction [*spaltung*] of the two wills. The omnipotent hidden God can by his secret will consign Peter to hell, and conversely raise Judas or Caiaphas to heaven. He would be doing no evil thereby; we are in his hands. But according to his revealed will, he does not want to drive away any struggling Jacob without a blessing (Gen. 32:26). He must [13] have pity on David, who

---

11 This scholastic reference to logical fallacy arising from the use of a word that might be taken in more than one sense appears in the margin.

12 On the exegetical significance of splitting and rumination, see n. 14.

13 A marginal notation "Muss, Muss" underscores the stricture laid on Deity. Cf. above p. 130," Muss, Muss, Muss." Cf. the later Federal theologians like William Ames.

cries out to him (Ps. 51:1); and must pardon his sins, and let him be found justified in his sentence when he is judged. He would not let the heathen woman go away unheard (Matt. 15:27 ff.). So great and powerful are the might and worthiness of the promises of God, who became man and was revealed by his word, which cannot fail, although heaven and earth fall to pieces (Luke 21:33). It is not because our will, our word, our work have any worth or distinction in themselves; but rather it is because the divine promises are so powerful and strong in all believers [cf. Mark 9:23] that God, by his own word, is caught (*gefangen*), bound (*gebunden*), overcome (*überwunden*) by the believers. This is called in Scripture, God with us and among us [Emmanuel] (Matt. 1:23).

[THE SECOND ARGUMENT]

God wills that all men be saved (I Tim. 2:4), and: Who hath resisted his will? (Rom. 9:19).

But my friends Eliphaz, Bildad, and Zophar say again: Listen! If God wants all men to be saved, let him enforce his will, for no choice or refusal depends upon me. Answer: Here [logical] equivocation and confusion of the wills is resorted to, for the first passage refers to the revealed will of God; the second, to his hidden will. Hence, because these are each half-truths, they must be kept distinct, lest they be undivided and swallowed without rumination. Otherwise we should be eating up death, as has already been said (Lev. 11:3).[14]

Let us leave the secret will of God (Rom. 11:34), in its worthy majesty, as something that we have no need to investigate. But let us take hold of his revealed will and divide it, according to the ordinance of Scripture, into an attracting and a repelling (*Zukherenden vnnd Abkherenden*) will. The attracting will of God is that God wills that all men be saved. Therefore he draws all men to him by the offer of his grace and mercy. He did not even spare his only begotten Son, but gave him up to death for us all (Rom. 8:2), to the end that we should not be lost, but should come over into eternal life (John 3:15).

This salvation God offers to us and invites us joyfully, saying: Come, buy without money and without price, wine and milk (Isa. 55:1); you are already bought and paid for, at a great

---

14 This reference to the Levitical distinction between animals is widely employed in Anabaptist exegesis. Cf. Hofmann, Selection IX, n. 42 and Obbe, Selection X, n. 60.

cost (I Cor. 6:20). Come, all who are heavy laden, and I will give you rest (Matt. 11:28). Now as soon as God turns to us, calls us and warns us to follow him, and we abandon wife and child, ship and cargo, everything that hinders our journey toward him (cf. John 1:11)—our help has already come to us, namely, his attracting, drawing will. By it, he wills and draws all men unto salvation. Yet choice is still left to man, since God wants him without pressure, unconstrained, under no compulsion (cf. II Cor. 9:7).

Such people who do not receive him, hear him, or follow him, God turns and averts himself from them, and lets them be as they wish to be. That is called now the repelling will, of which Daniel (cf. ch. 5:10) gives recognition when he says: O God, turn not thy countenance from me! Even as God is holy with the holy, so is he withdrawn from those who withdraw. The first will may be called in Scripture *voluntas conversiva*, from *convertendo*; the second, *voluntas aversiva*, from *avertendo*. Not that there are two wills in God, as said above. There is only one will in God, but we have to speak of God humanly and with human words, as if, for example, he had eyes, ears, a face, and a back. Turn to us, turn from us, we have to say on account of our poor understanding. This does not mean that God really has eyes, ears, hands, feet, as the anthropomorphists say. Of the first kind of revealed will, Scripture speaks, saying (I Tim. 2:4): God wants all men to be saved. Of the second kind, another part of Scripture says that God will harden and damn the godless (Ex. 4:1 ff.; Rom. 1:18); yet God's hidden will remains upright and omnipotent according to which He does whatever He wishes.

Nor can anyone ask Him (Rom. 9:20): Why dost thou thus? His attracting will is the will of his mercy. His repelling will is the will of his justice and punishment. We—not God— we, with our sins, are guilty before it.

VI

Trial and Martyrdom
of Michael Sattler[1]

ROTTENBURG, 1527

INTRODUCTION

MICHAEL SATTLER (C. 1490–1527) WAS AN outstanding leader of Swiss and South German Anabaptism. Stirred by the evangelical preaching in the Breisgau, he abandoned his position as prior of St. Peter's and went to Zurich, where under the influence of William Reublin he joined the Swiss Brethren and was present at the third magisterially authorized disputation on baptism on November 6, 1525. Expelled from Zurich, he turned to Strassburg, where he was received by John Denck and where he was enabled to discuss the Anabaptist position with Capito and Bucer. At the invitation of Reublin, Sattler made the upper Hohenberg region of Wurtemberg his missionary field with Horb as his headquarters. His success was so great that he was chosen to preside at the great Schleitheim conference on Anabaptist principles which drew up the influential Confession in Seven Articles, February 24, 1527. (This important document has been several times translated.) Shortly thereafter he was apprehended by the Austrian authorities. The record of the trial and martyrdom was carefully preserved with much of the simplicity and vividness of the authentic acts of the early Christian martyrs. The account as here translated is the version rendered familiar to generations of Mennonites in the *Martyrs' Mirror* of Tilman J. van Braght (1660). Van Braght took it over from the still earlier *Het Offer des Heeren* (1570). These two compilations are the Mennonite counterpart of the Hutterite

[1] The best orientation to the place of Sattler is the article of Gustav Bossert, Jr., translated by Elizabeth Bender, "Michael Sattler's Trial and Martyrdom in 1527," *MQR*, XXV (1951), 201. Most of the following notes are based upon this work.

Chronicle from which Selection I was taken. (The *Chronicle*, incidentally, has an independent account of Sattler's trial.) Thus Selection VI is doubly noteworthy, at once as a sampling from a stirring martyrology and as a document in its own right, illustrative of the martyr theology which sustained the whole Anabaptist movement. Here we behold the ideal Anabaptist in whom four formative Christian anthropological types are blended, namely, the monk as *miles Christi*, the missionary or apostle, the pilgrim to Jerusalem, and the martyr citizen of the heavenly Jerusalem.[2]

The court glimpsed here in session happens to be Catholic and the charge of disloyalty made against Anabaptists in general is here compounded by the seemingly irresponsible utterance of Sattler about the Turks. In warding them off, the Austrian authorities had immediate responsibilities as at once Catholic and imperial, for they were in direct contact with the common enemy of Christendom.

[2] Cf. Franklin Littell, "The Anabaptist Theology of Missions," *MQR*, XXI (1947), 5; Ethelbert Stauffer, "Anabaptist Theology of Martyrdom," *MQR*, XIX (1945), 179.

The Trial and Martyrdom [3]
of Michael Sattler

ROTTENBURG, 1527 [4]

THE TEXT

After many legal transactions [5] on the day of his departure from this world, [6] the articles against him being many, Michael Sattler . . . [7] requested that they might once more be read to

[3] There are four extant accounts of the trial and martyrdom. The first is that of the Swabian Protestant Nicholas von Graveneck, who had apparently been forced to proceed to Rottenburg with arms to protect the court. His account was written down, probably by his brother-in-law, and sent to Zurich. It is preserved in Wolfenbüttel. The second appears as an appendix to the Seven Articles of the Schleitheim Confession in the drawing up of which Sattler played the leading role, February 24, 1527. The third account, with some dramatic flourishes, was sent by William Reublin to the Brethren in Zollikon and elsewhere in Switzerland. (It has been most recently edited by Leonhard von Muralt and Walter Schmid, *Quellen zur Geschichte der in der Schweiz*, I [Zurich, 1952], No. 224.) The fourth, briefer account, is that of the Hutterite *Chronicle*. The Acts of Michael Sattler (Version 2) were translated into Dutch in 1560 and taken up in *Het Offer des Heeren* in 1570 (the only non-Dutch episode so honored)
[*Continued on next page.*]

[4] The trial opened on Friday, May 17, and continued on Saturday. The execution took place on either May 20 or 21.

[5] It was shortly after the Schleitheim conference that Sattler and his wife along with Reublin's wife and others were apprehended in and around Horb, the center of Sattler's mission, and to the congregation gathered therein he wrote his beautiful letter (preserved in the *Martyrs' Mirror*). The trial was several times postponed because of the danger of uproar from many who were sympathetic and also because the charges against the Anabaptists were ecclesiastical as well as civil and the attempt was made to secure at least two clerics from the university faculty of law (Tübingen or Freiburg).

[6] More accurately on the second day of the trial when the verdict against him was delivered.

[7] At this point the *Mirror*, in line with its general tendency to connect Anabaptism with an ongoing remnant of the faithful in the Middle Ages, asserts that Sattler belonged to the Waldensian brotherhood.

138

him and that he might again be heard upon them.[8] This the bailiff,[9] as the attorney [for the defense] of his lord [the emperor], opposed and would not consent to it. Michael Sattler then requested a ruling. After a consultation, the judges[10] returned as their answer that, if his opponents would allow it, they, the judges, would consent. Thereupon the town clerk of Ensisheim,[11] as the spokesman of the said attorney, spoke thus: "Prudent, honorable, and wise lords, he has boasted of the Holy Ghost. Now if his boast is true, it seems to me, it is unnecessary to grant him this; for, if he has the Holy Ghost, as he boasts, the same will tell him what has been done here." To this Michael Sattler replied: "You servants of God, I hope my request will not be denied, for the said articles are as yet unclear to me [because of their number]." The town clerk responded: "Prudent, honorable, and wise lords, though we are not bound to do this, yet in order to give satisfaction, we will grant him his request that it may not be thought that injustice is being done him in his heresy or that we desire to abridge him of his rights. Hence let the articles be read to him again." [The nine charges, seven against all fourteen defendants, two specifically against Sattler, are here omitted, as they are answered seriatim by Sattler.]

Thereupon Michael Sattler requested permission to confer with his brethren and sisters, which was granted him. Having conferred with them for a little while, he began and undauntedly answered as follows: "In regard to the articles

Footnote 3 continued]
and then reprinted in the *Martyrs' Mirror.* 'On the relation of *Het Offer* and the *Mirror,* see Gerald Studer, "A History of the *Martyrs' Mirror,* *MQR,* XXII [1940], 163 ff.) Because of the widespread influence of this version in the formation of Mennonite piety the present translation is based on it. The critical Dutch text is found in two places in *BRN,* II, pp. 62–67; V, pp. 645–50. Back of this lies the German original edited by Walther Köhler, *Flugschriften aus den ersten Jahren der Reformation,* II (1908) Heft 3, but slight alterations have been introduced to bring this version into general conformity with what Gustav Bossert, Jr., regards as the most accurate transcript of the proceedings.

[8] The trial had opened on the preceding day with the reading of nine charges, but naturally Sattler wished to have them fresh before him in writing, if possible, when called upon to respond.

[9] Jacob Halbmayer, mayor of Rottenburg, whom Sattler considered ultimately responsible for the outcome of the trial, although it was Hoffmann (n. 11) who did most of the speaking against him.

[10] There were twenty-four judges drawn from several towns and presided over by Landeshauptmann, Count Joachim of Zollern.

[11] Eberhard Hoffmann, a vindictive spirit, who had had much experience with Anabaptist trials in the seat of Austrian government in Alsace.

relating to me and my brethren and sisters, hear this brief answer:
"First, that we have acted contrary to the imperial mandate, we do not admit. For the same says that the Lutheran doctrine and delusion[12] is not to be adhered to, but only the gospel and the Word of God. This we have kept. For I am not aware that we have acted contrary to the gospel and the Word of God. I appeal to the words of Christ.

"Secondly, that the real body of Christ the Lord is not present in the sacrament, we admit. For the Scripture says: Christ ascended into heaven and sitteth on the right hand of his Heavenly Father, whence he shall come to judge the quick and the dead, from which it follows that, if he is in heaven and not in the bread, he may not be eaten bodily.

"Thirdly, as to baptism we say infant baptism is of no avail to salvation. For it is written [Rom. 1:17] that we live by faith alone. Again [Mark 16:16]: He that believeth and is baptized shall be saved. Peter says the same [I, ch. 3:21]: Which doth also now save you in baptism (which is signified by that [Ark of Noah]), not the putting away of the filth of the flesh but rather the covenant of a good conscience with God by the resurrection of Jesus Christ.

"Fourthly, we have not rejected the oil [of extreme unction]. For it is a creature of God, and what God has made is good and not to be refused, but that the pope, bishops, monks, and priests can make it better we do not believe; for the pope never made anything good. That of which the Epistle of James [ch. 5:14] speaks is not the pope's oil.

"Fifthly, we have not insulted the mother of God and the saints. For the mother of Christ is to be blessed among all women because unto her was accorded the favor of giving birth to the Saviour of the whole world. But that she is a mediatrix and advocatess—of this the Scriptures know nothing, for she must with us await the judgment. Paul said to Timothy [I, ch. 2:5]: Christ is our mediator and advocate with God. As regards the saints, we say that *we* who live and believe are the saints, which I prove by the epistles of Paul to the Romans [ch. 1:7], the Corinthians [I, ch. 1:2], the Ephesians [ch. 1:1], and other places where he always writes 'to the beloved

---

12 The Catholic authorities quite naturally assimilated Anabaptism to Lutheranism, but, of course, Sattler was keenly conscious of the difference. They were referring to the Edict of Worms (May 21, 1521) against Luther and Lutherans; Sattler skillfully appeals to the subsequent imperial mandate of the Diet of Nuremberg, February 9, 1523.

saints.' Hence, we who believe are the saints, but those who have died in the faith we regard as the blessed.

"Sixthly, we hold that we are not to swear before the authorities, for the Lord says [Matt. 5:34]: Swear not, but let your communication be, Yea, yea; nay, nay.

"Seventhly,[13] when God called me to testify of his Word and I had read Paul and also considered the unchristian and perilous state in which I was, beholding the pomp, pride, usury, and great whoredom of the monks and priests, I went and took unto me a wife,[14] according to the command of God; for Paul well prophesies concerning this to Timothy [I, ch. 4:3]: In the latter time it shall come to pass that men shall forbid to marry and command to abstain from meats which God hath created to be received with thanksgiving.

"Eighthly, if the Turks should come, we ought not to resist them. For it is written [Matt. 5:21]: Thou shalt not kill. We must not defend ourselves against the Turks and others of our persecutors, but are to beseech God with earnest prayer to repel and resist them. But that I said that, if warring *were* right, I would rather take the field against so-called Christians who persecute, capture, and kill pious Christians than against the Turks was for the following reason. The Turk is a true Turk, knows nothing of the Christian faith, and is a Turk after the flesh. But you who would be Christians and who make your boast of Christ persecute the pious witnesses of Christ and are Turks after the spirit!

"In conclusion, ministers of God, I admonish you to consider the end for which God has appointed you, to punish the evil and to defend and protect the pious. Whereas, then, we have not acted contrary to God and the gospel, you will find that neither I nor my brethren and sisters have offended in word or deed against any authority. Therefore, ministers of God, if you have neither heard nor read the Word of God, send for the

---

13 Sattler fails or perhaps disdains to take up what was the seventh article in the charge read against him, namely, that "he has commenced a new and unheard of custom in regard to the Lord's Supper, mingling the bread and wine together on a plate and eating and drinking the same." This is an understandable distortion of what the Catholic authorities had been told was a common meal in place of the Mass.

It is to the prosecution's eighth charge that Sattler is here responding, namely, that he had left his order and taken a wife. He had been prior of the Benedictine monastery of St. Peter's in the Breisgau.

14 He married a Beguine, called by Valerius Anshelm "a talented, clever little woman," *Bernische Chronik*, V, 185 ff.

most learned men and for the sacred books of the Bible in whatsoever language they may be and let them confer with us in the Word of God. If they prove to us with the Holy Scriptures that we err and are in the wrong, we will gladly desist and recant and also willingly suffer the sentence and punishment for that of which we have been accused; but if no error is proven to us, I hope to God that you will be converted and receive instruction."

Upon this speech the judges laughed and put their heads together, and the town clerk of Ensisheim said: "Yes, you infamous, desperate rascal of a monk, should we dispute with you? The hangman will dispute with you, I assure you!"

Michael said: "God's will be done."

The town clerk said: "It were well if you had never been born."

Michael replied: "God knows what is good."

The town clerk: "You archheretic, you have seduced pious people. If they would only now forsake their error and commit themselves to grace!"

Michael: "Grace is with God alone."

One of the prisoners also said: "We must not depart from the truth."

The town clerk: "Yes, you desperate villain, you archheretic, I say, if there were no hangman here, I would hang you myself and be doing God a good service thereby."

Michael: "God will judge aright." Thereupon the town clerk said a few words to him in Latin, what, we do not know.[15] Michael Sattler answered him, *Judica*.

The town clerk then admonished the judges and said: "He will not cease from this chatter anyway. Therefore, my Lord Judge, you may proceed with the sentence. I call for a decision of the court."

The judge asked Michael Sattler whether he too committed it to the court. He replied: "Ministers of God, I am not sent to judge the Word of God. We are sent to testify and hence cannot consent to any adjudication, since we have no command from God concerning it. But we are not for that reason removed from being judged and we are ready to suffer and to await what God is planning to do with us. We will continue in our faith in Christ so long as we have breath in us, unless we be dissuaded from it by the Scriptures."

---

15 Hoffmann may well have resorted to Latin when he observed the bad impression his intemperance was making on the court. The only word that our informant, Nicholas von Graveneck, could pick out was Sattler's "Give judgment."

The town clerk said: "The hangman will instruct you, he will dispute with you, archheretic."

Michael: "I appeal to the Scriptures."

Then the judges arose and went into another room where they remained for an hour and a half and determined on the sentence. In the meantime some [of the soldiers] in the room treated Michael Sattler most unmercifully, heaping reproach upon him. One of them said: "What have you in prospect for yourself and the others that you have so seduced them?"[16] With this he also drew a sword which lay upon the table, saying: "See, with this they will dispute with you." But Michael did not answer upon a single word concerning himself but willingly endured it all. One of the prisoners said: "We must not cast pearls before swine." Being also asked why he had not remained a lord[17] in the convent, Michael answered: "According to the flesh I was a lord, but it is better as it is." He did not say more than what is recorded here,[18] and this he spoke fearlessly.

The judges having returned to the room, the sentence was read. It was as follows: "In the case of the attorney of His Imperial Majesty vs. Michael Sattler, judgment is passed that Michael Sattler shall be delivered to the executioner, who shall lead him to the place of execution and cut out his tongue,[19] then forge him fast to a wagon and thereon with red-hot tongs twice tear pieces from his body; and after he has been brought outside the gate, he shall be plied five times more in the same manner. . . ."[20]

After this had been done in the manner prescribed, he was burned to ashes[21] as a heretic. His fellow brethren were

16 Another reading: "When I see you get away, I will believe in you!" In this same version it is another person who speaks the next part.

17 See above, n. 13, second paragraph.

18 Another version says that he went on to show his improved state from Scripture.

19 Actually only a piece was cut out because he continued to utter speech.

20 What the *Mirror* converts in the next sentence into narrative, other versions make a part of the original verdict.

21 Reublin (Version 3) reported that a sack of powder was mercifully tied around Sattler's neck to hasten his death. The Wolfenbüttel version (1) gives further details of the execution. From the ladder to which he was bound he admonished the people to be converted and to intercede in prayer for his judges. He then prayed: "Almighty, eternal God, Thou art the way and the truth; because I have not been shown to be in error, I will with thy help this day testify to the truth and seal it with my blood." When the ropes on his hands were burned, he raised the two forefingers in a promised signal to his group and prayed: "Father, into thy hands I commend my spirit." Köhler, *op. cit.*, p. 332, n. 2.

executed with the sword, and the sisters drowned. His wife, also after being subjected to many entreaties, admonitions, and threats, under which she remained steadfast, was drowned a few days afterward.[22] Done the 21st day of May, A.D. 1527.

[22] The Countess, spouse of the presiding judge, sought to dissuade her. She was drowned eight days after her husband's death.

VII

A Letter to John Campanus
By Sebastian Franck[1]

STRASSBURG, 1531

INTRODUCTION

JOHN CAMPANUS WAS A RADICAL LUTHERAN WHO turned Anabaptist under the influence of Melchior Hofmann (Selection IX). Campanus' ideas, carried by the Wassenberg preachers, were a factor in building up that fateful combination of restitutionism and millennialism which was the Münster theocracy. On the eve of this disastrous outburst within radical dissent, when the aberrant forces released by the Reformation were swirling toward a climax, Sebastian Franck, polyhistorian and free spirit, wrote the following memorable Letter to Campanus. It embodies in a remarkably complete form the Spiritualist's vision of the universal, invisible church of the Spirit and gives vivid expression to his philosophy of religion and history born of despair. Like Schwenckfeld (Selection VIII) and Obbe Philips (Selection X), Franck could not accept the claim of any one church because of the rival and mutually exclusive claims of all. He was most sympathetic with the Evangelical Anabaptists but their exclusiveness distressed him. He agreed with them that the apostolic church had disappeared in its accommodation to the state but deplored their feverish attempts to recover the worn-out sacraments and other practices from the infancy of Chris-

---

[1] The best accounts of Franck in English are those of Rufus Jones, *Spiritual Reformers*, Ch. iv, and J. F. Smith, "S. F., Heretic, Mystic, and Reformer of the Reformation," *Theological Review*, XI (1874), 163–179. The classical study is that of Alfred Hegler (1892). See introduction, above, p. 27. The extensive German literature on Franck is surveyed and evaluated by Eberhard Teufel in *Theologische Rundschau*, N.F., XII (1940), 99–179. The most recent biography is also by Teufel, *"Landräumig" Sebastian Franck: ein Wanderer an Donau, Rhein und Neckar* (Neustadt an der Aisch, 1954).

tianity. For God, as Spirit, had first declared and then historically demonstrated his preference for working spiritually rather
than sacramentally to achieve the mature fruits of the Spirit.
These fruits, faith, penitence, and self-denial, can be realized
by all peoples whether in or without organized Christianity.
Though, like Schwenckfeld, Franck looked for the visible
assembling of the church by God sometime in the future, he
like Obbe Philips was skeptical of the credentials of all contemporary reformers and restitutionists, holding that none were
called. His attendance upon the living Spirit was like that of
Thomas Müntzer (Selection II) but he was neither a revolutionary millennialist like him nor a martyr spirit like Sattler
(Selection VI); for although he was a pacifist (and teetotaler)
and understood the School of Christ to be the life under the
cross, he was not ready for an "untimely harvest." Franck's
universalism was akin to that of Denck (Selection IV). He felt
closest of all to John Bünderlin (rebaptized by Denck), of
whom he here gives a brief sketch. On the doctrine of the
Trinity, he says, he feels closer to Servetus than to Campanus.

This Letter and another of similar purport circulated widely
in left-wing circles and were of sufficient threat to the closely
disciplined Mennonite community to have elicited a full
refutation by Dietrich Philips (Selection XI).

A Letter[2] to John Campanus[3]
By Sebastian Franck

STRASSBURG, 1531[4]

THE TEXT

*1 Grace be unto thee, dear Campanus,[5] from the Father of Lights through the Lord Christ, for feeling and believing and

[2] This letter was written in Latin, and survives only in Dutch and German translations.

The Dutch translation by Peter de Zuttere (Hyperphragmus) is found in a miscellany in the Zurich Stadtsbibliothek, gal. I. 25 b. (The section of the letter bearing on Bünderlin is printed by Alexander Nicoladoni, *Johannes Bünderlin von Linz* [Berlin, 1893], 124 f.). This version, translated into German and at points paraphrased, with apparently some inaccuracies or misconstructions, is printed by Karl Rembert, *Die Wiedertäufer im Herzogtum Jülich* (Berlin, 1899), 218–226.

The German translation, published in 1563 by Johannes Ewich, is to be
[Continued on next page.

[3] John Campanus, born near Liege, identified himself with the Lutheran cause after studying at Wittenberg, but he antagonized both Luther and Melanchthon, especially when he obtruded himself into the Marburg Colloquy and insisted that his was the solution of the Eucharistic problem. Denounced, he wrote *Contra totum post apostolos mundum* (1530), which circulated in manuscript in both Latin and German. A popularization in German followed, wherein Campanus' special form of Unitarianism was clearly enunciated. His basic idea in church reform was restitution of which he was confident he held the key. He died in prison, 1575, generally regarded as mad. For his influence on Münster, see Selection X, n. 52.

[4] The date is in dispute. The Dutch (Zurich) translation dates it February 4, 1541. The German (Munich) translation dates it 1531. Hegler felt constrained to adhere to the earlier date because he did not know that Sebastian Franck was also in Strassburg in 1541 and that Bünderlin, referred to in the letter, was probably still living, for we know that Bünderlin met Schwenckfeld as late as 1538. The reference in the letter to the propriety of caution because of danger to his family might fit better into the period after the "Persecution" in Ulm than before. The references in the letter to a work of Servetus are not sufficiently distinctive to enable us to know whether *De Trinitatis erroribus* (Strassburg, 1531) or the *Dialogues on the Trinity* (1532) is meant.

[5] The Munich text has only "N."

preferring to stand alone[6] against all the doctors of the Roman or (if it please God[7]) the Christian church, who from the time of the apostles until this present hour have enjoyed great renown —for preferring to maintain thyself alone against all rather than to err with all or the larger part of them. It is my view that thou hast done rightly. I do not doubt but what with time the same opinion will please thee even more, and I pray to God that he will be pleased to strengthen thee therein.

*2 ¶ Indeed, I do not doubt but what all the highly famous doctors whose works are still available are [those] wolves which Paul [Acts 20:29] spiritually anticipated would fall in upon the flock and which John [I, ch. 2:18] calls antichrists, men who even in the days of the apostles fell away from them and indeed had never really been with them. This is proved by their works, especially [those] of Clement, Irenaeus, Tertullian, Cyprian, Chrysostom, Hilary, Cyril, Origen, and others which are merely utter child's play[8] and quite unlike the spirit of the apostles, that is, utterly filled with commandments, laws, sacramental elements and all kinds of human inventions. Jerome speaks of the seven [church] orders[9]; Clement, a pupil of Saint James—if one wants to believe it—writes something about purgatory and brings in more foolish nonsense. ¶ Right after [the apostles] everything unfolded in a contrary fashion.

Footnote 2 continued]
found in the Munich Stadtsbibliothek, 4o Polem. 1328. The text is interspersed with refutation but appears to be complete. From this text the present translation is made. Wherever possible the Dutch text and various excerpts have been consulted. The Munich sections, as divided up for refutation, are indicated thus: ¶.

The paragraphs of the Rembert text are indicated thus: * and are followed by a number. For ready reference I have numbered Rembert's paragraphs, the first, on p. 218, beginning "Franck lobt." Where Rembert's material covers less than the Munich text, an unnumbered asterisk is used to indicate where it leaves off in the fuller Munich text.

An independent German excerpt is preserved by J. G. Schellhorn, *Amoenitates literariae* (Frankfurt/Leipzig, 1729), 59–61. Dutch fragments occur in the refutation of two Franck letters (this and another) in a tract by Dietrich Philips. It is published by Cramer in *Bibliotheca Reformatoria Neerlandica*, X, 493–506, English translation by A. B. Kolb, pp. 473–86.

6 The reference is to Campanus' *Contra totum post apostolos mundum* (Strassburg, 1530), which provided the occasion for Franck's letter. This and a later reference favor the earlier dating for the letter, i.e., 1531. No copy of the book is known. Excerpts are to be found in a Bugenhagen MS. in Berlin. See *Zeitschrift für historische Theologie*, 1846, 535 ff.

7 The Munich text has "the gods." Here the Rembert reading is preferred.

8 Rembert text: "full of ravings and alien nonsense."

9 The printed text misreads the author as Irenaeus. The work is that of Pseudo-Jerome, *De septem ordinibus ecclesiae*.

Baptism was changed into infant baptism; the Lord's Supper into misuse and a sacrifice. What they have written is nothing but a shame and disgrace.[10]

*3 Therefore, I believe that the outward church of Christ, including all its gifts and sacraments, because of the breaking in and laying waste by Antichrist right after the death of the apostles, went up into heaven and lies concealed in the Spirit and in truth. I am thus quite certain that for fourteen hundred years now[11] there has existed no gathered church nor any sacrament.[12] For this is proved along with experience by the work, outward behavior, and misuse with which Antichrist has besmirched and spoiled everything.

*4 But[13] at the same time nothing has departed from the [inner] truth of baptism, the Supper, the ban, and gathering for worship. Instead, the Spirit has imparted all this in truth[14] to the faithful in whatever lands they be, although, of course, the betokening signs thereof, having been sullied by Antichrist, are left to the devil. For from the moment when the Sabbath, circumcision, and the commandment concerning the temple and offerings have been abrogated,[15] God recognizes them no longer as his ordinances although they were hitherto expressly ordained and says [Isa. 1:10 ff.]: What concern are the temple and sacrifices to me? I am full of burnt offerings, etc.

¶ Thus in the New Testament, although Christ in the beginning, not without reason, instituted baptism and the Supper, [he did so] not because he wished to serve himself thereby but rather because it might be serviceable and useful to us. This no one nowadays thinks of but rather everybody imagines that God has need of our work and service and takes a special pleasure in these things like children with their playthings. But nevertheless all this was surely in no sense arranged for God's sake but rather for our own, like circumcision and the Sabbath with our forefathers, in order that spiritual hearts

---

10 This sentence appears only in the Rembert text. The Schellhorn and Munich texts agree, a fact which would further confirm the reliability and relative completeness of the text being used for this translation.

11 This assertion places the fall, or, in one sense, the maturation of Christianity, exactly a century after Jesus' death, i.e., A.D. 131 (the date of the letter being 1531). The same dating is given below, p. 154.

12 To this point Schellhorn gives a German translation, not differing in sense from the Munich text.

13 The fourth paragraph in Rembert reduces the following material considerably.

14 Here in the sense of "in essence."   15 Literally: "cut off."

might out of these signs understand what God wants to have done by and permitted[16] to them.

Moreover, since the holy and omniscient Spirit anticipated that all these outward ceremonies would go under because of Antichrist and would degenerate through misuse, he gladly yielded these tokens to Satan and fed, gave to drink, baptized, and gathered the faithful with the Spirit and the truth in such a way that nothing would be lost to truth, although all outer transactions might pass away. Therefore even as the Spirit of God is alone the teacher of the New Covenant, so also he alone baptizes and alone avails himself of all things, namely, in the Spirit and in truth. And just as the church is today a purely spiritual·thing, so also is all law, promise, reward, spirit, bread, wine, sword, Kingdom, life—all in the Spirit and no longer outward, etc. *5 ¶ Therefore the unitary[17] Spirit alone baptizes with fire and the Spirit all the faithful and [all] who are obedient to the inner Word in whatever part of the world they be. For God is no respecter of persons but instead is to the Greeks as to the Barbarian and the Turk, to the lord as to the servant, so long as they retain the light which has shined upon them and gives their heart an eternal glow.

*6 To be brief, my dear brother Campanus, that I may say it in summary fashion and openly and be undersood by thee, I maintain against all ecclesiastical authorities that all outward things and ceremonies, which were customary in the church of the apostles, have been done away with and are not to be reinstituted, although many without authorization[18] or calling undertake to restore on their own the degenerated sacraments. ¶ For the church will remain scattered among the heathen until the end of the world. Indeed, only the Advent of Christ will at last destroy and make away with Antichrist and his church. He will gather together dispersed and ever fugitive[19] Israel from the four places of the world. Therefore, it is my opinion that nothing of these churches should be reinstituted which were once held in great esteem in the church.

*7 These are the things which the aforementioned wolves, the doctors of unwisdom, apes of the apostles and antichrists, have vigorously propagated. And they who understood the truth of these things—their writings and instructions were

---

16 In German: gelassen.
17 In German: einiger. Is this in contrast to the septiform Spirit of sacramental theology?
18 In German: sendung.   19 In German: ruchlos.

suppressed by these as godless heresies and nonsense;[20] and in their place in esteem come foolish Ambrose, Augustine, Jerome, Gregory—of whom not even one knew the Lord, so help me God, nor was sent by God to teach. But rather all were the apostles of Antichrist and are that still. I am a liar if all their own books don't prove as much, which never hold together and are far different from and unlike the apostles'. There is not a one of them, so far as can be seen from the books they have left, who appears to have been a Christian, unless it be that they, at last, felt differently in their hearts, being taught by God with something else and repented of their lost labor. For they teach nothing properly that concerns Christian faith. Yea, they have not known nor taught what God is [or] law, gospel, faith, baptism, Supper, true righteousness, Scripture, the church, and its law.

They mix the New Testament with the Old, as also today their descendants do. And when they have nothing with which to defend their purposes, they run at once to the empty quiver,[21] that is, to the Old Testament, and from it prove [the legitimacy of] war, oath, government, power of magistracy, tithes, priesthood; and praise everything and ascribe this all forcibly to Christ without his will. And just as the popes have derived all this from it, so also many of those who would have themselves be called Evangelicals hold that they have nobly escaped the snare of the pope and the devil and have nevertheless achieved, with great effort and sweat, nothing more than that they have exchanged and confounded the priesthood of the pope with the Mosaic kingdom!

But this remains a firm sentence[22]: If the priesthood cannot be re-established out of the old law, neither can [Christian] government[23] and outward government be established according to the law of Moses. *[8] Yet the Evangelicals at court are now fashioning for the princes another [rule] and nicely press the sword into their hands and, as the proverb has it, pour oil into the fire.

*[9] From this [inveterate confusion of the New and the Old Testaments] many intelligent people [i.e., the Anabaptists] are seized with a delusive idea, holding that at the time of Constantine and Constantius, Antichrist concurrently broke into the

---

[20] The word *tatmar* is of uncertain meaning.
[21] In German: *kocher*. [22] In German: *faste sententz*.
[23] The text has simply *Reich*, which can mean the Holy Roman Empire in particular or Christian government in general.

church and that the external polity of the church was at that same time reduced to ashes, especially because the worldly power and the princes of the pagans abandoned their pagan belief, were baptized, and were reckoned with the flock of Christ. Therefore the brothers[24] were courted, war was waged, heresies rooted out not with words but rather with swords, and the things of faith were defended with fist and force. The opinion of these people is not at all bad but they are in error nevertheless.[25] ¶ I, however, firmly believe that the outward church of Christ was wasted and destroyed right after the apostles.* This is what the wolves, that is, the Fathers amply prove for me, although Scripture gives no testimony on this point. For all that they teach is surely idle child's play, if they are compared with the apostles.

10 But now, since the outward arrangements and the sacraments were not wiped out by the laying waste of Antichrist after the time of the apostles, but rather were misused and sullied, God through the Spirit in truth provided by means of his spiritual church all things which the signs and outward gifts merely betokened. He leaves it to the devil, who seeks nothing other than the externals, to misuse the externals and control the sacraments, as [earlier] in the case of the [Old Covenant] externals: circumcision, kingship, Sabbath, Temple, sacrifices; and in the meantime he circumcises the hearts of his own with the Spirit and fire and in truth (which are not wiped away). With these also he causes them to sacrifice and makes and builds out of them at length a temple of God, baptizes scattered Israel, feeds and gives them to drink[26] without hands and external elements. Thus he establishes and perfects the whole New Testament and arranges all things in his fashion in the Spirit and in truth, so that nothing is fatuous or figurative, but rather all is truth. He closes it and no one opens.[27]

*11 ¶ Now, however, since experience teaches that the power of the external churches and all things external has fallen into

---

24 It is not certain whether by *den Gebrüderen* the two sons of Constantine are meant or the converted pagan "brethren." The latter is the interpretation of Rembert or his Dutch text, where also only one emperor is named, Constantine, hence construed as Constantine the Great.

25 Rembert's text does not give this sentence, wherein Franck clearly dissociates himself from the Anabaptist doctrine of the fall of the church in the reign of Constantine.

26 The German *speisen* and *trencken* refer to the Lord's Supper. Cf. below, p. 155, Schwenckfeld, below, p. 175.

27 On locking Scripture, cf. below, Selection IX, n. 41

decay and that the church is dispersed among the heathen, truly it is my opinion that no persons on earth can without a special call from God gather up the same and bring again its sacraments into use. For this is a work of external and special calling. And external things must have an external call.* For just as the inward man has an inward teacher, impulse,[28] nourishment, call, voice, and everything, so also the external things have an outward call, a special teacher, the word of mouth, and everything external. Therefore I have said that the outward ceremonies of the church ought not to be re-established unless Christ himself command it, who has not spoken orally to us but to the apostles and originally ordered the things that they should preach and baptize. But everyone is stealing the divine truth from his neighbors so that I do not [hesitate to][29] say that a number intrude themselves into this divine office without any calling or sending. And it is equally assured and certain that a heretic and one who has not been sent by God can handle nothing in the church, even though there still were sacraments and [even though] they, that is, these apes of the apostles, still baptized and did everything else. For God is not with them and they do not congregate with God. Therefore they scatter[30] everything like very apostles of Antichrist. This is what I am saying: They are restoring outworn sacraments, as I regard them, which no one should do unless he be especially sent for the purpose and [provided] with an outward sign and call.

*12 ¶ Even if the external church still stood intact and one could recover and use all the things mentioned, it is surely true that there would still be only one baptism, one Supper, one faith, one gospel, one God, and one Lord in the same church his bride. For it is impossible that the one undivided God with Christ, grace, and the sacraments should be in such different churches. Because of this [oneness], if Luther baptizes, Zwingli with his church does not baptize; if the pope and the Baptist Brethren had [validly] baptized, no one else would [really] baptize in addition—none, that is who did not belong to their conventicle or church, but instead [he] would be lost, since he would not be one of them.[31]

---

28 In German: zuck.
29 Only with this insertion can the sense of this sentence be given.
30 In German: zerstrewen.
31 This sentence is not entirely clear. It is, however, a recurrent theme in Franck's writings that the rival claims of the four "sects" (Papal, Lutheran, Zwinglian, and Anabaptist) in effect cancel each other* out.

Out of this [same presumption] the ancients also and especially Cyprian with the whole council of Carthage willed that one should baptize again or rather for the first time really baptize those who had been baptized by heretics, as though among the latter there were no [true] baptism—also no God, no faith, no grace, nor Holy Spirit among them. From this the saying has come: Outside the church, no salvation. Therefore either none of all the churches baptizes or only one. If only one, where, my friend, is this church? Perhaps in India, Greece, Germany, Armenia, at Rome, in Saxony, or in the mountains. But I believe nowhere. Instead, they all run uncalled and enter into the sheep[fold] unsent. So many come before the Lord that they are [surely] all thieves and murderers,[32] and even as they speak and teach on their own [authority], so also they baptize on their own and gather the scattered church as veritable servants of Antichrist.

¶ Along with this, I ask what is the need or why should God wish to restore the outworn sacraments and take them back from Antichrist, yea, contrary to his own nature (which is Spirit and inward) yield to weak material elements? For he had been for fourteen hundred years[33] now himself the teacher and baptizer and governor of the Feast,[34] that is, in the Spirit and in truth without any outward means—in the Spirit, I say, in order that he may baptize, instruct, and nourish our spirit. And does he wish now, just as though he were weary of spiritual things and had quite forgotten his nature, to take refuge again in the poor sick elements of the world and re-establish the besmirched holy days and the sacraments of both Testaments?* But God will remain [true] to his character,[35] especially [as disclosed] in the New Testament, as long as the world stands.

In the meantime the sacraments will also remain but, in respect to their truth and meaning, ensnared by Antichrist and trampled under his feet—the Antichrist whom the Lord by his Advent and by the Spirit of his mouth will tread on the ground and slay (II Thess. 2:8); and [he] will call the scattered church together (as I have said) from the four ends of the world. In the meantime, the Temple, sacraments, and all services and

---

[32] A rendering of John 10:1 common to the left-wing writers, not based on the Vulgate text, which has *fur* and *latro*, but rather on Luther (1522), who has *Dieb* and *Mörder*.
[33] The same dating given above, n. 11.
[34] I.e., Host at the inward Eucharist.
[35] In German: *weise*.

offices ought to remain with Antichrist. Nor should the Temple and the ceremonies of the scattered people [of God], driven by the heathen into misery, be reinstituted [contrary to what] Haggai testifies.

Yet many[36] in misconceived, though surely not (so I trust) ungodly, zeal are today very much concerned as to how they can recover church and sacraments, now that God has brought the fortunes of the church into a much better situation, so that now all things might take place in truth, which before were signified in figures. *[13]And[37] [yet they should be urged to see that] nothing has been taken from the child except its doll with which it has played long enough. One must leave the nest[38] and thereupon strive for greater and more serious things, namely, for faith, penitence, denial of self. This means the same as to be true Christians and to know Christ and [inwardly] to enjoy his flesh as food.

¶ God permitted, indeed gave the outward signs to the church in its infancy, just like a doll to a child, not that they were necessary for the Kingdom of God nor that God would require them of our hands. Instead, the church in its childhood did not want to dispense with such things as a staff; and [God therefore favored the infant church] as a father gives something to a child so that it won't cry. But when the child is at length strong enough and able to throw the staff away, the father does not thereupon become angry, but rather the same is pleasing to the father.

*[14] Therefore, my brother Campanus, it is indeed a very hard word and one which angers many and hardens those who are not from God. It pleases and wins me [over], however, so that I hold with thee, because thou writest against all the doctors of the church and their offspring since the time of the apostles, nay, more, against the whole world.[39] For this is my conviction also. But that thou dost have zeal for the outworn church is, I know for a certainty, in vain. For thou wilt not gather the people of God nor ever bring their polity and sacraments to the light of day. Cease therefore from thy enterprise and let the church of God remain in the Spirit among all

---

36 I.e., the Anabaptists.
37 The order of Rembert's material in paragraph 13 is different.
38 The word here is *nusz* and means *nut* and could thus be translated *kernel*, but the whole image is better rendered as above.
39 This is another reference to Campanus' *Contra totum post apostolos mundum.* (See above, note 6.)

peoples and pagans; let them be herein instructed, governed, and baptized by the Doctor of the New Covenant, namely, the Holy Spirit. And envy not and begrudge not thy mother the church her good fortune. Consider as thy brothers all Turks and heathen, wherever they be, who fear God and work righteousness, instructed by God and inwardly drawn by him, even though they have never heard of baptism, indeed, of Christ himself, neither of his story or scripture, but only of his power through the inner Word perceived within and made fruitful. For the Lord himself gives dispensation to such as these when he says [Matt. 12:32]: Whoever sins gainst the Son of Man will be forgiven. And therefore I hold that just as there are many Adams who do not know there was one Adam, so also there are many Christians who have never heard Christ's name.

*15 ¶ I[40] am sending thee a little book of my brother in faith,[41] which I should like to have thee accept from me as a present to read, evaluate, and judge. I tell thee for a certainty, he is a learned man, wonderfully God-fearing and utterly dead to worldly things. I would with all my heart that I might also be baptized with the same baptism.[42] If I learn that this has been of some use to thee, I shall send on others of his works and writings along with a copy of my own. For this Bünderlin associated himself with all the learned divines until he realized that it was all a lost cause with them. For by means of the Truth he discovered that they had completely stopped up their ears to Truth and with open ears hear nothing, so that they are the same dogs and swine as were the Pharisees in the time of Christ.

Further, if it should prove convenient for thee, I should like to send the man himself to thee sometime in order that ye might converse with one another face to face, or if it is more

---

40 The following section of the letter, concerning Bünderlin, is printed in the Dutch translation (in the Zurich Stadtsbibliothek) by Nicoladoni, *op. cit.*, 124 ff., and I have thus been able at this point to compare directly two translations of the original Latin letter.

41 The Dutch at this point seems to mean "a book of the faith of my brother." This reference is to John Bünderlin, born in Linz, who was apparently converted to Anabaptism in 1526 by John Denck, a kindred spirit. Like Denck he turned from the Anabaptists after serving as their missioner in Austria and Moravia. He was in Strassburg in 1528, leaving it in 1529 for Constance. The work referred to may be Bünderlin's *Erklärung durch Vergleichung der biblischen Geschrift*, 1530, or *Clare Verantwortung etlicher artikel*, 1531. The reference helps in dating the letter in 1531.

42 Allusion to Matt. 20:22, etc.

convenient, come rather thyself to see him up here. Truly he is a man profoundly grounded in the Scriptures and with uncommon clarity of mind to judge all matters, mighty in entangling and trapping his opponents. *16 Yet he is one who does not let himself or the matter of faith get into a disputation. For he says often that the Christian is no quarreler or disputer and that of such no word or example can be found anywhere in Christ or in the primitive church.* What need have I to say more? The Spirit will surely give testimony how Bünderlin judges all things. He takes special note of all the reasons in Scripture, what and to whom something is said, for he says that many learned divines go wrong who wish to understand Scripture according to the letter (as notably Luther does).*43 And in this also I think he's right. For the poor fools do not see what wrong they commit against God with this work, for they make him more unsteady and vacillating than Prometheus.44 God have mercy on us. Amen.

*17 Dear brother, I cannot indicate with the pen all that I have perceived very well through God's grace in my heart. And I should very much wish that I could myself be with thee some time and talk with thee face to face. For I should hope to work out many things with thee; and thou hast not yet closed thy ears and art still in quest. Do not give up. Thou wilt have need of no [other] person. God will probably not provide thee with a person but he will himself be thy helper to thy great advantage. ¶ Scripture and [another] person can only give to a person and a believing brother some testimony, but cannot teach what is divine [directly]. However holy they may be, they are nevertheless not teachers, only witnesses and testimony. Faith is not learned out of books nor from a person, however saintly he may be, but rather it is learned and poured in by God in the School of the Lord, that is, under the cross. *18 ¶ Where Bünderlin, my brother in faith, is I do not know.45 When he comes around again I shall send him to thee, God willing, that is, if I shall have learned that he will be welcome as a guest and a brother unto thee. He is much freer and—if

43 Rembert's paraphrase (paragraph 15) covers material up to this point, but he segregates two sentences to make his paragraph 16. A comparison of the Dutch text of this portion printed by Nicoladoni shows the extent of Rembert's paraphrasing.
44 Prometheus is not in the Dutch (Nicoladoni).
45 Rembert's German translation at this point is misleading. The Zurich and Munich texts agree that the question is not "whether" but "where" brother Bünderlin is.

should tell the truth—a more learned and pious person than I, poor fellow that I am. And therefore the chances are that he will be more useful to thee in many matters than I.[46] But, then, he is freer because he has no wife nor children as I have.*

*[19] Good luck, my brother, with thy wonderful theology. May it please God that it be as true as it is unbelievable to the world. Mine is not less wonderful. *[20] For I believe and am certain that at the present time not a single true and natural word of the Lord Jesus Christ, the Son of God, is acknowledged on earth, yea, that no one has begun to recognize the righteousness of faith. No one, I say, in the whole of Germany, nay, more, in the whole world—I speak of those who sound forth their falsified word from their pulpits to the common people, that is, of the swine and the dogs—no one has been called or sent. Of this I have absolutely no doubt. Therefore, they preach without any fruit, for they are not sent of God but instead retch out the Word solely according to the letter, soiled with human filth, not according to the divine sense. For they also don't know another word to say but what is Scriptural, and of no other teachers except their evangelists.[47]

Why should I say more? Our[48] scribes now with the Fathers do not ever compose a line interpreted according to the meaning of Christ. Thus there is the one and eternal error and blindness in all, especially in the learned divines, who have learned, not from God, but only from Scripture and from men who themselves have not learned from God. For hell, resurrection, Christ, truth, last judgment, damnation, knowledge of God, gospel, faith, love, and all things are of a much or have a much different meaning from what until now everybody has taught. But in the end learned men will arise from among the people and they will impart understanding (Dan., ch. 12).*

*[21] ¶ I have seen thy German edition, not thy Latin version, wherein thou makest two persons of Christ and the Father, but of one Spirit, just as husband and wife are one flesh.[49] *[22] Now

---

[46] This sentence in the Dutch version dropped out of the German.
[47] The German is *Evangeliesten*; Rembert understands his Dutch text at this point to mean the solafideist preachers of the day.
[48] This Zurich text sentence replaces a garbled one in the Munich version.
[49] Campanus held that bridegroom-bride, one flesh, constitutes the full image of God (Gen. 1:26f.; 5:1f.); for Father and Son are one (John 10:30). He was thus a Binitarian, and baptismal union was for him the basic sacrament. Cf. Selection IX, at n.21. See on Campanus' Binitarianism further, S. von Dunin-Borkowski, "Quellen zur Vorgeschichte der Unitarier," *75 Jahre Stella Matutina* (Feldkirch, 1931), pp. 113-115; W. Bax,

the Spaniard[50] of whom the bearer of this letter, thy brother, will speak postulates in his little book[51] a single Person of the Godhead, namely, the Father, whom he calls most truly *the* Spirit or most properly the Spirit[52] and says that neither of the [other] two is a Person. The Roman Church postulates three Persons in one essence. I should rather agree with the Spaniard.[53]

*23 It is my counsel that thou not publish thy books too speedily to the end that when afterward thou mightest be of a different opinion, thou wilt not rue the costs and the labor! For I know of a certainty that thy opinion in many matters will change. If thou art a disciple of God, thou wilt surely let people go their own way. I should wish, however, that thou wert not so addicted to the letter of Scripture, thus withdrawing thy heart from the teaching of the Spirit, and that thou wouldst not drive out the Spirit of God as though it were Satan, crowding him against his will into the script and making Scripture thy god (which has often happened and still happens). Thou shouldst much rather interpret the Scripture as a confirmation of thy conscience,[54] so that it testifies to the heart and not against it. Again, thou shouldst not believe and accept something [merely] reported by Scripture—and feel that the God in thy heart must yield to Scripture. It were better that Scripture should remain Antichrist's! ¶ Saint Paul speaks not in vain [II Cor. 3:6] that the letter killeth. And yet it is [precisely visible letters] which almost all and especially the learned

---

Het Protestantisme in het Bisdom Luik, I (The Hague, 1937), pp. 43–45. Campanus disputed with the Wittenbergers over both the Trinity and the Eucharist. Melanchthon reports that he wrote out his views and presented at Torgau a "*magnum acervum impiorum dogmatum*" (*Corpus Reformatorum*, II, 33 f.). It is the view of Karl Rembert that the damnation in the Augsburg Confession, Article I, of old and new Samosatenes is a reference to Campanus, and not, as hitherto supposed, a reference to Servetus (*Die Wiedertäufer in Jülich*, 201 f.). Campanus gave more explicit and extended formulation to his anti-Trinitarian views in *Göttlicher und Heiliger Schrifft . . . Restitution*, 1532. This is described and quoted extensively by J. G. Schellhorn, *Amoenitates literariae*, XI, 78 ff.

50 Michael Servetus.
51 The work sent was undoubtedly *De Trinitatis erroribus*, published in Strassburg at the time Franck wrote his letter, namely, 1531.
52 The German here is "*denselbsten oder eigentligsten.*" I have not been able to locate the corresponding Latin phrase in Servetus.
53 Actually, Franck in his other writings never made much either way of the Trinity. See Rembert, *op. cit.*, p. 225.
54 The German gives virtual synonyms: *conscientz und gewissen*; the Latin original probably had only the one term.

divines consider to be the sole, pre-eminent word of God—
supposing God's word really could be written—and the sole
teacher.[55]

*[24] In brief, all that we have learned since childhood from
the papists, we must all of a sudden again unlearn. Again, the
same for what we have received from Luther and Zwingli—
all must be abandoned and altered. For one will sooner make a
good Christian out of a Turk than out of a bad Christian or a
learned divine! For the veil of Moses[56] hinders them, that is,
the death-dealing letter of Scripture, which they receive as life
and as life-giving Spirit.* I, however, hold completely that
the intention of the Lord does not reside precisely in the rind
of Scripture. That is, Scripture is not so easy for everyone to
understand but what I would sooner believe that it were locked
with seven seals and knowable to none but to the Lamb. For to
such an extent does God hide his wisdom under the covering of
likeness and literary parable of letters that none but those who
are taught of God himself can understand them. And [he] does
not so lightly expose his secret to the godless world and all
scamps but rather conceals it beneath the rind so that only the
instructed of God, as I have said, may be able to grasp it.

*[25] ¶ But now, good night, my brother, and be sure not to
let this letter reach the canaille and swine,[57] so that thou [un-
wittingly] preparest for me an untimely cross and makest an
untimely harvest of me. For many by their inconsideration and
untimely talking bring themselves to the gallows. But also
Christ forbids this, [saying (Matt. 7:6)] that one should not
give that which is holy unto the dogs, lest they turn around to
the givers and rend them. One should speak prudently and
where it fits in. For everything has its time.* This advice of
Paul [Acts 17:26] should be observed, namely, that all things
should take place according to their [appointed] time and in
order.

Given at Strassburg in the year 1531.[58]

---

[55] The Lutherans make the Bible, which expressly states that the letter
kills, a source of deadly instruction when the pre-eminent Teacher,
from the point of view of Franck, is the living Spirit.

[56] II Cor. 3:13 ff.

[57] The harsh reference to the Protestant preachers as swine and dogs, here
and above pp. 156, 158, may be illuminated by comparison with Melchior
Hofmann's utterance on p. 200 below.

[58] The Dutch version gives February 7, 1541.

VIII

An Answer to Luther's Malediction

By Caspar Schwenckfeld[1]

BEFORE APRIL 23, 1544

INTRODUCTION

THE FOLLOWING SELECTION IS NOT ONE OF THE
basic works of the Silesian nobleman and lay theologian,
but it has the merit of illustrating several important
aspects of the thought of a leading and too-long neglected
Spiritualist. First there is the tone of the refutation. Schwenckfeld had learned much from Martin Luther, had been indeed
for a while the leading exponent of Protestantism in Silesia,
and had, even after his reluctant break with Luther, loyally

[1] The most recent biography is that by Selina Gerhard Schultz, *Caspar
Schwenckfeld von Ossig* (1489–1561): *Spiritual Interpreter of Christianity,
Apostle of the Middle Way, Pioneer in Modern Religious Thought* (Norristown,
Pa., 1946). As associate editor of the multivolume *Corpus Schwenckfeld-
ianorum*, Mrs. Schultz draws heavily upon her sources. Some of the longer
selections translated from Schwenckfeld are listed in the bibliography.
The most comprehensive theological analysis of Schwenckfeld's basic ideas
is that of Joachim Wach, "CS, a Pupil and a Teacher in the School of
Christ," *Journal of Religion*, XXVI (1946), 1; republished in *Types of
Religious Experience* (Chicago, 1951), Ch. vii. Among the German studies
the following may be mentioned. Karl Ecke stressed Schwenckfeld's ideal
of the spiritual church in *S., Luther und der Gedanke einer apostolischen Reformation* (Berlin, 1911); reprinted simply as *CS* (Gütersloh, 1952) in shortened
form without heed being taken to the intervening research of others. A
brief but far richer and discerning analysis is that of Emanuel Hirsch,
"Zum Verständnis Schwenckfelds," *Festgabe für K. Müller* (1922), wherein
he is seen as a proto-Pietist. Comparable efforts to locate the too-long
neglected Spiritualist in church history at large are the following essays or
chapters: Johannes Kühn, *Toleranz und Offenbarung* (Leipzig, 1923),
wherein Schwenckfeld is classified with Roger Williams *et al.* as a true
Spiritualist; Erich Seeberg, "Der Gegensatz zwischen Zwingli, S. und
Luther," *Festscrift Reinhold Seeberg, I : Zur Theorie des Christentums*
(Leipzig, 1929), 43–80; Heinrich Bornkamm, "Äusserer und innerer
Mensch bei Luther und den Spiritualisten," *Imago Dei: Beiträge zur
theologischen Anthropologie* (Giessen, 1932), 85–109.

161

sought the counsel of Wittenberg. Only years after Luther's violent and vulgar malediction was Schwenckfeld goaded into publishing his Answer, being obliged to defend himself against charges made by Matthias Flacius Illyricus. The reply takes up each point made in Luther's brief but pungent text. The characteristically irenic in Schwenckfeld here comes as close to being ironic as we ever find it in this indefatigable but always equable controversialist. Only the first sections of the reply, dealing with the Lord's Supper and Christology, are here translated. At the center of Schwenckfeld's life and thought was the mystical Eucharist of his conversion experience. He explained it and defended it repeatedly and was baffled that so few really understood him. Yet they, in their turn, were perplexed that for all its alleged importance he did not participate in the Supper after 1526, when he announced his policy of suspension until more light should be shed by God on its proper celebration. In the meantime he distinguished between the mystical Eucharist and the sacramental recollection both of the Last Supper itself and of one's personal experience of receiving the Bread of heaven. The mystical experience of the divine Bread was theologically based on John, ch. 6, and on Augustine, the "old Christian Fathers," and even the *Decretum*. Schwenckfeld was also drawing upon the mystical tradition in which the body of Christ and the bride of Christ become one in the soul's acceptance of the divine. His Eucharistic "realism" was all the more emphatic for the reason that he held to the doctrine of the celestial flesh or primordial humanity of Christ, which was in his mind not creaturely and therefore everywhere potentially available for the spiritually perceptive believer. Schwenckfeld claims to have been the first to revive this doctrine from antiquity. He surely studied the Greek Fathers and may well have come on to the doctrine associated with Apollinaris and Apelles. In one version or another the celestial flesh was accepted by most of the Anabaptists and many of the Spiritualists, i.e., Servetus, Philips (Selection XI), Menno (Selection XII), and Hofmann (Selection IX).

The first part of this selection was translated by Selina Gerhard Schultz.

An Answer[2] to Luther's[3] Malediction
By Caspar Schwenckfeld

BEFORE APRIL 23, 1544

THE TEXT

[34] That Dr. Martin Luther gives me such an abusive, harsh, unapostolic blessing in answer* to my friendly, Christian petition and request is really not surprising, as it also is well to consider in the case of such a famous teacher out of what a

* Schwenckfeld reproduced this answer in the form of a malediction, at the head of his own *Answer*, as follows: (It is addressed, not to Schwenckfeld directly, but to the messenger Hermann Riegel, who had presumed to deliver Schwenckfeld's letter and tracts, and who was later imprisoned at ·Nuremberg and held for questioning.)

Dear sir messenger: Tell your master, Caspar Schwenckfeld, that I have received from you the booklet and the letter and would to God he would be silent.

Formerly he kindled a fire in Silesia against the holy sacrament, which is not yet extinguished and will burn upon him forever [cf. Luke 12:49]. In addition to this he continues with his Eutychianism and creatureliness, misleads the church, though God gave him no command, nor sent him. And the mad fool, possessed of the devil, does not understand anything; does not know what he is babbling. But if he will not cease, so let him leave me unmolested with his booklets which the devil excretes and spews out of him. And give him this as my final judgment and answer:

The Lord punish Satan in you, and your spirit which has called you, and your course which you are following. May all those who have part with you, Sacramentarians and Eutychians, together with you and your blasphemies, be your destruction, as is written [Jer. 23:21]: They ran and I did not call them, they spoke and I did not command them. December 6, 1543.
Martin Luther, by his own hand.

2 The *Answer* is Document CCCCXXXIX of the *Corpus Schwenckfeldianorum*, IX (Leipzig, 1928), pp. 29–59. The manuscript upon which this critical edition of the text is based was not printed by Schwenckfeld until 1555 when he was obliged to defend himself against Matthias Flacius Illyricus. An earlier and shorter version of the *Answer* is also preserved and has been edited as the first draft, *ibid.*, pp. 76–84.
3 Luther's Malediction of Schwenckfeld was written on December 6, 1543. It came forth as Luther's intemperate response to what seems to have

mind and heart it comes and what more may be concealed underneath it, for it is written [Luke 6:45]: The good man brings forth good out of the good treasure of his heart, for out of the abundance of the heart his mouth speaketh.

Furthermore, the Lord Christ in his Gospel [Matt. 5:44 f.] taught us otherwise, yea, more than the contrary, namely, that we love our enemies, bless them that curse us, do good to them that hate us, and sincerely pray for those who despitefully use us and persecute us, that we may be children of our Heavenly Father. But Dr. Martin Luther has forgotten the Gospel to such an extent that he not only does not bless them that curse him, not only does not do good to them that hate him, nor pray for them that insult him and persecute him (one is quite accustomed to his reproach and anger toward such of his adversaries; almost everyone speaks of it), but he also curses those who bless him and does evil to those who love him, persecutes those who pray for him, yea, and despises those who honor him and desire instruction from him, which is grievous to hear from such a man.

However, we commend his unevangelical answer and unapostolic blessing to our Lord Jesus Christ, the kind, gentle, and only real teacher of all believing hearts, who by the blessing of his grace can turn everything to our good, as he also knows how to use all things to his honor and glory. To him alone be honor, praise, victory, and triumph now and forever. Amen. But unto us be ridicule, insult, hate, shame, and dishonor, for the sake of his glorious name and his glory, as it is today, thank God.

[35] In order, however, that the truth of this matter and in addition also my innocence may the more readily be known, in the name of the Lord Jesus Christ I will reply briefly, by way of refutation and vindication, to Doctor Luther's accusation and malediction, in six[4] points following. May it give him satisfaction.

been Schwenckfeld's last despairing effort to maintain some contact with one from whom he had learned so much. This last letter is Document CCCCXXIII, *CS*, VIII, p. 685, addressed to Luther, October 12 and embodying Schwenckfeld's reasoned corrections of Luther's most recent asserverations concerning Schwenckfeld in *Von den letzten Worten Davids* (Wittenberg, 1543). Schwenckfeld reproduced the Malediction at the opening of his *Answer*. The text is also printed in two variants in Luther's *Werke, WA, Tischreden,* V, 300 f. The language has been moderated in translation!
4 Only Points I to III are here translated. On Point II the best treatment in English is that of Frederick W. Loetscher, *Schwenckfeld's Participation in the*

I

That Dr. Luther writes that the messenger shall tell me in answer that he has received the booklets and the letters,[5] I was very glad to hear and I hope that if he diligently reads and considers everything well, he will be reminded in his conscience of sundry things which may be of service to him and others, although some did not like to see that all this was submitted to him.

Perhaps the poor messenger also received his blessing as a gratuity.[6] But the reason for it and whether it be just, will all be seen at that day when all of us shall be revealed before the judgment seat of Christ and each will receive according to his works (John 5:27–29; I Cor. 5:10; II Cor. 5:10; etc.).

Furthermore, Dr. Luther demands that I be silent, and writes: "Would to God he would be silent." What he means thereby is easy to understand, but if he would convince me by Holy Scripture and persuasive reasons that I am straying or mistaken in any point of Christian doctrine or faith, also with respect to life (which he had much better done than such malediction and indecency in answer to my friendly petition and request, according to the manner of Christian love), I would not only be willing to cease and desist from everything that is not right, but also praise and thank him for his love.

II. AN ACCOUNT OF FAITH CONCERNING THE HOLY SACRAMENT

To Dr. Luther's accusation that I kindled a fire against the holy sacrament which has not yet been extinguished and will burn upon me forever (although the apostles of Christ—for example, Peter with the sorcerer and Paul with the Corinthian and others who merited it—dealt far more mercifully), this in brief is my reply: I am not at all conscious of having ever transacted, spoken, done, or written anything against the holy sacrament or the Lord's Supper that was contrary or antagonistic to divine truth, the words of the Lord Christ, and his

Eucharistic Controversy of the Sixteenth Century (Philadelphia, 1906). On Point III the most helpful introduction to Schwenckfeld's Christology is Hans Joachim Schoeps, *Vom himmlischen Fleisch Christi* (Tübingen, 1951), 25–36.
5 Schwenckfeld's last letter to Luther was October 12, 1543; see above, n. 3; it is printed also in Luther's *Werke, WA, Briefwechsel,* X, 420 ff.
6 Allusion to Luther's possible implication in the arrest of the messenger in Nuremberg.

praiseworthy institution. Neither Martin Luther nor any other can prove this against me, and I hope that even today [36] I still hold and believe correctly and in a Christian manner about it. I am impelled to give account herewith of my opinion and faith as follows:

1. I let stand the words of the Lord about the meat and drink of his body and blood in the Supper, when, after the breaking of the bread, he says (I Cor. 11:24): This is my body which is broken for you, etc., and let them remain as God's words, words of life and spirit, in their simple, spiritual meaning and divine sense, unperverted and unchanged in every respect as they were spoken by Christ and described by the apostles and Saint Paul in the Holy Spirit. But I maintain that they are to be judged, interpreted, understood, and compared in accordance with the teaching and words of the Lord about his flesh and blood when he says (John 6:55): My flesh is meat indeed, etc., and (John 6:51) the bread that I will give is my body, etc.

2. I believe and confess that the body or the flesh of Christ which was given for us, and his blood which was shed for us in forgiveness of sin, is a true food, drink, and nourishment, yea, a true, quickening bread and drink, but not a corporal, corruptible food and drink, not an earthly and visible bread and wine, neither with, under, nor in, but intrinsically a heavenly, divine bread, a spiritual, everlasting food and drink unto eternal life for all souls believing in Christ and all children of God.

3. That such food and drink are truly eaten out of the living Word of God by the mouth of faith and partaken of in the Lord's Supper when the institution of Christ is rightly observed in the Christian church, according to his will, for the satiation of the soul and increase in the accessions of grace in the new, inner man.[7]

4. That the Lord Jesus Christ as the true heavenly high priest, through the Holy Spirit, himself invites to the Supper and himself gives and distributes to all believers his body and blood unto eternal life, as he previously promised such, saying (John 6:51): The bread that I will give is my flesh which I will give for the life of the world. And prior thereto (John 6:27): Work not for the food that perisheth, but for that food which

---

Schwenckfeld here refers marginally to Augustine's *Tracts on St. John*: Credere enim in eum, hoc est manducare panem vivum. Qui credit, manducat: invisibliter saginatur, quia invisibiliter renascitur. Infans intus est, novus intus est: ubi novellatur, ibi satiatur. Migne, *PL*, XXXV, col. 1607.

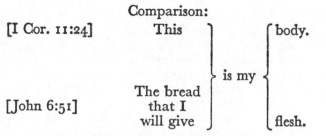

Comparison:

[I Cor. 11:24]   This ⎫   ⎧ body.
                        ⎬ is my ⎨
            The bread ⎪   ⎪
[John 6:51]   that I ⎪   ⎪
            will give ⎭   ⎩ flesh.

abideth unto eternal life which the Son of Man shall give unto you, for him the Father, even God, hath sealed.

5. For which reason also the visible, revered sacrament of the Lord's bread and cup[8] was instituted in the Supper by the Lord Jesus Christ before his departure, for thanksgiving and remembrance of the Lord, that the believers in Christ thereby might proclaim the death of the Lord and give praise, honor, and thanks for his bread and beneficence.

6. Therefore, it is essential that the divine work of the Lord Christ, that is, the feeding and the inner, spiritual eating in faith, be properly distinguished from the external, sacramental eating, the *gratias* or remembrance (or as Saint Augustine[9] has it: *sacramentum* and *res sacramenti*, the bread of the Lord and the bread which is the Lord himself), through a spiritual judgment and understanding, in order that these two kinds of bread and drink in the entire sacramental transaction of the Lord's Supper, one for the inner, the other for the external, believing man, each in its place (*Ordnung*), may remain unmingled with the other; that the inner, spiritual precede[10] and be contemplated, but the external, sacramental eating follow and be observed in proclaiming the death of the Lord; and that each be observed with fitting contemplation, earnestly and fervently, as is indicated by Holy Scripture.

This in brief is my understanding, faith, and confession of the Lord's Supper, of the spiritual nourishment of the soul, and of the holy sacrament of the body and blood of Christ.

It is, nevertheless, true that I, like many other goodhearted, God-fearing people, do not agree with Dr. Luther's [38] newly introduced understanding, practice, belief, and teaching

[8] Schwenckfeld refers to this on the margin as the Eucharist, i.e., the *poculum benedictionis* (I Cor. 10:16).
[9] Migne, *PL*, XXXV, cols. 1602; 1612; 1796.
[10] Schwenckfeld on the margin quotes Augustine: "Believe and thou hast eaten."

about the Supper in many points. Firstly, he interprets[11] the words of the Supper contrary to the thought and will of the Lord, and does not let them remain with the one spiritual eating and drinking of the body and blood of Christ in faith, but beyond that produces also a physical (*Leiplich*), oral eating, yea, two kinds of eating and drinking of the one body and blood of Christ, without certainty, without Scripture and proof; teaches about it thus, namely, that the body and blood of Christ is eaten and drunk in two kinds of, and different ways, once spiritually by the believing heart out of the Word, the other time physically by the physical mouth in the sacramental, visible bread which Paul [I Cor. 11:27] calls the bread of the Lord.

This, however, I regard as erroneous and false, because such physical eating of Christ and his body in external things not only cannot be authenticated by any Scripture, but such assertion is wrong because thereby the Christians are bewildered in the knowledge of Christ and are led away from the simplicity that is in Christ, contrary to Paul (II Cor. 11:3). Yea, the one Christ is made to be twofold and faith is divided, for we would have another Christ and also another way to salvation than the believing holy fathers, patriarchs, and prophets had under the Old Covenant who knew nothing of such physical eating of the body of Christ and the presence of his body in the bread, but as Paul says [I Cor. 10:3 f.; Heb., ch. 11; Eph. 4:5], One Lord, one faith.

Therefore, there is no other eating than the one spiritual eating and drinking of the body and blood of Christ which is done by faith. Moreover, it is directly contrary and opposed to the entire content of the Holy Scriptures as well as the Kingdom and glory of our Lord Jesus Christ, as I pointed out and proved some time past in a separate booklet,[12] which Luther may have seen, and which if God be willing, shall be repeated, confirmed, and—concerning the entire article about the Lord's Supper—brought further to the light. For to feed the soul, as well as teaching, sanctifying, regenerating, etc., are offices of the Kingdom of Christ which, without him, no one can administer.

The second point in which I cannot agree with Dr. Luther is

---

[11] *Dasz diese Wort Christi " Das ist mein Leib" noch fest stehen wider die Schwärmgeister, Werke, WA* 23, esp. pp. 258, 180, 188.
[12] *Refutation of the Opinion that the Corporeal Presence Is in the Elements,* Document LVI, January, 1528, *CS,* III.

that he claims[13] that the minister of the church can truly give, present, and distribute the body and blood of Christ [39] to the communicants, and not only the Lord Christ himself, but this is in direct opposition to the entire sixth chapter of John and the aforementioned words of the Lord when he (ch. 6:51) promises us a living bread which he (he himself) will give, and an incorruptible food which the Son of Man will give, who also alone is sealed thereunto by God the Father.

Some want to improve on this, writing and teaching that not the minister but Christ himself gives his body and blood, however, *with* the bread and wine and that he offers himself therewith. This as well as the previous is incorrect and false, against the heart and mind of Christ as well as against his divine glory.

The third controversial point is that Dr. Luther writes[14] and teaches that the physical mouth, also of the godless communicant, eats the body of Christ physically, yea, that the betrayer, Judas, and his crowd actually ate the glorious body and blood of Christ and that all unbelievers even yet may eat and drink him without faith. For, as Luther says, Christ himself is present in the sacramental bread and wine of the altar, alive in body and blood, in which again I can in no wise agree or harmonize with Luther against divine truth and the glory of the regnant Lord Christ, because he wants to make the body of our Lord Jesus Christ and the blood of the New Eternal Covenant common to the unworthy and godless men, contrary to all Scripture.

The fourth point of the disagreement is that he does not let the teaching of Christ about his flesh, body, and blood and of the heavenly food and drink of eternal life, remain one and the same doctrine, but divides it into multiplicity and makes it repugnant to itself in that he separates[15] the sixth chapter of John from the words of the Lord's Supper as if it did not belong thereto, contrary to all old teachings of the church, although the flesh and blood of which the Lord taught in John, ch. 6, is the flesh and blood of the body which he gives and distributes in the Supper to the believing disciples through his almighty living Word as a food unto eternal life.

The Lord Jesus Christ (John, ch. 6) spoke a prejudgment (*praejudicium*) with great earnestness and a certain and

13 *German Catechism* (1529), *Werke, WA*, 30, I, 224.
14 *On the Lord's Supper* (1528), *WA*, 26, 288.
15 *Das diese Wort Christi, WA*, 23, 182.

irreproachable one about the bread and drink [40] as well as about the manner of the eating and drinking of his body, flesh, and blood, which he in no wise changed or recanted before his death at the Last Supper, neither for the sake of the sacrament nor his death on the cross, nor for any other reason, but much rather renewed, repeated, clarified, and confirmed, as he is the eternal, unchanging truth which cannot deny itself. He is the Amen Amen. In him there is no yes and no. But in him is yes, also all promises of God are yes in him, and in him is the Amen, as Saint Paul (II Cor. 1:20) said: May he graciously grant that such be well recognized and considered.

Hence it is in no wise to be thought that Christ taught and held divine truth inconsistently, yea, two opposing opinions on one thing, about one food and drink of his one body, flesh, and blood, as little as he wanted to feed, give to drink, or nourish with his one body and blood in a twofold manner.

The fifth point is that without Scripture and proof I cannot agree with Dr. M. Luther when he writes[16] and teaches that our Lord Christ placed the strength and power of his passion in the visible sacrament, that one shall fetch, seek, and find it there and he who has a bad conscience because of sin shall fetch and seek there in the sacrament consolation, salvation, and forgiveness of sin, which also I do not consider right. For what is this other than crying out a new indulgence with the holy sacrament and establishing a false confidence thereby. The Lord Christ and his apostles taught nothing about this. It is also in direct opposition to the use and institution of the sacrament, for Christ says (I Cor. 11:25): This do in remembrance of me.

The sixth point wherein I do not know how to agree with Luther is that he writes[17] that the revered sacrament imparts life, grace, and salvation, yea, that it is a fountain of life and salvation. And as also others of his party,[18] out of want of understanding of the institution of Christ and the correct usage, write and teach quite ineptly that the communicants, through the receiving of the sacrament, satisfy the hunger of the soul, attain the righteousness of God, and receive a powerful impression for the betterment of life, all of which is quite wrong and does not harmonize with the truth, [41] as it also is contrary

---

[16] *Against the Heavenly Prophets* (1525), *WA*, 18, 203 f.
[17] *Von Anbeten des Sakraments* (1523), *WA*, 11, 443.
[18] Schwenckfeld on the margin refers to Gervasius Schuler, preacher in Memmingen, whom he met in 1534; cf. Document CLIX, *CS*, V.

to all Scripture, also to true faith. The effect or the consequences of the work sufficiently show such futility among the communicants of this time, because none of those things happen in their conscience which are being promised in, and ascribed to, the Supper.

Furthermore, in the booklet *Admonition for the Sacrament* Luther writes[19] that the sacrament is a fire which kindles the cold hearts; that it is a gracious, powerful thing full of benefit and healing, besides innumerable and unutterable heavenly riches of which one can partake without any cost and trouble if one attends; yea, if one merely thinks a little about it and prepares for it, it will kindle, incite, and draw a heart to it, says Dr. Luther.

But what is this other than perverting the laudable institution of Christ, binding salvation to the work out of the *opus operatum*, and making an idol out of the sacrament? It is setting up thereby a false confidence and fornication of the souls, if one wants to place the sacrament, symbol, or sign on a par with Christ Jesus, the only giver of all grace and salvation, with great offense to his honor and glory, in that one wants to appropriate that which is specifically Christ's, the ruler at the right hand of his Father, and also that one wants to appropriate it to the use of the sacrament and to teach that forgiveness of sin can thereby be sought or procured—not to mention the elevation or adoration which has been practiced this long time.

It also is unscriptural, incorrect, and false when Martin Luther teaches that Christ bound his bidding and doing to the words of the minister although the Lord does not command more than that one shall do this (namely, break the bread) in remembrance of him, as also Saint Paul clearly explains it, saying (1 Cor. 11:26): As often as ye eat of this bread and drink of this cup, ye proclaim the Lord's death until he come.

It is also incorrect and contrary to the Word of the Lord when Luther writes[20] that Christ binds himself to the Word in the sacrament, that one can find, lay hold of, and have him there and say: Here I have you, etc., which the [42] Lord himself calls a deception, and faithfully warned his disciples against it when he says (Matt. 24:23): If any man shall say unto you, Lo, here is the Christ, or there; believe it not, etc.; (Luke 17:23): And they shall say unto you, Lo, there! Lo, here!

19 *Vermahnung zum Sakrament des Leibes und Blutes Christi* (1530), *WA*, 30, II, 618; see exact quotation below in text at n. 24.
20 *Das diese Wort Christi*, *WA*, 23, 150.

go not away nor follow them. This has been written of elsewhere.

The seventh controversial point follows: That Dr. Luther's[21] and his colleagues' newly introduced interpretation and practice of the Supper undeniably is contrary to Paul's principle of probation (*Proba Pauli*) when he writes about the observance of the holy sacrament and about the feast or celebration of the Lord's Supper in a good, pious manner, and says (I Cor. 11:27–29): Let a man examine himself and so let him eat of the bread and drink of the cup. For he that eateth and drinketh, eateth and drinketh judgment unto himself, if he discern not the body of the Lord, and previously: Whosoever shall eat the bread or drink the cup of the Lord in an unworthy manner, shall be guilty of the body and blood of the Lord.

One no longer wants to consider such words and severe sentence of the Holy Spirit in Paul, but calls, allures, admonishes everyone, young and old, regardless of what is appropriate for such an act. And not much real reverence, love, and ardor are felt. Yea, one drives, threatens, frightens, and chases everything, without any sense, without any examination (*Proba*), also without any ceremony and discrimination, into the Supper, contrary to all Scripture, there to procure indulgence, grace, and forgiveness of sin, also even righteousness and the improvement of one's life. Yet actually nothing fundamental comes of it all, for everyone must confess that, with respect to the consciences, matters have scarcely ever been worse.

At one time it was taught that the spiritual eating must precede, as Luther himself in a *Sermon on John VI*[22] wrote, namely: "The bread on the altar is merely a symbol, like baptism, and is of no value, unless one has already eaten the living, heavenly bread inwardly." Thus wrote Martin Luther formerly [1524]. But now only the external sacrament is the important thing, with the *Hoc facite*[23] which is to accomplish it alone without any further reflection.

And [43] in order that one may warm oneself and lay off the cold and disinclination of the heart and awaken and strengthen faith, he offers consolation, mercy, and grace to all who attend (be they worthy or unworthy), yea, to all sinners.[24] "Here at

---

[21] Schwenckfeld on the margin says: Luther glosses [*WA*, 10, II, 38] right on the margin to the effect that proving one's self is to feel one's faith, etc. Now he has it that one should believe that grace and indulgence are first to be fetched at the sacrament.

[22] Cf. *WA*, 18, 136.   [23] "This do ye": I Cor. 11:25.

[24] *Vermahnung, WA*, 30, II, 618.

the sacrament you must rub yourself and hold onto it," Luther writes in his *Admonition*; "there is a fire which can kindle the hearts." He wants the sacrament to kindle the hearts, although the longer they remain [at the sacrament] the colder they become in their love of God and neighbor, in fact, the longer the worse they become, as is plainly evident. Furthermore, he also writes in the same place[25] that whoever only goes with him [Luther] to the sacrament is secure and free of all error and of all satanic deception. On the other hand, he curses all who do not attend, with pestilence, fever, and all kinds of sickness, hunger, war, dissension, discord, and unrest.[26]

In reality the Supper or sacrament of the altar has become not only a snare for the conscience and an offense to the Christ-believing soul, but a cloak for all error, all sin, and godless being, as well as a furtherance to and confirmation of the old unrepentant life and accursed way of the flesh (like the Mass). May God be graciously merciful! Do what you will [say the Lutherans], only go to the Supper and everything will be simple; and as soon and as often as you come again after falling, everything will be forgiven you! Thus do many at this time deal with the Supper.

Whoever notices such a grievous misuse and idolatry and the error therein and contradicts it by Holy Scripture or desists from it and points instead to the knowledge of Christ, and whoever also inquires about the correct understanding and basis of the Lord's Supper, must be a hypercritical ponderer, a sectary, or factious spirit, yea, a desecrater of the sacrament and not a Christian. He must be, as Luther writes, "a desperate heathen and worse than a Turk"; again, "a fanatic, devil, or child of the devil." In some places he is driven from country, city, wife and child, house and home, and decried and banned as an enemy of the gospel of our Lord Jesus Christ. When such a one dies, they would like with all their might to bury him under the gallows.

Should not a devout and God-fearing heart and conscience ponder over this? Yea, rightly have a horror of it, since all this is unapostolic, just as their assertion is in contradiction to the will and institution of the [44] Lord Jesus Christ: untheological and against the correct Christian observance of his holy Supper or sacrament.

All this, I say, which has been mentioned in the seven points, I shall not, nor can, with good conscience accept from Dr.

---

25 Cf. *ibid.*, 605. 26 *Ibid.*, 625.

Luther or any of his party, contrary to such bright, clear testimony of Holy Scripture, nor can I agree or harmonize with it. I also regard it as being very detrimental to our regnant (*Regirenden*) Lord Jesus Christ and his glory and office, also to the free course of grace and the nature of the New and eternal Covenant; in the first place because his holy, glorified, divine body[27] would be essentially in the earthly, visible bread, and the blood of Christ truly in the material corruptible wine; and in the second place because his body and blood would be received, eaten, and drunk in a twofold manner, both physically and spiritually, yea, even without faith, as Luther teaches,[28] by the unworthy and godless mouth.

For it would follow that the unique, single (*ainfaltige*) Christ would not always remain the same one Christ, and his body, flesh, and blood not always a true food and drink, nor a quickening flesh and blood. Indeed, the final conclusion and decision of the Lord about the food and drink of his body, flesh, and blood would be invalid when he says (John 6:56; 58): He that eateth my flesh and drinketh my blood abideth in me and I in him, and he that eateth this bread shall live forever.

This one conclusion of the Lord Christ proves sufficiently that Luther and others certainly must be teaching wrongly about the eating and drinking of the body and blood of Christ and are dealing quite censurably with the institution of Christ. For, whereas and since this examination (*Proba*) does not occur, nor show in the works of the communicants, there must necessarily (if the pronouncement of Christ is to be true and right, which it undoubtedly is) be something amiss; and nothing but God's judgment and chastisement is at hand.

Therefore, I cannot agree at all with Dr. Luther nor his colleagues in the article of the holy sacrament, for the above-mentioned reasons and for many others. For, according to the testimony of Holy Scripture, I know no other Christ than him who now reigns in the glory of God his Father and is full of life, spirit, grace, and blessedness, our high priest and the only forgiver of sin. In him also dwells all the fullness of God

27 Schwenckfeld does not in the present work more than as here advert to his characteristic doctrine of the heavenly flesh of Christ. But see below, Part III. Cf. Hofmann, below, p. 198. Schwenckfeld wrote: "They both [Hofmann, Franck] have taken their errors from our truth, like spiders who suck poison out of a beautiful flower." *CS*, V, pp. 522 f.
28 *Of the Lord's Supper, WA*, 26, 288.

bodily (Col. 2:9), who is made higher than the heavens and has nothing to do with the unbelieving, godless [45], and unworthy (II Cor. 6:15; Heb. 7:26 f.), but is righteousness, sanctification, food and drink, nourishment, and complete satiation unto eternal life of the chosen believers and is present in the Holy Spirit with grace, with them as the head of his body and members.

Moreover, according to the Holy Scriptures and the words of the Lord which are spirit and life, I know of no other eating and drinking of the body and blood of Christ in the Lord's Supper than of the one spiritual eating and drinking which takes place in the mystery of the true and living faith, as I have not otherwise written and maintained for many years and as I also today, God be praised, hold and believe with good assurance.

At the same time I in no wise disdain nor reject the visible sacrament of the Lord's Supper on account of the mystery and spiritual transaction of Christ's which he brings to the memory of the believers as in the words: "This do in remembrance of me," but in its place I regard it highly and reverently.

To remain [for the moment] with the commemoration, which is the *representatio*[29] of the Fathers, out of which they [Scholastics and Lutherans alike] have made a symbolical eating, etc. (of which, however, the Scripture says nothing), although I cannot regard or accept it [the elements] as God, nor as the Lord Christ himself [with the Catholics],[30] nor with Luther and his colleagues, as the fountain of life and salvation, nor as a divinely kindled fire and righteousness—nevertheless I give to Christ only and alone as is right the divine honor of justification and salvation due him, and I give to the holy sacrament (in correct usage) its benefit, office, place, and reverence, yea, all that the Holy Scriptures give. And as stated, I distinguish, through faith, the entire sacramental transaction of the Lord's Supper, spiritually, as also I point to and warn as to the proper understanding of the words and to the knowledge of Christ Jesus, according to my poor ability, and admonish thereto.

If, then, Dr. Luther calls this kindling a fire [cf. Luke 12:49], I should wish to God that it already burned in many hearts to the honor of Christ and the eradication of error, also that it illuminated every one in order that all kinds of misuse,

---

29 The meaning here is not entirely clear. One of the three manuscripts refers to Jerome's *Commentary on Matthew* for *representatio*. In Texts B and C this paragraph as far as "although" is omitted.
30 In the doctrine of transubstantiation.

false faith, violation, and idolatry would become manifest thereby, and that Jesus Christ the Son of God, our Saviour (who is the [46] only food and nourishment of our languishing heart, soul, and conscience), would be understood, recognized, and known according to the spirit in the glory of God his Father and, in his Heavenly Kingdom, as the ruling king of honor.

From this it is readily perceived what our dissension with Luther and his party is in this matter, and that it is not merely about the sacrament or Supper, but more about the real meaning and understanding of the words of the Lord about his body and blood in the Supper and about the correct observance of the holy sacrament, and also about that which Paul demanded of the attendants or guests, all of which they smear over and obscure in their vexation (*ahnfechtung*), as they also ignore the pure doctrine of the saving knowledge of Christ, and in its stead confirm and introduce a false reliance on the conscience,[31] that is, idolatry, together with an erroneous faith and a pernicious misuse and indulgence with the sacrament.

What, however, results from the idolatry and such misuse of the Supper? This: God's punishment with pestilence, sickness, famine, war, blindness, ignorance, and all kinds of evil, etc. This is amply described for us in Holy Scripture (as, specifically, I Cor. 11:17–22), although they will not take the blame and would like to put it upon other innocent ones who desist from such idolatry and misuse. Likewise they would like to make poor me suspect for everyone as though I opposed the holy sacrament simply because I admonished them concerning their misuse and error or also abstained from it.

But briefly, my booklets, and among others my *Confession of the Sacrament of the Body and Blood of Christ*,[32] particularly also an *Apology*[33] whereby I answered Dr. [John] Faber in this matter, are still extant. Herein I explained myself sufficiently about the true and the false understanding and faith, together with the reasons for the error and the apostasy in the article of the Lord's Supper, and also of the right understanding of the words: This is my body, etc. Up to this time no one has confuted these tractates, nor taught me better by Holy Scripture. In them it will also be found that I do not deny the food and drink

---

31 The text reads: *ain falsch vertrawen der gewissenn.*
32 *A Catechetical Confession of the Lord's Supper*, Document C (May–June, 1530), *CS*, III, 712 ff.
33 *The First Apology*, Document LXXX (January, 1529), *CS*, III, 391 ff.

of the body and blood of Christ in the Lord's Supper nor in any way disdain or abrogate the sacrament of the altar in correct Christian usage, but that, according to the evidence of Holy Scripture, through a spiritual judgment, I appropriately distinguish the spiritual [inward] eating and drinking of the body and blood of Christ from the [external] grace, that is, the thanks [47]giving [for the nourishment], the praise, and the remembrance of the Lord.

I also place together or compare the words of the Lord at the Supper about his body and blood with John, ch. 6, about the same body, flesh, and blood (as all old Christian teachers did and as is to be found in the *Decretum*)[34] and understand and interpret one through the other, the lesser through the greater, the last through the first; and one can readily see from the tracts and information mentioned and also from a comparison of the Gospels what I maintain concerning the holy sacrament, how I believe and confess it (and, as I hope, in the certainty of faith) according to the mind and meaning of the Lord—correctly, clearly, and Christlike.

Briefly, I also maintain and believe what Saint Augustine wrote about it, in *Tract XXVI on John VI*,[35] and subsequently in *Tract LIX*,[36] with clear, plain words, about two kinds of bread, thus: The believing disciples of the Lord ate the bread, the Lord, but Judas ate the bread of the Lord against the Lord; they received life, but Judas pain or punishment; for he who eats unworthily, eats damnation unto himself. Thus writes Augustine.

This is also, as stated, my understanding of and distinction between the two kinds of bread, food, and drink in the whole sacramental transaction of the Lord's Supper. [I stand] with Augustine, to whom, next to the Bible, I appeal; and since he has been accepted by the Christian church, I hope to remain unmolested therein with all Christians.

Therewith Luther's calumny about the fire kindled against the holy sacrament is refuted on the basis of truth. Also his misunderstanding and newly introduced conception of the Lord's Supper (of which he together with his associates is unable to give either a fundamental account or an argument

---

34 On the margin Schwenckfeld, who had studied canon law, cites the *Corpus juris canonici*, where it in its turn refers to Augustine's dictum: The sacrament is a visible sign of an invisible grace. *Corpus juris canonici* (Paris, 1705), I, 457.

35 Migne, *PL*, 35, col. 1611.   36 *Ibid.*, col. 1796.

from Scripture or necessity) has been briefly characterized and disproved.

[48] For certainly Dr. Luther has not, with understanding and truth, brought out the correct sense and the real meaning of the teaching of Christ about his body and blood in his Supper. The same is true in other matters. As his instability (which is noticed by many people and can be proven from their own books) obviously also shows, he and his associates up to this time have taught, before God, and written without foundation and without certainty in this matter.

Although they indeed boast that they have restored to the laity the other kind, namely, the cup, it can be shown that up to this day they have never understood nor correctly interpreted nor put into plain language the words of the Lord which he spoke to his disciples after passing the cup, as they also do not know wherein the eating of the body and the drinking of the blood of Christ truly and intrinsically consists. And if they should say that it consists or occurs in faith, they should explain well what such faith is, what its type and nature can do, and also which office that faith pursues; upon what and whither it directs itself; and what its object or aspect is; yea, how the eating is accomplished; how one eats a glorified body; where one must get it; how such eating is felt and perceived; again, how one presses through or comes to drinking the blood of the New, eternal Covenant; how it is drunk to the quickening and cleansing of the soul so that we are fed and satiated thereby unto eternal life.

The great rabbis should previously concern themselves about this and distinguish the body of the Lord correctly and consider well what kind of guests belong to the Supper of the Heavenly King, Jesus, and thereby clearly teach of an unchanging foundation, should also first learn for themselves in the Lord's School, if they would observe the Supper worthily and spread the Table of the Lord properly; for it is undeniable, and is found in all the old Christian teachers, that in the sacramental transactions one shall concern oneself first of all about that which is spiritual, and pay attention to the faith and the discrimination of the body of the Lord in the Supper, that is, to the knowledge of Christ according to the Spirit. . . .

III. OF THE HUMANITY OF CHRIST:

REFUTATION OF THE CHARGES OF EUTYCHIANISM

[49] Though Dr. Luther writes further in his answer: "In addition to this he continues with his Eutychianism and creatureliness, misleads the church, though God gave him no command, nor sent him" (he means me), I cannot understand what he means here with "Eutychianism" and whether or not, as with others, he means thereby the denial of the humanity of Christ. I know very well, however, that elsewhere, for example in *On the Councils and the Churches* published in 1539, he writes of Eutyches[37] that it was not Eutyches' view to consider Christ only a divine Person and nature and not a man, but rather that he held Christ to be true God and man and that he simply did not wish to ascribe the *idiomata* or properties of deity to his humanity. Thus all prophets, all Scripture, ascribing to Christ or the Messiah an eternal Kingdom and salvation from sins, are all against Eutyches; for all of them say that the seed of the woman will bruise the head of the serpent (Gen., ch. 3).—Thus Dr. Luther writes about Eutyches.[38]

Now if this is what it was for him and this is also what he further means by Eutychianism, then surely our antagonists or opponents, indeed, all who hold Christ the Man in glory as a creature under God and of less honor and power than God are much more to be accused of Eutychianism than I. Indeed, they must agree with Eutyches incontestably because they maintain and defend precisely this.

But if he now calls it Eutychianism when only one nature in Christ is believed in and his humanity is denied, then he himself proves, as also all others who read my writings or hear us, that he unjustly charges me therewith even against his own better knowledge. Since my whole activity and altercation has had to do exclusively with the humanity of Christ, with his true body, blood, and flesh and their properties, status, essence, and majesty in glory against those who want to rob his humanity of this splendor—how can I, then, deny the humanity of Christ and blood and flesh, or maintain only one nature, namely, only the Word in Christ, and make out of the human nature a divine nature, as they allege? This has never in my whole life come

---

[37] Eutyches was the Monophysite Archimandrite of Constantinople against whom the Council of Chalcedon in 451 defined Christ as one Person in two natures.

[38] *WA*, 50, 594 ff.

into my mind, that is, that I should not hold and confess Christ as a hero (*heldt*) with two natures to be true God and true man.

[50] Therefore, let M. Luther turn with his Eutychianism whichever way he will and at the same time seize upon whatever help he may; he will still not be able, with all other opponents, to make me out truthfully to be a Eutyches or any other heretic, thanks be to God! Indeed I have already cleared myself of this in a letter,[39] which should have been quite sufficient for him to have felt obliged to let drop the charge of Eutychianism in his [most recent] writing. But of what help is righteousness? For resentment and injustice have gotten the upper hand even though in the end, as the prophet says (Ps. 94:15): But right will remain right and all the upright in heart shall follow it.

But what did Luther himself write in his *Confession of Truth Concerning the Supper*,[40] also in the book against the fanatics on the body and flesh of Christ?[41] This: that the flesh of Christ is pure spirit and that his flesh was not born of flesh. Indeed, he writes that it is a blasphemy if one says that Christ's flesh is born of flesh and is flesh; and again, that the body of Christ must not be flesh but rather spirit because he was conceived of the Holy Ghost. Also that the body of Christ back in the days of his flesh was at once in heaven and on earth, indeed, that it was present in all the ends of the earth.[42] For all this I let him answer, although by any person it could well be looked upon and interpreted as much more of a Eutychianism or some other ancient heresy than my own belief and confession.

In addition to this, I recognize nothing of creation or creatureliness in Christ but rather a new divine birth and natural Sonship (*kindtschafft*) of God. Wherefore I cannot consider the Man Christ with his body and blood to be a creation or a creature. Rather, I believe and confess with Scripture that he is wholly God's only begotten Son and that Christ, the Son of God, his Heavenly Father, the whole Person indivisibly (*unzertailig*) God and Man, was born in time of the Virgin Mary; also that he suffered and died for us upon the cross in personal unity and wholeness, and as such rose again and ascended into heaven, that he sits at the right hand of God and rules also in his human nature wholly with God his Father

---

[39] The letter of October 12, 1543, Document CCCCXXIII, *CS*, VIII.
[40] *WA*, 26, 349 ff.
[41] *Das diese Wort Christi*, *WA*, 23, 200.   [42] *Ibid.*, 140; 144.

in divine glory, unity, and essence from which he will come to judge, etc.

But, as to what others with their purported creature in Christ have brought forth from their philosophy and the old scholastic opinions, corrupted or stirred up, that is, those who do not hold the Man Jesus Christ in [51] personal unity as the born Son of God but rather as a creation or a creature, and who do not want to accord to him the rank and honor of the other Person in the Trinity of God—maybe they would like to label me and others with "creature," as though we were causing an unnecessary squabble or introduced ancient errors, but the truth is now as clear as day, of which all unpartisan devotees thereof may easily avail themselves!

IX

The Ordinance of God
By Melchior Hofmann[1]

1530

INTRODUCTION

THE PROTESTANT "APOSTLE OF THE BALTIC," after turning from Lutheranism (on the issue of free will) and presently to Anabaptism, here presents in fiery passion his new understanding of the great spiritual transaction of the baptism of the reborn, a practice which he carried from the Swiss Brethren to Holland. Perhaps nowhere else in extant Anabaptist literature are we enabled to enter so deeply into the thought and religious experience that originally centered in believers' baptism. Surely the sober recital of the first rebaptism (Selection I) provides few clues to the source of the new religious vitality which was flowing over the channels surveyed and partly dug by the Reformers.

Here, however, we sense the intense heat and, as it were, the chthonic pressures beneath the crust of the magisterial Reformation and peer into the molten hearth from which Anabaptist volcanoes burst forth in Münster and Amsterdam. Not only Münsterites and Jorists traced their movement to Melchior but also the Mennonites, though by a different succession and a different appropriation of his ideas. Obbe and Dietrich Philips (Selections X, XI) are indebted to him. In characteristic

---

[1] There is no adequate treatment of Hofmann in English. A Dutch work by W. I. Leendertz (1883) is difficult to procure. The comparable German study is that of Friedrich Otto zur Linden, *M.H.: ein Prophet der Wiedertäufer* (Haarlem, 1885). Both these works contain excerpts and full documents, as does the much earlier work by Barthold Krohn, *Geschichte der fanatischen und enthusiastischen Wiedertäufer vornehmlich in Niederdeutschland: Melchior Hofmann und die Secte der Hofmannianer* (Leipzig, 1758).

Abraham Hulshof, *Geschiedenis van de Doopsgezinden to Straatsburg* (Amsterdam, 1905), has an excellent chapter on him. Obbe Philips gives a contemporary account of him, translated below, Selection X, at n. 12.

fusion of Biblical imagery Hofmann thinks of adult baptism and its immediate sequel as a recurrent epiphany of Christ. In the medieval church, the liturgy of Epiphany which commemorates the baptism of Christ at the Jordan was associated with Christ's first miracle, the marriage of Cana, itself (because of the wine) a symbol of the Eucharist. In Hofmann these same motifs are combined. Baptism is the betrothal of the soul to the heavenly Bridegroom. The Supper is at once the marriage (the bread being the presentation of the ring) and the marriage feast. Moreover, just as Christ after his baptism went directly into the wilderness to be tempted forty days, just as the Lover and beloved in the Song of Songs go into the wilderness together, and just as the Children of Israel after successfully passing through the Red Sea wandered forty years in the wilderness (Exodus and II Esdras), so every Christian must submit to the onslaughts of Satan. All are called to become the brides of Christ and corporately his church (cf. the universalism and the stress on free will in Denck, Selection IV, and in Hubmaier, Selection V), but there is always the temptation of spiritual adultery with the consequent ejection of the adulterous bride in the ban. Moreover, even those steadfast in the desert have not prepared for the full epiphany Christ the Lord until his body, as it were, is burned in them at the martyr's pyre; until at the blow of the executioner' sword his blood flows anew.

The Ordinance of God [2]
By Melchior Hofmann

1530

THE TEXT

[148] In the first place, the Lord Jesus Christ [Matt. 28:18] proclaims to his apostles and disciples that he has received from his Heavenly Father all power, might, strength, spirit, mind, and will and promises [Micah 5:2; Matt. 2:6] that he [will] be a king, prince, and captain [3] both in heaven and on earth, and that his rule extends over all, whatever it may be called. In this manner God speaks through his holy prophets [Ps. 110:1]: Sit thou at my right hand, until I lay thine enemies at thy footstool. And again in another place [Ps. 2:6]: I have set my king upon my holy hill of Zion. Of the same power and rule Saint Paul gives strong evidence in his epistles [Phil. 2:10 f.; Eph. 1:21 f.], namely, that he is a lord of all things and that nothing can be named which does not belong under his feet. Yea, he is a dispenser of all heavenly, eternal, and spiritual bounties of God. Just as Joseph in Egypt [dispensed] bodily and ephemeral [goods], so Christ Jesus dispenses spiritual, heavenly, and abiding riches.

---

[2] *The Ordinance* was written by Hofmann in Holland and first printed in Holland or East Frisia in 1530. Only a Dutch translation survives, first printed in Amsterdam in 1611. It is this text which is here translated from the critical edition of S. Cramer, *Bibliotheca Reformatoria Neerlandica*, V (The Hague, 1909), 148–198. The numbers in brackets refer to these pages.

   Only a selection of the Biblical references supplied in the margin of the text are here given (in brackets).

[3] The Vulgate has *dux*. Hence, among others, John Denck and Erasmus speak of Christ as Captain (*Herzog, dux*), *Ordnung Gottes*, B III b; *Enchiridion* (1516), ed. by Hajo Holborn, *Ausgewählte Werke* (Munich, 1933), p. 24. It is of note that Erasmus expressly connects Christ's captaincy over soldiers with the sacrament of baptism.

Thus is the Son of Man—a saviour of his people and the anointed peacemaker (*Salichmaker*) for all believers, a reconciler, advocate, and high priest, yea, the "mouth" of the spiritual Moses[4] and eternal Heavenly Father—[ever] sending forth his friends, servants, and apostolic emissaries in order to assemble for him his Bride[5] out of the bonds of darkness, out of the realm and all the power of the devil and Satan, out of all that belongs to this world—into the Kingdom of God and of the Lord Jesus Christ.

And the King of Kings shuts no one out [of the Kingdom]. He rejects not a single person but speaks rather and commands his servants that they should go thither and be his emissaries, and teach all people, yea, all peoples, pagans, tribes, tongues, and nations, just as it happened in the time of the apostles, until their noise went out into all lands, and their word unto the ends of the world. Just as the Lord Christ himself calls them, so also he says to them [Matt. 11:28]: Come unto me, all ye who are tired and burdened, I will refresh you. [149] For there[6] is a light which enlightens all men and gives understanding and a true knowledge; *it* also calls all, draws, and advances them. And such is also the true will of God which desires, through the anointed Saviour, that all men should be healed and made blessed, as the holy apostle Paul writes [I Tim. 2:1–2]. And it [is] surely not His will that anyone be lost. This also Saint Peter writes [II, ch. 3:9]. And in this sense the mouth of the Most High speaks to the prophet [II Esdras 8:59]: He has not willed that man should be brought to nought. Thereof also the Wise Man[7] and the High Prophet[8] write and proclaim.

---

[4] Christ is the mouth of the spiritual Moses, God, as was Aaron in respect to Moses.

[5] The bridal imagery, prominent in *The Ordinance*, comes not only from the New Testament but also from the Old Testament, principally, the Song of Solomon and II Esdras 7:26. In both places divine nuptials are connected with a withdrawal into a spiritual wilderness. In II Esdras the wilderness is connected with bondage in Egypt for four hundred years (cf. v. 28) and the wanderings in Sinai. In the Song of Solomon the "wilderness" of chs. 3:6 and 8:5 out of which the divine lover comes is apparently connected in Hofmann's mind with the withdrawal to the upland pastures of ch. 1:7 f.

[6] Or: He. The Dutch *het* may be a faulty translation of the German *es* or a typographical error for *hij*.

[7] Wisdom of Solomon 11:23.

[8] Hofmann refers loosely to Esdras, already cited, Ezek. 33:11, and Ecclesiasticus 15:20.

For Christ Jesus has given himself up for all peoples, yea, each individual, and he has paid for the sin of the whole world, taken it away, done away with it, and achieved an eternal salvation. And now again such a time has come that the proclamation of God's Word shall go out to all peoples as a witness and absolutely none shall be excepted. But rather to all tribes, pagans, tongues, and nations the gospel shall be revealed to their enlightenment, yea, the whole world shall be brought into a clarity of enlightenment and into a knowledge of the right understanding, taught, called, and drawn by God's Spirit and Word. And all those who hear this and do not stop up their ears but rather attend with alertness [will] inherit their salvation and [will] not despise it.

Thus it is the duty of every qualified apostle that they[9] go forth from the mouth of the Most High God—which mouth the Lord Christ Jesus is, and the true apostles the mouth of the anointed Saviour—in order to teach all peoples and to proclaim to them the friendly message and to bring the kiss rich in joys from the mouth of the Bridegroom, yea, this holy gospel of the crucified Christ Jesus, the Word of eternal life, who has paid for all misdeeds. And he has been established by his Father as a lord over all the creatures of God, both in heaven and on earth. And all those who wish to serve him and to confess him and take him for their King, Prince, and Lord may come unto him in freedom and assurance. These will he also eternally maintain with him in the Kingdom of God. The true apostles of the Lord reveal to all men, namely, that this teaching concerning [150] all the knowledge about Christ Jesus was the true nourishment along with the crucified, roasted, and baked paschal lamb which our spiritual fathers in that spiritual Egypt dispensed as food in their spiritual houses, assemblies, and congregations. So also now in our time there is a similar food available and a similar proclamation of the crucified Christ Jesus.

And it is further the order and command or law of the Lord for his apostolic emissaries, according to which they have also in fact instructed, called, and admonished the people, requiring and urging through the gospel and the Word of God that they also who have surrendered themselves to the Lord should lead themselves out of the realm of Satan and from the kingdom of darkness and from this world and that they should purify themselves and lead themselves into the spiritual wilderness and also wed and bind themselves to the Lord Jesus Christ,

9 Change of number in text.

publicly, through that true sign of the Covenant, the water bath and baptism. This to the end that ever thereafter they should remain obedient to, and follow the will and pleasure of, the Father, the Son, and the Holy Spirit and that their own will, life, desire, spirit, and passion be wholly slain, allowed to be quiescent, and allowed to die out, and that henceforth they live solely in the Spirit, and the mind, and the will and from the wisdom of God and the eternal Word of life, as a true bride, obedient to her dear spouse in all things, yea, [mindful of] his will and pleasure without any transgression or vacillation. In like manner also baptism and dying [to this world] were alluded to or portrayed in the Red Sea through which the Children of Israel were baptized and deadened [to this world][10] and covenanted with the divine Majesty under the semblance of a pillar of cloud, as also the holy apostle [I Cor. 10:2] clearly indicates.

And all of this was well acknowledged in the words of the Lord Jesus Christ [Matt. 28:19] as being a reference to the right ordinance of God [151] and of his faithful following. And they have[11] also taught and been taught and received all knowledge of Jesus Christ and wish to have him for Lord, King, and Bridegroom, and bind themselves also publicly to him, and in truth submit themselves to him and betroth themselves to him through the covenant of baptism and also give themselves over to him dead and crucified and hence are at all times subject, in utter zeal, to his will and pleasure. That is then such a true and certain covenant as takes place when a bride with complete, voluntary, and loving surrender and with a truly free, well-considered betrothal, yields herself in abandon and presents herself as a freewill offering to her lord and bridegroom.

Such a bride will no longer live unto herself, neither in darkness nor in the old Adam; again, neither of what is of the world nor what might be called of the world, but rather solely of the Lord Jesus Christ. In this manner also Saint Paul cries [Gal. 2:20]: I live, yet not I, but Christ liveth in me. They are the true "dead" who have the true salvation and liberation from sin, who are purified of all misdeeds through the blood of Jesus Christ, who have their life in Christ Jesus—all who are dead to themselves in the Lord, having routed out and laid aside the old Adam and having, through baptism, taken and

10 Literally "baptized" and killed (*ghedoopt ende ghedoodt*).
11 Literally "*has*," for the image is constantly shifting between the collective church and the individual bride.

put on the new Adam Christ Jesus; [all who] having crucified the old Adam with the urges and desires (who is now at leisure and rests from all sins and who must rest from all his works). And that sinful seed, being dead, cannot make unrighteousness fruitful, for he who has been born of God has the upper hand and victory, and therefore no sin can issue.

They therefore who have now in truth put on Christ Jesus through faith and in baptism in such a way that they are in Christ Jesus and Christ Jesus in them—in them there is nothing more to be condemned. The law has no sovereignty over them any more, because they live unto righteousness and no longer unto sin. Therefore the law cannot make them guilty, nor like a mirror show up blemishes and spots, because they are pure and live no more according to the flesh but according to the Spirit and have been found unpunishable before the judgment seat of God.[12]

[152] And now in this final age the true apostolic emissaries of the Lord Jesus Christ will gather the elect flock and call it through the gospel and lead the Bride[13] of the Lord into the spiritual wilderness, betroth, and covenant her through baptism to the Lord. Thus also Saint Paul (II Cor. 11:2) had betrothed the church of Corinth to the Lord as a virgin to her husband and bound it under the covenant. Now the Bride of the Lord Jesus Christ must be led by the true emissaries into the spiritual wilderness—through the forecourt of the spiritual Tabernacle of Moses,[14] through the antechamber of the Temple. For in the

12 Hofmann here follows the Epistle to the Hebrews, chs. 6:4-6; 10:26, in denying the possibility of forgiveness after believers' baptism. In consequence he is tempted to be excessive in his claim for purity. See Hulshof, *op. cit.*, 148. But he does not deny the persistence of temptation, which is the theme of the next paragraph.

13 The association of the Bride with the wilderness is based upon Song of Solomon 1:7 f.; see above, n. 5.

14 Hofmann's thought, here somewhat obscure, is amplified by Dietrich Philips in "The Tabernacle of Moses," *Enchiridion*, pp. 255 ff., where reference is made to an interpretation with which Philips disagrees, namely, that the court and Holy Place are for the children of Esau (the once-born) and the Holy of Holies for the children of Jacob (the twice-born, the victors). The meaning of the two principal divisions of the Tabernacle of Moses is discussed earlier. From the example of Esau, mentioned earlier, and the six hundred thousand who perished in the wilderness after having successfully passed through the Red Sea, it is clear that Hofmann thought of the "wilderness" experience after believers' baptism as fraught with danger leading to destruction rather than to the consummation of the full bridal relationship with God. Hofmann also identifies the Bride with the woman of Rev. 12:6 who flees into the wilderness for 1260 days.

New Covenant, the Third Day,[15] that third lunar festival, i.e., the spiritual Feast of Tabernacles, will be in the spiritual wilderness; and the last appearance of all that is lunar.[16]

Such a figurative meaning[17] the Lord Christ Jesus intends [when] he goes before his flock at the head to be a model. He comes to John the Baptist at the Jordan, covenants and betroths, yea, offers himself, his whole self, to his Heavenly Father, to whom he lets himself also through John the Baptist be baptized and betrothed [!] and covenanted through the

[15] The reference to a third day or period is an allusion to II Esdras 5:4, from which the original word *day* or its equivalent has dropped out and must be supplied. (*Kingdom, trumpet* are other substitutes.) The whole text, ch. 5:1–7, is very important for Hofmann's eschatalogical concept: Behold, the days come when the inhabitants of earth shall be seized with great panic. And the way of truth shall be hidden. . . . And the land that thou seest now to bear rule shall be a pathless waste; and men shall see it forsaken: if the Most High grant thee to live, thou shalt see it after the third [day] in confusion. Then shall the sun suddenly shine forth by night and the moon by day. And the blood shall trickle forth from wood. . . . And one whom the dwellers upon earth do not look for shall wield sovereignty. . . . And one whom the many do not know will make his voice heard by night; and all shall hear his voice. R. H. Charles, *Apocrypha and Pseudepigrapha* (Oxford, 1913), II, 569.

Echoes of Joachim of Flora's Third Age of the Spirit are here joined confusedly but significantly with strains of a primitivism based upon the desert of Sinai and its temptations and sufferings rather than on paradise and its bliss.

[16] The moon is interpreted by Hofmann as the symbol of the Old, the sun, of the New Testament. The Feast of Tabernacles is the third of the three historical, i.e., old covenantal or "lunar," festivals: Passover, Pentecost, Booths. The Feast of Tabernacles, of course, evokes the memory of the tents in which the Israelites dwelt in their flight from bondage to Egypt. After baptism in the Red Sea they had to endure the temptations of the wilderness. (Of the New Testament parallel he writes in the next paragraph.) In two other works Hofmann speaks of the lunar festival in reference to II Esdras 5:4: *Weyssagung* (1530), *quat.* A, iii *verso* and *Ausslegung der . . . Offenbarung, quat.* K, ii *verso:* ". . . also the Prophet Esdras declares (II, 5) that the same moon and faith will shine thrice in the day, and thereby the three lunar festivals are given spiritual expression."

[17] Hofmann's thought is that the forty years in the desert commemorated by the third lunar feast, Tabernacles, in the Old Dispensation corresponds to the forty days of temptation in the spiritual wilderness after baptism into the New Covenant. Cf. also the woman, clothed with the sun and moon, who fled into the wilderness (Rev. 12:1–6). Since for Hofmann the soul is the bride or beloved of the Lord who meets the bridegroom in the wilderness (Song of Solomon), it is not incongruous for him to speak of Christ himself, exemplar of all New Testament Christians, as himself betrothed to God the Father during the forty days in the spiritual wilderness.

water bath, during [which time he is] detached from his own will, and, through God's covenant, absorbed into the will of the exalted Father, [and prepared] to live eternally unto him. Thus the Father also accepts him and opens up the heaven over him, sends down upon him the simple Dove-Spirit and gives guidance to him, all his power, mind, and will. He adopts him moreover as his well-pleasing, beloved Son.

Thereupon, the anointed Saviour was led by the Spirit and the will of God into the wilderness[18] in order to fast forty days and nights and suffer all the temptations of Satan, but [he remained] steadfast and true to his believing, [153] devoted, trusting Heavenly Father, struggling through to the end and withstanding Satan and overcoming him in such a way that he [Satan] could not get any portion of him nor have or find anything according to his wish and liking.[19] There he becomes also an elect ambassador from the highest God, his Heavenly Father.

In just such a manner all children of God and brothers of the Lord Jesus Christ should imitate him and also covenant and betroth themselves to the Lord Jesus Christ, under the covenant of God, and give themselves over to him in truth, as a freewill offering, just as he has given himself over to him, his Heavenly Father. And so [it is with] the true apostolic emissaries who go forth and let themselves be betrothed through the same [Heavenly Father], under his covenant sign, and they go out from among their own, letting themselves be introduced by the servants of the Lord into the spiritual wilderness. They, being led and driven through the Spirit and the will of God and the anointed Saviour, spend forty days and forty nights in the wilderness, all of them according to the will and pleasure of the Lord with spiritual fasts—yea, [reminiscent of] the forty years long [in Sinai] and the forty cubits through the forecourt or through the nave of the Temple up to the Holy [of Holies].[20] They remain absolutely and fully in the good pleasure, spirit, mood, and will of the Lord Jesus Christ, and fight through unto the end and conquer. [Thereupon] they are found to be loyal and unblamable in all God's testings.

To such a victory all the promises of God tend, namely:

---

18 Similarly John came preaching in the *wilderness*.
19 The text is partly garbled at this point in translation from German to Dutch.
20 I Kings 6:17. For more on the spiritual meaning of the Tabernacle of Moses and the Temple of Solomon, see above, n. 14.

that to all such victors the true Kingdom of God is given here
and now as their inheritance; that the same enter into the
Holy [of Holies] and come to the Sabbath and the true rest[21]
completely naked and resigned to enter the bed of the Bridegroom where the righteous [re-]birth takes place and where one
is instructed by God and the Word. And the soul is completely
wedded by the grace of God. There the old Adam is put off
completely, the individual, quite naked, is rid of all. The old
Adam is at surcease from lusts and desires. He is crucified and
dead; slain to sin, and he reposes from all his works, so that the
sinful seed brings forth its fruits no more. These are then made
pious [154] and have the cleansing through the blood of Christ
Jesus, and in such there is nothing more that is blameworthy to
be found, as has already been said.

Of all such victorious struggles Saint Paul [Heb. 12:1, 22 f.]
makes sufficient mention, warning that one should lay aside all
that can weigh down, yea, the besetting sin, and make a good
race for the true Mount Zion and to the city of the congregation
of the living God, to the assembly of the perfectly righteous, to
the company of the angels, and to the blood of Jesus Christ.
And one may enter into the Holy [Jerusalem], into the true
new heaven of God. There [they] will become true newborn
children. There all is new and the old wholly wasted away.
There one is nourished at the true Supper of the Lord with the
bread of understanding and refreshed with the waters of life.

They also who now remain steadfast in the doctrine and the
School of Christ unto the end, through struggle and victory,
and who remain unwavering and are not overcome, the same
shall be saved. For as one believes and is enlightened and receives
the Lord, so is salvation and the inheritance of the Kingdom of
God promised in the first place; and if one pilgrimages toward
the spiritual land of promise, one will get and take possession of
the inheritance of the Kingdom. For they who believe in the
name of Christ Jesus, to them he gives in the first place the
force and power to become the children of God, to receive the
new birth and the eternal Kingdom.

For all such victors God himself will be the reward, and also
the Lord Christ Jesus, who gives himself as a prize to his own.
And this shall be as the Book of the heavenly revelations
[chs. 2:17; 3:5, 12] of the evangelist and apostle John has
sufficiently recounted, where the Spirit and the mouth of the
Lord Jesus Christ says that he will give all victors the crown of

21 On the true rest and Sabbath, see Heb., ch. 4.

life, yea, that they shall eat of the tree of life and of that hidden manna of heaven. Similarly he will give them a white stone with a new name, the morning star, a white garment, and he will enable them to be written down in the book of life. He will make them into a pillar in his temple, whom no suffering will befall, nor the second death. They will also sit with him on his throne and rule over the heathen.[22] With them also he [155] will hold the Supper and they again with him. For that purpose all such victors inherit all, says God the Almighty Lord through Christ Jesus.

O blessed are they who in this time are able to come to such an inheritance and also therein to acquire and to take hold of the Kingdom and also to attain that election. For all men are called and are still being called, but no one has been elected except for them who have struggled through to victory. And in case all of them struggle and conquer, all of them should also be elected by God, yea, even the whole world. For he has for all times suffered for all and has died for all. Moreover, God does not wish that any man be lost, nor that anyone receive damnation;[23] but his will rather is that all come to repentance, receive the knowledge of the truth, and be saved, as also Saint Paul [Heb. 3:7 ff.] truly warns that one should not stop the ears when the Spirit of God proclaims the gospel, as did the Children of Israel in the wilderness.

Such aforesaid promises, such an ordinace—this is the content of that high covenant of God and of the Lord Jesus Christ. It is the sign of the covenant of God, instituted solely for the old, the mature, and the rational, who can receive, assimilate, and understand the teaching and the preaching of the Lord, and not for the immature, uncomprehending, and unreasonable, who cannot receive, learn, or understand the teaching of the apostolic emissaries: such are immature children; such also are bells which toll for the dead, and churches, and altars and all other such abominations. For nowhere is there even a letter in the Old or the New Testament in reference to children. And there is absolutely no order enacted by the apostles or Jesus Christ nor have they taught or written a single syllable about it. And also it has not been discovered that they ever baptized any child, nor will any such instance be found in all eternity!

[22] Rule of the saints over the godless is never given prominence by Hofmann. This phase of his thought was developed later at Münster.
[23] II Esdras 8:59. The possibility of universal salvation is the same as in Denck and Hubmaier. Selections IV and V.

For that alone was enjoined upon them by Christ Jesus their Lord, namely, to baptize the nations who accept their word and preachment of the crucified Christ Jesus and give themselves over to him of their own free will. To such as these belongs the covenant and baptism. Thereafter, only that should be taught by our apostles[24] which the Lord has commanded them [156] and otherwise nothing. It is for this that Saint Paul also says [Rom. 15:18]: I dare say nothing unless Christ hath wrought the same by me. Thus now let every teacher and servant of the Lord hold to him and teach nothing more than he was taught by God and proceed according to this rule. Then it will go very well with him, and thus many countless souls will not be done to death by these blind leaders, who so very brazenly, without any fear, spit in the face of God Almighty, crucify the Son of God, and then tread upon him with their feet. O how heavily will such a one be visited by God with stern wrath and be tormented and made to pay with the eternal unending zeal of the Fire of the Almighty!

Accordingly, all human notions are sternly forbidden by the Lord, and pedobaptism is absolutely not from God but rather is practiced, out of willfulness, by anti-Christians and the satanic crowd, in opposition to God and all his commandment, will, and desire. Verily, it is an eternal abomination to him. Woe, woe to all such blind leaders who willfully publish lies for the truth and ascribe to God that which he has not commanded and will never in eternity command. How serious a thing it is to fall into the hands of God and willfully to mock and desecrate the Prize of God the Highest! Yea, all who do this will be stricken with heavy, great, and eternal blindness, and they will inherit the eternal wrath of God. For God is the enemy of all liars, and none of these inherits or has a part in his Kingdom. Their inheritance and portion is rather eternal damnation.

When now the bride of the Lord Jesus Christ has given herself over to the Bridegroom in baptism, which is the sign of the covenant, and has betrothed herself and yielded herself to him of her own free will and has thus in very truth accepted him and taken him unto herself, thereupon the Bridegroom and exalted Lord Christ Jesus comes and by his hand—the apostolic emissaries are the hand—takes bread (just as a bridegroom takes a ring[25] or a piece of gold) and gives himself to his bride

---

24 Text: *van den Apostelen.*
25 This comparison of the bread to the bridal ring is made also in Hofmann's *Weyssagung auss Heiliger Gotlicher geschrifft* (1550), *quat.* B, iii *verso.*

with the bread (just as the bridegroom gives himself to his bride with the ring) and takes also the chalice with the wine and gives to his bride with the same his true bodily blood, so that just as [157] the bride eats a physical bread in her mouth[26] and drinks the wine, so also through belief in the Lord Jesus Christ she has physically received and eaten the noble Bridegroom with his blood in such a way that the Bridegroom and the outpouring of his blood is [one] with hers—and the broken and crucified Christ Jesus. She [is] in him and, again, he is in her, and they together are thus one body, one flesh, one spirit, and one passion, as bridegroom and bride.

Yea, more. The bride is in truth assured the moment she takes the bread that she has accepted the true Christ for her Lord and Head and eternal Bridegroom in order that ever thereafter his will, spirit, mind, and good pleasure may be in her and that she on her part give herself over unto his will with all her heart, spirit, feeling, and will. It was in this sense that the disciples of our Lord Jesus Christ also ate when he sat bodily with them and they received him also bodily with the bread, as the bride receives the bodily bridegroom with the ring, that he in her and she in him may be one spirit, will, and mind. Moreover, a member and a bride of the Lord may well say, when she receives the bread, takes, and eats thereof, that she has bodily received, enjoyed, and eaten her Lord Jesus Christ, that the bodily Christ, who sits at the right hand of God, is in truth bodily her own and again that she is bodily his, yea with flesh and blood. And the two are thus one, and two in one flesh. While she has her house, habitation, tabernacle, and dwelling in Christ, for his part Jesus Christ has in her complete authority, sovereignty, habitation, and dwelling. Therefore Saint Paul writes to those of Corinth [I, ch. 11:28][27] that they should search themselves and prove whether Christ had his dwelling in them.

In such a manner as has been above recounted, a perky little bride, when she receives her engagement ring from her bridegroom, could speak to her childhood playmates and friends, showing it to them: Look here, I have my bridegroom Jack, Nick, or Peter. Now those who hear such words and see the ring understand very well how the bride intends this kind of

26 Literally, in her "stomach."
27 The juxtaposition in I Cor., ch. 11, of Paul's instructions concerning the relationship between Christ and man, man and woman, Christ's body in the Supper and the faithful, facilitates Hofmann's bold exegesis.

language, namely, that she does not mean that the ring is physically the bridegroom himself or that the bridegroom is physically [158] contained in the ring but that she has with all her heart, spirit, and emotion received a bridegroom by virtue of his will, word, spirit, and intention.

It was surely in this sense that the apostles of the Lord Jesus Christ likewise understood the words when the Lord took the bread and gave therewith his body and with the wine his own quickening blood. [They also surely understood] that he did not for this reason corporally exist in the bread, and that the physical bread was not he himself, that his blood was not in the wine, nor did the wine become his physical blood. Instead, [they understood] that through the bread and belief in the Word they should receive that body which sat by them there, that that same body should be their own which would be burned at[28] the cross. And [they believed] that theirs also was the physical blood which would be poured out from the cross. Such a simple explanation stolid fisherfolk could well understand even when they were still in the first birth, but one over which the wise and greatest scholars of Scripture for their part have become fools and madmen, and still are. They clash and break themselves over such simple words which were said and enacted in a quite straightforward way as by any other human being.

For all the reasons of God through Jesus Christ are for those who find [divine] knowledge and who fear God and to whom he reveals his will, spirit, meaning, and compassion, [namely, for] the simple, the illiterate, the guileless. But to the satiated, courtly, rich, and murderous spirits his simple word will become as blood and poison and even death, yea, a table,[29] whereat they are strangled and hanged and receive eternal damnation. And thereat they will be blinded, offending, provoking, and assaulting each other. As Saint Peter [II, ch. 3:15 f.] also writes, many of the writings of Paul as also the other Scriptures have been a confusion to unstable and inattentive spirits, unto their own destruction.

I think that this is a great horror that those learned in Scripture should thus reject such simple reasons. For surely the Lord Jesus Christ does not deal with his people other than a

---

28 The word is *gebraden*: "roasted." Has Hofmann allowed the common image of the heretic's pyre to replace that of the cross? Or is he thinking of martyrdom as the consummation of the imitation of Christ whereby one becomes the roasted paschal Lamb? Cf. above, p. 186.
29 Cf. Rom. 11:9; I Cor. 11:29.

bridegroom with a bride—with straightforward simple words. The shrewd and the wise for their part have become fools and daily more so. They write big [159] and thick books, and they always teach but themselves never come to the knowledge of the truth. And although they hold themselves to be wise and shrewd, they are become crazy and foolish. And the nonsense of such lunatics and fools must become evident to all men in a very short time. And then the cunning of Satan will not help them either, even though many such [theologians] have committed murder because of it. And how many thousands have caused blood to flow on account of it, whom the theologians have written onto the butcher's block, yea, judged, condemned, and given over [to the temporal authorities]. But in a short time they will see whom they have pierced; and all such courtly, rich, satiated, blind, and murderous spirits and bloodsuckers will be thrust into that eternal woe and be pilloried before the whole world.

And the bride has now so covenanted herself with the Lord under the sign of the covenant [baptism] and so given herself over to him, and he to them,[30] through his Word and again with the bread, that many brides are become one congregation and bride of the Lord, and he the husband and the Bridegroom. And if then the bride in the future should come to conduct herself improperly so as not to be fully obedient and faithful to her bridegroom but rather with a hard heart should come, against her vow, to attach herself to another and commit adultery with the same, and bespot herself (and be that whatever it may to which she attach herself) and thus turn away from obedience to her bridegroom and then if after warning no improvement should take place [—then, certainly the husband should eject her].

Likewise the [heavenly] Bridegroom [who], through his apostolic emissaries, would thereupon let her be thrown out of the congregation again, by his consent, yea, altogether out of his house, and would divorce her from his fellowship and would take from her the bread and wine, thereby indicating that she had no portion or should have any of him or of his blood, also that their vow had been broken, and that he had treated her, just as a bridegroom would take away his ring from his wayward bride and divorce her and spurn her.[31]

30 That is, the church.
31 Hofmann in his shift of tenses in this paragraph passes back and forth between the historic example of apostolic ex-communication to the

Therefore it has been held [in respect to] the ban from the time of the apostles that they who would live according to the will of Satan (as Saint Paul in Gal. 5:19–21 on the first fruits clearly indicated), after three warnings [Matt. 18:15–18] were ejected from Christ Jesus and his [160] Kingdom and delivered over into the Kingdom of Satan and the devil. But in so far as the same turned back in their hearts and gave themselves over to improvement of their wicked way of life, they were again accepted by the congregation through the servants of God and received again into the congregation of the body of Christ Jesus and into the fellowship of his blood. O how well it went when such an ordinance was maintained in the true fear of God!

With all such true apostolic servants and their followings the anointed Saviour has promised that he wishes to be all the days until the end of this transient world, that is to say: he with his word, Spirit, mind, will, and well-being in her; and she with her spirit, feeling, and all her heart in him. And such are then one temple, house, tabernacle, and true city of the entire divine, almighty sovereignty of God and of his eternal Word and high Holy Spirit and mind.

Into such a brotherhood and congregation of the heavenly band all peoples have been called wherever they are in the whole world in order that they may become the children of God and his Holy Spirit, and heirs of his eternal Kingdom. These, accordingly, go out now from the world and from the kingdom of Satan and from all which is still of the old Adam and thereupon enter into Christ Jesus in order to walk in the eternal living word of God, yea, and to do the whole will of God and of the Lord Jesus Christ. And in all things they are steadfastly to struggle through [to victory], free and with abandon, yea, completely strong to the end, to mount up the forty steps, grades, and cubits[32] in clarity [of purpose]. They fall aside neither to the left nor to the right, but with full strength press through in the struggle. . . .

O how much God would like to have all people saved, if only they would! And it was impossible that he could condemn anybody who did his will, which people could always very well

conduct of an offended husband and the practice of Christ as Bridegroom of the church.

[32] The forty cubits of the Temple in I Kings 6:17. Cf. the other references to the forty days of temptation in the wilderness after baptism, above, p. 190.

do. Surely it is not to be inferred that one cannot and may not [choose to do the will of God] as [could] Adam. Similarly, Moses asked that God should erase him from his book in case he would not also forgive the Children of Israel their sin. But the high, praiseworthy voice of exalted Deity declared that he does not erase from his book those who do his will, and also that he would never, yea, in all eternity, eject those who are of his will. They would never be erased by God. For God the merciful Father has sent by his power into the world, into flesh, his own eternal Word who has become himself flesh and corporal, in form like unto another man, without sin, and he became a physically visible Word before his death and also after his resurrection. As such he remains unto eternity. He did not take flesh upon himself but became himself flesh and corporal, in order that he might himself give salvation and pay for the sin of the whole world by means of his guiltless suffering, dying, and the pouring out of his blood.[33]

Therefore they blaspheme God grievously who lay it to him that he wishes sin, does and effects the same in man. But this will never be found to be so in all eternity. For God is none other than eternal good, and from him nothing but good comes, yea, verily he cannot create, work, and will other than what he is in himself and what he will also remain throughout eternity. No more can darkness issue or shine forth from the clear light of the sun than can anything other issue from God than what he himself is, namely, the eternal good, benevolence, and all-righteousness.

But there are those who, as has been said, ascribe this to God, namely, that [162] he should be a worker of sins and a desirer of the damnation of men. The same make the most high and eternal God into a devil and Satan and insult the high, praiseworthy good as evil, and the eternal light as darkness. . . .

I fear that many among them who do these things with words do them in part for the sake of their own honor, their own glory, and for the favor and the goods of this world, but in part also out of resentment, hate, and jealousy, as did the Jewish Pharisees in respect to Christ Jesus. For even as they did it they knew very well in their hearts, and were convinced that Christ Jesus drove out the demons by the finger and Spirit of God.

---

[33] This paragraph is the only place in *The Ordinance* which touches upon Hofmann's peculiar Christology. Cf. Schwenckfeld, below, Selection VIII, at n. 27 and Philips, Selection XI, at n. 10.

But they declared, out of resentment, jealousy, and hate that he drove out the demons through Beelzebub, the chief of demons. And in like manner when the watchmen came from the grave of Christ and announced that Jesus Christ had arisen, they promised them much money [on condition] that they say nothing to anyone but rather declare that in the night while they slept, he was stolen by the disciples of Christ.

Of all such intentional sins against the High Holy Spirit of God, the Lord Christ Jesus says [Mark 3:29] that neither now nor in the next world nor in all eternity can they ever attain forgiveness. Saint Paul also says the same in Hebrews [ch. 10:26 f.], namely, that no more sacrifice remains over for such sins but rather a fearful revenge and ordeal of [163] fiery indignation. In this manner God also speaks through Moses [Num. 25:8] that one shall without any mercy root out from the congregation all such willful sinners against the Spirit of God and shall accept for them no further sacrifices, for they will forever have no forgiveness. It was just such a stubborn one that Phineas the priest pierced to death without mercy, which [act] before God was so great a satisfaction that He swore unto him an eternal priesthood.[34]

And Saint John also writes in his epistle [I, ch. 5:16] that one shall never in all eternity pray for such a sin [unto death]. Also Saint Paul [II Tim. 4:14] calls down upon Alexander the coppersmith nothing but wrath and punishment, for with such [sin] this is always done, and therefore it cannot be that people should pray in behalf of such [sin], for they will get no more grace or mercy from God. There is also the terrible example of Saul the king of Israel, and also of Esau who sought mercy and nevertheless did not find it.

Yea, it was the same for the six hundred thousand in the wilderness, who bore suffering for forty years, and were unable to get grace from God. . . .

This is furthermore a sin of which Saint Paul writes [Heb. 6:4 ff.], namely, [that of] those who have once been enlightened and have received the taste of the wisdom of God, and who have delivered themselves up and given themselves over to the Lord Christ and who then fall away again and, after having confessed the truth, have departed from the faith and the true betrothal. It is impossible to restore these broken ones. In this sense also Christ Jesus speaks [Matt. 12:43 ff.]: Where Satan

34 Cf. n.22, above.

has been driven out and the house cleaned and swept and where also there is emptiness and vacancy and dead belief, where the Spirit is unfruitful in godly works and fruits, where the tree decks itself out in words and leaves without power and deed —here the spirit of Satan with seven spirits more wicked than himself takes possession of that empty vessel for his use according to his [164] lust and will, and the last [state] thereby becomes worse than the first. Similarly, against any such [relapse] Christ Jesus warned [John 5:14] the man who had stood up from his bed, [saying] that he should sin no more, lest a worse thing come unto him, lest the last [state] with him also be worse than the first.[35]

Of the same matter Saint Peter also writes [II, ch. 2:22] that [backsliders] do like pigs, which, after washing,[36] become involved again in the works of darkness and are besmirched with uncleanness, and like dogs which gobble up again the bad spirit, passion, and will, which they had once spewed out. Thus for all of these it were better had they never known the way of truth. Through such backsliders the way of truth was blasphemed in the first place and [therewith] the great good of eternal righteousness—as the apostle also thoroughly recounts in respect to all such as these.

And by the Spirit of God such falling away from Christ Jesus is now also indicated, such backsliding from his will, spirit, and mind, yea, the third part of the teachers.[37] O how many thousand have been eternally misled in this way by [teachers] such as these! For through them the strong delusion will first enter in, about which Saint Paul [II Thess. 2:11] writes, [coming] over all those who have heard and understood God's Word and Spirit, and also over all who have recognized his will, and [who], being enlightened in the true way of God, have not accepted that light and that good, but instead have the darkness. For them therefore the darkness will be overflowing, and eternal darkness will be their inheritance and portion.

For it will be so for all time that wherever the gospel is proclaimed, such great defection will arise and such great misleadings through the fallen stars and false apostles, [165]

---

35 Hofmann's appeal to this passage is particularly cogent since as an Anabaptist he could construe the pool of Bethesda as the waters of rebirth.

36 Rebaptism.

37 An allusion to third part of the trees burned up in Rev. 8:7.

teachers, and preachers, that even also the very elect, if it were possible, might be deceived—but that is impossible. For they who have once struggled through and conquered, they are then elected of God, so that they will not depart again from Christ and the eternal Temple of God. Over such as these the second death[38] can have no more power, for the first is completely passed away and in them all has become new; they are taught of God and he is their light and lantern, from then on and forever, through his Holy Spirit. These then come to Christ Jesus, these whom no one will ever be able to draw away from his hand and power, nor ever in all eternity be able to alienate. For such victors, having died in the Lord, cannot sin any more, for [a] new, true rebirth maintains them so that in very truth they cannot and will not fall in all eternity. For none can oppress him any more who has [once] conquered [sin], nor can anyone either save or help him who is destroyed.[39]

Therefore let everyone be warned that he regard carefully how and what he believes in order that he deceive not himself and go astray with the others. For the whole world[40] cries: Believe, believe; grace, grace; Christ Jesus. And therefore it does not choose the better part, for its hope is idle and a great deception. For such belief cannot justify them before God, as the holy apostle James writes [ch. 2:17]: Even so faith, if it has not fruits is in itself dead. Thus there were many of the leaders of the Jewish synagogue who believed in Christ Jesus, but nevertheless would not openly confess it, for they preferred the praise of men to the praise of God. What profited them such a faith? For all such timid ones will not inherit the Kingdom of God, as the High Spirit of God testifies. And as the Lord Christ Jesus says [Matt. 10:33; 16:25]: Those who deny him before men, them will he also deny before God, his Father, and before all the angels. For whoever wishes to save his life, he will lose it in eternity. Saint Peter denied the Word of truth on one occasion and bore remorse therefore all his life long. How then will it go with those who for so many years every day conceal the truth and deny it?

Therefore faith cannot make one justified, if [166] one does not bring in therewith his fruits. As Christ also says [Matt. 7:16 ff.] of all such strong belief, of all such who [will] confidently believe and confess him to be a Lord and say that they had prophesied in his name and cast out devils and had done

---

[38] Rev. 20:14; 21:8. [39] II Esdras 7:45.
[40] The reference is to the whole world of Lutheranism.

many mighty acts—these he will nevertheless not recognize. Such faith does not [by itself] bring about justification, nor again [that of] those who there [in Matt. 26:37 ff.] said: Lord, where have we seen you and not served you? The same also believed, but that is all in vain. Of the same kind Saint Paul also writes [I Cor. 13:1 ff.] that even if one had such faith that he could move mountains, yea, and spoke with the tongues of angels, and understood all mystery, and gave all his goods for God's sake, and let his body be burned—in all such cases belief would have absolutely no worth, if love were not present therein. For what kind of faith would that be in the case of a woman with her husband, to whom she publicly adhered and confessed to be her lord and bridegroom, and nevertheless continuously went out to commit adultery and illicit love-making with others? . . .

Therefore I warn all lovers of truth that they do not give themselves over to lofty arguments which are too hard for them, but that they hold themselves solely to the straight-forward words of God in all simplicity. Do not quarrel and struggle much over words and take a piece somewhere out of God's Word [167] and hold fast to it stubbornly and without understanding. Do not excoriate as lies all other words which are against it and thus abuse and make the apostles and the prophets along with the Holy Spirit of God into liars. For all words of God are of equal weight, also just and free, to him who acquires the right understanding of God and the Key of David.[41] The cloven claws and horns[42] [only] [168] the true apostolic

---

[41] In his *Ausslegung der . . . Offenbarung Ioannis* ad 3:7 Hofmann writes further about the Key of David: Christ has . . . received this Key of David (Isa. 22:22) from the Father, who reveals himself through the Spirit of God to his own, [unlocking] the door of grace which is he himself. . . . On him in whom he opens up the secret of God, none can thereafter close the door. Similarly for him to whom God closes the door of his word and therewith all the knowledge of God which his Spirit could create in him—for him none can open it, neither in heaven nor on earth, neither in the sea nor under the earth.

[42] On the horns see the *Vorrede zum ersten Capitel Matthäi*. The book is lost, but the Foreword is preserved ʊy Barthold N. Krohn, *Geschichte der fᵤ...atischen und eᵢ.....usiastischen Wiedertäufer vornehmlich in Niederdeutschland: Melchior Hofmann und die Secte der Hofmannianer* (Leipzig, 1758), 134–136. The altars of Ex., chs. 27 and 30 have four horns each. The altar signifies Christ, and the four horns, the fourfold nature of the divine Word. In the *Vorrede* Melchior gives several other examples of fourfoldness.

The expression "cloven claws" stems, of course, from Lev. 11:3 and Deut. 14:6. The same term is used in *Verclaringe von den gevangen ende vrien wil des menschen, BRN,* V, p. 188 and n. 3.

heralds can bear, because [to explicate] the Scripture is not a matter for everybody—to unravel all such involved snarls and cables, to untie such knots—but only for those to whom God has given [the power].

Who finds therein a lack, let him pray to God, as the apostle [James 1:5] teaches, and do not hurry or rush him. For to many in this day the Scripture will become a poison and eternal death, which nonetheless is in itself very good, because often it is misused without understanding, and leads the unwary and the willful into damnation and all who are without fear into abiding unbelief and damnation. And this is absolutely not the fault of Scriptures but the willfulness and misapprehension of the interpreters themselves.

For there are many in our time who continuously teach and regard themselves as masters of Scripture, and who nevertheless never really come to the understanding of the truth. Similarly the holy apostle thoroughly warns about such as these who also in that time inflated themselves, and there are now many such all around. Therefore let us—all of us who fear God in truth—earnestly pray to God that we may be saved through Christ Jesus from having to think beyond what is the will, the truth, and the command of the Lord to the end that we hold not to our own opinion and to the leaven of the Pharisees and to the manner of the doctors of Scripture, but rather regard it and flee from it as eternal death and follow only after the true understanding of Christ Jesus in order thus to be taught by God himself in our hearts and our conscience. Thereto may God help us, the gracious, merciful Father, through Christ Jesus, our Saviour and eternal Redeemer. Amen.

In general the significance of clovenness for Hofmann is that the Old and New Testaments are one, being from God as the two clefts constituting the one foot of a clean, cloven-footed beast, but that the interpreter must walk through Scripture clearly mindful of the division: All events in the Old Testament are images to which some happening in the New Testament, or yet to take place, corresponds.

Dietrich Philips and the Amsterdam bishop Jacob van Campen took over Hofmann's typological hermeneutics, but they were opposed by brother Obbe and one Hans Scheerder of Leeuwarden, the latter arguing that "Scripture stands on one claw." The deposition of Jacob van Campen before his martyrdom is given by C. A. Cornelius, "Die niederländischen Wiedertäufer während der Belagerung Münsters 1532 bis 1535," *Abhandlungen der königlich bayerischen Akademie der Wissenschaften*, hist. Kl. XI (1869), esp. p. 97.

X

A Confession
By Obbe Philips [1]

RECOLLECTIONS OF THE YEARS 1533–1536

c. 1560

INTRODUCTION

N O COLLECTION OF DOCUMENTS ILLUSTRATIVE OF the thought and action of representatives of the Radical Reformation could qualify in any sense as comprehensive without the inclusion of some material bearing on its revolutionary aspect. The editor has chosen to allow Thomas Müntzer (Selection II) to speak *for* Revolutionary Spiritualism and Obbe Philips to speak *about* Revolutionary Anabaptism as it came to a head in Münster. Obbe writes, however, as a disillusioned Melchiorite; and his personal convictions in the period of his so-called Confession are most akin to the Rational Spiritualism of Sebastian Franck (Selection VII) and the Contemplative Spiritualism of Caspar Schwenckfeld (Selection VIII). Like both these Spiritualists, Obbe Philips has come to despair of the inveterate divisiveness and the destructiveness of all attempts to establish a truly apostolic church; and he, like them, exposes to view the pretensions and the unseemly and even ungodly zeal of many who have enforced their wills as the will of God. Looking to some future action by or clear instruction from God, Obbe in the meantime is content with membership in an inward church of the Spirit. His defection from the very movement which for a while had borne his name (the Obbenites) was comparable among the Dutch Anabaptists to the "retractation" of John Denck (Selection IV), sometime "abbot" of the South German Anabaptists. His repudiation of the movement was all the more disconcerting for the reason

<hr/>

[1] There is no full-length study of Obbe Philips. See, however, below under Dietrich Philips, Selection XI, introduction, n. 1 and on the authenticity of the Confession, K. Vos, "Obbe Philipsz," *Doopsgezinde Bijtragen*, LIV (1917), pp. 124-138.

that the baptism and the ordination of several of the Anabaptist leaders, including his own brother Dietrich (Selection XI) and Menno Simons (Selection XII), derived from his, while his own authority in turn had stemmed from Melchior Hofmann (Selection IX). Hofmann is here pictured as a pitiable rather than as an execrable figure. But because Hofmann's prophecies remained unfulfilled, Obbe is sure that he did not have the apostolic authority which had been allegedly conferred in the pouring out of the Spirit in the last days of the world. The question of ministerial authority is thus uppermost in Obbe's mind when he opens his Confession with the question as to the divine credentials of a true apostle.

The Confession, in tracing the rise of the radical reform, the transfer of rebaptism to the Netherlands by Melchior Hofmann (Selection IX), and the tragedy of the Münsterite revolution, also provides this collection with an invaluable narrative as a supplement to Selection I, though it must be checked and emended. It will be observed, however (e.g., at notes 12 and 20 in the text), that the North Germans and the Dutch in the Melchior-Obbenite-Mennonite succession had a different conception of the rise of Anabaptism from that of the Swiss Brethren and the Hutterites.

The translation was made and many of the notes prepared by Christiaan Theodoor Lievestro.

A Confession[2]
By Obbe Philips

RECOLLECTIONS OF THE YEARS 1533–1536

c. 1560

THE TEXT

[121] Paul said in Rom. 10:14 f.: How shall they believe in him of whom they have not heard? and how shall they hear without a preacher? and how shall they preach except they be sent?

While no one can believe without hearing, so also no one can preach unless he is commissioned. And he who boasts that he is commissioned shall demonstrate his commission with strength and deed.

As we accepted this and brought this to light in our preaching, so must we and all impartial men with us examine ourselves by these previous ordinances (of Moses and Aaron, Joshua, Caleb,[3] Samuel, and all the prophets, and thereafter Christ,

---

[2] The *Confession* is translated from the first Dutch imprint edited by S. Cramer and F. Pijper, *Bibliotheca Reformatoria Neerlandica* (The Hague, 1910), VII, pp. 121–138. Numbers in brackets refer to the pagination of this critical edition.

An older MS. codex, of which a photocopy was kindly lent by the 'Goshen College Library, was consulted for certain preferred variant readings. Cf. Leonard Verduin, "An Ancient Version," *MQR*, XXII (1948), 120–122.

The *Confession* was written shortly before 1560. For a time, it was kept secret by Obbe's exiled companions in Rostock. When it made its way to a Reformed "seeker of the truth" in Holland, it first circulated in manuscript copies. In 1584, it was finally published by Cornelius Claesz. Another Dutch edition appeared in 1609.

When the *Confession* was published first, it was seized upon by the enemies of the Mennonites to demonstrate the gross errors and insidious threats which they found immanent in Anabaptism. Many followers of Menno Simons condemned it as a fraud. The *Confession* is not without error or miscalculation since it was written some twenty years after the events described. Indication has been made of those items of fact where doubt prevails.

[3] See especially Num. 14:1–12.

John, and all apostles, disciples, and followers of Christ), as to whether they are found to conform to them in all ordinances and commissions or whether they are not instead contrary in all these things. For the work, says Jesus ben Sirach [cf. Ecclesiasticus 9:17 (24)], praises the master, and a wise prince or ruler, his action.

In the first place, we must with all understanding concede and confess that the first church of Christ and the apostles was destroyed and ruined in early times by Antichrist. Of this one does not need to call forth many words or much testimony [121], since we ourselves are all in agreement and all who with us are called Evangelical know that the whole of the papacy is a Sodom, a Babylon, an Egypt, and an abomination of desolation, the work or service of Antichrist, and all its ordinances, ordinations (*sendinghe*), and teachings are false, according to prophecies of both Daniel (ch. 9:27) and Paul (II Thess. 2:3) by the testimony of the Holy Spirit.

Thus have we altogether let go all such offices and commissions and have not wished to re-establish the same, seeking only how each one might fear, serve, and honor his God and best pursue the way to service before God in righteous love, peace, and humility.

As these very devout hearts have resolved that they shall serve God in all such quiet simplicity after the manner of the Fathers and the Patriarchs, as already told, and therefore sought wholeheartedly to serve their God and followed without preacher, teacher, or any external assembly, so have some men not been content to serve God in the simplicity of the Spirit and with such quiet, pure hearts, but have wished to have visible gods which they could hear, touch, and feel and thus proposed that there must be established a congregation, assembly, ordination, office, and order, as though no one could be saved unless he stood in such a congregation or order.

And this was in time revealed, as it was in Israel, which could no longer exist without a king. Then would they establish a kingdom the same as the heathen and other peoples, and thereby angered God no little and so brought about their own chastisement (I Sam., ch. 8).

Thus in time this holiness was deceptive and the fieriness became apparent in some who could no longer contain themselves in such simplicity; and they presented themselves as teachers and envoys (*sendtbooden*) of God, professing to have been compelled in their hearts by God to baptize, preach, and teach, and establish a new church (*kercke*), since the ancient church had perished.

Among these were Doctor Balthasar Hubmaier,[4] Melchior Rinck,[5] John Hut,[6] John Denck,[7] Louis Haetzer,[8] and Thomas Müntzer.[9] Look in the *Chronica*[10] of Sebastian Franck[11] and in the letters and in many of their teachings about all these men.

Among these Melchior Hofmann[12] stood out. He came from upper [123] Germany to Emden to baptize around three hundred persons publicly in the church in Emden, both burgher and peasant, lord and servant.[13] This the old count[14] permitted to take place as long as Melchior was there. And it was said that the count was himself brought to the same belief.

This Melchior was a very fiery and zealous man, a very smooth-tongued speaker who was celebrated for his great calling and commission, and wrote heatedly against Luther and Zwingli concerning baptism[15] and other articles. And he interpreted the whole Apocalypse, in which everyone can hear of what remarkable and wonderful things are found therein, and

---

[4] See above, Selection V, introduction.

[5] Melchior Rinck (1493–1545), surnamed the Grecian, was the leading Hessian Anabaptist (sometimes confused with Melchior Hofmann). He was associated with Müntzer at Frankenhausen and with Denck and Haetzer at Worms.

[6] Hans Hut (d. 1527), Thuringia-born fiery apostle of the Anabaptists of Upper Austria, was associated with Müntzer at Frankenhausen, with Denck at Augsburg, and with Hubmaier at Nicolsburg (as an opponent).

[7] See above, Selection IV, introduction.

[8] See Selection I, n. 14.   [9] See above, Selection II, introduction.

[10] *Chronica, Zeitbuch und Geschichtbibel* (Stuttgart, 1531), esp. the famous description of the four sects of which the Anabaptists constituted one.

[11] See above, p. 145. It is possible that Franck's Spiritualism expressed in his *Chronica* and letters was a major factor in Obbe's withdrawal from the Anabaptists. His brother Dietrich Philips refutes two of Franck's letters in the *Enchiridion*.

[12] See above, Selection VII, introduction.

[13] This was denied by the preachers of Emden in their *Gründtlicker Warhaftiger Bericht* (1594), 42. Cf. W. I. Leendertz, *Melchior Hofmann* (Haarlem, 1885), 222.

[14] Count Edzard I (d. 1528)? The authenticity of Obbe's authorship of th *Confession* was questioned by Leendertz, *op. cit.*, in part because Coun Edzard I died prior to Melchior's arrival in East Frisia. F. O. zu Linden repeated the assertion and observed that Obbe confused the ol Count Edzard with Enno II. *Melchior Hofmann* (Haarlem, 1885), 236 Cf. Jehring's *Gründliche Historie* (1720), 96–98, 192. Certainly the allusior is an insufficient argument by which to deny Obbe's authorship. Cf. Abraham Hulshof, *Geschiedenis van de Doopsgezinden te Straatsburg van 1525 tot 1557* (Amsterdam, 1905), 119 note.

[15] Cf. above, *The Ordinance of God*, Selection IX.

of which I cannot thoroughly write or speak but which every-one may read for himself.

He also began to interpret the Tabernacle of Moses[16] with all the images of the Old Testament, from the flight of the Children of Israel out of Egypt to the Promised Land, with a book on the incarnation, how the Word became flesh and lived among us.[17] But this truth I must testify before God and my soul, that at this hour, however much I have read forward and backward and find that Martin Luther was very terribly calumnious in his writings, I know of no one who has so much calumniated and damned in his writings as this Melchior; whereby also we all taught many blasphemies and considered it was a true, pure, and saintly thing to denounce [others] as heretics and godless and to damn those who were not receptive or disposed to our belief. As such they were all Lutherans, Zwinglians, and papists; and all who did not say yes and amen were devilish and satanic spirits, godless heretics, and people damned to eternity. This [was done] in such a frightful way that the hair on a man's head would stand on end.

In short, this Melchior did not remain longer at Emden but set up as teacher John Trijpmaker,[18] who was well disposed in his eyes and who was a preacher at Emden. Whereupon, Melchior left him; and departed for Strassburg when his zeal drove him hastily on [124] to heed the prophecy of an old man of East Frisia who had prophesied of him that he would sit a half year in prison in Strassburg and thereafter would freely spread his ministry (*predick-ampt*) over the whole world with the help of his ministers (*dienaers*) and supporters.

Thus, through the mediation of this prophecy, Melchior removed to Strassburg and there began to preach and to teach here and there in the houses of the burghers. Then to be brief, the authorities sent their servants to take him prisoner. When Melchior saw that he was going to prison, he thanked God that

16 *Der Leuchter des alten Testaments uszgelegt, welcher im heylgen stund der hütten Mose* (Strassburg, 1529). See also above, Selection IX at notes 14 and 20 and the adaptation of Melchior's conception of the Tabernacle in Dietrich Philips, below, p. 258.

17 *Von der waren hochprächtlichen einigen Majestät Gottes und von der warhaftigen menschwerdung des ewigen worts und sons des Allerhöhsten, ein Kurzes zeugnisz.* Cf. Leendertz, *op. cit.*, Bijlage VIII, 386 ff., "M. Hofmanns Büchlein vom Fleisch Christi."

18 Jan Volkerts Trijpmaker, who was driven from Emden to continue baptizing in Amsterdam around Christmas of 1530, was a weaver of a nonsilk, mock-velvet fabric, i.e., tripe-de-velours.

the hour had come and threw his hat from his head and took a knife and cut off his hose at the ankle, threw his shoes away and extended his hand with the fingers to heaven and swore by the living God who lives there from eternity to eternity that he would take no food and enjoy no drink other than bread and water until the time that he could point out with his hand and outstretched fingers the One who had sent him. And with this he went willingly, cheerfully, and well comforted to prison.[19]

All this, dear friends, which I write here I heard and received orally from his own disciples who would daily come and go for him at Strassburg, and who were my companions and fellow brothers. We also received his letters every day, how his action, his visions, and revelations affected him. And this increased from day to day.

During this time the preachers of Emden rose up and condemned all those who were disposed to imitate Melchior in his manner of preaching against and calumniating baptism so severely that great dissension and insurrection daily broke out among the burghers; and the preachers resolutely got the upper hand.

Thus it happened that John Trijpmaker, whom Melchior had ordained (*veroordnet*) as a teacher, fled to Amsterdam, taught and baptized there and in other places those whom he found willing and ready. This he did until he was taken prisoner, as were six or seven others, and taken to The Hague to be condemned and put to death.[20]

[125] This was, in short, the commencement of the first commission and became the beginning of the movement. But who moved or commissioned Melchior to this or laid upon him such an offi.ᴗe or ordered him, or from whom was he sent or called? Or, in sum, whether he was sent by someone else or began by his own inspiration is entirely unknown to me, and I cannot testify any further about this because I have not heard about his commission from any of his disciples.

Now when John Trijpmaker was dead, there was no longer anyone who dared to take over or assume the office of apostleship (*sendinghe*), although there were many who were readily

---

[19] Martin Bucer similarly described this event in a little book which appeared December, 1533, in Strassburg: *Quid de baptismate*.

[20] December 5, 1531. G. Grosheide, using The Hague court records, established the names of ten men sentenced, including Jan Volkerts (Trijpmaker) of Hoorn. *Bijdragen tot de Geschiedenis der Anabaptisten in Amsterdam* (Hilversum, 1938).

baptized, for baptism came rapidly into vogue among many plain and simple souls. At the same time Melchior had written from prison that baptism should be suspended for two years. Only teaching and admonishing in quiet [were permitted] as with the Temple of Zerubbabel, Ezra, and Haggai, who, in the beginning of its construction, were obstructed for two years by their enemies, so that they could not build for two years until the time that God sent them stronger assistance in King Darius.[21] All such figures and images were much discussed and this caused much consternation among the others.

While Melchior was in prison and John Trijpmaker was dead and no one dared to take up or assume the office of apostleship, there rose up a prophet in Strassburg named Leonard Joosten, to whom Melchior was as much devoted as to Elijah, Isaiah, Jeremiah, or one of the other prophets.[22] Joosten had a pamphlet published in which were printed all his prophecies, which I have read through more than once, where so many remarkable things are found, and which I leave unchanged and in his words.

Shortly thereafter there also rose up two prophetesses in Strassburg, the one called Ursula, wife of Leonard Joosten, the other Barbara. These also prophesied and predicted remarkable things and had many visions, revelations, and dreams which Melchior also commanded to be placed with the prophecies of Leonard Joosten.[23] These prophetesses dealt with many remarkable visions among the brethren at Strassburg and could predict what deception[24] would arise, what attire, what features, faith, or form [it would have]; and all this through visions, images, and allegories [126]. One came dragging a wagon without wheels, another wagon had three wheels, one wagon had no shaft, some no horses, some no recognizable driver, some had but one leg, some were lepers and beggars, some wore a tunic or a cloak with a lappet of fur.[25] Some wore an unusually strange garment; and so forth with these shapes and appearances. All this they could interpret for the brethren in a spiritual sense and according to everyone's belief and the

---

21 The basic texts for the two-year *Stillstand* or suspension (found also in Caspar Schwenckfeld) are Ezra 4:24 and Hag. 1:1 f.
22 Joosten's vagaries soon drove the Strassburg authorities to lock him in chains in an insane institution.
23 See Leendertz, *op. cit.*, Bijlage VII, 384 ff.
24 The reference seems to be to the apocalyptic abomination of desolations (Matt. 24:15; Mark 13:14).
25 Another reading could be "parti-colored."

points by which everyone stood and the articles which many held. Thus they were held in wholly sacred regard by the brethren. And some of these things also proved true, as the brethren later reported when they came from them to me.

One of the prophetesses also prophesied—and that through a vision—that Melchior was Elijah. She saw a white swan swimming in a beautiful river or watercourse, which swan had sung beautifully and wonderfully. And that, she interpreted to apply to Melchior as the true Elijah. She had also seen a vision of many death heads on the walls around Strassburg. When she wondered whether Melchior's head was among them, and she tried to see, she became aware of Melchior's head, and as she gazed upon it the head laughed and looked at her in a friendly way. Thereafter she saw that all the other heads came alive, one after the other, and they all began to laugh. This and many suchlike visions and revelations they brought to light, but only for the brethren. What use and profit came from this I do not know.

She also saw a vision that occurred in this manner. She saw in the vision a great drawing room or beautiful salon, grand and stately, and full of brethren and sisters all sitting properly around the room in a row. And there stood a youth in the middle with a white garment draped about him. And he had in his hand a golden chalice full of a strong drink and he went along the row from one to the other offering each the chalice, but no one could touch the drink, so strong was it. At last he came to one brother named Cornelius Polterman,[26] who was Melchior's disciple. He took the chalice from the youth's hand and drank from it before all. This fantasy was interpreted to mean that Cornelius Polterman would be Enoch. Some among them held that Doctor Caspar Schwenckfeld[27] should be considered Enoch.

At that time it was also prophesied that Strassburg would be the [127] New Jerusalem,[28] and after Melchoir was in prison for a half year, according to the prophecy of the old man in East Frisia, he would leave Strassburg with 144,000 true preachers, apostles, and emissaries of God, with powers, signs and miracles, and with all such strength of the Spirit that no one could resist them.

[26] Cornelis Polterman of Zealand, preacher in Middleburg.
[27] See above, Selection VIII, introduction. Hofmann was never sure whom he should consider the rightful Enoch, as his adverse view regarding the false prophecies of one or another "Elijah" or "Enoch" indicates. Cf. Leendertz, *op. cit.*, 281.
[28] Melchior originally calculated that the millennium would begin in 1533.

Thereafter Elijah and Enoch would stand upon the earth as two torches and olive trees.[29] No one might harm or hinder them; and they would be dressed in sacks; and, if anyone should hinder them, fire would go from their mouths and devour their enemies. Thereupon the prophets would have such power as to strike the earth with many and manifold plagues, as often as they would. The 144,000 were interpreted as those in the Apocalypse (chs. 7:4; 14:1 ff.) who stood with the Lamb on Mount Zion. And all had harps in their hands and had the name of the Father written on their foreheads, and all sang a new hymn which was known only by the 144,000 who were redeemed from all peoples, the firstlings of God and the Lamb. In their mouths no guile is found, nor are they defiled with women, for they are virgins and follow the Lamb wherever it goes.

Now when these teachings and consolations with all the fantasies, dreams, revelations, and visions daily occurred. among the brethren, there was no little joy and expectation among us, hoping all would be true and fulfilled,[30] for we were all unsuspecting, innocent, simple, without guile or cunning, and were not aware of any false visions, prophets, and revelations. We supposed in our simplicity that if we guarded ourselves against the papists, Lutherans, and Zwinglians, then all was well and we need have no cares.[31] Thereby a man's experience brings him great wisdom.

Now, dear friends, before the half year of Melchior's prophesied imprisonment came to an end there arose a baker of

[29] Rev. 11:4.
[30] The pamphlet literature of the period reveals a marked frequency of prognostications beginning around 1528, dominating all other subjects in 1532–1535 and ceasing abruptly in 1536. In the midst of the most materialistic needs and anxieties of the populace appears a bright burst of hope and anticipation of the coming of Christ. See Louis D. Petit, ed., *Nederlandsche Pampfletten* (The Hague, 1882), 8, no. 47, 1532.
[31] K. Vos held that the chiliastic millennialists drew very substantial followings because a variety of material circumstances drove a tense and anxious populace to anticipate either the trumpets of doom or the heralds of Christ. He believed that the appearance of three comets (in 1531, 1532, and 1533) finally brought on the madness of the Münster debacle. "Revolutionnaire hervorming," *De Gids*, IV (1920), 434 ff. A vicious plague caused a strict ban to be imposed in Amsterdam on July 28, 1534. A famine threatened the populace and a series of disastrous floods may indeed have excited the people to cataclysmic anticipation. The combination of these factors and the increasing persecution of heretics brought about an exodus of religious dissenters to North Germany and to England in a stream that began around 1527 and reached its height

Haarlem named John Matthijs, who had an elderly [128] wife whom he deserted, and he took with him a brewer's daughter who was a very pretty young slip of a girl and had great knowledge of the gospel. He enticed her away from her parents with sacred and beautiful words and told how God had shown great things to him, and she would be his wife. He carried her secretly with him to Amsterdam and brought her to a clandestine place.

Now when he came there, he professed to have been greatly driven by the Spirit and [told] how God had revealed great things to him which he could tell to no one, that he was the other witness, Enoch.[32]

Now when the friends or brethren heard of this, they became apprehensive and knew not what they should best do. For Melchior, whom they regarded as Elijah, had written that they should follow Zerubbabel and Haggai in building the "Temple": they should refrain from baptizing for two years (as heretofore explained). They had also heard that Cornelius Polterman was Enoch.

When John Matthijs learned of this, he carried on with much emotion and terrifying alarm, and with great and desperate curses cast all into hell and to the devils to eternity who would not hear his voice and who would not recognize and accept him as the true Enoch. Because of this, some went into a room without food and drink, in fasting and prayer, and were almost all as disconsolate over such threats as if they lay in hell. For we were at that time all unsuspecting and no one knew that such false prophets could arise in the midst of the brethren.

Thus there came a youth of around twelve years of age, proclaiming peace, and hands were proffered and clasped in greeting. Then they again came to themselves and the fearful anxiety subsided among them. And therewith and after much negotiation they attached themselves to John Matthijs and became obedient.

---

about 1544. There was not, however, a steady increase in this flight. A distinct ebb occurred between 1530 and 1540. See A. A. van Schelven, *De Nederduitsche vluchtelingenkerken der XVIe eeuw in Engeland en Duitschland in hunne beteekenis voor de reformatie in de Nederlanden* (The Hague, 1909), 4. The decrease in emigration may be explained in part by the stricter enforcement of the ban on such movements at the time of Münster.

32 When the court of Holland in The Hague condemned Matthijs on July 14, 1534, the sentence recorded that Matthijs "declared himself before Christmas last (1533) in Amsterdam to be a prophet . . . sent by the Holy Spirit." Cornelius, *op. cit.*, 78.

John Matthijs as Enoch and an envoy of God (for so he professed to be) introduced them into the office of apostle and sent them out in pairs as true apostles and emissaries of Christ. Some, such as Gerard Boekbinder[33] and John of Leyden[34] departed for Münster.[35] Thereafter, through his corrupt activities, John of Leyden became king of Münster, all of which Gerard Boekbinder later told me in Amsterdam in the presence oi Jacob van [129] Campen[36] and several others. Now how

[33] Gerrit Boekbinder rebaptized Bernard Rothmann, the leading Lutheran preacher of Münster.
[34] Jan Beukelszoon van Leyden, later king of Münster. The ten other apostles listed in the *Successio Anabaptistica* (1603) are given by K. Vos and the lives of all twelve traced from various sources in *Doopsgezinde Bijtragen* (1917), pp. 98–100.
[35] Münster was taken by the Anabaptists in February, 1534. In Amsterdam the lenient magistrates were compelled by an apparent threat to civil order to league together to protect themselves against a possible revolution. Both in Antwerp and in Amsterdam the commercial interests feared an immediate cataclysm. It is noteworthy that the state of mind that led one segment of the population to hope for a New Jerusalem caused in the other half an equally vivid prospect of a material doom. Reynier Brundt, counselor and attorney general for the imperial court in The Hague, reported to Count Hoogstraten, imperial Stadholder of Holland, Zeeland, and Frisia, that the intensified search for the heretics had taken them into the swamps around the city and into the attics where the pursued had hidden themselves in Amsterdam. He complained, however, that many had fled, presumably to join the Münsterites, and he had, therefore, forbidden all ship captains to take the refugees aboard. See C. A. Cornelius, *Die niederländischen Wiedertäufer während der Belagerung Münsters* 1534 *bis* 1555, Bayerische Akademie, *Abhandlungen*, XI (1869), Abt. II, p. 90. Hoogstraten moved quickly to halt the migration. Altogether, some three thousand men, women, and children from the northern provinces attempted to join the Münsterites. Cf. J. S. Theissen, *De regeering van Karel V in de Noordelijke Nederlanden* (Amsterdam, 1912), 248–249.
[36] Jacob van Campen revealed in his confession (Cornelius, *op. cit.*, 98) that he had been acquainted with the young "king" of Münster while the gifted John of Leyden was a member of one of the rhetoricians' chambers (which openly mocked the priesthood and their indulgent habits). See J. le Petit, *La Grande chronique de Hollande* (Dordrecht, 1601), VII, 101 ff., and T. v. Domselaer, *Historische Beschrijving van Amsterdam* (Amsterdam, 1665), VI, 163 ff. The extensive examination made by G. Grosheide of the municipal records and court testimony on the Amsterdam uprisings reveals conflicting accounts of the role of Jacob van Campen. Cornelius (*op. cit.*, 97 ff.) exonerated van Campen from all implication in the attempted revolution. Van Campen consistently maintained in his confession at the repeated hearings that he had refused to heed the orders sent him by John Matthijs and John van Geelen. Testimony indicates that van Campen, like van Geelen, awaited some word or sign from Münster marking the deliverance of Amsterdam. The message that

everything—their activities and first beginnings in Münster[37]—unfolded is not entirely worth describing. Therefore I shall relate only the essentials.

During these events there came to us in Leeuwarden in Frisia two of these commissioned apostles, namely, Bartholomew Boekbinder[38] and Dietrich Kuyper.[39] And when some of us gathered together with the others, about fourteen or fifteen persons, both men and women, they proposed and proclaimed to us peace and patience with some words and instructions, and therewith they began to reveal the beginning of their apostleship and the compulsion (drijuinge) of the Spirit, and how John Matthijs had come to them with such signs, miracles, and agitation of the Spirit that words failed them to describe it enough to us, and they said we should not doubt but that they were no less sent forth with power and miracle than the apostles at Pentecost. Those same words I have reflected on a hundred times.

They also comforted us and said we need have no anxiety nor fear as we had long had because of the great tyranny since no Christian blood would be shed on earth, but in a short time God would rid the earth of all shedders of blood and all tyrants and the godless—which at that time did not please me too well in my heart and mind although I did not dare to contradict this because it was then the time that none dared to say much in opposition. And whoever spoke against this would immediately be resisting and slandering the Spirit, would be a Jannes or Jambres ([II Tim. 3:8; cf. Ex. 7:11] who, with their sorcery, had resisted Moses and Aaron). They also

finally came was that the brethren in Amsterdam had inherited the sword from Münster, to be appropriately used. Van Campen declared that he would use arms only to defend himself, not to harm others.

37 The interrelationship between the Münster and the Amsterdam Anabaptists is readily apparent. Cf. Walter J. Kühler, *Geschiedenis der Nederlandsche Doopsgezinden in de zestiende eeuw* (Haarlem, 1932), and John Horsch, "Is Dr. Kühler's Conception of Early Dutch Anabaptism Historically Sound?", *MQR*, VII (1933) 48; 97. C. A. Cornelius demonstrated the practical relationship between the two communities.

38 Bartholomeus Boekbinder is to be distinguished from Leonard and Gerard. All three were among the twelve apostles chosen by John Matthijs. *BRN*, VII, 31.

39 Willem (here incorrectly Dierick) Cuyper was one of the twelve commissioned by John Matthijs. He and Bartholomeus in turn baptized and commissioned Obbe. Obbe, in turn commissioned his brother Dietrich and Menno Simons. *BRN*, VII, 558. But it was Peter Houtzagher who baptized Dietrich. See below at n. 43. On Willem Cuyper, see Mellinck, *op. cit.*, 353.

frightened the hearts with damnation so that no one dared contradict them and each feared that he might in some way sin against them and speak against the commission or the ordination of God. For we were all guileless as children and had no idea that our own brethren, who were daily with us amid the perils of death and had to suffer persecution, would betray us.[40]

Thus did we on that day almost all permit ourselves to be baptized. The following day, when they were ready to go on, they summoned us along with John Scheerder,[41] at the suggestion of other brethren, and with the laying on of hands laid upon us the office of preaching, [commissioning us] to baptize, teach, and stand before the congregation, [130] etc. We could feel the laying on of hands and we could also hear all the words, but we neither felt nor heard the Holy Spirit, nor received any power from above, but [heard] many loose words which had neither strength nor lasting effect, as afterward we amply discovered; and after they had done these things with us, they immediately went forth the same day.

Eight days later came Peter Houtzagher[42] with the same commission, and baptized Dietrich Philips[43] and several others at the time when I was outside the town in the countryside to preach, so that I did not speak with this Peter. But they told me all about it and that there were many of the Zwinglians[44] there who contradicted him so that he did not accomplish much there. After a day or two he departed again for Amsterdam, and as soon as this Peter Houtzagher was outside

---

[40] It is not without justification that Obbe and his followers feared betrayal. John Trijpmaker himself had revealed the names of some fifty or sixty Anabaptists. Fortunately, informants in turn warned most of the betrayed so that only nine were arrested and consequently executed with Trijpmaker. Cf. G. Grosheide, *op. cit.*, 36. Charles V, who sought both to maintain religious unity and to take able men for the galleys, offered inducements to betrayal, typically in his edict published June 10, 1535: "He that delivers them up, or makes them known, shall have a third part of the confiscated estate." See T. J. van Braght, *Martyrs' Mirror*.

[41] Hans Scheerder, after 1535 a revolutionary. He is mentioned in Sel. IX, n. 42.

[42] Pieter Houtzagher (woodsawyer) was one of the twelve apostles of John Matthijs.

[43] Dirck Philips. See below, Selection XI, introduction.

[44] This designation is unusual and undoubtedly means the sacramentarians of Dutch origin. See critical Dutch edition, n. 3; cf. above, pp. 208 f., and below, p. 222.

Leeuwarden, all prophecy and spiritual braggadocio ceased. He himself was immediately and severely pursued and sought after, first in the town and then in the countryside and in all the villages, so that he only narrowly escaped, for the authorities had him hunted.[45] In the meantime Scheerder, my companion, and I set out again for Leeuwarden on a Sunday and when we arrived at the town gates around midday, there stood the gate-keeper, who was about to close the portals. He spoke to us as he saw us approaching and said that if we wanted to get in, we must enter quickly. When we heard this we were much alarmed and we asked what the trouble was. He said: There are Anabaptists in the town who will all be taken prisoners. Then we became even more frightened and thought of the prophecies. Nevertheless, we had not reckoned on this and we gathered up courage and went into the town in the bright mid-day. In entering the house I found my wife much distressed, and she told me of the business about Peter Houtzagher, that some had strongly spoken out against his word and commission, which resulted in a great clamor and persecution, begging me to get out of the way [131] to some other house until it was dark (for it was winter, between Christmas and Candlemas).[46]

These three men, dear friends, who boasted to us of such commission and apostolic offices and told us that no more blood would be shed on earth, themselves shortly thereafter through the driving of the Spirit, walked through Amsterdam [March 23, 1534]. One cried out: The new city is given to the children

---

[45] The procurator general Reynier Brundt appealed to Stadholder Hoog-straten on February 14, 1534, to impose his imperial authority in Amsterdam where, wrote Brundt, "all these troubles have come about principally [through] the fault and negligence of the officers [of the city]" (Cornelius, op. cit., 76). Hoogstraten toured Holland in April and May of 1534 with the result that about a hundred persons were executed by fire, sword, and water. The confession of Jannetgen Thys, January 23, 1535, confirmed Brundt's worst fears. Some sixty of the Amsterdam militia were secretly Anabaptists, she reported, and two magistrates and one burgomaster were counted among the brethren. She also asserted that the signal would soon be given from Münster for the Amsterdam brethren to use the sword and take the city. Differences of doctrine and purpose, however, split the leaders of the group, she added. Had they been able to reach an accord, they would already have taken the city. Cornelius, op. cit., 86 f.

[46] The winter of 1533–1534.

of God; another called: Repent ye, repent ye and do penance; the third cried: Woe, woe to all the godless.[47]

Now, as they were captured in the midst of these outcries, they and some fifteen or sixteen other teachers and brethren were taken as insurrectionists and Anabaptists to Haarlem where they were all condemned and tortured to death.[48] Some were smothered and put on a pike; then the others were beheaded and set on the wheel. This I myself thereafter saw and stood among the executed with some brethren who had traveled with me because I was curious to know which in the heap those three were who had baptized us and had proclaimed such calling and promise to us. But we could not identify them, so frightfully were they changed by the fire and smoke, and those on the wheels we could not recognize either, nor tell one from the other.

See, dear friends, so did it come to pass with the first commission among us and such was the reliability of their prophecies.[49]

Now one may really wonder what the courage of our hearts was when we thought of the highly daring and boastful words, which I did not read in a book nor receive or hear in roundabout ways, but which I received from their own mouths. O God! Their message to us was entirely opposite: and all they told us would come upon the world, the tyrants and the godless on earth, *that* came upon us and upon them first of all, for we were the very first who were persecuted and put to death. O man, how can the great consternation among us be expressed— we are oppressed by the world [132] and severely persecuted

---

[47] Dietrich Kuyper, Bartholomew Boekbinder, and Peter Houtzagher marched through Amsterdam, brandishing swords, on March 23, 1534, and were executed on or about March 26. The "new" city was the west side of Amsterdam, where most of the Anabaptists resided or gathered. The chronicles reported that they cried out: "In the name of the Lord: God's blessing over the new side, God's curse over the old city!"

[48] Hoogstraten was officially informed from The Hague on March 26, 1534, that seven Anabaptists, among them Peter Houtzagher, were executed on that day. Cf. Cramer's comments in BRN, VII, 106 f.

[49] This event may have been the moment of the Obbenite defection from the Melchiorite movement in The Netherlands. It appears that the execution of Peter Houtzagher and the others shocked Obbe into seeing their promises ("henceforth no Christian blood will be shed on earth") as lies and false prophecies, betrayed in the violence of their miserable deaths. Eventually, the legality of his ordination by these men, and thus his own authority to ordain and to preach, was cast in doubt.

and even by our own brethren we are every day deceived and betrayed.

After this some others arose who were made teachers by the previous ones mentioned and who had been ordained by John Matthijs—such as Jacob van Campen, a teacher of Amsterdam, Damas of Hoorn, Leonard Boekbinder, Cornelius from the Brielle, Nicholas of Alkmaar, Maynard of Delft,[50] and many others, with all of whom I have spoken and dealt much with—and such strange instruction was heard among them! One corrupted marriage. The second taught nothing but parables. The third would pardon no one nor recognize him as brother who fell into apostasy after baptism and herewith referred to the willful and knowing sin unto death.[51] The fourth would have the baptism of John before the baptism of Christ, etc. Others stood firmly by visions, dreams, and prophecies. Some also were of the opinion that when the brethren and teachers were put to death, they would immediately be resurrected and would rule on earth with Christ a thousand years, and all that they left behind them would be restored to them a hundredfold. Thus there were almost as many meanings as there were teachers, each comforting himself with lies and false promises, visions, dreams, and revelations. Some had spoken with God, others with angels—until they got a new trek under way to Münster. During this business, those at Münster accepted the teaching and commission of the emissaries [apostles] of John Matthijs, namely, Gerard Boekbinder and John of Leyden; and in time, with the message and their apostolic role, they took Münster with the sword and by force.

In this business, the most prominent in Münster were John Matthijs and John of Leyden, who later became king of Münster, also Bernard Rothmann.[52] If one were to describe the beginning and end of all those events and how it all transpired, one would have to write a book about it—of the books, writings, and letters they daily sent to us, of the great signs, wondrous visions, and rev[133]elations they had daily—since such highly celebrated prophets and prophecies came so quickly to an end and misrepresented themselves. One may perceive of

---

50 Others of the twelve. *BRN*, VII, 31.
51 Cf. Heb. 6:4–6 and 10:26; also see Melchior Hofmann, Sel. IX, n. 12.
52 Bernt Rothmann, popular Lutheran preacher, was converted to restorationism by the Wassenberg refugees who carried into Münster certain ideas of John Campanus. See above, n. 33, and Sel. VII, n. 3.

which spirit they were the children and by which spirit they were led and driven. Thus we leave this and look further to how they represented themselves to us in order that we may clarify a little the trek to Münster.

This lively interchange with Münster took place rapidly through letters and through diverse teachers from Holland who professed that Münster and not Strassburg was the New Jerusalem. For Melchior was forgotten with his prophets and prophetesses, with his apostleship of 144,000 true apostles of Christ out of Strassburg, with his Elijah role, and all his boasting. In time we gave the matter little belief; rather, it was for the most part forgotten, for Melchior was and remained imprisoned until death and died in prison. All his apostleship, prophecy, Elijah role, and his dispatch of apostles from Strassburg all went to nought and to shame. And so it was told to me by the brethren that Melchior even had to break his own fast, using other food and drink because of the weakness of his condition, for he could no longer keep alive on water and bread. The ever gracious God must take pity on his poor soul and be merciful, for a truly reasonable person can clearly imagine what the courage of Melchior's heart must have been when the time of the prophecies had elapsed and no deliverance, help, or comfort came to him. Everything that he so boldly professed from the mouth of the prophets and prophetesses he, in the end, found it all falsehood and deception, in fact and in truth; and he was so deceived with all their visions, prophecies, commission, dreams, and Elijah role that my heart today feels pity for his on account of this distress of his soul, which indeed was much more severe for him than all the persecution and tyranny, as all sensible people can readily comprehend. This Melchior, who was to have been Elijah, was soon scorned and forgotten by the brethren, as already described, when they had Enoch in the Netherlands.

Just as John Matthijs was truly Enoch with the true commission [134] and apostolic office, so he also came to his end and received his reward according to his works. Melchior died in prison and did not come out again as the prophets and prophetesses had predicted, and all his intentions with all his following toppled to the ground and came to nothing more. John Matthijs, as an apostle and Enoch, was beaten before the gates of Münster in a skirmish or hostile encounter, for he daily strode there in his armor and with his musket like a wild man out of his senses. He was so fierce and bloodthirsty that he

brought various people to their deaths; yea, and he was so
violent that even his enemies for their part were terrified of
him, and when finally in a tumult they became too powerful
for him, they were so incensed that they did not just kill him
like other people but hacked and chopped him into little
pieces, so that his brethren had to carry him in a basket
when the tumult was over. Yet some of the brethren
insisted that, following the prophecy of Enoch and Elijah, he
would be resurrected on the fourth day and before all people
he would rise up to heaven or be carried away by a cloud.
So blind with such frightful blindness were some of them smitten.

See, dear friends, how we have here the beginning and end of
both Elijah and Enoch with their commissions, visions, prophecies, dreams, and revelations. What spirit compelled this
performance, office, and commission, I will let each judge for
himself.

Thus it continued with muskets, pikes, harquebuses, and
halberds. Thus would they fight and no longer suffer. They
would put on the armor of David; they would deal out to the
godless double their tyranny according to the Scripture.
Münster and not Strassburg was then Jerusalem. Amsterdam was
given to the children of God. There one insurrection followed
another [notably May 10, 1535].[53] There the godless would
meet their end and be punished. But all that came to nothing.
All prophecies were false and lying, for the tables were always
turned the other way. Those who denounced others as godless
[135] were such themselves. And those who would exterminate
the others were themselves annihilated. Everywhere it was
dealt out to them twofold. And still we poor people could not
yet open our eyes, for it all happened so crudely that we were
not able to put our hands on the lies and obscurities. But God

---

53 The spectacle of seven "naked walkers" in February, 1535, was a con-
vincing example to the city that the treacherous madness of Anabaptism
must be finally and completely destroyed. This little coterie of wild
visionaries proclaimed the "naked truth" of an apocalyptic judgment
and the coming of a communistic paradise. Cf. Selection IX, at n. 21. The
final explosion occurred on May 10, 1535. A group of thirty-three insurrectionists took possession of the town hall where they were subdued by
cannon and militia in a day and a night. Such reinforcements as had been
hoped for by the rebels from Flanders and Frisia arrived too late. By
holding back their followers from joining the Anabaptist rebellion,
Obbe and Jacob van Campen ultimately determined the failure of
the abortive revolution in Amsterdam. The Münsterite leader, John
van Geelen, was fatally wounded; and his followers were promptly
executed.

knows that Dietrich and I could never find it in our hearts
that such onslaughts were right; we taught firmly against this,
but it did us no good, for most of the folks were inclined to this.
Some men always wanted to answer this and turn it to good
account, making the shame into an honor, and attach to it a
nice flaxen beard.[54]

O how many times were some of us so distressed to death
that the heart in our bodies turned cold, and we did not know
where to turn, nor what best to do; the whole world pursued us
to death with fire, water, sword, and bloody tyranny for our
belief. The prophecies deceived us on all sides and the letter of
the Scriptures took us prisoner. The false brothers whom we
punished and spoke out against vowed our deaths and yet the
love of so many hearts caused such pity in us that the all-
highest King of Glory knows that my heart was often grieved
to death. Were it not for the love I felt for the simple hearts
who were daily misled by the false brethren, I would long
ago[55] have left them and departed from all my acquaintances
with some of these innocent hearts. For a time there was no one
among the teachers who would help me to resist the false
brethren against all insurrectionists, except Dietrich Philips,
since *we* were never in our hearts given over to such seditious
inspiration and false prophecy. Indeed, I may well say with
truth that my love of the brethren in the zeal for the house of
the Lord very nearly engulfed me.

I am still miserable of heart today that I [136] advanced
anyone to such an office while I was so shamefully and miserably
deceived that I did not stop forthwith, but permitted myself
to bring poor souls to this—that I through the importuning of
the brethren commissioned to the office [apostleship] Dietrich
Philips[56] in Amsterdam, David Joris[57] in Delft, and Menno
Simons[58] in Groningen.

54 I.e., to prettify their intentions.
55 Obbe broke from Menno and Dietrich only c. 1539–1540, whereupon
the former branded him a Demas (II Tim. 4:10).
56 It was the apostle Peter Houtzagher who had baptized Dietrich Philips
(above, at n. 43), but it was Obbe who ordained or commissioned him.
The question of orders and the ministry remains an obscure chapter in
Anabaptist history. See "Ministry," *Mennonite Encyclopedia.*
57 David Joris, who regarded himself as the third David in succession to
King David and Christ, misled the more fanatic remnants of the Münsterite debacle from his new base in Basel where he lived splendidly under
a false name. The most recent study is that of Roland Bainton in *The
Travail of Religious Liberty: Nine Biographical Studies* (Philadelphia, 1951).
58 Menno Simons (1496–1561) could not have been ordained before

It is this which is utter grief to my heart and which I will lament before my God as long as I live, before all my companions, as often as I think of them. At the time that I took leave of those brethren I had warned Menno and Dietrich and declared my commission unlawful and that I was therein deceived. I wished from my heart that they had not touched or assumed such an office. I wanted to free my soul in a confession of this before God, acknowledging my guilt and deception. They might then do what they wished and may still do what they will. I thank the blessed, gracious, and merciful God with all his mercy, who opened my eyes, humbled my soul, transformed my heart, captured my spirit and my downcast mind and soul, and who gave me to know my sins. And when I still think of the resigned suffering[59] which occurred among the brethren in Amsterdam, in the Old Cloister [in Bolsward], in Hazerswoude, in Appingedam, in the Sandt [in Groningen], and above all at Münster, my soul is troubled and terrified before it. I shall be silent about all the false commissions, prophecies, visions, dreams, revelations, and unspeakable spirit[137]ual pride which immediately from the first hour stole in among the brethren. For those baptized one day cried on the morrow about all the godless, that they must be rooted out. And actually, as soon as anyone was baptized, he was at once a pious Christian and slandered all people and admitted no one on earth to be good but himself and his fellow brethren. Was that not a great and terrible pride? And who can express the great wrangling and dissension among the congregations, of debating and arguing about the Tabernacle of Moses, the cloven claw,[60] about the commission, the armor of David, about the thousand-year Kingdom of Christ on earth, about the incarnation, baptism, belief, Supper, the promised David,[61]

December, 1536, or January, 1537. He neither acknowledged nor denied the ordination. Menno led the remnants of the Obbenites (themselves, the pacifistic dissidents from among the Melchiorites) into a firmly disciplined international Anabaptist fellowship bearing his name and using his *Foundation Book* as their guide. Obbe Philips' brother, Dietrich, and Leonard Bouwens were the chief associates of Menno in this endeavor.

59 The Dutch word here is *verbeydinghe*. This could be a misprint in the early editions for *verleydinge*, in which case it should be translated "deception."

60 On the Tabernacle, see Hofmann, Sel. IX, at n. 14 and *passim* and Dietrich Philips, *ibid*. On the cloven claw, see Hofmann, Sel. IX, n. 42; Hubmaier, Sel. V, at n. 12; "Gespauwde Klauw," *Mennonite Encyclopedia*.

61 Above, n. 57.

second marriage (*dubbelde Echte*), free will, predestination, the conscious sin unto death.[62] And all this occurred with ban, condemnations, blasphemy, slander, the blackening of reputation, backbiting, judging, and adjudication, [the labeling of others] as heretical, godless, papistical, Lutheran, Zwinglian. And this the brethren did among each other, the one as much as the other, the one this and the other that.

Thus it is that a reasonable, impartial Christian may truly say that it is no Christian congregation but a desolate abomination, that it can be no temple of God but a cave of murderers, full of hate, envy, jealousy, spiritual pride, pseudo piety, hypocrisy, contempt, defamation. They could suffer neither the love nor benefit of another who was not of their belief, sect, opinion, and who did not say yes and amen to all their enterprises and onslaughts.

Thus was the beginning of the commission and apostolic office of Elijah and Enoch continued by the teachers and its end revealed and sufficiently exhibited. So also can one who is not otherwise blind easily see that the one errs and fails here, the other there; the one promotes an offense and tumult here, another there; one fetes[63] and lauds God here, the other there. If I were to tell everything in full that I know of all this, of the commission, doctrine, office, and the teachers whom I have known and of the positions which they actually held, it would be much too much, yes, grievous, to hear and also would not be appropriate to relate.

[62] Cf. Hofmann, Sel. IX. at n. 12.
[63] The rather extraordinary word (*bancketiert*) may refer to the holding of the Lord's Supper and love feast.

XI

The Church of God
By Dietrich Philips [1]

c. 1560

INTRODUCTION

HERE WE HAVE IN THE WORK OF THE YOUNGER brother of the foregoing Obbe Philips (Selection X) a more constructive reaction to the confusions and miscalculations of the Münsterite Anabaptists. Here is a vigorous delineation of the church, organized strictly on the apostolic pattern (as the Münsterite commonwealth had not been) with a programmatic suppression of any claim to its being the Kingdom of God.

In the following Selection from Dietrich's *Enchiridion*, which has had a place in Mennonitism comparable to that of Melanchthon's systematic *Loci communes* within Lutheranism, the whole of Mennonite theology can be glimpsed in concentrating on one aspect of it.

The Church of God may be conveniently divided into three parts: (I) the creation of the church and its restoration among angels and men, (II) the seven ordinances of the true church,

[1] There is no full-length study of Dietrich Philips in English. Besides brief descriptions of the two Philips brothers in the general and regional histories cited in the introduction, n. 1, mention may be made of an article by John Horsch, "The Rise of Mennonitism in the Netherlands," *MQR*, VIII (1934), 147, and the most recent general study of Dutch Anabaptism by Walter Kühler, *Geschiedenis der Nederlandsche Doopsgesinden in de zestienden eeuw* (Haarlem, 1932). Kühler's stress on the humanist strand supplied by the *devotio moderna* and Erasmus as well as Kühler's willingness to grant a fairly close connection originally between Amsterdam and Münster was vigorously assailed by John Horsch, "Is Dr. Kühler's Conception ... Sound?", *MQR*, VII (1933), 48; 97. The most recent study of Dutch Anabaptism is by A. F. Mellink, *De Wederdopers in de Noordelijke Nederlanden, 1531–1544* (Groningen, 1953). See the brief references to Dietrich in Obbe's *Confession*, Selection X, at notes 43, 55, and 56.

and (III) the ten marks of the church. Part I is indirectly indebted to Augustine, though Augustine's seven periods of sacred history are allowed to fade behind the more typical Anabaptist stress on the distinction between the Old and the New Dispensation. Dietrich does not find occasion here to date the fall of the New Covenant church; and though, like Brait-michel in the Hutterite *Chronicle* (Selection I), he apparently holds to a continuity of the faithful remnant down through the Middle Ages, he cites no names. In contrast to Obbe (also Schwenckfeld, and Franck, Selection VII) Dietrich holds that the church of the apostles has truly been restored (Part II). At the same time its marks (Part III) partake of the bright hues of the eschatological church of the Apocalypse. In fact, the magnificence of the conception is due to the fact that after the debacle of the Münsterite theocracy the Dutch Anabaptists appropriated the Apocalyptic language of the church triumphant for their own conventicles militant. The cogency of this treatise depends in part upon the strong and resourceful undergirding supplied from Scripture at every juncture. Nevertheless, to reduce its bulk, the editor has removed many of the Scriptural references. The text has also been slightly reduced at points indicated by ellipses but at two points expanded in the notes with material taken from another part of the *Enchiridion* (*On Becoming Man*) to allow Dietrich to speak more fully on the heavenly flesh of Christ and the implications of the doctrine for the observation of the Supper (cf. Schwenck-feld, Selection VIII).

The Church of God [2]
By Dietrich Philips

c. 1560

THE TEXT

[I. THE ORIGIN AND PRIMORDIAL FALL AND RESTORATION OF THE CHURCH]

The church (*Gemeynte*) of God was originally begun by God in heaven with the angels, who were created spirits and flaming fire (Ps. 104:4; Heb. 1:7), to stand before the throne of God praising and serving him, and also that they should minister to and be fellow servants of the believers (Rev. 22:9). For, although they are such high and exalted creatures of God, they are nevertheless one and all ministering spirits, as the apostle says (Heb. 1:14), sent forth to minister for them who shall be the heirs of salvation. For they guard the children of God, they encamp round about the camp of those who fear God (Ps. 34:7; Ex. 14:19). They went before Israel, they led Lot out of Sodom (Gen. 19:16; Ps. 20:6[3]; 34:22; Matt. 18:10). In short, they serve the saints and chosen people of God, they preserve them in all their ways, yet always beholding the face of the Father in heaven. Hence the church (*Gemeynte*) had its origin in the angels in heaven.

Afterward the church (*Gemeynte*) of God was begun in

---

[2] *Van die Ghemeynte Godts*, first published c. 1560 without indication of date or place, was later taken up into the *Enchiridion* (1563). The critical edition of the text is published by F. Pijper, *Bibliotheca Reformatoria Neerlandica*, X (The Hague, 1914), pp. 377–414. (These pages are referred to in brackets.) The whole of the *Enchiridion* was translated from the German edition by A. B. Kolb (Elkhart, Ind., 1910). The present translation is indebted to that of Kolb but is based upon the Pijper text. As to the numerous Scriptural references, a few have been dropped as not particularly pertinent; a few (in brackets) have been added to fix an obscure allusion. Where the Scriptural reference of the Pijper text has been faulty it has been corrected without comment.

[3] It is in the Vulgate text, Ps. 19:7 b, that this reference has significance: "The salvation of his right hand is in powers [=angels]."

228

paradise with Adam and Eve, who were created after the image of God and in his likeness (Gen. 5:2), upright and pure creatures of God, incorruptible and immortal (Gen. 2:7; 9:6; Wisdom of Solomon 2:23), and in whom there was an upright devout nature and a divine [381] character, and in whom was a true knowledge (Ecclesiasticus 16:25) of God and the fear and love of God so long as they remained in their first creation and ordinance and bore the image of God.[4]

Therefore the church of God is a *congregation*[5] of holy beings, namely, of the angels in heaven and of the believing reborn men on earth, who have been renewed in the image of God. These are all united together in Jesus Christ (Eph. 3:6; Col. 1:27), as Paul well explains in his epistles, especially to the Hebrews (ch. 12:22–24), when he writes: Ye are come unto Mount Sion, and unto the city of the living God, the heavenly Jerusalem, and to a company of many thousands of angels, to the congregation of the first-born, who are written in the heavens, to God, the Judge over all, to the spirits of just men made perfect, to Jesus the Mediator of the New Covenant, and to the blood of sprinkling, that speaketh better things than that blood of Abel.

From these words it is to be clearly understood that the company of angels, the congregation of the first-born, which are inscribed in the heavens, and the spirits of just men made perfect, together with all believers who have been added thereto, all together comprise the congregation of God, over which God, the righteous Judge, rules, of which Christ is the Head (Eph. 1:22), and in which the Holy Spirit dwells (I Cor. 3:16; 6:19).

But the first falling away from God in his congregation occurred among the angels in heaven, who sinned (Job 4:18) and were untrue to their Creator, and were therefore cast out of heaven, and bound with chains of darkness (II Peter 2:4), so that they can no longer do anything but what God suffers them to do (Luke 9:1), although they are evil spirits and angels, who now rule in the air (Eph. 2:2), warring against Christians, seeking their destruction (Matt. 4:1; I Peter 5:8; James 4:7), operating in the children of unbelief and possessing the world; but they are preserved, up until the Day of Judgment, unto

---

[4] As in Hubmaier (Selection V) man originally had the knowledge of good and evil sufficient to his needs.

[5] Hereafter the Dutch word *Gemeynte* will be more accurately rendered "congregation."

eternal pain and damnation, yea, for the hellish fire, which shall never be quenched (II Peter 2:4; Matt. 25:30).

The second falling away from God in the congregation occurred through Adam and Eve in paradise, who were deceived by the craftiness of the [382] serpent (Gen. 3:6) and corrupted by sin (Rom. 5:12; I Cor. 15:21), by which they lost the image of God, the holiness of their immaculately created nature and pre-eminent reason; full of exalted wisdom and knowledge of God and of his creation; and which was fervent in love and obedience toward God. All this they lost. Yea, from righteousness they passed into unrighteousness, from that immortal state into corruption and condemnation, and out of eternal life into eternal death.

The first restoration of corrupted man, and the renewal in him of the divine image, and the reconstruction of the ruined church (*Kercken*) occurred in the promise of the coming seed (Gen. 3:15) of the woman, which should crush the serpent's head. This seed is principally (*principalijck*) Jesus Christ, and he is called the seed of the woman because he was promised to Adam and Eve by God and is, according to the flesh, born of a woman (Matt. 1:25; Luke 2:7). For although Mary conceived him by the Holy Spirit and brought him forth as a pure maiden, she is nevertheless called a woman in the Scriptures (Luke 2:5; Gal. 4:4), and in the same way Christ is also called her seed and the fruit of her body. And this Jesus Christ is the Crusher and Conqueror of the crooked old serpent (Rev. 12:17), who by his death redeemed the human race from the tyrannical power of Satan, sin, and eternal death (Rom. 5:1; Col. 1:20; Heb. 2:14).

This was the first preaching of the gospel of Jesus Christ, the only Redeemer and Saviour of the world, by whom Adam and Eve were again restored and again got back the lost image of God (John 3:36); for they were created anew of God, born anew of him, because they accepted the gracious promise of the gospel in true faith by the power and enlightenment of the Holy Spirit.

Of this Adam and Eve, his housewife, came Cain and Abel, two brothers, one upright, the other godless (Gen. 4:1); Abel, a child of God and a fellow member of the Christian church; in contrast, Cain, a child of the devil (I John 3:12) and embraced in his fellowship. The devout and righteous Abel was hated by the wicked and murderous Cain and slain because of the envy of his wicked heart. This is a clear representation and testimony that from that time on there were two kinds of people, two kinds of children, two kinds of congregations [383] on earth, namely, the people of God and the devil's people, God's children and the devil's children, God's congregation and the synagogue or assembly (*Vergaderinghe*) of Satan, and that the children of God had to suffer persecution from the children of the devil, and that the congregation of Christ must be suppressed, hunted, and put to death by Antichrist's assembly (Matt. 23:38; John 8:44), which fact God also made known in this, that he has put enmity between the serpent's seed and the seed of the woman, and that the serpent's seed would lay a snare for the seed of the woman, or bite him in the heel; for Christ Jesus is the true promised seed of the woman, as said above (and I say again, of a promised seed, and not of a natural seed, or else the serpent's seed also would be natural [John 16:33]), and he is the only conqueror of the devil. Besides this, all believers are the seed of the spiritual Eve, just as the unbelievers are the seed of the crooked old serpent, and that in a spiritual sense. And between the children of the aforementioned Eve and the serpent has been put an eternal enmity by God so that the children of the devil all the time hate, envy, and persecute the children of God (Gen. 3:15); and, on the other hand, the children of God overcome the serpent and its seed, the world and all that is in it, by the blood of the Lamb, by their faith in Jesus Christ, by their confession and testimony to the truth, and by their steadfastness in the Word of God unto death (Rev. 7:14; 12:12; I John 5:4).

Further, God gave Adam and Eve another son in Abel's stead, the God-fearing Seth (Gen. 4:25). And from him descended other devout people up to Noah who found favor before the Lord at a time when God punished with a deluge the children of men along with those children of God who had intermingled with the daughters of men and thus transgressed. Thereupon he destroyed, removed, and annihilated all flesh except Noah and those that were with him in the ark. What this figure signifies, however, we have explained in our *Confession*[6] and in *Spiritual Restitution*.[7]

God made a covenant with Noah and his two sons Shem and Japheth, or at least renewed it, and these at that time constituted

---

[6] First published separately in 1558 and taken up into the *Enchiridion*, critical Dutch edition, *BRN*, X, pp. 60–111; English translation, pp. 18 ff.
[7] First published separately in 1558 and taken up in the *Enchiridion*, critical Dutch edition, pp. 339–376; English edition, pp. 321–65.

his congregation. But Ham, the third son of Noah, though he had been in the ark, was a mocker of his father and was [384] cursed by him, and so, in Cain's stead, became a new beginning of the congregation of Satan upon earth, the father of Canaan and his seed, the wicked children, who have always tormented and mocked the children of God and fought against God.

From Shem in direct line Abraham came forth, the father of all the faithful with whom God renewed and confirmed his covenant. . . .

So then the covenant of God with all its gracious promises descended from Abraham to Isaac and Jacob, upon the twelve patriarchs, and afterward upon Moses and Aaron, upon David, and upon all the God-fearing who lived then and afterward and who in upright faith served God. These constituted the congregation of God, the commonwealth of Israel (Eph. 2:12), the temple of the Lord, the testament and sanctuary of the Most High. Here wisdom had her abode in Jacob and her heritage in Israel (Ecclesiasticus 24:8) until the time of Christ, in which time there were many devout and God-fearing people among the Jewish nation in Jerusalem and throughout Judea, such as Zacharias and Elizabeth, Joseph and Mary, the aged Simeon and Anna the widow, etc.

Besides these there were many God-fearing people among the Gentiles, such as Melchizedek, king of Salem, a priest of the Most High, whose pedigree is suppressed by the Spirit; Abimelech, king of Gerar (Gen. 14:18; Heb. 7:1; Gen. 20:2); Job an Idumean, his friends, and many others. Therefore Paul writes [to the same effect in] Rom. 2:14–16;26–29 . . . [385]. . . .

Moreover the promise of God to Abraham was that in his seed all the nations of the earth should be blessed, and that he should become the father of all nations and of the Gentiles. And there God changed his name, so that he should be no longer called Abram, but Abraham. There are likewise also many prophecies in the Pentateuch (Gen. 15:5; 17:3–5; 22:18), the psalms (Ps. 18:43), and the Prophets (II Sam. 22:44) concerning the Gentiles, that they should be called by Jesus Christ into the flock of Israel, and that many should believe in God and be obedient to the gospel (Rom. 11:25).

Therefore the Jews and Israelites cannot be counted alone as the congregation of God, but all who truly confessed, feared, honored God, and lived according to his will, by the law of nature inscribed by God in their hearts; and all among the heathen who have believed in Jesus Christ, are in their uncircumcision of the flesh (Rom. 2:26) and in their heathendom counted as the spiritual seed of Abraham and of the promise (Gal. 3:20). Hence it follows that they have been of God and of Christ.

[386] Thus the congregation of God from the beginning existed in Christ, by whom all things are renewed. Indeed there are united into one body all that are in heaven and on earth (Col. 1:16), by whom the congregation of God was made more glorious and also was multiplied; for then figures had an end, but the true realities came into being (Col 2:9; Rom. 10:4); grace and truth came by Jesus Christ (John 1:17). Then the lost sheep of the house of Israel were sought and led by Christ into the right sheepfold (Matt. 10:6). Then did the Gentiles of all nations come unto Mount Sion to learn the law of the Lord our God, and to hear the gospel of Jesus Christ, and to walk in the way of the Lord. Then was the prophecy fulfilled that the desolate should be comforted, and the shame and contempt of the unfruitful be forgotten (Isa. 54:1; Gal. 4:27) because he who created her became her husband, his name is the Lord Sabaoth, the Redeemer and Saviour of Israel, the Lord and God of the whole earth. Then did Jerusalem arise and shine, for her Light came (Isa. 60:1), and the glory of God illumined her and his radiance shone over her, so that the Gentiles walked in her light, and the people of the earth in the brightness that had risen upon her. Then were given to the believers, through the knowledge of Jesus Christ, by God, the most precious promises, that they through the same [knowledge] should be made partakers of the divine nature (II Peter 1:4), if they but escape the corrupting lusts of this world. In short, the true knowledge of God and Christ then appeared like a bright morning star (Rev. 22:16), grace flowed then like a living stream of water out from the paradise of God, then was the Holy Spirit poured out abundantly by God upon his sons and daughters (Rev. 22:1; Joel 2:28; Acts 2:17), then was the New Testament of the Lord completed with the house of Israel and Judah according to his promise by the prophet Jeremiah [ch. 31:31–34]; yea, then was the congregation extended and the Kingdom of God increased throughout the whole world (Matt. 28:19; Mark 16:15) by the true messengers (emissaries) of the Lord (Col. 1:28), prepared and endowed with many precious promises and ordinances, thus becoming a glorious house of the living God.

But how this came to pass, and how this building up of the

congregation of Jesus Christ took place the Scripture shows us with great clearness, namely, by the right teaching of the divine Word and by the faith that cometh out of the hearing of the divine Word (Rom. 10:17 f.). It is because of this that the enlightenment of the Holy Spirit comes; for no one can enter into the Kingdom of God, into the heavenly Jerusalem, that is, into the [387] congregation of Jesus Christ, unless he from the heart amend his ways, sincerely repent and believe the gospel (Matt. 3:2). For just as God founded his congregation on earth in paradise with pure and holy people, who had been created in his image and made and begun after his likeness, so he still desired such as are created in Christ Jesus and have been renewed by the Holy Spirit in his congregation. Although the salvation promised to man has been wrought by Jesus Christ the Saviour, and although the forfeited life has been redeemed by the blood of the unique sacrifice, and is offered to all men by the gospel (Titus 2:13; Heb. 2:2; 10:18–20), nevertheless, not all men enjoy this eternal salvation and eternal life, but those alone [a] who in this life here are born again by the Word of Jesus Christ, who allow themselves to be sought and found by the light of the divine Word, and who obey the voice of their Shepherd (I Peter 1:23–25; James 1:18–19; John 3:3; 8:32; 12:46); [b] who are enlightened with the true knowledge of God and his will and in sincere faith accept the righteousness of Christ.

[a. Spiritual Rebirth]

Christ testifies of this to Nicodemus and says (John 3:3, 5): Verily, verily, I say unto thee, except a man be born again, he cannot see the Kingdom of God. Verily, verily, I say unto thee, except a man be born of water and of the Spirit, he cannot enter into the Kingdom of God.

Here the Kingdom of God is absolutely denied by the Lord himself to all who are not born again of God, and who are not created by him anew in the inner being in his image. Hence those who desire to enter the Kingdom of God (I here speak of intelligent beings) must be born again.

This rebirth does not take place outwardly, but in the understanding (Verstant), mind (Sin), and heart of man. It is in the understanding and the mind that man learns to know the eternal love and gracious God in Christ Jesus who is the eternal image of the Father (II Cor. 4:4; Col. 1:16) and the brightness of the divine being (Heb. 1:3). It is thus in the heart that man loves this same almighty and living God, fears, honors, and believes in him, trusts in his promise, which cannot take place without the power of the Holy Spirit, who must inflame the heart with divine power which must also give faith, fear with love, hope, and all good virtues of God.

[388] Neither are we regenerated by flesh and blood, nor by any temporal or corruptible things, but—as Peter (I, ch. 1:23) and James (ch. 1:18) testify—viz., by the Word of the living God, just as we have written in our booklet *Of Regeneration and the New Creature*[8] and every one who desires may read there.

Moreover, the Word of God is twofold, viz., the law and the gospel.[9] The law is the word of command, given by God through Moses on Mount Sinai with such a terrifying voice, with such quakings, storm, thunder, and lightning that the Children of Israel could not bear it, but said to Moses (Ex. 20:19): Speak thou with the Lord, and we will hear; and let not God speak with us, lest we die. Even Moses himself had become afraid and trembled (Heb. 12:21), which shows the sternness of the law; for it shows to us sin and condemnation, since it demands perfect righteousness in the inner man (Rom. 4:13–15; Deut. 4:1–6; 6:1–3; Matt. 19:17–21) and the holiness of the whole created nature and of the higher understanding, full of true knowledge of God—and added to this: a holy, pure heart that is fervent in love to God.

Moreover, the law condemns the inward uncleanness of nature, that is, the damage and loss of the created wisdom and knowledge of God and the inwrought righteousness and holiness of the heart (Ps. 51:6–12; Eph. 2:1–3). Again, it condemns the wicked desire and inclination that are contrary to the law of God; for whoever reads the law with unveiled countenance must be terrified at God's wrath (Rom. 3:20; 7:7; II Cor. 3:13–16; Ex. 34:33, 35; 20:19 f.; Heb. 12:19) and be humbled, just as has been pictured to us in the case of Israel and indeed in the case of Moses himself.

Therefore the law is given by God, not that it might bring with it to man perfect righteousness, salvation, and eternal life (for by the deeds of the law shall no flesh be justified, Rom. 3:20; Gal. 2:16), but that it might, by revealing sin, teach man to fear God, to know and humble himself under the mighty hand

---

8 First published separately, after 1556; in critical Dutch edition, pp. 313–337; English translation of the *Enchiridion*, pp. 293–321.
9 The *BRN* edition includes this sentence in the preceding paragraph.

of God, and thus be prepared with penitent heart to accept Jesus Christ the only Saviour and by his grace and merit alone seek and hope for salvation (I Peter 5:6; I Tim. 2:6; Eph. 2:13; Acts 15:8).

[389] Inasmuch then as the law teaches the knowledge of sin and as from such knowledge comes the fear of the Lord, which is the beginning of all wisdom (Rom. 7:7; Ecclesiasticus 1:16), without which no man may be justified, and as from the fear of the Lord comes a broken and contrite and humbled heart, which is acceptable to the Lord (Ps. 51:10), therefore the law serves or is conducive in part to, the new birth, in view of the fact that no one can be born again or spiritually quickened and no one can believe the gospel, except he first sincerely repent, as the Lord Jesus Christ himself testifies (Matt. 3:2); for he taught the people repentance first of all, and then faith, and so he also commanded his apostles to do (Luke 24:47).

But the gospel is the word of grace. It is the joyful message of Jesus Christ, the only begotten Son of God, the only Redeemer and Saviour (I Tim. 2:5; Titus 2:14) who gave himself for us that we might be ransomed from the power of Satan, sin, and eternal death, and made us children and heirs of our Heavenly Father, to be a royal priesthood (Gal. 1:4; Heb. 2:15; Rom. 8:14; Eph. 1:5), to be a holy people and an elect race and a possession of God in the Spirit (I Peter 2:9). Therefore he also says in the gospel (Matt. 11:28–30): Come unto me, all ye that are heavy laden, and I will give you rest. Learn of me; for I am humble and meek in heart. Take my yoke upon you, for my burden is light and my yoke is easy. Again (John 5:24): Verily, verily, I say unto you: He that heareth my word, and keepeth it, hath everlasting life, and shall not come into condemnation; but is passed from death unto life; (John 11:25 f.): I am the resurrection, and the life; he that believeth in me, though he were dead, yet shall he live: and whosoever liveth and believeth in me shall never die; again (John 3:16–18): God sent not his Son into the world to condemn the world; but that the world through him might be saved. . . .

This is the true gospel, the pure doctrine of our God, full of grace and mercy, full of comfort, salvation, and eternal life, given to us by God from grace without our merits and works of the law, for the sake of the only eternal and precious Saviour Jesus Christ, who made himself [390] subject to the law for our sakes and became the fulfillment of the law unto eternal salvation for all believers, if it be that we accept it in true faith. . . .

Now, all who from the teaching of the law learn to fear God, recognize sin, sincerely repent, turn away from their sinful life and godless being and with penitent heart believe the gospel and accept Jesus Christ as their Saviour (Matt. 3:8; Mark 1:5; Luke 3:8) are born anew of God by his eternal Word (I Peter 1:23) in the power of his Holy Spirit, by whom they are renewed and also sealed unto the day of their redemption; and they have free access to God and to the throne of grace by faith in Jesus Christ (James 1:18; Eph. 4:30; Heb. 5:3, Rom. 3:24). Here the law, which once condemned, now becomes silent. Here are silenced the peals of thunder, the earthquake, the storms, and the dreadful manifestations on Mount Sinai (Ex. 19:16). Here shines a clearer light of the gospel and the Sun of righteousness into believing hearts (John 3:19; 12:46), here is an entirely new man, a new heart, mind, and feeling (*Ghemoet*), a child of God, and an heir of the Kingdom of Heaven convenantcd (*verbonden*) with God, born anew of God, strengthened by his power and ready for everlasting life (Wisdom of Solomon 5:6).

And that is the spiritual rebirth out of God's Word wherein we get or receive that lost image of [391] the knowledge of God, of his will, and that image of the divine righteousness whereby we are able to stand before God through Christ. And this is the will of God and the right ordinance of the Lord that thus we should be born again by the Word of God and grow daily in the knowledge of God, in faith, in love (Eph. 4:15), and proceed in all obedience to the Word of God, to the praise of the Lord, and to our salvation (Matt. 10:22).

[b. The Knowledge of the Triune God]

Of necessity connected with this rebirth is a true knowledge of the one God, that is, of the Father, Son, and Holy Spirit (Matt. 28:19; I John 5:8). The Father is the fountain spring of all good (Ex. 3:6), the Essence of all things, the Creator of all being, the eternal, invisible God, who dwelleth in light (as the apostle says, I Tim. 6:16) which no man can approach unto; whom also no one hath seen, neither Moses on Mount Sinai nor John the Baptist at the Jordan, nor the apostles on Mount Tabor, nor Paul in the third heaven (Ex. 20:21; Matt. 3:16; 17:5; II Cor. 12:1–8). But in a devout and pious condition of mind believers have always beheld and confessed God in Christ Jesus, who is the image of the invisible God, the brightness of his glory, the mirror of his divine clarity, the only begotten of the Father, the Word, by whom all things are made, in whom is life, the Life that is the light of men (II Cor. 4:4; Col. 1:15; Heb. 1:3; Wisdom of Solomon 7:26; John 1:3), and which has come into the world and shineth into the darkness, and the darkness has not comprehended that light. This Word was made flesh, was received in the maiden Mary from the Holy Spirit, and was born of her a Son of the Most High (Matt. 1:18; Luke 2:7), but the world did not comprehend the great mystery that God has been revealed in the flesh (I Tim. 3:16), that wisdom has appeared upon the earth (Baruch 3:20–23), and that the Word of life has become man (I John 1:1 f.), and has yet remained the Word of life; for since he was to be the Mediator between God and man, and also make reconciliation between us and the Father (I Tim. 2:5; Eph. 2:16; Col. 1:20), therefore he had to be both God and man in one person. Inasmuch as he was to take away the sin of the world (John 1:29) and with his righteousness make nought all unrighteousness and to swallow death (I John 3:14; I Cor. 15:34; Heb. 2:15; Jer. 21:8; John 14:6), therefore he had to be himself righteousness, eternal life, and salvation. Again inasmuch as he was to give his flesh for the life of the world, therefore his flesh had to make alive. For this reason Christ himself calls his flesh the bread of life, that came down from heaven (John 6:33); therefore it is not of the earth, nor of the flesh and blood of any mortal man.[10]

10 In the foregoing paragraph Philips becomes as explicit as anywhere in this tract concerning his adaptation of the Melchiorite doctrine of the celestial flesh of Christ. His thought at this point may be amplified with the following excerpt from another tract in the *Enchiridion*, namely, *Van der Menschwerdinghe, BRN*, X, pp. 140 f.:

"But if the body of Christ had been made by Mary (as the world thinks and says with such want of understanding regarding it), then there would be no difference between the body of Christ and that of Adam, because like as Christ was conceived of the Holy Spirit in Mary, so also Adam was made by God and had no other Father than God. What difference would there be, then, between the body of Christ and the body of Adam, if the body of Christ had been made of the earth, the same as the body of Adam? . . . Far from it! God, the Heavenly Father, prepared for Jesus Christ, his only begotten Son, a body (Heb. 10:5), but not of corrupt human seed (Luke 1:35), rather of his incorruptible seed, with which he caused Mary, the pure virgin, to conceive through the power of his Holy Spirit. . . . Therefore Christ everywhere testifies that he came down from heaven, but he speaks of his origin especially in John 6:51. . . .

"Now, if Christ is the bread of heaven, and if the bread of heaven, moreover, is the flesh of Christ, it is impossible for the flesh of Christ to

[392] In this great work of redemption, by which God redeemed the lost human race, there is represented to us and set before our eyes the picture of divine majesty, wisdom, righteousness, mercy, and friendliness, in this that God sent his only begotten Son (who was in the divine form) in the form of sinful flesh (Phil. 2:6), made him subject to the law, made him to be sin, and cast him under the curse. And he who was immortal, yea, he who rules all things with his powerful word, became weak and mortal (Gal. 4:4; Rom 8:3; II Cor. 5:21; Gal. 3:13; Heb. 1:3); nevertheless he rose again from the dead, and by his divine power he overcame all his enemies (Rom. 4:25; I Cor. 15:25).

This is not the wisdom of the world, nor yet of the angels in heaven, but is the wisdom of God, hidden in mystery, which was preached by the apostles, not with words of human cleverness, but with such words as the Holy Spirit taught them (I Cor. 2:6). That is also the stern, exalted, and courageous (*dappere*), yea, eternal, righteousness of God that he inflicted punishment and expiation for our sins (which could be redeemed and taken away by no other means) on his own beloved Son with such severity that it is [clearly] not [of] human love and mercy but [of] God's eternal love, God's fathomless grace and mercy,[11] that Jesus Christ died for us when we were yet sinners, godless, and enemies of God (Isa. 53:9; I Peter 2:24; Gal. 1:4; Rom. 5:8). This is the mystery of godliness (I Tim. 3:16) that is so great and so wonderful, of which Paul writes (I Cor. 2:10), that it cannot be apprehended except by the Holy Spirit, which searches all things, yea, the deep things of God. And since the world cannot receive the Holy Spirit (as Christ himself says, John 14:17, because it sees him not, neither knows him), therefore also it does not understand the mystery of godliness in its power. It does not rightly know Jesus Christ and does not believe in him, as the Scripture testifies (John 7:27; I John 2:22). But some deny his true divinity, some argue against his holy, spotless humanity, and some reject his salvation—godly teachings, etc.

The Holy Spirit is the third name, person, power, and

be formed of the seed of Mary; for neither the seed of Mary, nor that of any earthly creature can by any means be the true living bread that came down from heaven, or be so called."

11 The doctrine of the celestial origin of the flesh or humanity of Christ (cf. n. 10 above) intensifies the divine as distinguished from the human action in the atonement.

operation in the Godhead, one divine being with the Father and the Son (Matt. 28:19); for he proceeds from the Father through [393] the Son and also with them wrought creation, and he is the Spirit of truth, a Comforter of the conscience (I John 5:8; John 16:13), and a Dispenser of all spiritual gifts (I Cor. 12:1, 11), which are poured out by God the Father through Jesus Christ and infused into the hearts of believers by which they are enlightened, renewed, and sanctified (Titus 3:6; I Cor. 6:11) and become a possession of God (Eph. 1:14), and new creatures in Christ, and saved unto everlasting life, and without whom no one knows God, nor believes in Jesus Christ (I Cor. 12:3), since all good gifts come from the eternal Father (II Cor. 5:16; Gal. 6:18; James 1:17), and are divided to us by the Holy Spirit (Matt. 7:11).

The Father, Son, and Holy Spirit, then, is the only true and living God and Lord (Isa. 40:28; 42:5), beside whom there is no other God and Lord, neither in heaven nor upon earth; the first and the last, the only, eternal, wise and just God, Redeemer and Saviour (Rev. 1:17; 22:13). And this knowledge of God must exist in connection with the new birth, in a good conscience with true faith from the Word of God (John 3:36), comprehended by the enlightenment of the Holy Spirit, of which we have written at more length at another place,[12] and of such reborn people and new creatures Jesus Christ has gathered his congregation, and for them he has set up several ordinances[13] and has given several commandments which they must keep, and thereby be known as his congregation.

[II. THE SEVEN ORDINANCES OF THE TRUE CHURCH]

The *first ordinance* is that the congregation above all other things must have the pure and unfalsified doctrine of the divine Word (Matt. 28:19 f.) and along with it correct ministers (*Dienaers*); both are regularly called and chosen by the Lord and the congregation of the Lord. What the true and plain Word of God is and that it is twofold, namely, the law and the

---

12 The reference is apparently to *The True Knowledge of Jesus Christ* and especially to *Of Regeneration*.
13 There are seven such ordinances. These may be related to the traditional seven gifts of the Holy Spirit (Isaiah 11:2 in Septuagint and Vulgate). The seven ordinances are placed in polemical parallelism to the seven sacraments. Sebastian Franck in his letter to Campanus (see p. 148) refers to the seven orders of the Catholic Church prescribed by (Pseudo-) Jerome.

gospel, we have already explained above. Likewise as to the manner in which the calling, choosing, and ordaining of the true ministers is to take place, Scripture teaches us very clearly [where it speaks of] the calling of the prophets by God, the sending forth of the apostles by Jesus Christ (John 20:21), and the ordaining of the elders by the Holy Spirit and the Christian congregation, through the united, common (*gelijcke*) voice, over the flock of God [394] to pasture and to tend them (Matt. 10:1; Acts 13:2; 20:28; I Tim. 3:2–7; Titus 1:5 ff.).[14] And we have in our booklet *On the Sending of Preachers*[15] explained this very well, in part, and therefore here again say only briefly that the true ministers of the divine Word are easily recognized by the saving teachings of Jesus Christ, by their godly walk, and by the fruits which they bear, and moreover by the persecution which they must suffer for the sake of truth and righteousness. For whoever speaks the Lord's Word is sent of God (John 3:34), and he that doeth righteousness is born of God (I John 2:29), and he that converts men from unrighteousness to the living God remains in the counsel of God and declares to the people the Lord's Word (Jer. 23:3), and he that is persecuted because he teaches and bears witness to the truth fares just as the Scripture says, and as all good prophets and apostles, yea, as the Lord himself fared (Matt. 5:11, 12; 10:22–25; 12:14; 21:46; John 15:19).

Again, how the ministers are ordained and how they must be sent may be well observed and noted from the Old Testament figures of Aaron and his children. . . .

Aaron and his children [are] as a figure pointing to the reality, to the teachers in the congregation of God, especially so far as the sons of Aaron are concerned. For Aaron is really a figure of Jesus Christ, our only High Priest (Heb. 2:17; 5:6; 8:1; 10:11). Nevertheless, in view of the fact that Christ sends forth his ministers, even as the Father sent him (John 20:21), it follows that the ministers of Jesus Christ and of his holy Word must be conformed to his image (Rom. 8:28 f.). Hence the figure of Aaron and his children [395] may properly be understood, according to the Spirit, to mean that the ministers of Christ who preach his Word and proclaim his gospel must be washed

14 Note the Triune sanction of the threefold ministry of prophet, apostle (emissary), and elder (all called *Dienaers*).
15 *Of the Sending of Preachers or Teachers*, first published as a separate booklet in 1559, incorporated into the *Enchiridion*, critical Dutch edition, *BRN*, pp. 205–248; English translation, pp. 173–221.

with the pure water of the Holy Spirit and sprinkled with the precious blood of the spotless Lamb Jesus Christ who offered himself for us (Heb. 10:18–22; John 1:29; I Peter 1:24), first on the right ear, that the ears of their understanding may be opened to hear what God speaks to them; secondly, on the thumb of their right hand (Heb. 12:12 f.), that they may lift up holy hands to God (I Tim. 2:8); and thirdly, on the great toe of their right foot, that they may walk uprightly before the Lord, in the way of righteousness. They must put on the holy garments, that is, they must be clothed with Christ Jesus (Rom. 13:14; Gal. 3:27; Eph. 6:11), girded with the band of love and of truth, and adorned with the silk of righteousness (Rev. 19:8). The breastplate with Urim and Thummim and with the twelve precious stones must be hung on them, that is, they must have the treasure of the divine Word in their hearts, for they are ministers of the Lord (Gal. 6:16) over the spiritual Israel in order to teach Jacob the judgments of God and Israel his law (Deut. 33:10). The cap with the golden frontlet of the holy crown is upon their head, that is, they rightly divide the Word of God between the Old and New Testaments, between the letter and the Spirit, with a clear understanding of the divine mystery (Matt. 13:52; I Tim. 3:9; Eph. 6:19). They have also a living hope of salvation, and there is laid up for them the crown of righteousness for that day (II Tim. 4:8). They enter the sanctuary of God (Rom. 12:1; I Peter 2:5), and their prayers ring out and are heard by the Most High, so that he remembers his congregation. The anointing oil is poured out upon them, for they have received the anointing of him who is holy, and they are thereby sanctified (I John 2:27) . . . [396]. . . .

The *second ordinance* which Christ established in his congregation is the proper, Scriptural use of the sacraments of Jesus Christ, that is, of baptism and the Supper. For the penitent, believing and reborn children of God must be baptized and for them the Supper of the Lord pertains (Matt. 3:16; 28:19; Mark 1:9; Acts 2:41; 8:12; 10:48; 16:15; 18:8; 22:16). These two symbols Christ gave and left behind and subjoined to the gospel because of the unspeakable grace of God and his covenant, to remind us thereof with visible symbols, to put it before our eyes, and to confirm it. In the first place [he ordained] baptism, to remind us that he himself baptizes within and in grace accepts sinners, forgives them all their sins, cleanses them with his blood (Matt. 3:11; John 3:5), bestows upon them all his righteousness and the fulfilling of the law, and sanctifies them with his Spirit (Rev. 1:5; I Cor. 3:23). In the second place, [he ordained] the Lord's Supper, which testifies to the truth of the divine acceptance and redemption by Jesus Christ (Matt. 26:26–28; Mark 14:22; Luke 22:19); namely, that all believing hearts, who are sorry for their sins, hasten to the throne of grace (Jesus Christ), believe and confess that the Son of God died for us and has shed his blood (Rom. 3:25; 4:25; 8:3), do obtain forgiveness of sin, deliverance from the law, and everlasting justification and salvation by grace without the merits of works through Jesus Christ (Gal. 3:13; Eph. 1:7; Rom. 11:6).[16]

These two tokens [baptism and the Supper] are left us by the Lord that they might admonish us to a godly walk (Col. 2:6; Rom. 16:18), to a mortification of the flesh, to a burial of sin, to a resurrection into the new life, to thanksgiving for the great benefits which have been given us by God, to a remembrance of the bitter suffering and death of Christ, and to the renewing and confirming of brotherly love, unity, and fellowship (Matt. 26:26; Mark 14:23; Luke 22:20; I Cor. 10:17; 11:25);

16 The thought of the writer may be amplified at this point with the following excerpt from another part of the *Enchiridion*, p. 140. It is the immediate sequel of the matter similarly introduced above, at n. 10.

"Christ says much, according to John, of the eating of his flesh and the drinking of his blood. It, therefore, behooves us to see and consider, how the flesh of Christ shall and must be eaten and his blood drunk, namely, thus, that we accept and obey the Word of God with pure hearts and in true faith. Why do we eat the flesh of Christ and drink his blood? Because God's Word was made flesh, and hence the Word of God and the flesh of Christ are one and the same, as Christ himself shows with these words (John 6:51): I am the living bread which came down from heaven; and the bread that I will give is my flesh, which I will give for the life of the world. And the living bread (which is Christ and his flesh) is beyond all doubt and contradiction the Word of God, and therefore if any man believes and obeys the word of God, receives Christ, the Word of life and the bread of heaven, yea, he eats the flesh and drinks the blood of Christ. And because of this, Jesus calls his flesh 'meat indeed,' and his blood, 'drink indeed,' because the Word of God is really meat for the soul. But inasmuch as the Word was made flesh (John 1:14), and therefore the Word and the flesh of Christ are the same, therefore also the flesh of Christ is meat indeed, and his blood drink indeed.

"Lastly: Christ Jesus is the living bread which came like dew or manna from heaven, and what was the food of angels has also become the food of men (Ps. 78:25). But the bread, which he is himself, and gives men—that is, believers—to eat, is his flesh, which he has given for the life of the world."

The close connection between Christology and the Eucharist is apparent. Cf. Schwenckfeld, Selection VIII.

again, that they should distinguish the congregation of God from all other sects, who do not make right Scriptural use of the sacramental symbols of the Lord Jesus Christ, although they have the appearance of doing so, and in their hypocrisy profess much about them, and commit and perpetrate shameful sacrilege therewith. For they do not use the sacraments of Jesus Christ according to his Word, nor according to his command and example, nor according to the precepts and practices of the apostles, but according to the world's establishment and the ideas of men. Besides this, they remain impenitent in the old sinful life [397], full of unrighteousness, covetousness, uncleanness, pride, envy, slander, and all manner of wickedness, which is a sure evidence that they have not the pure Word of God and the true faith, with the proper use of baptism and the Supper of Jesus Christ according to the Scripture. For wherever the gospel that is testified to with such solemn vows of God, confirmed by the precious blood of Jesus Christ, and sealed by the Holy Spirit, is rightly taught and believed, and the sacraments of the Lord are thereupon regularly (*ordineerlijck*) received with true faith in heartfelt devotion and meditation upon the mysteries which are hidden therein, as this should be done, there the Spirit of God comes into the heart, there he renews daily the lost image of God, there he imparts the knowledge of the Father in his image, Christ, there he increases faith, hope, love, patience, and all the virtues of God (Heb. 6:3; Gen. 15:18; 17:7; John 3:16; 5:43; Acts 2:46; Titus 3:5; Eph. 4:23; Rom. 3:24; John 15:10; Gal. 4:5). Again he comforts the consciences, cleanses the hearts and makes them fruitful in the knowledge of God and Christ and endows them with all manner of spiritual wisdom and understanding in heavenly things. He gives boldness to the mind to call upon God and to address the exalted majesty of God, saying, Abba, dear Father (Col. 1:9; Rom. 8:15; Gal. 4:5, 6). He teaches true humility, meekness, patience, kindness, and brings the peace of God to the conscience (Gal. 5:22). Here, then, the adversary, the devil, must flee; here the flesh is crucified with its lusts and desires (James 4:7; Gal. 6:14, 16); here by the power of faith in Jesus Christ the world lies trodden under feet (I John 5:4). Where this does not take place and cannot be seen, there is neither God, nor Christ, nor Holy Spirit, nor gospel, nor faith, nor true baptism, nor the Lord's Supper. In short, there is no congregation of God.

The *third ordinance* is the foot washing of the saints, which

Jesus Christ commanded his disciples to observe, and this for two reasons. First, he would have us know that he himself must cleanse us after the inner man, and that we must allow him to wash away the sins which beset us (Heb. 12:1) and all filthiness of the flesh and the spirit, that we may become purer from day to day, as it is written (Rev. 22:11): He who is pure let him be even purer; he who is holy, let him be even more holy, and he who is righteous, let him be even more righteous, and this is necessary, yea, it must be done, if we would be saved; therefore Christ says to Peter (John 13:8, 10): If I wash thee not, thou hast no part with me. Then [398] Peter answered: Lord, not my feet only, but also my hands and my head. To this Jesus replied: He that is washed needeth not save to wash his feet, and is clean every whit. By this Christ makes it evident that the washing of feet (wherewith Christ washes us) is very necessary, and what it signifies, inasmuch as those whom he does not wash shall have no part with him, and that those who have been washed by him need no more than that their feet be washed, and they are wholly clean, for it is Christ who must cleanse us from our sins with his blood. And he that is sprinkled and washed therewith needs have no more than that the earthly members, the evil lusts and desires of the flesh, be mortified and overcome through the Spirit; and by grace he is wholly clean and no sin is imputed to him (Rom. 3:24; Eph. 1:4–7; Col. 3:5; I John 1:7; Rev. 1:5; Rom. 8:13).

The second reason why Jesus instituted foot washing is that we should humble ourselves toward one another (Rom. 12:10; Phil. 2:3; I Peter 5:5; James 4:10, 11), and that we should hold our fellow believers in the highest respect, for the reason that they are the saints of God and members of the body of Jesus Christ, and that the Holy Spirit dwells in them (Rom. 12:10; Col. 3:13; I Cor. 3:16). This Jesus teaches us in these words (John 13:13–17): Ye call me Master and Lord: and also ye say well: for so I am. If I then, your Lord and Master, have washed your feet, ye also ought to wash one another's feet. For I have given you an example, that ye should do as I have done to you. Verily, verily, I say unto you, The servant is not greater than his lord; neither the apostle greater than he that sent him. If ye know these things, happy are ye if ye do them. Now, if they are happy or blessed who know and do this, how void of blessing those remain who profess to be apostles or messengers of the Lord and do not know these things; or, if they know, do not do them, nor teach others to do them. But their heart is altogether too proud and puffed up, so that they will not humble themselves according to the command and example of Christ. Because of this they are either ashamed to do so, or else it appears like folly to them (exactly as the divine wisdom has always been looked upon by the world as foolishness, I Cor. 1:18-21; 3:19). But they greatly prefer to have the honor of men—they love to be called Doctors, Masters, and Sirs (John 5:44)—rather than the honor that comes from God, which is obtained by upright faith and a holy conduct. This they do not aspire to, yet they want [399] to be the church of Christ and be so known, yea, held exclusively as such. But God, who resisteth the proud and giveth grace to the humble (I Peter 5:5; James 4:10), knows them well and will at the last day reveal what kind of assembly or congregation (yea, I might more properly say sect) they have been.

The *fourth ordinance* is evangelical separation, without which the congregation of God cannot stand or be maintained. For if the unfruitful branches of the vine are not pruned away they will injure the good and fruitful branches (John 15:6). If offending members are not cut off, the whole body must perish (Matt. 5:30; 18:7-9), that is, if open sinners, transgressors, and the disorderly are not excluded, the whole congregation must be defiled (I Cor. 5:13; I Thess. 5:14), and if false brethren are retained, we become partakers of their sins. Of this we have many examples and evidences in the Scripture (II John 10 f.).

In Joshua we have the terrible example of Achan, who had stolen some of the condemned goods in Jericho and hidden them in his tent. Because of this the Lord's anger was stirred against Israel, so that he permitted a number in Israel to be slain in battle, and among other things he said to Joshua (ch. 7:12): The Children of Israel could not stand before their enemies, but turned their backs before their enemies, because they were under the ban: neither will I be with you any more, unless ye destroy the ban[ned] from among you. Therefore Achan and all that belonged to him were destroyed and rooted out of Israel. And Joshua (ch. 7:25) said to him: Seeing thou hast troubled us, the Lord must trouble thee this day, etc.

We have likewise in Numbers (ch. 16:11) a notable example in Dathan, Abiram, and Korah, who set themselves up against Moses and Aaron, and many of the most prominent or esteemed in Israel took their part. But Moses said to the congregation of the Lord (Num. 16:26): Depart from the tents or tabernacles of these godless men, and touch nothing that belongs to them, lest ye be consumed in all of their sins.

From such and like historical incidents and examples given in Holy Writ it may be easily observed and understood that no congregation or assembly can be maintained before God that [400] does not properly and earnestly exercise the ban or separation according to the command of Christ and the teaching and example of the apostles, but that they will fare according to the common proverb that (I Cor. 5:6) a little leaven leaveneth the whole lump, and that one scabby sheep contaminates the whole flock; yea (Hos. 4:9): Like the priest or the prophet, so also is the people.

Separation or exclusion must also be practiced for the reason that thereby the offender may be chastised in the flesh and be made ashamed, and so may repent that he may be saved in the day of the Lord Jesus (I Cor. 5:5), which is the highest love, and the very best mastery or medicine for his poor soul, as may be observed in the case of the Corinthian fornicator. Moreover, necessity demands that there be a separation from apostates and wicked persons, that the name of God, the gospel of Jesus Christ, and the congregation of the Lord be not on their account put to shame (Ps. 50:21; Ezek. 36:20–24; Rom. 2:24).

Now, what those sins are which must be punished with the ban are shown us by the Evangelists and apostles in express words (Matt. 18:13–17; Rom. 16:17; I Cor. 5:10; I Thess. 5:14; I Tim. 3:1–7; Titus 3:10; II John 10), and we have also in our confession[17] regarding the evangelical ban carefully explained it. And what the congregation of the Lord determines with his Word, the same is judged[18] before God, for Christ gave his congregation the keys of the Kingdom of Heaven (Matt. 16:19) that they might punish, exclude, and put away the wicked, and receive the penitent and believing. What the congregation binds upon earth shall be bound in heaven, and,

---

17 The reference is to *A Loving Admonition*, first published separately, 1558, and taken up into the *Enchiridion* as Book Six; critical edition, *BRN*, pp. 250 ff.; English edition, pp. 223 ff. Philips also wrote another work with the title *A Plain Presentation of the Evangelical Ban and Shunning*, first published in French and after his death in Dutch, critical edition, *BRN*, pp. 657 ff.; English edition, pp. 519 ff. Since Philips here calls his work specifically Evangelical, he may well refer to the French-Dutch work which at the time circulated in manuscript. Cf. Menno, Selection XII with its greater stress on New Testament practice.
18 In the sense of "confirmed."

on the other hand, what they loose on earth shall be loosed in heaven. This must not be understood as meaning that men have power to forgive sins or to retain them (John 20:23), as some imagine and assume, and therefore deal with the confessional and absolution as with merchandise. But no minister of Christ is to do this, neither is the congregation of the Lord to permit any simony (Acts 8:9, 13, 18), for to no prophet or apostle on earth has it been given to forgive sin, to hear confession, and to absolve the people, although Christ said to his disciples (John 20:22 f.): Receive ye the Holy Spirit: whosoever sins ye remit, they are remitted unto them; and whosoever sins ye retain, they are retained. The holy men of God did not [401] assume divine honor, but were perfectly conscious of the fact, through the prompting of the Holy Spirit, that God alone forgives sin, as the Scripture unanimously testifies. But the congregation has received the Holy Spirit and the gospel from Jesus Christ (Isa. 43:25; Matt. 9:6; Ps. 51:4) in which is proclaimed and promised forgiveness of sins, reconciliation with God, and eternal life to all who truly repent and believe in Jesus Christ. On the other hand, disfavor, wrath, and damnation are threatened and promised toward all unbelievers, disobedient and perverted ones.

This word, together with the Holy Spirit, is the judge in the congregation over all false brethren (Titus 3:10), over all heretical people (Rom. 10:16) and all disorderly and disobedient persons who after sufficient warning do not better themselves; and on the Judgment Day no other sentence will be pronounced, as the Lord himself says (John 12:48). And this word the congregation has received from God, by which, in the name of Jesus Christ, and in the power of the Holy Spirit, it testifies, judges, receives, and expels, and what it thus binds or looses on earth with the Word and Spirit of the Lord is bound or loosed in heaven.

The *fifth ordinance* is the command of love which Christ gave his disciples, saying (John 13:34, 35; 15:12, 17): A new commandment I give unto you, that ye love one another, as I have loved you, that ye also love one another. By this shall all men know that ye are my disciples, if ye have love to another. From this it is easy to understand that pure brotherly love is a sure sign of genuine faith and true Christianity. But this is true brotherly love, that our chief desire is one another's salvation, by our fervent prayers to God, by Scriptural instruction, admonition, and rebuke, that thereby we may instruct him who is overtaken in a fault, in order to win his soul. And all this [we do] with Christian patience (Gal. 6:3; II Thess. 1:11; James 5:19; I John 5:16), having forbearance toward the weak and not simply pleasing ourselves.

Then again brotherly love is shown in this, that among ourselves we serve one another by benevolently reaching out our hand, not only with spiritual, but also with temporal, gifts, which we have received from God, that we take it upon ourselves to give richly according to our ability because of the needs [402] of the saints (Rom. 12:13); yea, that it be done among us as it was done under the literal Israel, namely, he that gathered much manna had nothing over, and he that gathered little had no lack (Ex. 16:18; II Cor. 8:15). Thus then, the rich, who have received many temporal possessions from the Lord, are to minister to the poor therewith (Rom. 15:27; II Cor. 8:9) and supply their lack, so that the poor in turn may come to their aid as they have need. Therefore Christ says, in the Gospel (Luke 16:9): Make to yourselves friends of the mammon of unrighteousness; that, when ye fail, they may receive you into everlasting habitations. And Paul writes to Timothy (I Tim. 6:17–19): Charge them that are rich in this world, that they be not high-minded, nor trust in uncertain riches, but in the living God, who giveth us richly all things to enjoy; that they be communal (*gemeynsaem*), that they give gladly in order that they lay up a treasure for the future, that they may obtain eternal life. And John writes in his epistle (I John 3:16–18): Hereby perceive we the love of God, because he laid down his life for us: and we ought to lay down our lives for the brethren. But whoso hath this world's good, and seeth his brother have need, and shutteth up his heart from him, how dwelleth the love of God in him? My little children, let us not love in word, neither in tongue; but in deed and in truth. How necessary love is, the apostles show us everywhere in all their writings, especially Paul to the Corinthians (I, ch. 13:1–4). . . .

From this it may be easily understood how widely those differ from the upright faith and Christianity who do not love one another, who do not prove their love toward one another by their works, but allow their poor to suffer want and openly beg for bread, against the command of the Lord (Deut. 15:4; Rom. 12:13; II Cor. 8:14; Gal. 6:8), contrary to all Christian nature and contrary to brotherly love and fidelity. And, what is worse, they trespass upon, hate, envy, backbite, defame, scold, blaspheme, persecute, throttle, and kill one another, as is seen before our eyes and as their deeds amply show; and although they do this, nevertheless they want to be called Christians and the congregation of God. But if they do not repent, they will find out, on that day when they appear before the judgment seat of Jesus Christ, what fine Christians they have been. For where love is not, God is not, seeing that God is love (I John 4:8), as John (ch. 4:16; 2:11) says: He that dwelleth in love dwelleth in God, and God in him. But he that dwelleth not in love is in darkness, and walketh in darkness, and knoweth not whither he goeth, because that darkness hath blinded his eyes.

The *sixth ordinance* which Christ has instituted for his congregation is the keeping of all his commandments (Matt. 28:20); for he demands of all his disciples a godly life, that they walk according to the gospel, openly confess the truth before men (I Cor. 7:19; Phil. 1:27; Matt. 10:32), deny self, and faithfully follow in his footsteps (Matt. 16:25; I Peter 2:21), voluntarily take up his cross, forsake all things, and earnestly seek first the Kingdom of God and his righteousness (Matt. 6:16, 20), the unseen heavenly things, and eternal life. He also teaches his disciples to be poor in spirit (Matt. 5:3, 11), have godly sorrow, meekness, purity of heart, mercy, peacemaking, patience in persecution for righteousness' sake, and happiness of conscience when they are despised and rejected for his name's sake (Luke 9:24; 17:33). He also instructs his own in true humility and warns them faithfully against all spiritual and carnal pride. Moreover, he holds before them the fact that they must hear and keep God's Word, hunger and thirst after righteousness, beware of false prophets (Luke 8:14; John 8:47; Matt. 5:6), follow not the hireling, and should flee from the strange voice (Matt. 16:6; John 10:12); also that they are to fast, and to pray without ceasing, that they are to guard against overabundance of food, drunkenness, and anxiety regarding temporal nourishment (Matt. 6:5; Luke 21:34); that they must watch, and prepare for his appearing (Matt. 24:32; 25:13), and they must beware of the leaven of the Pharisees, which is hypocrisy (Matt. 16:6), so that they will not glory in their own works and seek a false righteousness therein; that they shall not watch for the mote in their brother's eye and not be aware of the beam in their own eye (Matt. 7:3); also, not swallow camels while they strain at gnats (Matt. 23:24); etc. Yea, he prescribes to his own the rule of perfection (Matt. 5:48), how they [404] must love their enemies, do good for them who do them evil, pray for their persecutors, bless those who curse them (Matt. 5:44), and from the heart forgive their debtors just as they desire forgiveness from God for their debt; and avenge not themselves, but leave the matter to God (Rom. 12:19).

Also, they are not only to guard against the works of the flesh which are manifest, such as murder, adultery, false swearing, etc., but also against anger, bitter words, inordinate lusts unbecoming of the heart, and they are to guard against all kinds of swearing, and not do this in any manner, on pain of hell-fire, as may be seen in Matthew (ch. 5). The apostles likewise teach in their epistles that Christians must in all things show themselves obedient children of their Heavenly Father as the elect and chosen ones of a holy God (Col. 3:12; I Peter 1:1; II Cor. 6:4), as the servants[19] of the Lord Jesus Christ, as the instruments of the Holy Spirit, as a royal priesthood (I Peter 2:9), as a chosen generation, a peculiar people, zealous of good works (Eph. 5:27; Titus 2:14), as the children of light, who must walk no longer in darkness, but in the light, having been called out of darkness into the wonderful light that they might declare the power of God, and are therefore delivered from the hand of their enemies to serve God in holiness and in righteousness all the days of their lives (Luke 1:70 ff.).

This is the heavenly philosophy, which Jesus Christ, the Son of God, received of his Father, brought down from heaven, and taught his disciples. This is the counsel and will of God, the saving doctrine of Jesus Christ (Acts 20:27), and the testimony of the Holy Spirit; and in all this the Lord Jesus Christ is to his own a master sent of God, whom they must hear (Matt. 3:17; 17:5); a leader (*Voorganger*), whom they must follow (I Peter 2:25); an example, to which they must conform (Rom. 8:29). This is the rule of Christianity, of which Paul writes (Gal. 6:16): As many as walk according to this rule, peace be unto them, and mercy, and upon the Israel of God. But those who will not walk according to this rule are not Christians, let them profess what they will.

The *seventh ordinance* is that all Christians must suffer and be persecuted, as Christ has promised them and said thus (John 16:33): The world shall have joy, but ye shall have tribulation: but be of good cheer, for your sorrow shall be turned into joy; again (Matt. 24:9): Ye [405] shall be hated by everyone for my name's sake; again (John 16:2): The time cometh, that

19 The word here is normally translated in this text "ministers" (*Dienaers*) and might be so rendered here.

whosoever killeth you will think that he doeth God service. Paul concurs with this and says (Rom. 8:17): If so be that we suffer with him, we shall also be glorified together, and inherit our Heavenly Father's Kingdom; again (II Tim. 2:12; 3:12): All that will live godly in Christ Jesus shall suffer persecution. Again Paul and Barnabas testified (Acts 13:50) in all the congregation that they must through much persecution and suffering enter the Kingdom of Heaven. In short, the entire Holy Scripture testifies that the righteous must suffer and possess his soul through suffering (Luke 21:19). Where there is a pious Abel, there does not fail to be a wicked Cain (Gen. 4:1 f.); where there is a chosen David, there is also a rejected Saul to persecute him (I Sam. 18:11); where Christ is born, there is a Herod who seeks his life (Matt. 2:16); where he openly preaches and works, there Annas and Caiaphas, together with the bloodthirsty Jews, gather together and hold counsel against him (Matt. 26:3 f.; Mark 14:1; Luke 22:1; Acts 4:6), nor can they cease until they have killed him and force Pilate to do their will.

Thus must the true Christians here be persecuted for the sake of truth and righteousness, but the Christians persecute no one on account of his faith. For Christ sends his disciples as sheep in the midst of wolves (Matt. 10:16); but the sheep does not devour the wolf, but the wolf the sheep. Hence they can nevermore stand nor be counted as a congregation of the Lord who persecute others on account of their faith. For, in the first place, God, the Heavenly Father, has committed all judgment unto Jesus Christ (John 5:22), to be a judge of the souls and consciences of men and to rule in his congregation with the scepter of his word forever. In the second place, it is the office or work of the Holy Spirit to reprove the world for the sin of unbelief (John 16:8). Now it is evident that the Holy Spirit through the apostles and all pious witnesses of the truth did not administer this reproof by violence nor with an outward sword, but by God's word and power. In the third place, the Lord Jesus Christ gave his congregation the power and established the ordinance that she should separate, avoid, and shun the false brethren, the disorderly and disobedient, contentious and heretical people, yea, all in the congregation who are found wicked, as has already been said (Rom. 16:17; I Cor. 5:10; I Thess. 5:14; Titus 3:10); what is done over [406] and above this is not Christian, evangelical, nor apostolic. In the fourth place, the parable of the Lord in the Gospel proves clearly to us that he does not permit his servants to pull up the tares lest the wheat be pulled up also; but they are to let the wheat and the tares grow together in the world until the Lord shall command his reapers, that is, his angels, to gather the wheat into his barn and cast the tares into the fire (Matt. 13:29).

From this it is evident that no congregation of the Lord may exercise dominion over the consciences of men with the outward sword, nor seek by violence, to force unbelievers to believe, nor to kill the false prophets with sword and fire; but that she must with the Lord's Word judge and expel those in the congregation who are found wicked; and what is done over and above this is not Christian, nor evangelical, nor apostolic. And if someone ventures to assert that the powers that be have not received the sword in vain (Rom. 13:1), and that God through Moses commanded that the false prophets be put to death (Deut. 13:5), I will give this answer in brief: The higher power (*Ouerheyt*) has received the sword from God, not that it shall judge therewith in spiritual matters (for these things must be judged by the spiritual, and only spiritually, I Cor. 2:13), but to maintain the subjects in good government (*Policie*) and peace, to protect the pious and punish the evil. And that God commanded through Moses to kill the false prophets is a command of the Old, and not the New Testament. In contrast to this we have received another command from the Lord (Matt. 7:15; John 10:5; Titus 3:10) that we are to beware of false prophets, that we are not to give ear to them, that we are to shun a heretic, and thereby commit them to the judgment of God. Now, if, according to the Old Testament command, false prophets were to be put to death, then this would have to be carried out, first of all, with those who are looked upon as false prophets and antichrists by the God-fearing and understanding persons, yea, by almost the whole world. Likewise the higher powers would be obliged to put to death not only the false prophets but also all image worshipers, and those who serve idols, and who counsel other people to commit sacrilege (Ex. 22:18), and all adulterers, and all who blaspheme the name of the Lord, and who swear falsely by that name, all who curse father and mother and profane the Sabbath (Ex. 20:7; Deut. 27:16); for they are all alike condemned to death by the law as well as the false prophets are.

[407] It is therefore nothing but an effort to sew fig leaves together to hide their shame, on the part of those who would

decorate their tyranny with Scripture and propose that they do not put Christians to death, but only heretics, and that God thus commanded through Moses. Yea, the world even looks upon the most pious Christians as the most wicked heretics, just as all good prophets were always looked upon by the world as liars, agitators, demented persons, and deceivers (Jer. 11:21; Amos 2:9; Matt. 5:11; 23:30; Acts 6:14), and Christ himself was numbered with the transgressors (Mark 15:28). And the apostles are set forth as the least, and as it were, appointed unto death, made a curse of the world, and a purgatory sacrifice (*veechoffer*) of the world (Ps. 44:13 f.; I Cor. 4:9). And this is still the case with all upright Christians; but they are comforted herein. For they trust in the Lord their God and comfort themselves with the glorious promises given them by God, namely, that they are saved (Matt. 5:10 ff.), that theirs is the Kingdom of Heaven and that the Spirit of God rests upon them when they are persecuted for righteousness' sake, when men say all manner of evil against them falsely and for the sake of the name of Christ, if they have become partakers of the sufferings of Christ and for his sake are despised, knowing that they shall also be made partakers of his glory (I Peter 4:14; Rom. 8:17; II Tim. 2:12).

I have now briefly pointed out and discussed what the congregation of God is, how and by what means it is built up, what ordinances are included, by what symbols it is portrayed, how it may be recognized, and how distinguished from all sects; for in all false and anti-Christian congregations these things are not found; namely: no real new birth; no real distinction between law and gospel, that brings forth fruit, and by which people truly repent and are converted from unrighteousness unto the living God (Matt. 3:8; Luke 3:8); no true knowledge of the eternal and only God, who is life eternal, the fullness of wisdom and of righteousness, that is manifested by the keeping of the commandments of Christ (John 17:3; Wisdom of Solomon 15:3); no true confession of the pure, holy, and spotless humanity of Jesus Christ; no faith that produces fruits; no Scriptural baptism or Lord's Supper; no Christian washing of the feet of saints (John 13:5–17) in the quietness of true humility; no key to the Kingdom of Heaven; no evangelical ban or separation; no shunning of the temples (*Tempelen*) of [408] idolatry nor false worship, no unfeigned brotherly love; no God-fearing life nor keeping of the commands of Christ; no persecution for righteousness' sake. All these ordinances and evidences of true Christianity are found in no anti-Christian congregations in correct form, but everywhere the reverse and opposite, as may be clearly seen in these days, if so be that a man has eyes to see, ears to hear, and a heart to understand (Matt. 13:9; Rev. 2:7; 3:6).

[III. THE TWELVE NOTES OF THE CHURCH]

Furthermore, the congregation of the Lord is easily recognizable from its description, namely, that she is the Holy City, New Jerusalem, coming down from God out of heaven, prepared as a bride adorned for her husband (Rev. 21:2), having the glory of God: and her light is like unto a stone most precious, crystalline jasper; and has high and great walls, and has twelve gates, and at the gates twelve angels, and names written thereon, which are the names of the twelve tribes of the Children of Israel (Rev. 21:12); and the building of the wall of it is of jasper; and the city is pure gold, like unto clear glass. And the foundation of the wall and of the city is garnished with all manner of precious stones. [Here follows Rev. 21:18–27 complete except, significantly, for v. 24 b.]

[409] This is a description or lifelike portrait of the Christian congregation, how it goes on here in the first place in the Spirit, and hereafter in the perfection of heavenly existence. For, in the first place, the Holy City is the congregation, whose citizens are the Christian believers and members of the household of God (Eph. 2:19), and it is called a city for the reason that as in a city there must be concord; the citizens must hold firmly together, living and conducting themselves according to the same polity, law, and statutes, if the city is to continue to exist. So it must also be in the congregation: there must be unity of Spirit and of faith (I Cor. 1:9; 10:21; Rom. 12:16); there the same rule of the divine Word must govern the walk of its members, and the divine polity which this city has received of God must be concordantly observed. Therefore also the prophet (Ps. 122:3) declares that Jerusalem is built as a city whose citizens are united, whereby there is portrayed to us the unity of the congregation of God, of which the Scripture says much (Eph. 4:3; Col. 3:5; Gal. 3:28; John 17:11).

In the second place, the congregation is the New Jerusalem (Rev. 21:2) because all things have become new through Jesus Christ (Rom. 7:6); the oldness of the letter and of the flesh has passed away, and the upright new being of the Spirit has been ushered in by Jesus Christ (II Cor. 5:17). Jerusalem is as much as to say a vision of peace, and therefore the congregation of the Lord is the true Jerusalem, for it is at peace with God through Jesus Christ, and peace is within her walls, and no disturbers against evangelical teaching may be suffered to remain therein; for God is a God of peace in all his congregation. Christ is the Prince of Peace and has given and left with us his peace. The Holy Spirit gives peace and joy to the consciences of believers, and the apostles admonish us to this peace in all their epistles, that it get the upper hand in our hearts (Rom. 5:1; 14:8; 12:19; Heb. 12:15; Eph. 4:4; Phil. 4:1).

In the third place, this New Jerusalem has come down from heaven, for the Christians are not of this world, just as Christ also is not of this world (John 17:14), but they are born from above. Therefore also they are not carnally, but spiritually minded and by faith seek those things which are above (I John 3:6; Rom. 8:5), where Christ sitteth at the right hand of the Father (Col. 3:1). With Abraham, Isaac, and Jacob they are content to dwell in tents, and to be strangers here on earth; for they seek for a city which hath foundations [410], whose Builder and Creator is God (I Peter 1:1; 2:11; Heb. 11:10). Those who by the grace of the Lord and by the power of their faith are thus minded are the congregation of God, the Jerusalem that is above, of which Paul writes to the Galatians (ch. 4:26).

In the fourth place, the congregation is prepared as a bride adorned for her husband; for by faith she is espoused and wedded to Jesus Christ, and is the glorious, beautiful bride (Hos. 2:19; II Cor. 11:4) of the Lamb, adorned with many virtues of God and gifts of the Holy Spirit. Here is the great mystery of Christ and his congregation, of which Paul writes to the Ephesians (chs. 5:23; 1:22), namely, that Christ is the head of the congregation, flesh of his flesh, and bone of his bones; therefore he loved it and gave himself for it, and cleansed it with the water bath in the word, that he might present it to himself a glorious congregation, in order that she would not have spot nor wrinkle, nor any such thing, but that she should be holy and unblamable, yea, partaking of the divine nature (II Peter 1:4), if she hold the beginning of the nature of Christ steadfast unto the end (Heb. 3:14). Therefore also the congregation in turn must love Christ and surrender herself wholly to him, for his sake forsake everything and cleave unto him alone, and wholly avoid all spiritual adultery, that is, idolatry, and flee therefrom (Matt. 10:37; 16:24; I Cor. 6:18; 10:14).

In the fifth place, this Holy City has in it the glory of God, and she has no need of the sun nor moon to give light unto her, for the glory of God lightens her, and her light is like the most precious stone, like crystalline jasper; and the heathen of them which are saved shall walk in the light of it (Rev. 21:11 f.; etc.); that is, the congregation is a kingdom of the Most High, exalted above all the kingdoms of the earth, in which the saints shall have spiritual dominion (Dan. 7:27), and are the conquerors over the whole world by their faith; and Jesus Christ, the brightness of the everlasting light, the express image of the Person of God, is the light of his congregation, which is enlightened by his appearing, yea, with the clarity of his Word, so that she needs no other light, and the Gentiles who shall be saved are called from darkness to this light and walk in this light, as children of light, and shine as lights in the world in this, that they hold fast to the Word of life. Therefore also Tobit says in his song of praise (Tobit 13:11): O Jerusalem, thou holy city, thou shalt [411] shine in glorious brightness, and in all the ends of the earth thou shalt be honored.

In the sixth place, this city of Jerusalem has walls great and high, and the building of the wall is of jasper, and the foundations of the wall of the city are garnished with all manner of precious stones. This represents to us that the congregation is built upon the precious foundation of the apostles and prophets, of whom Jesus Christ is the chief cornerstone (Eph. 2:20); and this same congregation has had from the beginning many glorious ministers, preachers of righteousness (I Cor. 3:5; I Peter 5:1), adorned with exalted gifts of the Spirit, which are like a wall round about the city of God to protect them from her enemies, and as a fence round about the vineyard of the Lord, because of the little foxes, that is, to keep out of it the false prophets who would creep in, so that they destroy not the vineyard of the Lord (Isa. 5:1; Song of Solomon 2:15).

In the seventh place, there are twelve gates to this city Jerusalem, and twelve angels, and names written thereon, which are the names of the twelve tribes of the Children of Israel. This indicates to us that the congregation of the Lord has the doctrine of the apostles, which leads to the heavenly Jerusalem, and that there is entrance by no other way; for the apostles have preached to us the true gospel, and beside this no other may be preached (Gal. 1:9). And if we would enter into the congregation of the Lord we must enter in through these gates, for Christ is the only way to the Father, the only door to the sheepfold, that is, the only means of entrance into the congregation, and into the Kingdom of God (Luke 13:22; John 10:7; 14:7). And in view of the fact that the apostles preached Christ, proclaimed the gospel, and thus brought the people to Christ, they are therefore called gates, by which one enters into the Holy City. They are also angels of the Lord, and the emissaries of the Most High, the sealed servants of God, and the names of the twelve tribes of the Children of Israel are written upon them (Mal. 3:1; Ps. 103:20), for to them they were sent first by Christ, and they were first called to the fellowship of the gospel, and they take precedence; and from them came the apostles of the Lord.

In the eighth place, the aforementioned city is of pure gold, as it were clean glass, and there is no temple therein, for the Lord God Almighty is its Temple and the Lamb. This [412] reveals to us the fact that the congregation of the Lord is clean and pure, purified by much tribulation (Ecclesiasticus 2:5; Wisdom of Solomon 3:6), even as the Scripture points out to us that God tries his saints, as gold is tried in the fire, with many trials, that the trial of their faith may be found much more precious than [of] gold that perisheth. Neither does the congregation need any external temple made with hands, which does not avail before God, and therefore none is found in the congregation, but the tabernacle of God is with them (Acts 7:48; 17:24), and the dwellings of the Most High are therein (Ps. 48:9; Rev. 21:22). Moreover, the congregation herself is the temple of the living God, as it is written (II Cor. 6:16; I Cor. 3:16): I will dwell in them, and walk in them; and they will be my people and I will be their God, says the almighty Lord.

In the ninth place, the gates of the city shall not be closed by day; and there is no night there. That is: the entrance to the congregation of God is always open to penitents and believers; for them the door of grace is always open, for them the day of salvation always shines (II Cor. 6:2), and there is no darkness; since God, who dwells in eternal light and in whom is no alteration nor changing of the light nor of the darkness, is in his congregation and enlightens her with his divine brightness, here in the heart, by his Word and Spirit, which is accepted in true faith; and hereafter in the eternal Kingdom, in which the justified shall gleam as the sun forever.

In the tenth place, a stream of living water, clear as crystal proceeds from the throne of God and of the Lamb through the midst of the streets of the heavenly Jerusalem, and on either side of the stream are the trees of life, which bear fruit every month, and whose leaves are for the healing of the heathen. This clear stream of living water represents the Holy Spirit, who proceeds from the eternal Almighty God and Father (John 15:26) through the Son and is a spirit of the Father and the Son, and he is in the congregation. He quickens and comforts the believing souls with the everlasting comfort of the divine grace, and by this same Spirit Jesus Christ is glorified (I Peter 1:11; John 16:15), the Word of life, the comforting gospel, is proclaimed, which becomes fruitful in the hearts of the believers, and is conducive and profitable for eternal salvation to all who [413] have been converted from heathendom to the Almighty God and led into his congregation (I Cor. 2:10).

In the eleventh place, the glory and honor of the heathen shall be brought into this holy city. And there shall in no wise enter into it anything that defileth, neither whatsoever worketh abomination, nor maketh a lie: but they who are written in the Lamb's book of life (Rev. 21:26 f.) that is the Gentiles, who through the hearing of the gospel that was preached to them have, by the power and working of the Holy Spirit, believed, have praised God (as the prophets testify in many places, Rom. 15:9; Deut. 32:43) and have made the congregation of God glorious, because many thousands of Gentiles have been added to the congregation. But the impure and the liars and those that work abomination may not enter into this Holy City; for the ungodly, says the prophet (Ps. 1:5), shall not stand in the judgment, nor sinners in the congregation of the righteous. Yea, they shall have their part with the dragon in the lake that burneth with fire, as it is written (Rev. 21:8): But the fearful, and unbelieving, and the superstitious, and the abominable, and murderers, and all liars, shall have their part in the fiery lake which burneth with fire and brimstone: which is the second death. O Lord! where shall those remain who now with such proud and haughty words profess to be the congregation of the Lord, and yet are wholly intoxicated with carnal pleasures and are openly the servants of idols, and liars against the truth and commit all manner of abomination before the Lord?

Lastly, the servants of the Lord in this Holy City serve the Most High, and his name is on their foreheads, and they shall see his face, and shall reign from eternity to eternity. These servants are the true Christians who serve the Lord faithfully in his congregation, who have yielded their members to the service of righteousness in order that they might be holy (Rom. 6:19) and in the end acquire the salvation of their souls (I Peter 1:9). These have the mark on their foreheads, the name of their God. They openly confess the truth, as those whom the Holy Spirit has sealed, and rejoice in the mercy of the Lord and are not ashamed of their praise of him (Ecclesiasticus 51:29); they do what God has commanded them to do with upright [414] confidence. Therefore God will reward them in due season, and the Lord Jesus Christ will transfigure them, and they shall be like him, for they shall see him face to face in the resurrection of the just and shall reign with him from eternity to eternity (John 12:28; 17:5; I Cor. 13:12; Phil. 3:21).

Thus has the Holy Spirit portrayed to us in the Scripture the congregation of Jesus Christ, from which we may understand how the congregation here must be qualified, how glorious she is, and how she shall be eternally in heaven, when all these things shall come to pass and be fulfilled in the fullness of power and glory. And now, in whatever congregation this is begun in the Spirit and may be seen and found, there is the true congregation of the Lord, the city of the living God, the New Jerusalem, come down from above. Blessed are they that do the commandments of the Lord, that their strength be in the tree of life, and that they may enter in through the gates into the city. For without are dogs and sorcerers, and idolaters, and whosoever loveth and maketh a lie (Rev. 22:14 f.).

May God, the Father of all mercy, who by his grace has called us into the congregation of his dear Son, preserve us therein and strengthen us unto his Heavenly Kingdom, through Jesus Christ. Amen.

Deus est, qui operatur omne quod bonum est in omnibus.

XII

On the Ban: Questions and Answers
By Menno Simons [1]

1550

INTRODUCTION

B APTISM AND THE BAN WERE THE TWO KEYS
controlling the entry to and the exit from the regenerate
church of Anabaptism. By [re]baptism one entered the
church. By the ban the wayward member was extruded. Only
the pure could participate in the communion of the celestial
flesh of Christ (cf. Dietrich Philips, Selection XI and Caspar
Schwenckfeld, Selection VIII). The ban was, of course, based
on Matt. 18:15–18. With it came to be associated the practice
of avoidance or shunning, based on I Cor. 5:11. Paul's injunc-
tion not to eat with the faithless could be interpreted as limited
to the Supper of the Lord or it could be extended so as to
exclude all social intercourse with the banned. And as the
movement passed from the phase of widespread baptismal
recruitment in the spirit of Conrad Grebel (cf. Selection III,
at n. 21), George Blaurock (Selection I), and Melchior Hofmann (Selection IX) to that of disciplined consolidation
(cf. Hutterite Ulrich Stadler, Selection XIII), the problem of
the extent to which the faithful might properly associate with
former members who had been banned, including spouses,
became acute. In the Netherlands the rigoristic interpretation
of avoidance set in after the defection (c. 1540) of Obbe

---

[1] The best biography in English is that of John Horsch, *Menno Simons:
His Life, Labor, and Teaching* (Scottdale, 1916). Horsch apparently did not
know at the time the work of Karl Vos, *Menno Simons, 1496–1561:
Zijn leven en werken en zijne reformatorische denkbeelden* (Leyden, 1914).
Cornelius Krahn built upon both in his *Menno Simons: Ein Beitrag zur
Geschichte und Theologie der Taufgesinnten* (Karlsruhe, 1936). A major
source for the biography is Menno's own reminiscence in his *Reply to
Gellius Faber*. See also Selection X at nn. 55 and 58.

Philips (Selection X) and the banning of Adam Pastor in 1547 for incipient Unitarianism. Among the rigorist leaders were Menno's two chief lieutenants, Dietrich Philips (cf. Selection XI, at notes 55 and 58) and Leonard Bouwens. Menno himself, however, wavered on the question of shunning a banned spouse, bed and board. Whereupon he was himself threatened with excommunication. By 1555 a schism opened on this issue with Menno leading the slightly moderated rigorists over against the laxist or mild-banner Waterlanders, who became the forerunners of the liberal *Doopsgezinden*. From the following Selection it is clear that the Anabaptists could be fully aware of the vindictive, spiteful, and otherwise uncharitable motives which might get mixed up with the religious acts of banning and shunning. Menno was much concerned to have Christ's second key turned with as much care as the first and "with vigilant love" both for the sake of the sanctity of the church and the ultimate salvation of the wayward.

The editor is tempted to take note of the antiquity of the ban as a persistent motif in religious history. The Dead Sea Manual of Discipline supplies an instructive parallel to the "Rule of Christ" (Matt. 18:15–17 = col. vi, 1).

On the Ban: Questions and Answers[2]
By Menno Simons

1550

THE TEXT

QUESTION 1. Is separation a command or is it a counsel of God? *Answer.* Let everyone weigh the words of Christ and of Paul [1 Cor. 5: 11] ... and he will discover whether it is a divine commandment or whether it is a counsel. Everything which Paul says in regard to separation he generally speaks in the imperative mode, that is, in a commanding manner. *Expurgate,* that is, purge, I Cor. 5:7. *Profligate,* that is, drive out. *Sejungere,* that is, withdraw from, I Tim. 6:5. *Fuge,* that is, flee, Titus 3:9. Again (II Thess. 3:6): We command you, brethren, in the name of our Lord Jesus Christ. I think, brethren, these Scriptures show that it is a command; and even if it were not a command but an advice of God, should we not diligently follow such advice? If my spirit despise the counsel of the Holy Spirit, then I truly acknowledge that my spirit is not of God. And to what end many have come who did not follow God's Spirit, but their own, may be read in many passages of sacred history and may be seen in many instances, at the present time.

QUESTION 2. If any person should not observe this ban and yet be pious otherwise, should such a one be banned on that account? *Answer.* Whoever is pious will show his piety in obedience, and not knowingly or willfully despise and disregard the word, commandment, will, counsel, admonition,

2 This is a portion of a larger series of questions and answers (*Sommige Vragen*) printed in the Amsterdam edition of 1681 (pp. 473–474) and translated into English at Elkhart, Indiana, in 1871. The present selection is adapted from the Elkhart translation compared with the Dutch. The most recent treatment of the subject is by Frank Peters, "The Ban in the Writings of Menno Simons," *MQR*, XXIX (1955), 16.

and doctrine of God. For if anyone willfully keeps *commercium* with such whose company is forbidden in Scripture, then we must come to the conclusion that he despises the Word of God, yea, is in open rebellion and refractoriness (I speak of those who well know and acknowledge, and yet do not do). For rebellion is as the sin of witchcraft and stubbornness is as iniquity and idolatry (I Sam. 15:23).

Since the Scripture admonishes and commands that we shall not associate with such, nor eat with them, nor greet them, nor receive them into our houses, etc.; and then if somebody should say, I will associate with them, I will eat with them, I will greet them in the Lord, and receive them into my house— he would plainly prove that he did not fear the commandment and admonition of the Lord, but that he despised it, rejected the Holy Spirit, and that he trusted, honored, and followed his own opinion rather than the Word of God. Now judge for yourself what kind of sin it is not to be willing to hear and obey God's Word. Paul says (II Thess. 3:6, 14): Now we command you, brethren, in the name of our Lord Jesus Christ, that ye withdraw yourselves from every brother that walketh disorderly, and not after the tradition which ye received of us; again: And if any man obey not our word by this epistle, note that man, and have no company with him, that he may be ashamed. Inasmuch as the ban was so strictly commanded by the Lord, and practiced by the apostles (Matt. 18:17), therefore we must also use it and obey it, since we are thus taught and enlightened by God, or else we should be shunned and avoided by the congregation of God. This must be acknowledged and confessed.

QUESTION 3. Should husband and wife shun each other on account of the ban—as also parents and children? *Answer.* First, that the rule of the ban is a general rule, and excepts none: neither husband nor wife, neither parent nor child. For God's word judges all flesh with the same judgment and knows no respect of persons. Inasmuch as the rule of the ban is general, excepts none, and is no respecter of persons—therefore it is reasonable and necessary to hear and obey the Word of the Lord in this respect; no matter whether it be husband or wife, parents or children.

Secondly, we say that separation must be made in the congregation; and therefore the husband must consent and vote with the church in the separation of his wife; and the wife in the separation of her husband. If the pious consort must give his consent, then it is also becoming that he also shun her, with the church; for what use is there in the ban when the shunning and avoiding are not connected with it?

Thirdly, we say that the ban was instituted to make ashamed unto reformation. Do not understand this shame as the world is ashamed; but understand as in the conscience, and therefore let it be done with all discretion, reasonableness, and love. If then my husband or wife, parent or child is judged in the church, in the name of and by the power of Christ, to be banned, it becomes us (inasmuch as the evangelical ban is unto reformation), according to the counsel of the Holy Spirit, to seek the reformation of my own body, namely, of my spouse, and also of our nearest kinsfolk as parent or child; for spiritual love must be preferred to anything else. Aside from this I would care for them and provide the temporal necessaries of life, so far as it would be in my power.

Fourthly, we say that the ban was given that we should not be sullied by the leaven of false doctrine or unclean-living flesh, by apostates. And as it is plain that none can corrupt and leaven us more than our own spouses, parents, etc., therefore the Holy Spirit counsels us to shun them, lest they leaven our faith and thus make us ashamed before God. If we love husband or wife, parent or child more than Christ Jesus, we cannot possibly be the disciples of Christ.

Some object to this, saying that there is no divorce but by reason of adultery. This is just what we say; and therefore we do not speak of divorce, but of shunning, and that for the aforementioned reasons. To shunning, Paul (I Cor. 7:10) has decidedly consented, although this is not always coupled with adultery; but not to divorce. For divorce is not allowed by the Scripture except by reason of adultery (Matt. 5:32; Luke 16:18); therefore we shall never consent to it for other reasons.

Therefore we understand it that the husband should shun his wife, the wife her husband, parents their children and the children their parents when they apostatize. For the rule of the ban is general. They [the godly] must consent, with the church, to the sentence; they must aim at Scriptural shame unto reformation and diligently watch, lest they [themselves] be leavened by them, as said above.

My beloved in the Lord, I would here sincerely pray you that you would make a difference between commandment and commandment and not consider all commandments as equally weighty. For adultery, idolatry, shedding blood, and the like shameful and abominable works of the flesh will be punished more severely than a misunderstanding in regard to the ban, and particularly when not committed willfully and perversely. Therefore beware that in this matter of matrimony you press no one farther than he is taught of God in his heart and that he in his conscience can bear, lest you boil the kid while it is still sucking its mother's milk [cf. Deut. 14:21]. On every hand the Scriptures teach that we should bear with the weak. Brethren, it is a delicate matter. I know too well what has been the result of pressing this matter too far by some in my time. Therefore I advise you to point all to the sure and certain ground. And those consciences that are, through the Scripture and the Holy Spirit, free and unencumbered will freely, without the interference of anyone, by the unction of the Holy Spirit and not by human encouragement, do that which he advises, teaches, and commands in the Holy Scripture, if it should be that one's spouse should be banned. For verily I know that whoever obeys the Holy Spirit, with faithful heart will never be made ashamed.

QUESTION 4. Should we greet one that is banned, with the common, everyday greeting, or return our respects at his greeting? For John says (II John 10 f.): If there come any unto you, and bring not this doctrine, receive him not into your house, neither bid him God speed; for he that biddeth him God speed is partaker of his evil deeds. *Answer.* Mildness, politeness, respectfulness and friendliness to all mankind becomes all Christians. If, then, an apostate should greet me with the common greeting of Good Morning or Good Day and I should be silent; if he should be respectful to me and I should turn my face from him, and bear myself austerely and unfriendly toward him, I might well be ashamed of myself, as Sirach says. For how can such a one be convinced, led to repentance, and be moved to do better by such austerity? The ban is not given to destroy but to build up.

If it should be said that John has forbidden such greeting, I for myself would answer that, before my God, I cannot understand that John said this in regard to the everyday greeting, but that he says, if some deceiver should come to us who has left the doctrine of Christ, that we should not receive such a one into our houses, lest he mislead us; and that we should not greet him as a brother lest we have communion with him. But not so with the worldly greeting. For if the worldly greeting have such power in itself that it causes the communion of the vain works of those whom I greet, then it must follow that I would have communion with the fornication, adultery, drunkenness, avarice, idolatry and bloodshed of the world, whenever I should greet a worldly man with the common greeting or return his compliment. Oh no! But the greeting or kiss of peace does signify communion. Yet if one should have conscientious scruples in this matter, with such a one I do not dispute about it. For it is not worth contending about. But I would much rather see all scruples in regard to this matter removed and have Christian discretion, love, politeness, and respectfulness practiced for [our] improvement rather than stubbornness, unfriendliness, malice, and unmercifulness unto disruption. Brethren, beware of discord and controversy. The Lord grant every God-fearing person a wholesome understanding of his holy Word. Amen.

QUESTION 5. Are we allowed to show the banned any charity, love, and mercy? *Answer.* Everyone should consider, (1) the exact meaning of the word *commercium*; (2) for what reason and purpose the ban was ordained by the Holy Spirit in the Scriptures; (3) how a real true Christian is reborn, bred, and endowed[3]; (4) how the merciful Father himself acts with those who are already worthy of his judgment and wrath.

All those who can rightly see into these will doubtlessly not deny necessary services, love, and mercy to the banned. For the word *commercium* does not forbid these, but it forbids daily company, conversation, society and business, as was explained above. The ban is also a work of divine love and not of perverse, unmerciful, heathenish cruelty. A true Christian will serve, aid, and commiserate with everybody; yea, even with his most bitter enemies. Austerity, cruelty, and unmercifulness he hates with all his heart. He has a nature like his Father of whom he is born: for he maketh his sun to rise on the evil and on the good, and sendeth rain on the just and on the unjust. If I, then, be of a different nature than he, I show that I am not his child.

Therefore I say with our faithful brother Dietrich Philips[4] that we should not practice the ban to the destruction of mankind (as the Pharisees did their Sabbath) but to its improvement; and thus we desire to serve the bodies of the fallen, in love, reasonableness, and humility, with our temporal goods when necessary, and their souls with the spiritual goods of the holy Word. And we should rather, with the Samaritan, show mercy

3 The text has "uyt geboren, geaert ende genatuert."
4 See Selection XI, the fourth ordinance.

to the wounded than to pass by him with the priest and Levite. James says (ch. 2:13): For he shall have judgment without mercy, that hath showed no mercy, and mercy rejoiceth against judgment. Be ye therefore merciful as your Father also is merciful. Blessed are the merciful; for they shall obtain mercy. In short, if we understand the true meaning and nature of the word *commercium*, we understand for what reason and purpose the ban was instituted, how a true Christian is and should be minded; and if we conform ourselves to the example of Christ and of God, then the matter is all helped along. And if we have not this grace, we will shamefully err in this ban and be cruel, unmerciful Christians; from which error and abomination may the gracious Father eternally save all his beloved children.

My brethren, I tell the truth and lie not when I say that I hate with all my heart such unmercifulness and cruel-mindedness. Nor do I wish to be considered a brother of such unmerciful, cruel brethren, if there should be such, unless they desist from such abomination and discreetly follow, in love and mercy, the example of God and Christ. For my heart cannot consent to such unmerciful action which exceeds the cruelty of the heathen and Turks; and by the grace of God I will fight against it with my Lord's sword unto death. For it is against the doctrine of the New Testament, and contrary to the Spirit, mind, and nature of God and Christ, according to which all the Scriptures of the New Testament should be judged and understood. All those who do not understand it thus are already in great error.

But in case my necessary service, charity, love, and mercy should become a *commercium*, or that my soul should thereby be led into corruption, then we confess (the Lord must be praised) that our daily intercourse is forbidden in the Scripture, and that it is better to leave off our charity, love, and mercy than to ensnare our souls thereby and lead them into error. The unction of the Holy Spirit will teach us what we should best do in these matters.

QUESTION 6. Are we allowed to sell to, and buy of, the apostates inasmuch as Paul says (I Cor. 5:11) that we should not have intercourse with them? And yet the disciples bought victuals in Sychar, and the Jews dealt with the Gentiles (John 4:5). *Answer.* That the apostles bought victuals in Sychar proves nothing at all; for many of the Samaritans were a remnant of the ten tribes, as we have sufficiently shown above, from the Holy Scripture. But we do not deny that the Jews dealt with the Gentiles, yet they shunned their *commercium*, that is, their daily association, company, and conversation, and did not eat or drink with them, as the writings of the Evangelist sufficiently and plainly show in many Scriptural passages.

And inasmuch as Christ points us to the Jewish ban or shunning, namely, that as they shunned the Gentiles and sinners, so we should likewise shun an apostate Christian; and as the Jews had dealings with them, although they shunned their daily intercourse in company, association, and conversation; therefore we say that we cannot maintain, either by the Jewish example to which Christ points or by any explicit Scripture, that we should not in any manner deal with the apostate, if no such daily intercourse arises therefrom. For such intercourse with the apostate is strictly prohibited by Scripture; and since it is prohibited, it is manifest that a pious, God-fearing Christian could have no apostate as a regular buyer or seller. For as I have daily to get my cloth, bread, corn, salt, etc., and exchange for it my grain, butter, etc., it cannot fail but that intercourse will arise therefrom. But with a trading which is conducted without such intercourse this is not the case.

And because such business which is carried on without intercourse cannot be shown to be disallowed by virtue of the Scripture, as was said, therefore we would pray all God-fearing brethren and sisters in the Lord, for the sake of God and of love, to act in this matter, as in all others, as reasonable, good, discreet, wise, and prudent Christians and not as vain, reckless, self-conceited, proud, obdurate, and offensive boasters; for a true Christian should always strive after that which is the best and the surest, and follow the pure, unfeigned love, lest he abuse the freedom which he seems to have, to the injury and hindrance of his own soul, to the affliction and destruction of his beloved brethren, to the scornful boasting of the perverse, and to the shameful defamation of the holy Word and the afflicted church of Christ. Besides, I pray and desire in like manner that none will thus in the least be offended at his brother and mistake and judge him by an unscriptural judgment; as he has in this case no reproving example among the Jews nor forbidding word [in the Scriptures].

O my sincerely beloved brethren, let us sincerely pray for understanding and wisdom that all misunderstanding, error, jealousy, offense, division, and untimely reports may be utterly exterminated, root and branch; that a wholesome understanding, doctrine, friendship, love, edification, and a sound judgment may get under way and prevail. Let everyone look with pure eyes and impartial hearts to the example to which Christ points, and to the wholesome, natural meaning of the holy apostles, and let true, Christian love take precedence; and everyone will know, by the grace of God, how he should act and proceed concerning this matter.

QUESTION 7. Are we allowed to be seated with an apostate in a ship or wagon, or to eat with him at the table of a tavern? *Answer.* The first part of this question . . . we deem childish and useless, since this so often happens without intercourse and must needs happen. As to the second part, namely, [whether] to eat at the table with an apostate, while traveling, we can point the questioner to no surer ground and answer than this, namely, we advise, pray, and admonish every pious Christian, as he loves Christ and his Word, to fear God sincerely, and follow the most certain way, that is, not to eat by or with him; for thereby none can be deceived; and if perchance some God-fearing brother might do so, then let everyone beware, lest he sin against his brother by an unscriptural judgment; for none may judge unless he have the judging word on his side.

Whosoever fears God, whosoever desires to follow after his holy Word, with all his strength loves his brother, seeks to avoid all offense and desires to walk in the house of God in all peace and unity, will act justly in all things and will not offend or afflict his brethren.

QUESTION 8. Who, according to Scripture, should be banned or excommunicated? *Answer.* Christ says (Matt. 18:15–17): If thy brother trespass against thee, etc., and will not hear thee or the witnesses, nor the church, let him be unto thee as a heathen man and a publican. And Paul (I Cor. 5:11): If any man that is called a brother be a fornicator, or covetous, or an idolater, or a railer, or a drunkard, or an extortioner; with such a one do not eat. To this class also belong perjurers, thieves, violent persons, haters, fighters and all those who walk in open, well-known, damnable works of the flesh, of which Paul enumerates a great many (Rom. 1:29; Gal. 5:19; I Cor. 6:9; Eph. 5:5). Again, disorderly persons, working not at all, but who are busybodies; such as do not abide in the doctrine of Christ and his apostles and do not walk therein, but are disobedient (II Thess. 3:11, 14). Again, masters of sects. Again, those who give offense, cause dispute and discord concerning the doctrine of Christ and of his apostles. In short, all those who openly lead a shameful, carnal life, and those who are corrupted by a heretical, unclean doctrine (Titus 3:10), and who will not be overcome by the wine and oil[5] of the Holy Spirit, but remain, after they have been admonished and sought to be regained in all love and reasonableness, obdurate in their corrupted walk and opinion. They should, at last, in the name of our Lord Jesus Christ, by the power of the Holy Spirit, that is, by the binding Word of God, be reluctantly but unanimously separated from the church of Christ and thereupon, according to the Scriptures, be shunned in all divine obedience, until they repent.

5 Cf. Hubmaier, Selection V, introduction and p. 130.

XIII

Cherished Instructions on Sin, Excommunication, and the Community of Goods

By Ulrich Stadler[1]

PROBABLY IN BUCOVICE, MORAVIA, C. 1537

INTRODUCTION

THIS SELECTION ILLUSTRATES THE RELIGIOUS motivation of Hutterite communism as a way of achieving selflessness and abandonment in the Lord, *Gelassenheit*, variously translated as "resignation," "yieldedness." We have already encountered this characteristic religious term, notably in Grebel (Selection III), in Denck (Selection IV), and in Hofmann (Selection IX). The first outward step in dying to self is submission to rebaptism; withdrawing into the wilderness and living the communal life of paradise and the primitive church consummate the abandonment of self in the Lord. (We have already encountered the wilderness motif in Hofmann, Selection IX.) The regenerated life is felt by the Hutterites to be that of a colony of heaven or of the Saints of the Most High, sojourning in misery and exposed to hardships and to martyr death in the Last Days. Outside of membership in this pilgrim community of mutual suffering and love there is no salvation. Indeed, in the language of Cyprian, Stadler holds that whoever is outside the covenantal commonwealth of the twice-born "has no Father in heaven."

Moravian communism as a restitution of the usage of the primitive church is, of course, inspired also by the model in

---

[1] There are only brief notices of Ulrich Stadler. He died in 1540, bishop (*Vorsteher*) of the Hutterite settlement in Bucovice in Moravia. He had been a mine official in Sterzing in the Tyrol and was briefly a Lutheran before becoming a member of the Hutterite community in Austerlitz. On the Hutterite epistles in general, see Robert Friedmann, *MQR*, XX (1946), 93; for recent research in Hutterite Anabaptism, *ibid.*, XXIV (1950), 353–363; and for a recent analysis of Hutterite theology, Franz Heimann, "The Hutterite Doctrines of the Church and Common Life," *ibid.*, XXVI (1952), 22; 142.

Acts, chs. 2 to 5. Likewise the Fifth Letter of Clement of Rome was no doubt influential. Detached from the Pseudo-Isidorian Decretals, it was popularized in the *Geschichtsbibel* of Sebastian Franck (Selection VII) as supposedly reflecting the apostolic communism in Rome and Jerusalem. The Decretals (themselves a ninth-century forgery) embodied Pseudo-Clementine material from the third century in which the communism of The Acts, the Golden Age, and Biblical paradise were mingled. By way of Campanus (Selection VII) Franck's evaluation of Pseudo-Clement reached Bernard Rothmann in Münster.[2] By what specific way Clement's ideal reached Moravia has not yet been fully worked out, but the phrasing of his Letter is echoed by Stadler. His *Instruction* occupies a place in the long history of the community of *disciplined friends* who have dreamed of or practiced in love the communion in goods from Platonism and Stoicism through medieval monasticism to what Luther excoriated as the "new monachism" of the Anabaptists.

The Selection is illustrative of the mood and organization of the Hutterite congregation-commonwealth (*gmain*). It dates from the period when, after the dissolution of the Hutterite colony in Austerlitz under persecution in 1536, Stadler's following joined a colony under Hans Amon, one mile to the east. The amalgamating groups are known to have agreed upon certain articles of which our document may well be the echo.

[2] See Hans von Schubert, *Der Kommumismus der Wiedertäufer in Münster und seine Quellen*, Sitzungsberichte, Heidelberger Akademie der Wissenschafte, phil.-hist. Kl., 1919, 11. Abh. Clement is quoted in the Hutterite *Article Book* (1547). See Friedmann, "Eine dogmatische Hauptschrift," *Archiv für Reformationsgeschichte*. XXVIII (1931), 135.

The Clementine letters were published by John Sichard in Basel, 1526. The Fifth Letter can be read in the Decretals as edited by Paul Hinschius (Leipzig, 1863) on pp. 65 f. where the reading, so important at Münster, remains intact: . . . communia debere esse amicorum omnia . . . sine dubio et *coniuges*.

Cherished Instructions on Sin, Excommunication, and the Community of Goods[3]

By Ulrich Stadler

PROBABLY IN BUCOVICE, MORAVIA, C. 1537

THE TEXT

[EXCLUSION][4]

... One speaks[5] without any distinction just as though one could not miss God's grace and as though the door of grace always stood open to be entered whenever one wished and to let the Lord in whenever he should knock. [But] he also turns away and after [such conduct] does not allow himself to be found in time of trouble. And, moreover, a person can become so blinded and hardened that he will no longer see or hear. Thus people are not taught rightly to recognize the pure fear of God and his divine severity in judgment.

Though he is, to be sure, merciful indeed and gladly takes mercy on the sinner, helps him out, and lifts him in Christ out of his filth like the prodigal son, nevertheless he is also at the

---

[3] The German title is *Eine liebe unterrichtung Ulrichen Stadlers, diener des worts, der sünd halben und des ausschlusz, wie er darinen stehe, auch gemainschaft der zeitlichen güeter halben.* ... It is printed by Lydia Müller, *Glaubenszeugnisse oberdeutscher Taufgesinnter*, I (Leipzig, 1938), 215 ff. The numbers in brackets refer to the pagination of this text. The document is colloquial and not tightly constructed. The *Instruction* opens with the problem of original sin. Only the last section of this portion is here translated, but the remaining two portions of the work are complete.

Another writing by Stadler on the same subject but not ascribed to him is published by Rudolf Wolkan, *Die Hutterer: Oesterreichische Wiedertäufer und Kommunisten in Amerika* (Vienna, 1918). Five other writings besides our selection are edited by Müller, and there is a long letter of his to the rulers in Poland preserved in the Hutterite *Chronicle*, ed. Ziegelschmid, pp. 166-170.

[4] Exclusion (*ausschlusz*) is more than the ban of the noncommunitarian Anabaptists, because the whole of the exile's economic and social as well as his religious life is involved.

[5] The reference is to the foregoing query of critics, possibly from within the Hutterite group, as to why God will not forgive many times.

274

same time a pure and holy God, [who] wills[6] that man sin no more but that he serve and laud him, [a God who is] often a consuming fire above those who thus sin against him and defile themselves after he has cleansed them. Thus let him who, after being once helped, gladly, wittingly, brazenly sins against him according to recognized truth, seek an expiatory offering wherever he will; I do not know where to find one to show him in Christ, the High Priest. Rather, God's Spirit testifies that a terrifying judgment and the zeal of fire await him, which will consume all the perverse. For the seeding with the Lord's Word takes place once. Thereafter the Lord waters it continually with rain. Now when the ground which is seeded and receives rain continually bears only thistles and thorns, it must for the best be burned up. Again, one does not always haggle (*dinget*) over a planted tree, but rather cultivates it for several years [220] [to see] whether it bears fruit, and if not, it is cut down. This the Lord also testifies in Christ [John 15:2 ff.]: Every branch in me which beareth not fruit the Father will cut off. Whoever abideth not in me is cast forth as a branch of the vine and is withered and men gather it and cast it into the fire and it is burned. Whoever exceeds and does not abide in the doctrine of Christ has no God.

Therefore, whoever proclaims and promises mercy to such a persistent sinner, who blasphemes the Spirit of grace and treads the Son of God under foot, let him be answerable for himself rather than [maintaining] that God's Spirit ever so testified.

But it is said, if someone is able to do penance, God will not fail him. Yea, but it is not of one's (own) willing and running; in short, it is not in the hands of man to convert himself but rather of God the long-suffering. But that he is merciful to them who consider the blood of the New Covenant impure by which they have been purified, God's Spirit does not testify —declares, in fact, just the opposite, namely, it is impossible that such a one should be renewed by repentance. Therefore, ye elect saints of God, be on your guard, watch and fear God. For now is the time when the Lord will lead out his own in tribulation and thereafter receive them with everlasting joy and splendor, to the glory of the Father in heaven. It is so in Christ.[7]

Further, it is adduced against me that I do not wish to

6 Stadler on free will and divine chastisement is similar to Hubmaier and Denck (Selections IV and V).
7 The sentence is mutilated.

receive anybody in the communion of the saints in Christ. To this I say to my sons in Christ our Lord: It is proper for the true deacons [of the Word][8] of the Lord to have watchful eyes in all this and to judge and treat everybody in his community according to the mind and Spirit of Christ, lest that one be bound and not accepted who before God has been loosed. For the truth itself testifies concerning someone who unwittingly or in haste stumbled, and so forth, and the children of truth as his witnesses testify [in his behalf]. So it is, indeed, possible to receive [someone] in the Lord with the consent of the whole brotherhood. Paul also warns the Corinthians [II, ch. 13:1] that in the mouth of two or three witnesses every matter should be confirmed in the Lord; the same, John in Epistle III [v. 12] concerning Demetrius. Otherwise the wicked, malicious impure, unrepentant hearts could also weep, holler, and implore, acknowledge and confess, but still show no improvement in force and thus deceive the innocent children of God.

In the matter of the exclusion of such I hold as before, namely, that the deacons should exercise the power in the house of the Lord and with severity punish all who are disorderly, disobedient, and obstinate and not put up with them in the house of the Lord, ban them also from the house of the Lord with the consent of the whole people of God, yea, all sinners who work unrighteousness. For what's the purpose of a steward and deacon in the church (kürchen) of the Lord who has no power or authority in the Lord, nor the righteous severity and zeal to ban and punish what is unrighteous? He bears the name of a deacon of the Lord without any strength [221] and vitality. The people, however, as zealous for the Lord should unanimously concur with him and he with them; and this is, according to the command of Christ and his holy apostles, the real truth and correct usage. Defame it however

---

[8] In the Hutterite communities there were two diaconates: that of the *Diener der Notdurft*, which I am translating as "deacon of welfare," and the *Diener des Wortes*, "deacon of the Word." Of the latter there were at least two kinds: the apostle who preached and gathered the saints and the minister of the Word who remained within the community. Stadler himself was deacon of the Word at Austerlitz and died as bishop (*Vorsteher*) or chief minister in Bucovice. On Stadler's ministry specifically and on the organization of the Hutterite church-commonwealth in general, see Joseph Beck, ed., *Die Geschichts-Bücher der Wiedertäufer* (=*Fontes Rerum Austriacarum*, 2. Abt., XLIII), (Vienna, 1883), 149 and Introduction; and on the latter point also Lydia Müller, *Der Kommunismus der mährischen Wiedertäufer*, Verein für Reformationsgeschichte, *Schriften*, No. 142 (Leipzig, 1927).

one may, may God grant it to them to see it. For it is said we [deacons] have stolen the power of the congregation (*gmain*) of the Lord! I should rather be a swineherd than a deacon of the Lord, if I did not have in the Lord power and authority to punish. Surely, I might, at least, strike a miscreant pig and drive it back to the herd! Once someone is recognized as fitted for such an office of the Lord and that the Lord honors him with appropriate gifts of his Spirit, and he is true and also pure in his life, then he should be fully entrusted with his office, as already said. Where not, let it be abandoned. It would not be possible that deacon and community could die and recover together. There would never be peace and concord among them, but instead the congregation would be full of suspicion toward the deacon, the deacon would have a malevolent heart against the congregation. God protect us from this. I know in part what pains this can bring.

THE TRUE COMMUNITY OF THE SAINTS

There is one communion (*gmain*) of all the faithful in Christ and one community (*gmainschaft*) of the holy children called of God. They have one Father in heaven, one Lord Christ; all are baptized and sealed in their hearts with one Spirit. They have one mind, opinion, heart, and soul as having all drunk from the same Fountain, and alike await one and the same struggle, cross, trial, and, at length, one and the same hope in glory. But it, that is, such a community (*gmain*) must move about in this world, poor, miserable, small, and rejected of the world, of whom, however, the world is not worthy. Whoever strives for the lofty things [of this world] does not belong. Thus in this community everything must proceed equally, all things be one and communal, alike in the bodily gifts of their Father in heaven, which he daily gives to be used by his own according to his will. For how does it make sense that all who have here in this pilgrimage to look forward to an inheritance in the Kingdom of their Father should not be satisfied with their bodily goods and gifts? Judge, O ye saints of God, ye who are thus truly grafted into Christ, with him deadened to the world, to sin, and to yourselves, that you never hereafter live for the world or yourselves but rather for him who died for you and arose, namely, Christ. [They] have also yielded themselves and presented themselves to him intimately, patiently, of their own free will, naked and uncovered, to suffer and endure his will[9] and, moreover, to fufill it and thereafter also to devote themselves in obedience and service to all the children of God. Therefore, they also live with one another where the Lord assigns a place to them, peaceably, united, lovingly, amicably, and fraternally, as children of one Father. In their pilgrimage they should be satisfied with the bodily [222] goods and gifts of their Father, since they should also be altogether as one body and members one toward another.

Now if, then, each member withholds assistance from the other, the whole thing must go to pieces. The eyes won't see, the hands won't take hold. Where, however, each member extends assistance equally to the whole body, it is built up and grows and there is peace and unity, yea, each member takes care for the other. In brief, equal care, sadness and joy, and peace [are] at hand. It is just the same in the spiritual body of Christ. If the deacon of the community will never serve, the teacher will not teach, the young brother will not be obedient, the strong will not work for the community but for himself and each one wishes to take care of himself and if once in a while someone withdraws without profit to himself, the whole body is divided. In brief, one, common builds the Lord's house and is pure; but mine, thine, his, own divides the Lord's house and is impure. Therefore, where there is ownership and one has it, and it is his, and one does not wish to be one (gmainsam) with Christ and his own in living and dying, he is outside of Christ and his communion (gmain) and has thus no Father in heaven. If he says so, he lies. That is the life of the pilgrims of the Lord, who has purchased them in Christ, namely, the elect, the called, the holy ones in this life. These are his fighters and heralds, to whom also he will give the crown of life on the Day of his righteousness.

Secondly, such a community of the children of God has ordinances here in their pilgrimage. These should constitute the polity (policeien) for the whole world. But the wickedness of men has spoiled everything. For as the sun with its shining is common to all, so also the use of all creaturely things. Whoever appropriates them for himself and encloses them is a thief and steals what is not his. For everything has been created free in common (in die gmain). Of such thieves the whole world is

---

[9] This same bridal imagery (cf. also n. 14, below), derived in part from medieval mysticism, is prominent in Melchior Hofmann. Selection IX, at n. 5 and passim.

full. May God guard his own from them. To be sure, according to human law, one says: That is mine, but not according to divine law.[10] Here in this ordinance [in our community] it [the divine law] is to be heeded (*gilt es aufsehens*) in such a way that unbearable burdens be not laid upon the children of the Lord, but rather ones which God, out of his grace, has put upon us, living according to which we may be pleasing to him. Thus only as circumstances dictate will the children of God have either many or few houses,[11] institute faithful house managers and stewards, who will faithfully move among the children of God and conduct themselves in a mild and fatherly manner and pray to God for wisdom therein.

ORDINANCES OF THE SAINTS IN THEIR COMMUNITY AND LIFE HERE TOGETHER IN THE LORD WITH THE GOODS OF THEIR FATHER

In order to hold in common all the gifts and goods which God gives and dispenses to his own, there must be free, unhampered (*ledige*), patient (*gelassene*), and full hearts in Christ, yea, hearts that truly believe and trust and in Christ are utterly [223] devoted. Whoever is thus free, unhampered, and resigned in the Lord from everything, [ready] to give over all his goods and chattels, yea, to lay it up for distribution among the children of God—it is God's grace in Christ which prepares men for it. Being willing and ready—that makes one free and unhampered. But whoever is not thus at liberty to give over and lay up in Christ the Lord, as indicated, should nevertheless not hold back, nor conceal, nor disavow anything but instead be willing and ready to give even when there is nothing at hand, yea, even to let the deacons in to collect in order that [at least] they might have free access in the Lord to them and at all times to find a willing, open heart ready to share. The house

10 The remainder of this paragraph is not entirely clear. One might expect Stadler to distinguish between two laws, the one for the worldlings (even when they might call themselves Protestant or Catholic) and one for the elect. But instead, he seems to be moderating the divine law of the complete community of goods as in paradise in its application to the saints, recognizing their inherited inequalities and their insufficiently eliminated imperfections.

11 The Austrian and Moravian authorities were slightly less alarmed if the Anabaptists managed to avoid concentrations and the appearance of a threat of revolution. But it was precisely their faith as well as their misery which induced them to live together.

managers who have devoted themselves to the Lord and his people with body and substance in the service of, and obedience to, the Lord in his community should not be changed where they are recognized as fitted for the work and found faithful nor the [management of] the necessities withdrawn from them in the Lord, as long as they deal faithfully. Where, however, avarice or selfishness is detected, it should not be permitted. They must also be more community-minded with all the wretched of the Lord.

[As] deacons of welfare, true men should be ordained who take care that everything proceeds equally in the whole house of the Lord, everywhere in all the households, lest one have and another want. They also should be fatherly with all the little children of God; and also do all the buying and selling for the community.

The children of God should group themselves and hold together here in misery after they have been driven out in the worst sort of way—if they can achieve this, for it is good and purposeful; however, if it [can be managed] without hardship they should not make big concentrations[12] but rather, as opportunity affords, they should have many or at least a few [separated] houses. In brief, it belongs to all the children of God to live, to serve, to work, to seek not their own benefit but that of another, since we are all of the Lord. [Such] is their behavior on their pilgrimage.

Again, the brethren ought not to do business with each other, buy and sell like the heathen, each being rather in the Lord the Lord's own. Finally, everything should be arranged for the good of the saints of God in the church of the Lord according to time, place, propriety, and opportunity, for one cannot set up a specific instruction for everything. The hearts which are free, willing, unhampered, patient, [ready] to serve all the children of God, to have everything in common with them, yea, to persevere loyally and constantly in their service, shall remain always in the Lord. Where such hearts of grace exist, everything is soon ordered in the Lord. But whoever goes about in the congregation and the community of the saints with cunning and deception, untruth or lies, the Lord will bring to ruin[13]. . ., however long postponed—[also him] who seeks himself or does not work faithfully as for the Lord himself or as with the goods of the Lord, and does not rightly go about in the fear of the Lord.

[12] See n. 11.   [13] Small gap in the MS.

[224] Now follow the counterarguments.

Someone says that it is better, because of bickering and complaining, to be separate from each other, and that if everyone takes care of and lives unto himself, it stays more peaceful.

Answer: The complainer and grumbler, of course, who have never mortified the flesh, who do not control their desires and lusts, who have indeed abandoned the patience and the true love of God (whoever has this love of God in his heart is long-suffering and patient along with the rest of the pious here in these troubled times lest he lose himself too far in the world), yea, because of these things it is difficult or even impossible [for them] to live along with and in the midst of the others— [for them] who seek themselves, [who seek] to maintain their own life here comfortably, and to cultivate their body, as they have since childhood learned and been accustomed to doing according to the perverse manner [of the world]. Indeed, for such unmortified, carnal, natural men without the Spirit, it certainly is a heavy, bitter, unbearable life. Such persons seek freedom only to dwell someplace unto themselves in order that they might live pleasantly according to the flesh and unto their corruption. Otherwise they would surely be captured by the snares of blessedness and love. Those who had not been constrained to love within their hearts would nevertheless endure it in order not to become obvious, but upon such as these, God's severity should be visited.

Secondly, it is said that the children of God cannot all dwell in the same place. They cannot all be even in one land; nor is this really necessary, for the whole earth is the Lord's and it makes no difference where one dwells, so long as it is in the fear of God.

Answer: This is indeed true, but as far as it can be had and achieved, it is very good and purposeful to be together as well as can be so that all is possessed as by sojourners who seek another habitation. For to wander in the world and to have much to do with it and still to keep from being unsullied is possible for only a few and very hazardous. But whoever likes danger very likely comes to disaster thereby, especially in these times, which are much more full of danger than ever before. In this time a place has been given to the bride of the Lamb in which to dwell amid the wasteland of this world, there to put on the beautiful bright linen garment and thus to await the Lord until he leads her after him here in tribulation and afterward receives her with eternal joy.[14] The time is now. Whoever has ears to hear, let him hear.

But when some are with others in one place even in misery and nevertheless do not live communally as friends and brothers in the Lord (as even children driven out hold together), but rather seek excuses—the one on account of his stomach, the other because of his wife and child, the third with another excuse, as it has gone on now for some time—they [obviously] do not recognize the other in their heart as one of their own, for whom they have as much love as for self. Otherwise they would surely bear and suffer one another. And also the well and the strong would surely be considerate of him who is ill and [225] has a weak stomach and distribute to each one what is necessary for him to maintain the poor, miserable body. There are, in fact, several gross members of the community without understanding, who think that everyone has a good stomach and can digest anything [but due care should be given the weak].[15] May the deacons of welfare have, in this [whole matter], faithful supervision, so that on neither side is too much done for anybody lest the body be coddled with faithless eating and drinking! In brief, wherever things are as described and each one sets up his kitchen, there it can[not] be said in truth that there is the one heart, soul, and body which must, however, and always should be among the children of God. If that is not the case, it must be remedied in the house of the Lord.

Thirdly, it is alleged for the time of the apostles that the congregations of Christ were not so ordered and were not thereby thrown upon one another, having all in common, as their letters show, except for a brief period in Jerusalem up to the separation [from Judaism].

Answer: I say there is a great difference in the times. There, they [the primitive Christians] were left in their homes and not at once driven into misery, but now the children of God have no place in the whole Roman Empire.[16] For the Babylonian whore who sits on the dragon with seven heads, I mean the Roman Church, a synagogue of the living devil, spews out all the

---

[14] Again (see above, n. 9) the bridal imagery as in Hofmann and the motif of withdrawal into the desert or wasteland. The allusion is to Rev. 19:8. Here also is the mystic's and notably Müntzer's motif of the bitter preceding the sweet in the experience of Christ.

[15] Supplied as certainly necessary to make sense of the whole section.

[16] Moravia, as distinguished from the Kingdom of Bohemia, lay outside the Holy Roman Empire.

children of God and only drives them into the wilderness, unto their place, as declared above. Nonetheless, truth is truth and must so stand. And, moreover, all the elect follow it. She [truth] says this: We are never for ourselves but of the Lord. We have in truth nothing of our own, but rather all the gifts of God in common, be they temporal or spiritual, except that they [the deacons] should adapt the ordinances to the circumstances of time, place, and situation for the good of the children of God and not rule [autocratically] over the children of God, but rather they should at all times be ordered and interpreted for the improvement of the people. So judge all ordinances according to propriety and opportunity for the good of the saints and take hold with strength and bring it to pass that property, that is, *his, mine, thine,* will not be disclosed in the house of the Lord, but rather equal love, equal care and distribution, and true community in all the goods of the Father according to his will.

I say also of our own times if there were so many faithful allowed to remain in their homes as with the communities of Paul, they should but be true, faithful house managers and dispensers, and all things would be nicely arranged, as Paul shows. But the free, unencumbered, community-minded and yielded hearts must still be and remain precisely those who have everything in common with the children of God, gladly distribute and dispense, and who also gladly endure and suffer with the pious.

[226] Fourthly, it is said that not all are so free and resigned that they are able to be one with the community of all the elect, and these should not be expelled.

Answer: Such a selfful, unsurrendered heart must be hewn and circumcized; and only then will it be useful for the construction of the house of the Lord. He must be forthrightly shown his retarded behavior and insufficiency in order that it [the dressed rock] may be like-minded and of one color with all the other resigned, holy children of God.

Further, it is said that God wishes to have a joyful giver, indeed, unencumbered, [giving] out of love and desire, not out of pressure and coercion.

Answer: Wait until one finds such grace in the Lord in a person and take nothing that is proffered joylessly and despondently. It is proper, however, for the deacons of the Lord in such a case to instruct, guide, and admonish with all patience, neither coddling nor rejecting, like Paul in whom one has an ideal pattern. There is a lack of mortified, free, unencumbered, yielded hearts. In the beginning they were [present] in the Lord, but now that the pilgrimage is postponed, they nestle down again in the world; and therewith there are few who long to leave the world. Indeed, they really prefer to live than to die [in Christ]. The saying: Death is my reward,[17] becomes rarer among them, among many of them.

In conclusion, it is very good for the children of God, while they make their pilgrimage in misery, to assemble and hold themselves together, as well as can be achieved in the Lord, and not to take counsel concerning this with the flesh, for the flesh would never recommend it but rather wants to be and have only its own and not suffer it out with the pious.

Again, it is contended that nowhere in holy Scripture can it be read that it is a command of the Lord to bring together all the goods and to place deacons and stewards over them.

Answer: It is true abandon[18] to yield and dispose oneself with goods and chattels in the service of the saints. It is also the way of love. Moreover, true friends have all things in common; indeed, they are called two bodies with but one soul. Yea, we learn it in Christ to lose oneself in the service of the saints, to be and become poor and to suffer want, if only another may be served, and further, to put aside all goods and chattels, to throw them away in order that they may be distributed to the needy and the impoverished. That is the highest part and degree of divine abandon and voluntary surrender to the Lord and to his people through the Spirit of grace.

In brief, a brother should serve, live, and work for the other, none for himself; indeed, one house for another, one community[19] for another in some other settlement in the land, wherever the Lord grants it that we gather together, one communion, as a body of the Lord and members one to another. This we see in all the writings [227] of the holy apostles, namely, how one brother, one congregation, serves the other, extends assistance and supplies to the other in the Lord. Such is the life of the elect, holy children of God in their pilgrimage. Amen.

17 The Anabaptist motif of martyrdom, which combined the mystic's impulse to die to self with the radical evangelical's urge to imitate Christ unto the cross.
18 *Gelassenhait.*
19 *Versammlung.*

BIBLIOGRAPHY OF MATERIAL IN ENGLISH TRANSLATION WRITTEN BY REPRESENTATIVES OF THE RADICAL REFORMATION (1524–1575)*

Acontius, Jacob (1492–1566?), *Satan's Stratagems* (1565), translated by Walter T. Curtis, with an introduction by Charles O'Malley, Sutro Branch, California State Library, *Occasional Papers*, English Series, No. 5 (San Francisco, 1940); a historically important translation of the first four books is that of John Goodwin (London, 1647).

Anneken of Rotterdam (1511–1539), *Letter*: to David Joris (1538), in *Martyrology*, I, 204–207.
   Testament to her son Isaiah (1539), in *Martyrology*, I, 196–201.

Blaurock, George (c. 1492–1529), *Memorial* and *Exhortation* (1529), in *Martyrology*, I, 92–96.

Braght, T. J. van (1625–1664), *The Bloody Theatre or Martyrs' Mirror* (1660), translated by Joseph F. Sohm (Scottdale, Pa., 1938); translated by Edward B. Underhill as *A Martyrology*, 2 vols. (London, 1850). Some of the longer documents (up to 1550) contained in the *Martyrs' Mirror* are separately listed in this bibliography.

Castellio, Sebastian (1515–1563), *Concerning Heretics* (1554), introduction ("Martin Bellius") and excerpts translated by Roland H. Bainton, *Concerning Heretics* (New York, 1935), pp. 121–251; also included are excerpts from other works: *Preface to the French Bible* (c. 1553); *Counsel to France in Her Distress* (October, 1562); *Reply to Calvin's Book* (1562); *Concerning Doubt and Belief, Ignorance and Knowledge*, pp. 257–305.

Claeson, John (1544), *Testaments* (c. 1544), in *Martyrology*, I, 251–59.

*A few English Anabaptist and early General Baptist tracts are also included.

285

Cooche, Robert (fl. 1550), *The Confutation of the Errors of the Careless by Necessity* (c. 1557); edited by Baptist Historical Society, *Transactions*, IV, 2 (1915), 88.

Denck, John (1495–1527), *Confession*: to the City Council of Nuremberg (1524), paraphrased by Frederick L. Weis, *The Life of Johannes Denck* (Strassburg, 1924), pp. 23–25.

He Who Really Loves the Truth (1525), translated by Weis; typescript copy in Andover-Harvard Theological Library, Cambridge, Mass.

Letter to Augsburg Council (1526), translated by Weis, *op. cit.*, pp. 31–32.

Brief excerpts from various works, compiled by Harry E. Fosdick, *Great Voices of the Reformation* (New York, 1952), pp. 300–302.

Dortrecht Confession of Faith (1632), text in the *Martyrs' Mirror*, and more recently reprinted in John Wenger, *Glimpses of Mennonite History* (Scottdale, Pa., 1947), pp. 215–226; printed separately as a *Christian Confession* (Philadelphia, 1727).

Elizabeth Dirks the Beguine (c. 1518–1549), Acts of (c. 1549), in *Martyrology*, I, pp. 294–98.

Felbinger, Nicholas (? –1560), *Confession*: to the Council of Landshut (1560), translated by Robert Friedmann, *MQR*, XXIX (1955), pp. 144–161.

Franck, Sebastian (1499–1543), *The Forbidden Fruit* (1534) [London], 1640, under pseudonym A. Eleutherius and 1642 by T.P. and M.S. for Benjamine Allen.

Grebel, Conrad (c. 1498–1526), *Letter to Zwingli* (Sept. 8, 1517), translated and edited by Edward Yoder, *Goshen College Record*, XXVII (1926), pp. 33–37.

Poem (1521), translated by Samuel S. Jackson, *Zwingli, Selected Works*, I, p. 292; translated by Yoder in Harold Bender, *Conrad Grebel* (Goshen, Ind., 1950), p. 281.

Letter to Vadian (May 30, 1525), translated by Edward Yoder. Reprinted by John Wenger, *Glimpses of Mennonite History and Doctrine*, 2d ed. (Scottdale, Pa., 1947), pp. 202–203.

Letters to Andreas Castelberger (May, 1525), translated by Yoder, *MQR*, I (1927), pp. 41–53.

Testimony before the Zurich Court (November, 1525), translated by Bender, *Conrad Grebel*, p. 293.

On Baptism (1526), as recoverable from Zwingli's *Elenchus*, translated by Jackson and assembled as a unit by Bender, *Conrad Grebel*, pp. 294–296.

Epistolae Grebelianae, translated by Yoder; typescript

deposited in Goshen College Library, Goshen, Ind.; excerpts therefrom printed by Bender, *Conrad Grebel*, pp. 281–282; 288–293; several printed in full in *MQR, passim*.

Haetzer, Louis (1500–1529), *Hymn* (1529), translated by Weis, *The Life of Ludwig Hetzer* (Dorchester, Mass.), pp. 207–210.

Martyrdom (1529), in *Martyrology*, I, pp. 97–100.

Helwys, Thomas (?1550–1616), *The Mistery of Iniquity* (1612) (London, 1935).

Persecution for religions judg'd and condemn'd in a discourse between an antichristian and a christian (1615).

Hubmaier, Balthasar (?1482–1528), *Concerning Heretics and Those Who Burn Them* (1524), translated by Henry C. Vedder, *Balthasar Hubmaier* (New York/London, 1905), pp. 84–88.

Form for the Celebration of the Lord's Supper, translated by W. J. McClothlin, *The Baptist Review and Expositor*, III (1906), pp. 82–97; reprinted in Fosdick, *op. cit.*, pp. 311–315.

A Dialogue between Hubmaier and Zwingli on Infant Baptism (1526), extensive extract in Henry Burrage, *History of the Anabaptists in Switzerland* (Philadelphia, 1883), pp. 148–152.

On the Sword (1527), translated by Henry C. Vedder, *Balthasar Hubmaier* (New York/London, 1905), pp. 275–311.

A Song in Praise of God's Word, translated by Vedder, *op. cit.*, pp. 311–321.

A Dialogue Between the Preachers at Basel and Balthasar Hubmaier of Friedberg Concerning Infant Baptism (1527), translated by Vedder; manuscript in the Library of the Colgate Rochester Divinity School, Rochester, New York.

Concerning Brotherly Discipline: Where it is not there certainly is no church though water baptism and the supper of Christ be observed (1527), translated by Vedder; manuscript in Rochester.

Ground and reason why each one though baptized in infancy is bound to be baptized rightly according to the order of Christ even if he is a hundred years old (1527), translated by Vedder; manuscript in Rochester.

A Synopsis of Christian Doctrine which each man should know before he is baptized in water (1526), translated by Vedder; manuscript in Rochester.

A Short Apology: To all believers in Christ that they should not be scandalized by the untruths invented and charged upon him by his enemies (1526), translated by Vedder; manuscript in Rochester.

The twelve articles of Christian belief set forth as a prayer in the water-tower at Zurich (1527), translated by Howard Osgood in Vedder, *op. cit.*, pp. 130–136.

The Complete Works, collected and photographed by W. O. Lewis; translated by G. D. Davidson, William Jewell College, Liberty, Missouri. Typescript. Copies in several Baptist libraries. The copy the editor used was from the Southern Baptist Theological Seminary Library, Louisville, Ky.

Hutter, Jacob (? –1536), *Letter of Remonstrance to John Kuna of Kunstadt* (1535), in *Martyrology,* I, pp. 149–153.

John of Overdam (? –1550), *Confession, Letter, and Acts* (c. 1550), in *Martyrology,* I, pp. 314–336; 339.

Joris, David (1501–1556), *The Plea for Servetus,* a letter, translated by R. H. Bainton, *Concerning Heretics* (New York, 1935), pp. 305–309.

Langenmantel, Eitelhans (? –1528), *An Exposition of the Lord's Prayer* (c. 1527), translated by J. C. Wenger, *MQR,* XXII (1948), pp. 40–42.

  A Sermon (c. 1521), *MQR,* XXII (1948), pp. 36–40.

  A Prayer (c. 1528), in *Martyrology,* I, pp. 86–88.

Mantz, Felix (c. 1480–1527), *Petition of Protest and Defense to the Zurich Council* (late 1524), translated and edited by E. H. Correll and H. S. Bender, *GQR,* XXVII (1926), pp. 23–31; reprinted in part by Bender, *Conrad Grebel,* p. 287. It is here ascribed to Grebel, but more recently it has been reassigned to Mantz by Leonhard von Muralt and Walter Schmid, *Quellen zur Geschichte der Täufer in der Schwerz,* I (Zurich, 1952), p. 23.

Marpeck, Pilgram (?1495–1556), selections from *On the Sword,* translated by John Horsch, *The Principle of Nonresistance* (Scottdale, Pa., 1940), 24 f. This book is a collection of similar excerpts from the early Anabaptists.

Ochino, Bernardino (1484–1563), *Certaine Godly and Very Profitive Sermons, of Faith, Hope and Charitie* (1530), translated by William Phiston (London, 1580).

  A Dialogue of Polygamy (London, 1548).

  Sermons (1541–62), translated by R.C. (London, 1548).

  A Tragaedy or Dialoge of the iniuste usurped primacie of the Bishop of Rome, translated by John Ponet (London, 1549); reprinted and edited by C. E. Plumtre (London, 1899).

Paracelsus (1493–1541), selected writings, edited by Jolande Jacobi (New York, 1951).

Philips, Dietrich (1504–1568), *Enchiridion or Handbook* (1564), translated from the German translation from the Dutch by A. B. Kolb (Elkhart, Ind., 1910).

Reublin, William (c. 1480–after 1559), *Letter to Pilgram Marpeck* (1531), translated by J. C. Wenger, *MQR*, XXIII (1949), pp. 67–75.

On Original Sin and the Way of Redemption, *MQR*, XXVI (1952), p. 210.

Ridemann, Peter (1506–1556), *Appeal to the Lords of Lichtenstein* (1545), condensed; translated by W. J. McGlothlin, *Baptist Confessions* (Philadelphia, 1911), pp. 19–23.

Account of Our Religion, Doctrine, and Faith (1565) (London, 1950), Rinck. Melchior (1493–1545), *Letter and a Note: Allow the Children to Come to Me*, etc., *Mark* 10, translated by J. C. Wenger, *MQR*, XXI (1947), pp. 282–84.

Rothmann, Bernard (1495–1535), *Earthly and Temporal Power* (c. 1530), translated by George A. Moore, mimeograph (Chevy Chase, Md., 1950).

Rys, John de and Lubbert Gerritsz (1534–1612), *A Brief Confession of the Principal Articles of the Christian Faith* (1580, Alkmaar, 1610). McGlothlin, *Baptist Confessions*, pp. 26–48.

Letter from the Waterland Church (c. 1610), B. Evans, *The Early English Baptists*, I (London, 1862), pp. 211–213.

S. B., an English Anabaptist, *A Conference Between a Christian* [*William White*] *and an English Anabaptist* (1575), edited by Albert Peel, Baptist Historical Society, *Transactions*, VII (1920), pp. 78–128.

Sattler, Michael (c. 1495–1527), *Concerning the Satisfaction of Christ* (c. 1527): an Anabaptist tract on true Christianity, translated by J. C. Wenger, *MQR*, XX (1946), p. 234; also in *Mennonite Historical Bulletin*, VII (1946).

The Hearing of False Prophets or Antichrists, translated by J. C. Wenger, *MQR*, XXI (1947), p. 276.

Concerning Evil Overseers, ibid., p. 280.

Concerning Divorce, ibid., p. 116.

Two Kinds of Obedience, translated by J. C. Wenger, *MQR*, XXI (1947), p. 18; reprinted by Fosdick, *op. cit.*, pp. 296–299.

Letter to the Congregation in Horb (1522), in *Martyrology*, I, pp. 27–34.

The Schleitheim Confession of Faith (1527), translated by W. J. McGlothlin, *Baptist Confessions of Faith* (Philadelphia, 1911), pp. 3–9; also translated by J. C. Wenger, *MQR*,

XIX (1945), pp. 243–53; reprinted in Fosdick, *op. cit.*, pp. 286–295.

Schwenckfeld, Caspar (1490–1561), *Letter to Johann Hess* (October 14, 1521), Document II (Latin) *Corpus Schwenckfeldianorum*, I, pp. 13–15.

Letter to Johann Hess (June 13, 1522), Document III (Latin), *CS*, I, pp. 39–41.

Letter to a friend who is on the point of losing his faith (March 31, 1523), Document IV, *CS*, I, pp. 64–66.

A Missive and Reminder to the Sisters in the Cloisters at Naumberg am Queis: How they shall conduct themselves in the present changeful time, and how they may profitably use the cloistered life according to the freedom of the Spirit (September, 1523), Document VI, *CS*, I, pp. 124–129.

A Christian Exhortation for the Furtherance of the Word of God: an open letter to Jacob von Salze, Bishop of Breslau (January 1, 1524), by C.S. and Hanns Magnus von Langenwalde, Document VII, *CS*, I, pp. 284–304, reproduced by Selina Schultz, *Caspar Schwenckfeld von Ossig* (Norristown, Pa., 1946), pp. 33–53.

The [Lost] Twelve Questions or Argument Against Impanation (July, 1525), Document XI, *CS*, II, pp. 132–139; this is a translation by C. D. Hartranft of what is presumably the embodiment of the lost Questions in the larger Document LXXXVII (August, 1529); the Hartranft translation is reproduced by Selina Schultz, *Schwenckfeld*, pp. 151–152.

Extract from the *Diary* [concerning the discussion with Luther about the Eucharist] (December 1–4, 1525), Document XVIII, *CS*, II, translated by Selina Schultz, *Schwenckfeld*, pp. 75–97.

Circular Letter [on the suspension of the Supper] (April 21, 1526), by C. S. Valentine Crautwald, and the Liegnitz Pastors and Preachers, Document XXVIII, *CS*, II, translated by Selina Schultz, *Schwenckfeld*, pp. 106–109.

De cursu verbi Dei: A Letter to Conrad Cordatus (March 4, 1527), Document XLI (Latin), *CS*, II, pp. 583–599, translated up to p. 596, line 6, by Selina Schultz, *Schwenckfeld*, pp. 130–135.

Appendix to *De cursu verbi Dei* (autumn, 1527), Document LII, *CS*, II, pp. 675–79, line 18. Paraphrased by Selina Schultz, *Schwenckfeld*, pp. 135–136.

A Criticism of the Augsburg Confession (c. 1530), introduction, Document CVIII, *CS*, III, pp. 866–884; see below, *A Deliberation on Christian Liberty*.

Letter to Landgrave Philip of Hesse (after May 18, 1534), Document CLXIV, *CS*, V, pp. 99–103, paraphrased by James L. French, *The Correspondence of Caspar Schwenckfeld von Ossig and the Landgrave Philip of Hesse* (Leipzig, 1908), p. 1.

Letter to the Landgrave Philip of Hesse (before September 26, 1535), Document CCIV, *CS*, V, pp. 387–400, paraphrased by French, *op. cit.*, pp. 64–65.

Letter to the Landgrave Philip of Hesse (September 26, 1535), Document CCVI, *CS*, V, pp. 402–403, paraphrased by French, *op. cit.*, p. 6.

Seventh Letter to Helena Streicher and Her Godfearing Daughters (before September 25, 1537), Document CCXXIX, *CS*, V, pp. 697–709. Translated by Selina Schultz as "Christian Patience and Humility," *The Schwenckfeldian*, L (1953), pp. 116; 131; 145; 157.

Letter (and Treatise) to the Landgrave Philip of Hesse (January 1, 1542), Document CCCLV, *CS*, VIII, pp. 5–10, paraphrased by French, *op. cit.*, p. 11–12.

Letter to the Landgrave Philip of Hesse (January 5, 1542), Document CCCLVI, *CS*, VIII, pp. 26–28, paraphrased by French, *op. cit.*, p. 18–19.

Letter to the Landgrave Philip of Hesse (July 20, 1542), Document CCCLXX, *CS*, VIII, pp. 138–146, paraphrased by French, *op. cit.*, pp. 39–40.

Letter to the Landgrave Philip of Hesse (September 7, 1542), Document CCCLXXVII, *CS*, VIII, pp. 263–265, paraphrased by French, *op. cit.*, p. 49.

Letter to the Landgrave Philip of Hesse (April, ?, 1543), Document DCCCCXXXVII, (1555), *CS*, XIV, pp. 437–446, paraphrased by French, *op. cit.*, pp. 53–54.

The Heavenly Balm and the Divine Physician (December 18, 1545), Document DXIV, *CS*, IX, pp. 512–624. Translated by F. R. Anspach in *The Heavenly Balm and the Divine Physician* (Baltimore, 1858).

The Three Kinds of Human Life (c. June 21, 1546), Document DXXXIV, *CS*, IX, pp. 826–940. Translated by F. R. Anspach in *The Heavenly Balm*.

True and Heretical Faith [*in respect to predestination*] (August 24, 1549), Document DCCXX, *CS*, XI, pp. 887–906 (omits pp. 906–913). Translated by F. R. Anspach as "A Letter to Some Christian Friends" in *The Heavenly Balm*.

A Deliberation on Liberty of Belief, Christian Doctrine, Opinion, Conscience (before August, 1561), Document MCLIX, *CS*,

XVI. Translated by Selina Gerhard Schultz; typescript in Pennsburg. The first five paragraphs reproduce almost verbatim Schwenckfeld's *A Criticism of the Augsburg Confession* (c. 1530), Document CXVIII, *CS*, III, pp. 863–864, while the whole is in effect a concise restatement of the whole of that introduction: pp. 866[19]–884[15].

A Summarized Statement concerning the Non-Observance of the Lord's Supper (August 1, 1561), Document MCLXI, *CS*, XVI. Translated by Selina Gerhard Schultz, *Schwenckfeld*, pp. 112–114 (apparently complete except for ellipses in respect to Zwingli and Calvin, p. 114).

Statement of Doctrine and Calling (after August, 1561), Document MCLXVI, *CS*, XVI.

Servetus, Michael (1511–1553), *On the Errors of the Trinity* (1531), translated by E. W. Wilbur, *Harvard Theological Studies*, XVI (Cambridge, Mass., 1932).

The Christianisimi Restitutio (1553). Selections translated by Roland Bainton, *Hunted Heretic* (Boston, 1953). Section on the lesser circulation translated by Charles D. O'Malley, *Michael Servetus: A Translation of His Geographical, Medical and Astrological Writings with Introduction and Notes*, Memoirs of the American Philosophical Society, XXXIV (Philadelphia, 1953), 202–208.

Simons, Menno (1496–1561), *The Complete Works* (Elkhart, Ind., 1871), translated from the Dutch edition of 1681; excerpts therefrom systematically arranged by John Horsch and Harold Bender, *Menno Simons' Life and Work* (Scottdale, Pa., 1944), pp. 55–110; *A Foundation* (1539), translated by Daniel Rupp (Lancaster, Pa., 1863); *The Complete Writings*, translated by Leonard Verduin (Scottdale, Pa., 1956).

The Cross of Christ (1556), newly revised translation by Peter van Tuinen (Scottdale, Pa., 1946).

A Letter to a Troubled Christian; John Horsch, *Menno Simons* (Scottdale, Pa., 1916), pp. 214–16; reprinted by John C. Wenger, *Glimpses of Mennonite History and Doctrine*, 2d ed. (Scottdale, Pa., 1947), pp. 204–205.

Smuel, Andrew (Dietrich Peterson) (? –1546), *Confession* and *Testament* (c. 1546), in *Martyrology*, I, pp. 278–291.

Socinus, Faustus (1539–1604), *The Racovian Catechism* (1605), embodying his influence, translated by Thomas Rees (London, 1818).

An Argument for the Authority of Holy Scripture (1570), translated by Edward Combe (London, 1731).

Socinus, Laelius (1525–1562), *Confession of Faith* (1555), translated by Edward M. Hulme in *Persecution and Liberty: Essays in Honor of George Lincoln Burr* (New York, 1931), pp. 216–218.

Thomas of Imbroich (1533–1558), *Confession concerning Baptism and Two Letters* (1558), in *Martyrology*.

Walpot, Peter (Peter Scherer) (1519–1578), *Reason and Obedience*: Letter to the Apothecary Simon (1571), translated by Harold Bender, *MQR*, XIX (1945), pp. 29–37.

 School Order (probably by Walpot, 1578), translated by Harold Bender, *MQR*, V (1931), pp. 232–241.

 Address to Schoolmasters (1568), translated by Harold Bender, *MQR*, V (1931), pp. 241–244.

Walter of Stoelwijk (? –1541), Epistle (c. 1541), in *Martyrology*, I, pp. 211–236.

Weigel, Valentine (1533–1588), *Of the Life of Christ* (1578), translated (London, 1648).

PART TWO

EVANGELICAL CATHOLICISM AS
REPRESENTED BY JUAN DE VALDÉS

Introduction

LIFE AND DEATH OF JUAN DE VALDÉS

THE SUBJECT OF THIS CONCLUDING PORTION OF A volume devoted to "Spiritual and Anabaptist Writers" is Juan de Valdés, the greatest of the Spanish Reformers. His theological point of view as well as his personality was closely related to contemporary Spanish historical and cultural events. The first purpose of this introduction is to place Valdés in the historical and cultural environment within which his development as an original thinker may best be seen.

The life of Juan de Valdés spanned the first half of the sixteenth century. Those years, embracing the reign of Charles I (Charles V as Roman emperor), 1517–1556, were perhaps the most decisive in the history of Spain, because it was during this time that Spain suffered what I have elsewhere called "a change of direction" in its national life.[1] Up to this time, the people, the real Spanish nation, and their sovereigns had not come to a serious clash. This is exactly what happened in the reign of Charles.

"This, the key period of Spanish history," says Madariaga, "cannot be understood unless the spring motive which animates it is appraised at its true value.

"Charles V was the greatest monarch of the Austrian dynasty. His very hesitations toward the Reformation should be read in relation to the high and noble dream which animated him. He heard on the one hand the duke of Brunswick, in the name of the Catholic princes and the prelates at Mainz, urging him to take strong action; on the other, the wise and generous advice of his Spanish secretary (Alfonso) Valdés, whose leanings were not un-

[1] A. M. Mergal, *Reformismo Cristiano y Alma Española*, Ch. 22, pp. 17–32, and Ch. 5, pp. 73–86.

297

favorable to the Reformation. His policy was not definite, but it was clear. He wished to save the unity of Christendom while remaining faithful to the purity of his faith; hence, while uncompromising as to dogma, he tried to compromise as much as he could in every other way."[2]

Upon arriving in Spain, Charles found himself in the current of a complex and rich tradition. Spain had become catholic in the fullest sense of universality. That which was Spanish did not fear the most versatile diversification. But very soon Spain closed all its frontiers. The narrow circle of an exclusive Hispanicism suffocated the very essence of the Spanish soul.

An observation of Benjamin Wiffen, upon the death of Alfonso de Valdés, which occurred in Vienna on October 5, 1532, sums up the essence of this change:

"With him (Alfonso) seemed to come to an end the policy of the party of freedom, which had caused Spanish affairs to arrive at so prosperous a promise. . . . Two powers in the state became successively absolute, neither of which paid any deference to the people, who in all countries form the real basis of the commonweal—the court and the church. The latter was more oppressive than the former, because freedom of the mind became more enthralled than freedom of the person."[3]

The main events of this important period are all meaningful for a correct interpretation of the momentous change that was going to take place in Spanish history. Let it be noted first that, from the very beginning, Charles clashed with the Spanish people, as represented by the Cortes, by the *Comuneros*, or by such a typical Spanish character as Cardinal Ximenes de Cisneros.[4]

Although the Cortes were a very poor representation of the people, the fact that Charles was unable to handle them was very significant, revealing in him a profound misunderstanding of the Spanish genius. Then, to check the revolt of the Castilian *Comuneros*, Castile being the real soul of Spain, he had to pit them against the northern and southern provinces.

García de Loaysa, cardinal of Osma, Charles's confessor and personal envoy to Pope Clement VII, voiced the feelings of that half of the Spanish people that annihilated, in the name of their emperor, the revolt for freedom of the other half. In Loaysa's

---

[2] Salvador de Madariaga, *Spain*, pp. 46 and 66.
[3] B. Wiffen, *Life and Writings of Juan de Valdés*, pp. 91, 92.
[4] William Robertson and William H. Prescott, *The History of the Reign of the Emperor Charles the Fifth*, pp. 416–422.

own words, the defeat of the Commons had shown the procedure to be followed with the Protestants.

"I never found any better cure for heretics than the force of the Catholic princes, because since heresy originates in the will only, reason has no part in its cure.

"I always compared them (the Protestants) with the Castilian *Comuneros*, following the path of soft dealings and less than honest means; we lost our time, until the sure and only remedy was applied to them, war.... Your Majesty had better quit that fancy of converting souls to God and from now on convert bodies to your obedience.... Even if they are heretics, let them be your servants.... Don't be afraid even of buying their faith."[5]

Although not so outspoken, such were and had been the feelings of other advisers. But if many agreed with Loaysa's opinion: "Let him part company with that ominous enterprise of the Council,"[6] his secretary of Latin correspondence, Alfonso de Valdés, had quite different ideas. He championed the Erasmian feelings of tolerance and peace, and with him the archbishop of Seville and General Inquisitor Manrique, university scholars, and deeply religious people all over the nation. The idea of an ecumenical council where all things would be arranged by peaceful and reasonable means was the chief concern of Alfonso de Valdés. Nobody had any doubts concerning the ends; the world must be saved for Catholic Christianity; but concerning the means, Spain was a house divided against itself. Some wanted tolerance in dogma and intolerance in morals; some wanted it the other way around; some wanted tolerance in both.

Quite clearly, two opposite tendencies in the religious sphere, and two corresponding tendencies in the political sphere, developed side by side during the Middle Ages, and during the reign of Charles were coming swiftly to a sharp issue. These two religious tendencies were faith by compulsion and authority emanating from Rome, and faith by personal and free concern for God. The first tendency follows the line: Saint Augustine, Gregory VII, Saint Thomas Aquinas, Council of Constance, Council of Trent, to mention only a few outstanding landmarks, culminating with the proclamation of papal infallibility by the Vatican Council in 1870. The second tendency runs from Saint Paul to Saint Augustine, from Augustine to the nominalists

---

[5] *Cartas Inéditas de Juan de Valdés al Cardenal Gonzaga*, p. LXXXIX.
[6] *Ibid.*, p. XC.

and mystics of the Middle Ages, to pre-Reformers, to Luther, culminating, perhaps with the modern Friends.

The two outstanding political issues may be expressed thus: the nationalistic ideal and the idea of a Catholic monarchy. These two ideals fought each other within political ideology developed from Augustine to Charles the Great, to Otto the Great, and culminating with Charles V. No wonder that, at the critical moment, all strong nationalistic realms sided with Luther, and even the Castilian secretary, Alfonso de Valdés, expressed a veiled sympathy for the German attitude, even if not for Luther himself.[7]

The political development of Spain is so tied to the development of the religious and intellectual life that it is almost impossible to separate these three aspects. Erasmus of Rotterdam and Adrian of Utrecht were the two most influential figures in the spiritual formation of the emperor. Erasmus was also the person of greatest religious and intellectual influence in the lives of the Valdés brothers. The Erasmian influence and the Erasmian controversy, indigenous spiritual movements like "alumbrismo,"[8] the Cisneros' reform, the progress of the Inquisition, the religious personalities all over the nation, were the most important events of this period as far as intellectual and religious life is concerned.

The life of Juan de Valdés runs parallel to these profound transformations in the Spanish scene. In the work of de Valdés one can see his contributions to the desideratum of liberty, the efforts that he made to preserve and enrich this policy, and the effect all this had on his own inner life, and its influence on Italy and on other reform currents in Europe.

Students of Juan de Valdés' life and work up to the present have considered him either as a product of foreign influence, Lutheran and Erasmian, or as a unique deviation from the Spanish tradition. Without disregarding the self-evident Erasmian influence upon Valdés' early thought, we consider his best work an expression of a pure Spanish genius. In the same line stand Raymond Lull, Cardinal Ximenes de Cisneros, Queen Isabel I, Ignacio de Loyola, and Santa Teresa de Jesús.

Juan and his brother Alfonso are two authentic representatives of the Spanish soul. In his time, Alfonso was not only

[7] B. Wiffen, *Life and Writings of Juan de Valdés*, pp. 30–35 and 45–47.
[8] "Alumbrismo" is considered as an indigenous Protestant movement in Spain. The followers were called "alumbrados" because they considered themselves to be "illumined" or "enlightened" by the Holy Spirit.

better known, but also more important because of the political influence which his position permitted him to exert. As secretary of Latin correspondence for the emperor, Alfonso enjoyed the intimate friendship of the sovereign and many relationships throughout all of Europe.

Nevertheless, the influence of Juan has been more profound. Alfonso was an Erasmian in his political action as well as in his books. Juan succeeded in bringing to maturity an original orientation within Hispanicism. Although he wrote incessantly, only one of his books, the *Dialogue on Christian Doctrine*, saw the light during the lifetime of the author. Of his other books, published after his death, only one, the *Dialogue on Language*, has been published in its entirety in the original Spanish. The rest of his works, with the exception of some fragments, were published in Italian translations made by the followers of the author.

The greatest work of Juan, nevertheless, was realized through his personal contact with his followers. One of these followers, Peter Martyr Vermigli, exerted a great influence in the English church. About this, John T. Betts has written:

"The Zurich letters witness with what reverence both Archbishop Cranmer and Bishop Jewell held Peter Martyr as the master-spirit in Israel; and can it be otherwise than deeply interesting to the English reader to study the sentiments of Juan de Valdés who molded the mind, in Evangelical doctrine, of Peter Martyr, the arch-counselor of the recognized founders of the English Church?"[9]

At the close of the sixteenth century, the contribution of Juan de Valdés to thought and reform attitudes was known all over the Continent. When his thought was absorbed by the Reform current, the author was forgotten, like so many others, until he was rediscovered by a small group of Quaker scholars about the middle of the nineteenth century.

The Valdés family, probably of Asturian origin, came to live in Cuenca during the closing days of the reign of Alfonso VIII.[10]

[9] John T. Betts, Introduction to *One Hundred and Ten Considerations*, p. 200.
[10] E. Cione, *Juan de Valdés*, p. 15. Juan Pablo Martir Rizo, in his *History of the City of Cuenca*, Madrid, 1629, p. 284, says: "The house of Valdés is one of the most ancient and distinguished of the kingdom of León. A gentleman of this name and family, called Hernando de Valdés, came somewhat more than three hundred and fifty years ago to settle in the City of Cuenca, where he left magnificent houses, a chapel, and entailed estates; he had many children and from them many noble descendants." Cuenca is situated between Madrid and Valencia, about thirty miles south of Madrid.

The two persons who exerted the most powerful influence in the determination of the character, ideas, and spirit of Juan de Valdés were his father, don Ferrando, and his lord Diego López Pacheco, marquis of Villena and lord of Escalona. Both of them were supposed to be connected with the political movements of the *Comunidades*, with the Italian humanistic movements, and with the clerical reform movement which had as its goal the deepening of Christian faith.

We have no reports of the childhood of the Valdés brothers, but there is an autobiographical passage in the *Dialogue on Christian Doctrine:*

"You must know that my father had this habit. Each morning, as soon as he got up, he used to hold a reunion of his sons and daughters and members of the household, and there he instructed them about almost all these points that I have considered. And after that, he would ask in more or less the same fashion what you have questioned me. Because he said that in the same way that a bishop must instruct the members of his diocese in Christian doctrine, and the curate the members of his church, in much the same way was it his duty to instruct the members of his household, especially so, since he was a man of letters, and since he did not become learned in order to earn a living, but for the edification of his soul and of the members of his household.

"Besides this, my father had a teacher at home . . . who was also a friend of every good Christian thing; and with the continuous communication and conversation of this one, I found that I was much benefited and I learned many of the things I have told you."[11]

In 1524, Juan de Valdés was living at Escalona in the service of the marquis of Villena. A pious atmosphere with strong reform tendencies reigned at the court of the marquis.[12] In 1527, Juan was at the University of Alcalá, dedicated to the study of the humanities. Here he published in 1529, at the press of Miguel de Eguía, his *Dialogue on Christian Doctrine*. Between 1527 and 1529 his brother Alfonso had written and circulated his two dialogues, *Mercurio and Charon* and *Lactancio and the Archdeacon*, which together constitute the book *Dialogue on the Things Which Happened in Rome*. These two *Dialogues*, in which Alfonso made Pope Clement VII responsible for the sack of Rome by the troops of the emperor, brought upon the Valdés brothers the enmity of the papal nuncio, Count Baldassare Castiglione.

11 J. de Valdés, *Diálogo de Doctrina Cristiana*, Madrid, Librería Nacional, 1929, p. 121.
12 M. Bataillon, Introduction to the *Dialogue on Christian Doctrine*, pp. 67, 79.

When the *Dialogue on Christian Doctrine* came out, the sound of Castiglione's angry voice was still in the air. Although the book was dedicated to the illustrious lord, Diego López Pacheco, marquis of Villena, hardly had it seen the light when it was attacked by the Anti-Erasmians. A lawsuit against its author was begun.[12]

By August, 1531, Juan de Valdés was in Rome. In Spain he was sought by the officials of the Inquisition. Although in December, 1529, Alfonso had obtained a breve from Clement VII[13] which absolved the imperial secretary and all the members of his family, Juan did not dare return to Spain. Juan de Vergara, his former Greek teacher at Alcalá, and many of those who, as members of a commission appointed by the Inquisition, had examined the works of Erasmus and the works of the Valdés brothers, had been, in their turn, judged and condemned by the Holy Office.

After the death of Alfonso in Vienna, in October of 1532, Juan lived some time at the court of the emperor in Mantua and in Bologna. Through the mediation of Secretary Cobos, the emperor paid Juan the salary of his brother from October on, and assigned him to the post of filer of Naples, for which Alfonso had been named. Juan resigned this appointment in December, 1533.

During his stay in Mantua, Juan established a close relationship with Cardinal Ercole Gonzaga, a near relative of the countess of Fondi, Giulia Gonzaga. Then, while Juan lived in Naples, he sustained private correspondence with the cardinal from December 1, 1535, until January 12, 1537. This correspondence affords an excellent opportunity through which to contemplate something of the spiritual biography of Valdés.

Juan served as chamberlain to Pope Clement VII until the latter's death in 1534. Then he moved to Naples, where he lived for the rest of his life. The Neapolitan epoch, from 1535 until his death in 1541, was the period of his most creative religious activity. Cardinal Pietro Carnesecchi, on whom Valdés had a profound influence, was much surprised to find him in Naples, devoted to such spiritual exercises.

"Although I had known Juan de Valdés at Rome in the time of Pope Clement, I cannot say that I knew him as a theologian before the year 1540 in Naples. For when in Rome . . . I knew him only as a modest and well-bred courtier, and as such I liked him very

13 John E. Longhurst, *Erasmus and the Spanish Inquisition*, p. 12.

much. . . . At Naples, however, the friendship grew to be a spiritual one, for I found him entirely given up to the Spirit, and wholly intent on the study of the Holy Scripture. This, however, would not have been sufficient with me, to give him the credit I did, now that the *gentihomo di spada e cappa*, the layman and the courtier, had, for me, suddenly become the theologian, had I not observed what a high place he occupied in the eyes of Fra Bernardino Ochino, who then was preaching, to the admiration of everybody, at Naples, and who professed to receive the themes of many of his sermons from Valdés, from whom he used to get a note on the evening preceding the morning on which he was to ascend the pulpit; and if Fra Bernardino's opinion would not have been in harmony with that of Flaminio, whom I thought was such a prudent and learned man, that he would not have been imposed upon; and so sincere and worthy, that he would not have wished to delude others."[14]

From the inquisitorial lawsuit of Pietro Carnesecchi we learn of the numerous people of distinction on whom Valdés exerted a profound influence.

Bernardino Ochino di Siena was a preacher at the church of Giovanni Maggiore. Charles V, upon returning from his African expedition, heard him and was profoundly impressed. Ochino came to England, invited by Cranmer, and stayed at Oxford together with Peter Martyr Vermigli, who belonged also to Valdés' circle.

Giulio da Milano was a professor of theology. He published a volume of sermons and founded some churches at Puschiavo, in the Grisons.

Fabio Mario Galeota, a Neapolitan gentleman, was a prisoner of the Inquisition at Rome and escaped the eighteenth of August, 1559, when, on the death of Paul IV, the populace attacked the prison. Garcilaso de la Vega, the famed Spanish poet, was a friend to both Galeota and Valdés.

Benedetto Cusano was Peter Martyr's fellow student at Padua. Both of them became great Greek scholars.

Giovanno Mollio, of Montalcino, near Siena, was lecturer at the monastery of San Lorenzo at Naples.

Lorenzo Romano, a Sicilian, recanted under the persecution by the Inquisition.

Giambattista Folengo, prior of the Benedictines of Monte Casino, wrote a commentary on the Psalms, published in 1542.

Pier Paolo Vergerio, bishop of Capo d'Istria, was papal nuncio, and a member of the Council of Trent. He preserved

14 Edward Boehmer, *Lives of Juan and Alfonso Valdés*, pp. 23–24.

the manuscript of the *One Hundred and Ten Considerations* and published this work in Basel in 1550.

Giovanni Francisco de Aloys, named Caserta, was Flaminio's intimate friend. In March, 1564, he was beheaded and burned in the market place of Naples.

Marc Antonio Flaminio was a distinguished Latin poet.

Jacopo Bonfadio was the author of the famous letter to Carnesecchi, quoted below.

Pietro Carnesecchi, the papal prothonotary, secretary of Clement VII, was of a distinguished Florentine family; he was a man of great learning and deep piety. In 1546 he was called to Rome by the Inquisition to defend himself, but was acquitted. In 1565 he was summoned for a second time, and on October 3, 1567, was burned alive.

Among the famous women influenced by Valdés, three are especially renowned in the Italian Renaissance. Constanza d'Avalos, duchess di Amalfi, of noble Spanish ancestry, gave her mind to the love and study of poetry.

Vittoria Colonna, marquesa di Pescara, daughter of Fabrizio Colonna, grand constable of Naples, was the youthful widow of Ferrante d'Avalos, marquis of Pescara, Charles V's commander at the battle of Pavia. After the death of her husband, she dedicated her life to sacred studies, poetry, and retirement. She was also a friend of Michael Angelo Buonarotti, who addressed several sonnets to her.

Giulia Gonzaga, duchess of Trajetto and countess of Fondi, was Valdés' closest friend. It was Giulia who inspired not only *The Christian Alphabet*, but also most of Valdés' Commentaries on the Holy Scripture; and it was probably she who preserved the manuscripts of the works of Valdés.

The last years of Valdés' life, spent in Naples, were not only years of the deepening of his Christian piety, but also of feverish literary production. Pacheco, one of the speakers in the *Dialogue on Language*, describes this period thus:

"I have never in my life seen a man more given to writing, always in his home, who became a veritable Saint John the Evangelist, pen in hand, so much so that I think he writes at night as well as by day, and by day he writes what he dreams at night."[15]

Valdés possessed a villa in Chiaja, one of the most beautiful quarters of Naples. There he gathered his friends on Sundays. The mornings were dedicated to prayer, meditation, and pious

15 J. de Valdés, *Diálogo de la Lengua*, p. 16.

conversations. In these meetings the *One Hundred and Ten Considerations* arose. Also his translation and Commentary in Spanish on the Hebrew Psalms, the Commentaries on Romans and Corinthians, and his Commentary on the Gospel of Saint Matthew are from this period. These are the works that have come down to us. Probably he wrote commentaries to the other three Gospels and to other Epistles of Paul.

Those who were contemporaneous to Valdés felt, at his death, the emptiness that the disappearance of a great leader always leaves. Jacopo Bonfadio, in a letter to Cardinal Pietro Carnesecchi, has expressed this feeling with eloquence, rendering at the same time a high tribute to the Spanish Reformer:

"May it please God that you may return. Yet, thinking on the other side, where shall we go, since Signor Valdés is dead. This has been truly a great loss for us, and for the world, for Signor Valdés was one of the rare men of Europe, and these writings he has left on the Epistles of Paul and the Psalms of David will fully confirm it. He was, without doubt, in his actions, his speech, and in all his conduct, a perfect man. With a particle of his soul he governed his frail and spare body; with the larger part and with his pure understanding, as though almost out of the body, he was always exalted in the contemplation of the truth and of divine things."[16]

The poet Daniel Rogers, writing an epigram on John Jewell, includes Juan de Valdés among the great names of the Reformation.

"The Italians will evermore assert the claims of the
    divine Martyr,
France may extol their Calvin to the stars;
Germany may boast and pride herself over Melanchthon,
And Luther drag in the same triumphal car with him. . . .
May John Knox's teaching characterize all Scotland,
Of Valdés, as an author, let all Spain be proud."[17]

This line of Rogers, "Valdesio Hispanus scriptore superbiat orbis," was selected by the Valdesians of the nineteenth century, Wiffen, Boehmer, Usoz, and Betts, as the theme of all their works newly published. Thus it was that a writer, practically forgotten for almost two centuries, once again came to life to occupy the place that belonged to him not only in the history of

16 Giuseppe Paladino, *Opuscoli e Lettere di Riformatori Italiani*, Vol. 1, p. 96.
17 Lawrence Humphrey, *Life and Death of John Jewell, Bishop of Salisbury*.

Spanish culture, but also in the history of that spiritual revolution called the Reformation.

VALDESIAN THOUGHT

Those who have read with attention and with impartiality the works of Juan de Valdés have always found reasons to admire him. Some have admired him for his spiritual depth, others for his literary style and contributions to Spanish letters, others for his humane attitude, but all have admired him. José Montesinos called him "the most well-balanced and sensitive spirit of our sixteenth century."[18]

Benjamin Wiffen, comparing him with Luther, wrote: "His doctrine of justification by faith alone is an acceptation deeper and more intimate, although less demonstrative than that which Luther himself enunciated to reform Europe."[19]

Perhaps Montesinos himself offers the best explanation of this admiration which Juan de Valdés awakened among his contemporaries and awakens even among present-day readers. "In the history of culture," he says, "one counts not only the works, but also the attitudes, and today, when theology so little interests us, we are attracted above all by his humanity."

This thing that Montesinos calls "his humanity," nevertheless, is the expression of his thought and deepest emotion. We should like to be able to give an idea, although merely schematic, of the development and structure of this thought, which, in our judgment, is the most profound source of his spiritual poise.

There are three dates that mark prominent milestones in the mental life of Juan de Valdés: 1529, the year in which he published his *Dialogue on Christian Doctrine*; 1537, when his correspondence with Cardinal Ercole Gonzaga ceased; and the four remaining years of his life, dedicated to meditation and spiritual conversation.

The first period could be called "Erasmian." If it is true that Spanish humanism precedes that of Europe, and above all that of Erasmus, by several years, it is also true, perhaps for the same reason, that Erasmus was generally accepted among the Spanish humanists, and, above all, in the recently founded University of Alcalá. When Juan entered this university, his brother Alfonso had already established intimate intellectual relations with Erasmus and with all those Spanish Hellenists,

---

[18] J. Montesinos, *Diálogo de la Lengua*, p. XLVI.
[19] B. Wiffen, *Alfabeto Christiano*, p. LII.

Latinists, and Hebraic scholars who were admirers of the humanist from Rotterdam.

Erasmus is alive in the *Dialogue on the Things Which Happened in Rome*, and also in the *Dialogue on Christian Doctrine*. To the optimism of the humanistic position belongs not only the understanding of the religious problem as a pedagogical problem, but also his way of understanding the exterior and interior imperial policy, the ecclesiastical reform, and the most complicated theological and cultural affairs. The superficial and ironic humor of the *Praise of Folly* is present, although strongly affected by the natural Spanish gravity, in the *Dialogue on Christian Doctrine*.

The fundamental antithesis which animates the *Dialogue* is not yet the "oldness of the letter" face to face with the "newness of the spirit" (Rom. 7:6), but "the verbal formula" face to face with rationalistic or humanistic thinking.

Nevertheless, a new category, called by Valdés "contemplation" already appears. It is not that first step or plane of medieval mysticism, called by the same name. The Valdesian "contemplation" is like an insight into a personal, spiritual truth, not communicable through any resource of mediation or gradation of a Catholic type—but humanistic. The "archbishop" describes it for "Eusebio" in the following manner:

"Read the psalm of David which begins, 'Blessed are the undefiled in the way' (Ps. 119), and there you will see how all contemplation and exercise of that most holy prophet was to think on the commandments and on the law of God, and in the same way you will find this in many other psalms. Then if you will read some of the Epistles of Saint Paul, in all these you will not find any other way of contemplation. Hold, then, for certain that this is the true contemplation; because from it the soul takes all knowledge of the greatest good, the grandeur and mercy of God; from it come to our knowledge, our own smallness and misery. Here one learns what is that which we ought to do for God and what we should do for our neighbors, and what for ourselves; there is, finally, no good which cannot be reached through this constant contemplation."[20]

Marcel Bataillon thinks that in spite of the evident Erasmian spirit in this work, one can appreciate the way in which the Spanish thinker differs from Erasmus.

"An irreversible movement from one to the other of these works (*Dialogue* and *Alphabet*) separates Valdés from Erasmus."

[20] J. de Valdés, *Diálogo de Doctrina Cristiana*, p. 124.

In the *Enchiridion*, for example, Erasmus places the emphasis on the adhesion of man to the divine will, on the assimilation that makes him a member of Christ and a participant of the benefit granted once for all to humankind. He who allows himself to be carried away by the eloquence of the *Enchiridion* must notice a kind of wisdom, easily communicable, sufficient to make him understand the horror of the judgment and the disgust of false piety.

For Valdés, on the contrary, regeneration is at the same time more free and less easy. One is not worthy of divine help until he has understood, from the most profound depth of his being, that without this help, no one can do anything that is truly good. To find oneself miserable and at the same time obliged to seek perfection is, for Valdés, the fertile paradox which nurtures unceasingly the Christian life. At the same time that he imitates Erasmus, Valdés moves in these dangerous regions of grace which the Flemish humanist surrounded with prudent barriers. In the transition from the *Dialogue* to the *Alphabet*, Erasmus disappears.[21]

Between one work and the other run these years from 1531 to 1537, when his correspondence with Cardinal Gonzaga ceased. In this correspondence Valdés still appears jovial, the same who, in correspondence with Gracian de Alderete, is pleased to send him fables, sayings, and jokes about monks. We could say that this Valdés is a paradigm of human prudence which later will deserve his disgust. He described himself as "a poor man, a courtier, who likes to live royally."

The letter of March 1, 1536, is revealing of a deep preoccupation, perhaps of a spiritual process in gestation:

"It is indeed true that thus for the stimulus that the letters of your illustrious lordship give me to attain knowledge of what passes in the world as knowing how man should govern his own business, I have desired that your illustrious lordship should have the grace to command me to write sometime on whatever you think of importance; be it of a general nature, as to say what we could promise ourselves about the pope, but I have not dared to ask because I have never wished to aggravate him whom I must serve. About what is going on now in this court, I have failed to advise your illustrious lordship, holding it certain that you are always most well informed from don Fernando as from the ambassador of the lord duke; but from here on I wish to find what to say, even though it

---

21 M. Bataillon, Introduction to the *Dialogue on Christian Doctrine*, p. 149 *et passim*.

be nothing more than the relations which Neapolitan ladies have with gentlemen of the court, of which I shall not now say anything through reverence of ashes. Of the rest, according to what I am able to understand, we shall be here, more than many think, because in order to tell your illustrious lordship the truth as I understand it, we have neither prudence to rule, nor the will to exercise it, and thus everything goes out of hand, which neither human prudence nor advice has any part in what is well done. God is the one who guides us and who does everything, and I hope that thus everything will come to a good end."

This "human prudence" in which Valdés places such confidence will fail very soon. Perhaps this failure illumines a new turn in the path undertaken already in the *Dialogue on Christian Doctrine*.

The correspondence with Cardinal Ercole Gonzaga ceased on January 11, 1537. But in the letters addressed to the secretary Francisco de los Cobos, even if the vigor of his tone is still the same, he already confessed that in relation to political matters, "I take very little interest."

In the introduction to *The Christian Alphabet*, Valdés tells us that this book originated as he was coming out, escorting the countess of Fondi from a religious service, where the general of the Capuchines preached. In this work, the author of the *Dialogue on Christian Doctrine* gives himself over to the same religious contemplation described so many years before.

It seems strange to Montesinsos that Valdés, in his letter to Ercole, hardly mentions religious matters. Yet the letter dated March 1, 1536, already quoted, seems to us to point to this change, which to Carnesecchi seemed sudden. The biographer Fermín Caballero is right when he says that it is not a usual thing in a man of talent and good judgment, given to philosophy and the humanities, to change in the last years of his life to an austere mysticism, to devote himself to religious teaching and to the exclusive exercise of piety, unless a catastrophic revolution has taken place in his spirit so that if it is not converted into a mania, it must be considered as a real fanatical urge.[22] It is neither mania nor a fanatical urge which possesses, during his last years, this man who was judged by Montesinos as "the most levelheaded and sensitive man of the sixteenth century." It was a slow and mature penetration into the meaning of his own life which precipitated the spiritual crisis which to the rest seemed a sudden change. Valdés' perfect

[22] Fermín Caballero, *Conquenses Ilustres*, Vol. 4, p. 220.

intuition of the inadequacy of "human prudence" to enable man to understand the mystery of existence, to show man how to govern his own affairs, revealed to him finally the truth of the gospel. He followed that same road, dimly seen already in the *Dialogue on Christian Doctrine*, and fully known now as the royal road to truth.

"It seems," wrote Montesinos in his unpublished Letters, "as if the consciousness of his political failures again activated his religious doubts, if it be that they were ever asleep" (p. CXII).

"These letters are as a division between his official activity and his apostleship" (p. CIII).

"The obscurity in which the documents leave us almost imposes the conjecture that the turn which Valdés' life took later is the result of his failure" (p. CXII).

The translation and Commentary on the Psalms helps to illuminate this "obscurity" which Montesinos laments. This is the first work dedicated to the countess; and it is worth noting the similarity of style in his secular letters to Ercole Gonzaga and the first work dedicated to Giulia Gonzaga. Here are some samples:

"Men judge according to what their prudence teaches them; they are deceived in almost everything" (Ps. 41, p. 244).

"The wicked sheep will be much pleased with ruling and governing himself by himself, and the good sheep enjoys more being ruled and governed by God. The wicked sheep has as a jewel free will, and the good one has it as a defect" (Ps. 23, p. 132).

"If indeed the pact with God is described, it will not be understood except by those who reach the secrets of the Lord. 'Human prudence' thinks that with ingenuity and with human smartness, it will be reached; the more we weary ourselves and work hardest for it, the least we understand it" (Ps. 25, p. 140).

"As happens when a good prince wishes with holy constitutions to govern a people, but he is frustrated by those who are gross and fat with the blood of the people; who, I understand that first they lose the fear of God, renouncing and casting aside piety; then they lose the shame of the world; and thus, daringly they place themselves against their kings, princes, and superiors" (Ps. 143, p. 74).

"The people in whom the Holy Spirit abides, then trust more, when they find and when they see less to trust in, doing the opposite to what those who are controlled by human prudence do, who then trust less when the danger is greater, when they see less in whom to trust. . . . In this house of God the pious must pretend to reach the Holy Spirit, who instructs and teaches in all truths and in all the secrets which can be understood and reached of God, to which *human prudence never attains*; rather it is thus that finding them written, they do not penetrate into them nor feel them, even if they pretend to penetrate them and feel them" (Ps. 27, p. 149).

"God illustrates his presence among Christian people, *taking away their love of the world and making them fall in love with him*, making them renounce the governing of 'human prudence,' and that they should accept that of the Holy Spirit. But from this illustration men see and understand as they feel and experiment" (Ps. 21, p. 170).

That kind of contemplation which in the *Dialogue on Christian Doctrine* was an ideal seen from the distance has become a living experience, a warm intuition of the mystery of the love and the wrath of God. This immediate experience of the judgment of God, in the sense of justification of some and the condemnation of others, precipitates the revolution of his preceding experience. There are the same ideas, the same doctrines, but his personal intelligence is new and different.

A passage from *The Christian Alphabet* will serve as a key to comprehend this fundamental insight.

"You must know, my lady, that the human heart is naturally inclined to love; in such a way, it must either love God and all things for God, or it must love itself and all things for itself. That which loves itself does all things for itself. I mean to say that it is so far moved to them as its own self-interest invites it, and thus if it love anything beyond itself, it loves it for itself and for its own interest, and if it have any love toward God, it has it for its own interest and in no other respect. Such a one, friar or nonfriar, because he has his affection in a state of disorder, having placed it in himself, never knows how, or in what manner, he ought to love created things. Rather when he desires to dispose himself to love God, because he does not conceive how to go out of himself, he never discovers the way, and therefore goes continually wandering in mere appearances, and thus being always confused and variable in his affections, bad or good, he lives far away from the life of Christian perfection; and so much the more will he live farther from it as the more he becomes enamored of himself, although he may be very perfect in outward observances; because God requires the heart.

"He who loves God performs everything he does for him. I would say that he is moved to this by the love he bears to God, and this he does with as much warmth and earnestness as the degree of affection moves or incites him. And thus if he love anything besides God, he loves it for the sake of God, and because God wills it so, and he likewise loves himself because he knows that God wills that he be loved. Such a one, friar or nonfriar, because he has his love ordered in God, takes hence the mode and manner how he should love all created things, and is most regulated and ordered in his love, and loves nothing inordinately. And now his good works please and are grateful before God, because he is moved to work by the impulse of love, because as God is love, so no work is grateful to him that is not done by love."[23]

The Contradictions in Natural Man

The tendency to see the relation between God and man, between the Christian life and the non-Christian life, in the form of contradictions or antitheses, is already manifested very clearly in Valdés' Commentary on the Psalms.

"When human prudence is illumined by the Holy Spirit, all the interior of man is resplendent; and when it is obscure, without the Holy Spirit, all the interior of man is dark. Thus as the eye serves man to see the light of the sun, but he cannot see it except with the same sun, so human prudence serves man to see and know God; but he cannot see or know Him except through the same God; because God lets him see and know. Also I understand that, thus as it would be great foolishness for one who wishes and presumes to see the sun with the light of candles, trusting in the clarity of his eyes, so it is most great temerity on the part of those who wish to know God in the light of the writings and persuasions of men. It is necessary that God light our candle, that he himself make our clouds disappear, without which all that man knows of God is by opinion, is through the imagination, which always has more of the false in it than of truth."[24]

This analogy, similar to that used by Thomas Aquinas in his *Treatise on Grace*, Question 109, Article 6[25], seemed to Valdés so adequate that he elaborated it in his Consideration XII, and in other lesser writings. In it is reflected an intellectual cautiousness in contrast to his profound faith in the illuminating grace. It is this which imparts to his spirit that equilibrium so admired by Montesinos and that certainty confused by Caballero with fanaticism.

The point of departure in the thinking of Valdés is his perception, as much emotional as intellectual, of a fundamental contradiction of man and God. In his Commentary on the Epistle to the Romans he emphasizes this contradiction upon pointing out the incapacity of man to obey the absolute commandment of love.

[23] J. de Valdés, *Alfabeto Cristiano*, p. 69.
[24] J. de Valdés, *Salmos*, p. 100.
[25] *Basic Writings of Thomas Aquinas*, ed. by Anton Pegis, Vol. 2, p. 979.

"And I understand that Saint Paul touches first upon self-esteem because it is so united with and so natural to man, that it insinuates itself into all man's operations and exercises, and seeks, if not the whole, at least the greater part, for its own sister to self-love; it being so that where there is self-love, there is self-esteem, and the converse. . . .

"There are some who naturally will that which is good; but because that will of theirs ever springs from self-love, it being a carnal will, it does not operate to disculpate either the work or the mode of doing it, this being peculiarly the privilege of those who will that which is good through the Holy Spirit, and because God has given them the will. . . .

"Self-knowledge consists of a man's knowing that 'there dwells no good thing in his flesh,' so that a man's self-knowledge does not consist in knowing himself to be, as is vulgarly said, a sinner but in knowing the wickedness and the perversity of the root whence these evils issue. This is natural depravity, aggravated by the acquired, the iniquity together with the ungodliness which is rooted in man from his mother's womb."[26]

The perception of this contradiction may be considered as the origin of *The Christian Alphabet*. Valdés points this out to his friend the countess.

"If you do not know yourself, you can never cease to love yourself inordinately. And while you have this self-love you cannot love God. And while you do not love him, you cannot do, say, or think anything that may be to his honor; and not being to his honor, consider whether it would be to the service of your soul. And still in this, *signora*, consists the deception, that not knowing yourself, you think you do. I give you to know that he must be a very spiritual person who entirely knows himself."[27]

This contradiction is resolved when the believer learns, through Christ, to put the honor of God above his own human honor.

"I do understand that incorporation into Christ produces this effect upon the man who accepts the grace of the gospel: that just as he, prior to the time at which he accepted it, took pleasure in and enjoyed, both mentally and bodily, the honors and dignities of the world, seeking and courting them, neither relishing nor enjoying those which are chief among divine things, nor at all aiming at them; so after he has accepted the grace of the gospel, he hates in his mind

26 J. de Valdés, *Romans*, p. 235 and p. 109.
27 J. de Valdés, *Alfabeto Cristiano*, p. 96.

what he previously thought and courted, and loves what he previously condemned and avoided, altogether changing his purpose."[28]

From the point of view of this basic contradiction, Valdés considers the other antitheses that make up his thought. These are sin and virtue, the wisdom of God and human prudence, unfaithfulness and faith, the kingdom of the world and the Kingdom of God, the old man and the new man. Of these, the most important is the antithesis faith = human prudence. It is in relation to this antithesis that he reflects on the theme of natural light in contrast to the light of grace, or supernatural light.

The faith that wins the victory over human prudence is the work of the Holy Spirit in the penitent. It is the sovereignty of the Holy Spirit which constitutes, for Valdés, the pure essence of the Kingdom of God. Consequently, the contradiction between the kingdom of the world and the Kingdom of God disappears only by submittance of the human spirit to the Holy Spirit.

"By the 'Kingdom of God,'" says the Commentary on Rom. 14:16–19, "he means the rule of the Holy Spirit, for it is through God's ruling us by his Holy Spirit that we begin to enter, meaning that we, in this present life, take possession of the Kingdom of God, and that in the life eternal we shall continue it, rising again glorious, impassible, and immortal."

In relation to this final victory of the Holy Spirit over his four moral enemies, the devil, the flesh, honor, and death, Valdés wrote Consideration LXV. In this is found the beautiful comparison of the glass of water, in which Valdés describes in a simple but penetrating way the theme of the Benefit of Christ in relation to the Kingdom of God.

"These very persons, if their desire to enter into the Kingdom of God be a call of God himself and not their own caprice, accepting the justice of God executed upon Christ as their own, do in this present life escape from the tyranny of three of the tyrants; they pass from the kingdom of the world, and through Christ enter into the Kingdom of God. I mean to say that Christ reigns as the Son of God, he being in those who are in his Kingdom, and with them properly, what the head is to the members of the body; for just as virtue and efficacy descend from the head to the members of the body, they being ruled by it, so virtue and efficacy descend from Christ to those who are in the Kingdom of Christ, with which they

[28] J. de Valdés, *Consideraciones*, p. 229.

combat the tyrants who despotically rule other men. And thus they are ruled by Christ in this present life, and through him they shall attain to the resurrection and life eternal; and thus they shall be brought from subjection to the tyranny of the fourth tyrant, which is death, and shall enter into the Kingdom of God, where God himself will reign.

"In the meanwhile, they who have passed from the kingdom of the world, having felt the tyranny of the four tyrants, feel the charm and sweetness of the Kingdom of Christ; experiencing inwardly the virtue and efficacy of Christ and the guidance of the Holy Spirit, and feeling themselves to be lords and masters of their sensual appetites, and of the worldly affections of honor and ambition; having determined their own course of conduct, and their bearing to the world, forasmuch as being incorporated into Christ, they find their flesh to be dead, and their regard for the world to be dead likewise, and being assured of their resurrection, immortality, and eternal life. Such assurance works this effect in them, that though they experience death as far as the body is concerned, yet through an assured hope of the resurrection they do not feel it as to the soul. I understand the Kingdom of Christ to consist in this.

"And because when the resurrection of the just shall have been accomplished we shall no longer have to resist the devil, nor will it be necessary to mortify the flesh, nor to oppose the world, nor will it then remain to conquer death, I understand what Saint Paul says, that then 'Christ will deliver up the Kingdom to his eternal Father, and that God shall be all in all' (I Cor. 15:24–28), ruling and governing everything himself. So that the Kingdom of Christ, according to Saint Paul, shall last until the universal resurrection, and the Kingdom of God in men shall then commence, and be permanent, men continually acknowledging the benefit received from Jesus Christ our Lord.

"As it happens to a thirsty traveler to whom a glass of spring water is presented; while drinking he feels the use of the vessel which holds the water given him and, having drunk, when the glass is laid aside, he thanks the individual who gave him drink, though he knows that he received that benefit by means of the glass. And just as the grateful traveler who is refreshed with a glass of cold water experiences, while he drinks, the use of the glass and, after he has drunk, feeling and acknowledging the kindness of the individual who gave him the glass, knows likewise the advantage of the glass, so men, while they are in this present life, experience the Kingdom of Christ, knowing by experience the benefit of Christ, and in the life eternal they will feel and know the kindness of God, who has given them Christ, and they will acknowledge the benefit rendered by Jesus Christ our Lord."[29]

29 J. de Valdés, *Consideraciones*, pp. 145–147.

The Benefit of Christ signifies for the believer, according to Valdés, the solution of the contradictions or antitheses inherent in human life.

Originality

In Consideration CX, Valdés calls attention to the fact that truth is revealed to man according to the measure of his living faith. Piety, regeneration, and knowledge are connected "to such an extent that it is scarcely possible to understand whether the distinctness of views be assignable to the perfection of practice, or whether the perfection of practice be assignable to the distinctness of views; and therefore, it is to say that both one and the other are due to the Christian spirit, which marvelously operates, both the one and the other, in those persons who accept the gospel of Christ. I have stated this for this reason: that having regarded the matter of Christianity not as a science, but as experience, I have endeavored to make this truth intelligible to individuals by numerous illustrations. I never satisfied my own mind so that it could appear to me that I had expressed my views in my own way until now, when to my own judgment, having apprehended it more distinctly, it seems to me that I am better enabled to express it. . . . But they are incapable of understanding these Christian truths who are inexperienced in Christian subjects; and this experience they alone possess who, through the gift of God, and through the Benefit of Christ, possess faith, hope, and charity, and hence are pious, holy, and justified in Christ, and are intent upon apprehending the piety, righteousness, and holiness in which they are apprehended (Phil., ch. 3), being like to God, and to the Son of God, Jesus Christ."

Free both from medieval rational tyranny and from medieval asceticism, Valdés is, undoubtedly, in the tradition of the Spanish religious spirit that had produced, three centuries before, a Raymond Lull, and which produced a few years after Valdés the profound and beautiful *Dialogues on the Names of Christ* by Fray Luis de León. Valdés is as far from Aquinas or Calvin's dogmatic *Summas* as from the excesses of all sectarians. In the particular constellation of contemporary thinkers, Valdés had a position of his own, holding in common with others those things which originate in the Biblical background and philosophical currents running through the Middle Ages from Augustine to Luther. At the same time he was within the renascent philosophy running from Scotus Eriugena to the Spaniards León Hebreo or Baruch Spinoza.

Concerning his orthodoxy, Fermín Caballero, Menéndez y Pelayo, Ludwig Pastor, Benedetto Croce, and Edmondo Cione admit that he is not a Catholic. That question was decided officially by both the Italian and the Spanish Inquisition by placing all his religious books in the Index. But, furthermore, Menéndez y Pelayo, Pastor, and Rafael Altamira think that he was influenced by Luther. Benjamin Wiffen admits the possibility that he was influenced by Tauler's *Institutes*.

Edward Boehmer, after many years of careful research, affirms that "a man of such overpowering originality should not be considered Lutheran or Calvinist, and much less an Anabaptist."[30] Manuel Carrasco and Eugène Stern, both disciples of Boehmer, studied Valdés as a Protestant theologian who was very original in his points of view.

Benedetto Croce has said that a proposition is valid only within its context and "this doctrine of faith, as it was presented by Juan de Valdés and accepted by Giulia Gonzaga, implied a negation of the papal church, of its juridical decisions in things pertaining to moral conscience, of its sacramental system, of indulgences, and of everything else."[31]

That opinion of Croce, I believe, is true. Even if, according to Giulia Gonzaga and Fermín Caballero, Valdés died in the faith in which he had lived, his faith was no longer Roman Catholic. But what is not true is that Valdés was an Anti-Trinitarian. The question is as old as the Christian church itself, since even today it is very difficult to determine who is and who is not an Anti-Trinitarian. In Consideration XCV, he admits "that men are incapable of comprehending the divine generation of the Son of God, and the spiritual generation of the children of God," yet he believed in one as well as in the other, the benefit of Christ being the essential experience on which all his thought is based.

Valdés' originality does not consist in pretending to invent, or in having discovered, new truth. He realizes that truth is eternal reality, the ground of all being. But the originality consists in his approach to truth, in that he is apprehended by the Origin of all truth and reality, in that he places himself at the root of all being, and only in this sense he is original and radical. Self-knowledge and knowledge of God, the inquiry

[30] M. Menéndez y Pelayo, *Heterodoxos*, Vol. 4, p. 250.
[31] B. Croce, *Introduction to the Alfabeto Cristiano*, pp. XVIII–XIX.

into the image of man as he is and the image of man as he ought to be according to the image of God as revealed by Jesus Christ—this is his point of departure from which he approaches all reality. He finds evil in man as a whole, body and mind. The capacity for discriminating good from evil is the essence of human personality, yet even that is the consequence of original sin. To get beyond the limitations that evil places upon man's judgment, a restitution of the original image of God is necessary. This is done by the acceptance of the gospel as a personal experience of pardon. Only then is truth unveiled to man, even if not fully.

As may be easily appreciated from the pattern of thought that we have endeavored to sketch above, spiritual motivation and impulse is more important for Valdés than intellectual constructions. His *One Hundred and Ten Considerations* is much more a spiritual diary than a treatise of systematic theology. Education is, for Valdés, the leadership of the Holy Spirit, experienced by those who are elected and under God's grace. In his *Opuscules*, he has given a description of his method of preaching: "If he had to give regulations for preaching the gospel of Christ, he would prescribe that penitence (self-knowledge) should be preached first; secondly, justification by faith; and connected with this article, thirdly, the necessity of testifying to Christian faith by Christian works, which works, he says, will be rewarded in the present life by corporal and spiritual benefits and in the future life by greater glory."[32] This method, combined with great clearness and charm of style, and freedom of spirit, is followed throughout all his works. And this is the method that imparts originality to Valdés' thought —an originality that springs from a radical change of all his being.

[32] J. de Valdés, *Trataditos*, p. 162.

I

A Dialogue on Christian Doctrine

INTRODUCTION

THE TEXT OF THE *DIALOGUE ON CHRISTIAN DOCTRINE* THAT has been translated for this Library of Christian Classics is the facsimile edition published by Marcel Bataillon in 1925, by the press of the University of Coimbra, Portugal. It was in the National Library of Lisbon that the French scholar discovered a copy of the first edition, published by Miguel Eguía, in Alcalá de Henares, probably in 1529.[1]

Although this work is anonymous, from the very beginning it was attributed to Juan de Valdés, the brother of the imperial secretary, Alfonso, who two years before had published his *Dialogue of Lactancio*. Bataillon characterizes the work as a "moderate Erasmian catechism." Because of his Erasmian sympathies and because of his relation to the *Dialogue on Things Which Happened in Rome*, Juan de Valdés brought upon himself and his work the hostility of the Inquisition. Already in 1532 the reading or possession of the book was considered bad by the Holy Office and it was included in the first Index of Portugal in 1547 and in the first Index of Toledo in 1551.

There are in existence two other editions of the *Dialogue*: an ordinary copy of that of Coimbra, printed in Madrid in 1929 by the National and Foreign Library, and another published in Buenos Aires in 1946 by La Aurora publishing house.

This work and the Commentary on the Psalms are the only religious works of Valdés the Spanish text of which has been preserved. I have tried to preserve in my translation the Spanish idioms and the particular style of the author.

[1] Juan de Valdés, *Diálogo de Doctrina Cristiana*, Reproduction en facsimile, de l'exemplaire de la bibliothèque nationale de Lisbonne (Edition d'Alcalá de Henares, 1529) avec une introduction et des notes por Marcel Bataillon. Coimbra, Imprensa da Universidad, 1925, p. 68, *et al.*

I

A Dialogue on Christian Doctrine
Newly Composed by a Churchman[2]

THE TEXT

Dedicated to the most illustrious gentleman Don Diego de López Pacheco, Marquis of Villena[3]

A DIALOGUE ON CHRISTIAN PRAYER[4]

Antronio: Then, according to your opinion, you would not have us pray from books, if we are not compelled to do so, nor with beads.

Archbishop: I do not say that. Let anyone who wishes pray like that as much as he wants, but, to tell you the truth, I will not consider it evil if he does not pray from a book, provided he were not compelled to do so, neither with beads, provided he were living properly. Neither will I consider a good man he that prays much in both ways, if I do not see in him some other sign of being a Christian. I say this, because I know many that if you see them in church with their books and beads, you would think they were some Jeromes, and when they come out, and even in the church, as soon as they finish a number of Pater Nosters and psalms, their tongues are so quick to gossip about their neighbors, to utter lies, lowliness and slander as to be a great pity.

Eusebio: Since they train their tongues to speed the Psalms, maybe that is the cause that they are unable to keep them still with respect to these other things.

---

[2] "A churchman" is not the best translation, but the only one available for the Spanish "un religioso," which means a person given exclusively to the religious life, as a clergyman, monk, or otherwise.

[3] The marquis of Villena, lord of Escalona, was the Spanish nobleman to whose court Juan de Valdés was attached until 1525. He was a deeply devoted person, dedicated to scholarly pursuits. In 1527, Francisco de Osuna addressed to him the famous *Tercer Abecedario,* a book that exerted a great influence on Spanish mysticism, very especially on Santa Teresa de Jesús. Cf. Marcel Bataillon, *op. cit.,* p. 28.

[4] Praying without audible words, and without the ordinary helps provided by the church, was one of the suspected practices of the *alumbrados,* as the Spanish heretics of the time were known.

Ar: Be that as it may, at last they will discover themselves deceived, no matter how well they work, if they do not cease their low habits. I find consolation in knowing that there is a happy and eternal life for the good and a sad and endless death for the wicked.

An: In spite of all that you have said, I think you will consider it good that all Christians pray the Pater Noster, and that for this purpose it should be explained very well to them.

Ar: I surely do, and even more than good; but only after they learn what I have said. It is much more important and more convenient for them to know so that their prayer be agreeable to God, what we have said above. Then it is very good for them to know how to pray, and also what they pray, and for this purpose it is needed to explain to them in few words, as you say, the Pater Noster, so that they would know both the prayer and its meaning.

An: In that respect I say you are very right; but, pray, tell us how do you think that brief exposition should be made?

Ar: I will tell you as far as God lets me understand it; God will that it should be so to the point that you and I be happy and satisfied.

An: It could not be any other way, but that what you say will make us happy and satisfied.

Ar: Then, trusting thus, I say it is a good thing that everybody should know and feel about the Pater Noster in this way:

Let the first thing be for every Christian to know that this prayer was composed by our Redeemer, Jesus Christ. And it was thus that his disciples came to him, asking him to teach them to pray. Then, after telling them not to multiply words when praying, he taught them this prayer, and for this reason it should be esteemed more than all others that are written. In this prayer our Lord Jesus Christ teaches us how we ought to pray. And by its own example the prayer teaches us that it should be brief in words, but abundant in content; and this kind is the Christian's prayer. Besides, the prayer should be more spiritual than verbal. We are already in that time that Jesus Christ said would come, when the true worshipers would worship their eternal Father in spirit and in truth; because with this kind of worshipers, says he, the eternal Father finds pleasure. Also the prayer must be said with much attention and very great fervor, with complete and strong faith, with perseverance and finally with full knowledge of God, and ourselves. In short, here you see how every Christian should pray. It is also shown to us what we should pray for, considering all the prayer, that is nothing more than those things pertinent to the glory of God and the salvation of our souls and our fellow men. Having said this, we should also ask what every Christian should consider when he prays this prayer and with this exposition, you would have the way in which it should be taught, since it is in this way that I have ordered it to be taught. You should know that all this prayer consists of seven petitions, which we shall point out as we repeat it. So when the Christian says:

Father, after having considered God's greatest benignity by which he takes pleasure when his enemies, who every day offend him, yet call him *Father*, he should consider if his works are those of a true son, and if he finds that they are not so, he should be confused and humbled before God, acknowledging his misery and smallness. When he says: *our*, he should remember that through this word he shows that all those who call upon this same name, and can do so, are his brothers. Then he should search well if he does with all of them brotherly works and if he loves them with all his heart as brothers. If he finds himself lacking in these things, he should ask God for, not only with tears in his eyes but also in his heart, a spirit of love with which to love his brothers.

When he says: *who art in heaven*, he should remember the banishment in which he is, and sigh truly after that heavenly home where he will go to enjoy the beatific vision of the eternal and sovereign God, where joy and rest is perfect and complete, since you enjoy it without fear of losing it. Of this joy, even here on earth, God gives the soul some taste so that, enthralled by its sweetness, he will despise all worldly things and hold as deceitful and vain all its pleasures and enjoyments.

When he comes to say: *Hallowed be thy name*, think that he asks God here not to let that neither he nor anybody else think, say, do, have, nor purpose any other thing but only that which is directed toward the glory of God, and that in all things, by his grace, he should be respectful of his love and fear. This is the way in which God's name is sanctified, when we sanctify ourselves. This is the first petition, and I explain it as briefly as I can, since if it is going to remain in the memory of all, it should be declared like that, in few words, to the people and especially to the children.

E: The order which you follow seems to me the best in the world, and since it is so, Sir, proceed further.

Ar: I am agreeable, but on condition that you pay close

attention. Since the name of God cannot be hallowed unless the Spirit abides and rules in our souls, the second petition follows, where we ask in this fashion: *Thy kingdom come.* Here it is convenient for every Christian to know that with these words he is asking God to redeem all men from the most cruel tyranny that the devil, the world, and the flesh hold over all, under which they are brought anywhere, as dragged by the hair, to do the will of these three, and would that God allow his spirit to rule and be the absolute Lord of us all. They need to know also that this Kingdom of God in our souls is but a voluntary subjection and whole obedience to God, a true peace, a marvelous rest and perfect satisfaction. Let them also know that the reason for asking this from God is to break the tyranny of the devil, and with sin cast off as far as possible, his soul will be free and agreeable before his majesty, and be a temple of the living God and having God only as ruler, so that through exterior and interior obedience it will be a kingdom where God reigns. This is a very great truth that if we come to know how great and how priceless is the good the soul possesses when God is its Lord and King, we would say these words with such an ardent desire and great fervor as to rend our hearts, wishing for their fulfillment. For the love of the only God, I require from you, father, that you will charge everybody with earnestness to look after this, since their life and even much more than their life is at stake. And thus because God does not reign in our souls except when they are very obedient, both inside and outside, and in order to attain this Kingdom the will of God must be done, for this reason Jesus Christ, our God and Lord, taught us to ask in the third petition in this fashion:

Thy will be done on earth as it is in heaven. Here the Christian should consider that because of his own nature he is inclined to do evil and to be disobedient to God, and thus he regrets it when God corrects and punishes him; he asks God to give him grace so that with good will he will agree that God's will be fulfilled in him. It is as if he were to tell God: Eternal Father, even if my sensitive flesh should resist, be not mindful, but do as you do, punish me as you will, be thy will and not mine fulfilled. In no way be my will fulfilled since it is always contrary to yours, which only is good, even as thou alone art good, and mine is always evil, even when it seems to me very good.

E: I know that it is not only in that respect where we should wish the will of God to be done.

Ar: True, indeed, but I said this first because it is there where to do the will of God is most difficult and because he who obeys God in this will be able to obey him very well in all other things. Thus, the Christian asks that in all things the will of God be absolutely fulfilled, here on earth, as it is in heaven, where all are obedient to God with great joy and with the whole will, since theirs is at one with God's. So, he who in truth says the words of this petition and wishes the fulfillment thereof as I have told you, I assure you his accomplisment is not small.

An: As far as I am concerned, it seems to me I pray these words in truth.

Ar: I believe it indeed, but I am not sure if you feel them as truly as you say you pray them. But coming back to our theme: since to be wholly and firmly in agreement with God's will is something beyond human strength, God advised us to present the fourth petition in this way:

Give us this day our daily bread. When the Christian says these words, let him see well that what he asks for here is grace to be able to fulfill God's will, which is the spiritual bread that supports and imparts life to our souls. This bread is the grace of the Holy Spirit, without which our souls cannot be pleasing to God, not even for a moment. The soul is wonderfully sustained by this grace. When by means of this bread our souls will have impressed upon them the image of Jesus Christ, who is the true and heavenly bread, they would be able to break their wills completely and gladly, and they will feel as delicious and sweet any suffering God may send. Finally, the Christian ought to include in this petition that God send us true and holy doctors that may distribute among the Christian people the bread of evangelical doctrine, clean and clear and not soiled and dirty with human opinions and affects. You see what a great need we have of this bread.

E: So great it is that it cannot be greater and, since you speak so well, I do not want to interrupt you. Proceed further; I am extremely pleased with the order you follow.

Ar: Because it is not convenient to give this heavenly bread to the dogs, nor should it be given to them, who are the people that are soiled by sin, for this reason, in order to cleanse us from these sins, God enjoins us to say in the fifth petition:

Forgive us our debts, as we forgive our debtors. This petition should be carefully considered by every Christian since what he asks here must be asked with full understanding of his guilt and defects that he asks God to forgive. Freed from guilts and defects he could sit at the table with the sons of God and eat of this heavenly bread, from which eat only those to whom God has forgiven their sins, accepting them as his own. And because without this support our souls are unable to move through the vicissitudes of this world; and since this support is not given but to those whom God accepts as his own, and he does not accept as his own any but those whom he forgives; and since everybody, no matter how holy he may be, has something for which to be forgiven, it is necessary that every day we ask for forgiveness and that we acknowledge at the same time that we need to be forgiven something. And something else should be kept in mind here: we are not worthy to have our sins forgiven just because we forgive our debtors, those who offend us, but because God wanted to forgive us through his infinite goodness and mercy; under these conditions we are forgiven. So, it is necessary to forgive our neighbors in order that God may forgive us, but let us not think that God forgives us because we forgive, because this will amount to attributing to ourselves what should be attributed only to God. I know some people that, even though thinking of themselves as very holy and wise, when they feel some enmity against somebody, not wishing to forgive them, they do not pray this part of the Pater Noster, but skip it. Have you ever seen greater foolishness or nonsense? They are not afraid of calling God "Father," being sons of Satan, and they want and ask for the heavenly bread which is given only to the pure of heart, and they are afraid to ask God for forgiveness because he would require from them the fulfillment of that condition for which they ask.

An: By my health, I did that whenever I was not in good relations with any of my colleagues, and I did not even think much of it.

Ar: See that you do not do it again from now on.

An: I accept it; but would it not be better if I abstain from praying the whole Pater Noster instead of this part only?

Ar: Yes, for the sake of avoiding this new superstition, as long as you do not want to stop being angry with your brother, but on condition that you keep on asking for God's grace, that through it you may overcome your anger, although it would be much better to forsake your anger and forgive, and then you could pray the whole prayer.

An: And if it is not within my power and I could not help being angry?

Ar: If you feel sorry for not being able to overcome resentment, then you could say the whole prayer and beg God to help your good will, and since he gave you grace to wish the good, he will give grace to attain it.

An: As true as I live, you have given me life by telling me this, because I shall take advantage of this for myself and for others.

Ar: May God so help you. And now, give me your attention and we shall proceed. Since we have asked God's forgiveness, and since perseverance in doing good is rewarded, and by ourselves we will never attain it, since we are by nature fickle and faithless and so we fall easily in temptation, for this the sixth petition tells us:

Do not let us fall into nor be vanquished in temptation. When the Christian utters these words it is convenient, in order to obtain the results for which they are said, that he know the great weakness of his flesh, and also the great power and diversity of temptations with which the devil, the flesh, and the world tempt us. And then, with this knowledge, he should consider that what he asks from God in this petition is to be protected and guided by His hand and never to let him be vanquished by any temptation, nor to sin again, but on the other hand, to give him persevering grace with which to fight like a man until death. Since we know that God is just and that he should punish us for our sins and we should endure our punishment, and since the evil in us, the sin that governs our bodily members, is the cause of it all, the last petition advises us to say:

Deliver us from evil. It is necessary that the Christian, if he possesses the aforesaid knowledge, should emphasize here that, since this evil that abides in our flesh is the cause that we should be tempted, should fall, and be punished for it, then God with his supreme power delivers him from this evil. Free from all evils and sins, the Christian will then be, together with all those who love Jesus Christ, a sanctifier of the name of God, will be part of the Kingdom of God. Then he will do God's will in all things; he will eat of and support himself with the daily bread of God's grace and the Holy Spirit, and no sin will abide in him that will not be then forgiven, and also he will not be vanquished by temptations, from which we cannot be completely saved while we live in this world.

E: That seems to me a very new way of explanation.

Ar: It is not as new as you think, and in my opinion it is better than all those I have read and more practical.

E: In what respects?

Ar: I shall tell you, and in order that you may see it better, I shall tell you first two other explanations. The first is about the meaning of *deliver us from all evil.* Here theologians make their distinctions saying that it is not the evil of punishment but the evil of guilt. I do not want to meddle in this, but, according to those who know Greek, the language in which the Evangelists wrote, this explanation and distinction is beside the point. This is the reason why Erasmus, in his translation of the New Testament, says: *Deliver us from the evil one,* that is, from the devil. And this is the second explanation. Both of them, in my opinion, are holy and good, but in my judgment the one I have told you is more to the point; otherwise it would seem that in this petition we do not ask anything further than in the previous one.

E: In what way?

Ar: He who asks God to keep him and deliver him from falling into temptations, is he not asking at the same time to be delivered from the devil?

E: Yes, doubtless.

Ar: Then, the same is true of the other explanation.

An: By your life, sir, do not trouble yourself any more talking about this; I am very well satisfied with what you have said; do not trouble yourself with any more answers.

Ar: I will do what you say, and in conclusion I say it is to the point that after asking God in the previous petition not to let us be defeated in temptation, we should ask him afterward to deliver us from that evil which brings temptation, that bad tendency that comes to us from the sins of our ancestors.

E: I assure you that although I have replied to some of these explanations, I have been extremely satisfied with them.

Ar: Very well. Let the end be that the word "Amen" is a sort of confirmation and general petition of all that has been said. Besides, if we want to obtain the fruit of this petition, it is necessary to remember that Jesus Christ taught us this way of praying, and that he promised to grant us what we pray for if we know how to ask him, and, keeping this in mind, we should have steadfast hope that God will grant us, in order to keep his word, what we ask for in this prayer.

An: Let us see, and if I cannot believe that God will hear me?

Ar: Do like the one who brought to Jesus Christ his son possessed by a demon, who when Jesus Christ said to him, "If you are able to believe, all things are possible to the believer," he answered, "Lord, I believe, but help thou and be gracious with my incredulity and little faith."

E: By my life, you have given a wonderful answer and you have declared very well the Pater Noster; I am certain that anyone who thinks of all these things will be greatly edified in his soul whenever he prays.

II

One Hundred and Ten Considerations

INTRODUCTION

I N HIS *DIALOGUE ON LANGUAGE*, JUAN DE VALDÉS OFFERS us some indications as to how the themes originated which were later collected in *One Hundred and Ten Considerations*.

"We, in order to obey you and serve you, have spoken this morning about what you have wished, and very obligingly we have answered you all that which you have asked. It is just that, since you are so courteous and well-behaved to everyone, as everybody says you are, you should be so with us too, taking pleasure that we speak this afternoon about that which will most please us, answering us and satisfying us with the answers to the questions that we may propose to you, as we have done to those which you have proposed."[1]

Juan de Valdés owned a country house in the quarter of Chiaja, one of the most beautiful spots in Naples. Every Sunday a select number of his friends resorted to hear him speak upon sacred subjects. After breakfasting and enjoying themselves amidst the beauty of the surrounding scenery, they returned to the house, where he read some selected portion of the Scripture and commented upon it. Sometimes a theme would be proposed and he would explain it. These subjects on which he conceived that his mind had obtained a clearer illumination are called "Divine Considerations" and constitute the content of his book.

Clearness of thought, sincerity of feeling, and peace of soul seem to be the main objectives of these pious meditations. There is no pretense of systematic presentation and no polemic intention. Yet, practically all the most important themes of

[1] J. de Valdés, *Diálogo de la Lengua*, p. 1.

Reformation thought and practice are touched upon in these Considerations.

Celio Secondo Curione, in his "Letter to Christian Readers" which precedes the first Italian edition of this work, has made some pertinent observations, some of which are worth reproducing here. In them is revealed not only the great admiration of the pupils for their master, but also the profound influence of Valdés on the most outstanding Reform thought of Italy.

"Many, both ancients and moderns, have written upon Christian topics, and some of them have done so better than others; but it would be difficult to find out the man who, since the days of our Lord's apostles and Evangelists, has written better, more soundly, and more divinely, than Juan de Valdés. . . .

"For bringing to our knowledge and into our possession this great and heavenly treasure, we are all indebted to Maestro Pietro Paolo Vergerio, who was, in the course of divine providence, instrumental in causing it to be printed. Coming from Italy, and leaving a feigned bishopric to come to the true apostolate to which he was called by Christ, he brought with him many beautiful compositions. . . . He left with me the *One Hundred and Ten Considerations* in order that I might get them printed. . . . These Considerations, as is known to many, were originally written by the author in Spanish, and afterward translated by a pious and worthy person into Italian, and hence it is that they are not wholly divested of the Spanish idiom peculiar to them. . . ."

This is the work of Valdés which had the greatest influence in Europe. This may be judged by the many translations which were quickly made of this work to Dutch, French, and English. In continuation we offer a bibliography of this work, chronologically arranged.

Le cento e dieci divine considerationi del S. Giovanni Valdesso, nelle quali si ragiona delle cose utili, piú necessarie e piú perfette della christiana professione. I Cor. II. Noi vi ragioniamo della perfetta sapientia, non della sapientia di questo mondo. ec. (con lettera introduttiva de Celio Secondo Curione). In Basilea, MDL.

Cent et dix consyderations divines de Juan de Val D'Esso. Traduites premièrement d'espaignol en langue italienne & de nouveau mises en français par C. R. P. Durer, morir e non perir. Lyon, Claude Senneton, MCLXIII. (Colophon.) A Lyon, par Jean d'Ogerolles, 1563.

Cent et dix consyderations de Jan de Val D'esso. Paris, Mathurin Prevost, à l'escu de Venise, 1565.

Cent et dix considerations de Jan de Val D'Esso. A Lyon, par Jan Martin, 1565.

Jo. Valdessi. *Godsalige Anmerckingen uyt het Italiansche* overgeset. (Trad. di Adriano Garino) (s.i.e.t.?) 1565.

Les divines considerations, saintes meditations de Jean de Val d'esso, gentilhomme espaignol. Touchant tout ce qui est nécessaire pour la perfection de la vie chrestienne. Traduites par C. K. P. Reveûes de noveau & rapportées fidelement à l'exemplaire espaignol & amplifiees de la table des principales matieres traictées par l'aucteur. Lyon, Pièrre Picard, 1601.

The hundred and ten considerations of signor John Valdesso, treating of those things which are most profitable, most necessary and most perfect in our Christian profession. Written in Spanish, brought out of Italy by Vergerius, and first set forth in Italian at Basel by Coelius Secundus Curio, anno 1550. Afterward translated into French, and printed at Lyons, 1563, and again at Paris, 1565. And now translated out of Italian copy into English, with notes. Whereunto is added an epistle of the author's, *upon the Romans*. I Cor., ch. 2. Nowbeit we speak wisdome amongst them that are perfect, yet not the wisdome of this world. (Translation by Nicholas Ferrar.) Oxford, Leonard Lichfield, 1638.

Divine Considerations, treating of those things which are most profitable, most necessary, and most perfect in our Christian profession. By John Valdesso. Cambridge: printed for E. D. by Roger Daniel, Printer to the University, 1646. (Ferrar's translation revised.)

Ziento y diez Considerazones de Juan de Valdés. Ahora publicadas por primera vez en castellano. Valdesio hispano scriptore superbiat orbis. (Dan. Roger Epigr. in Tum. Juelli Humphr. Vita Juel. 4to. 1573.) Ed. e Trad. de Luis Usoz i Río.) S. l. e. t. Año de MDCCCLV. (Reformistas Antiguos Españoles, tomo IX.)

Le cento e dieci divine considerazioni di Giovanni Valdesso. (Ed. of E. Boehmer) Seguono: l'Epistola del primo editore (Celio Secondo Curione) et i "Cenni biografici sui fratelli Giovannie Alfonso de Valdesso" dello stesso Boehmer. Si aggiunge un "Documento inedito," é alcuni "Supplimente." Halle in Sassonia, MDCCCLX.

Ziento i diez considerazones leídas i explicadas hazia el año de 1538 i 1539. Por Juan de Valdés. Conforme a un ms. castellano escrito el a. 1558 existente en la biblioteca de Hamburgo, i ahora publicado por vez primera con un facsímile.

Valdesio hispanus scriptore superbiat orbis. Expaña. Año MDCCCLXII. (Reformistas Antiguos Españoles, tomo XVI.) *Ziento i diez consideraziones* de Juan de Valdés. Primera vez publicadas en castellano el a. 1855 por Luis de Usoz i Río i ahora corregidas nuevamente con mayor cuidado. . . . Londres, G. A. Claro del Bosque, 1863. (Reformistas Antiguos Españoles, tomo XVIII.)
Le cento e dieci divine considerazione de S. Giovanni Valdesso. . . . Londres, Claro de Bosque, 1863.
Life and writings of Juan de Valdés, otherwise Valdesso, Spanish reformer of the sixteenth century, by Benjamin B. Wiffen. With a translation from the Italian of his *Hundred and Ten Considerations,* by John T. Betts. London, Bernard Quaritch, 1865.
Juan de Valdés. *Hundertundzehn Göttliche Betrachtungen.* Aus dem Italienischen (übersetzt von Hedwig Boehmer, Frau des Ausgebers Eduard Boehmer). Mit einem Anhang Ueber die Zwillings brüder Juan und Alfonso de Valdés von Eduard Boehmer. Halle a. s., Georg. Schwabe, 1870.
Juan de Valdés, *Göttliche Betrachtungen,* Uebersetzt von Otto Anger. Leipzig, Buchh. des vereinshauses, 1875.
Consideraciones y Pensamientos de Juan de Valdés. Escogidos y prologados por Juan Orts González. Editorial Juan de Valdés, Madrid, n.d.

Nicholas Ferrar, first translator of Valdés into English, sent the manuscript of his work to the poet George Herbert. Upon returning the book, Herbert wrote an interesting letter from which we quote:

"You owe the church a debt, and God hath put this into your hands (as he sent the fish with mony to S. Peter) to discharge it: happily also with this (as his thoughts are fruitfull) intending the honour of his servant the Author, who being obscured in his own country he would have to flourish in this land of light, and region of the Gospell, among his chosen. It is true there are some things which I like not in him, as my fragments will expresse, when you read them; neverthelesse I wish you by all means to publish it, for these three eminent things observable therein: First, that God in the midst of Popery should open the eyes of one to understand and expresse so clearly and excellently the intent of the Gospell in the acceptation of Christ's righteousnesse (as he sheweth through all his Considerations), a thing strangely buried, and darkened by the Adversaries, and their great stumbling-block. Secondly, the great honour and reverence, which he everywhere beares towards our deare Master and Lord, concluding every Consideration almost with his holy Name, and setting his merit forth so piously, for which I doe so love him, that were there nothing else, I would print it, that with it the honour of my Lord might be published. Thirdly, the many pious rules of ordering our life, about mortification, and observation of God's kingdome within us, and the working thereof, of which he was a very diligent observer."

The present version in English has been made taking into account the Italian version of Celio Secondo Curione, the Spanish versions of Usoz, and the English version of Betts.

One Hundred and Ten Considerations

THE TEXT

Consideration I

HOW IT IS TO BE UNDERSTOOD THAT MAN WAS CREATED IN THE IMAGE AND LIKENESS OF GOD[2]

Oftentimes have I decided to understand in what that image and likeness of God properly consists of which the sacred Scriptures speak, when they declare that man was created in the image and likeness of God. So long as I strove to understand it by reading books, I did not achieve anything at all, because I was led by reading, at one time to entertain one opinion, and at another time another; until attempting it by the way of reflection, it appeared to me that I apprehended it, or at least that I began to understand it; and I feel certain that the same God who has given me the knowledge I possess will give me that which I still want.

I understand the image and likeness of God to consist of his own particular being, involving his impassibility and eternity, as likewise his benignity, mercy, justice, faithfulness, and truth. I understand that God created man in the terrestrial paradise with these qualities and perfections, where, prior to his disobedience to God, he was impassible and immortal—he was good, merciful, just, faithful, and true.

[2] Both, in the *Considerations* as well as in *The Christian Alphabet*, Valdés begins by a meditation on the image of God in man. As we have pointed out, in the Introduction, Valdés seems to depart from the reflection on man's Fall, from original sin. God and man, considered as antithetical beings, and the recovery of God's image by man through the benefit of Christ, seem to be the mainspring of all Valdés' thought. This approach to the Christian doctrine is surprisingly similar to Calvin's. The French thinker, nevertheless, produces an absolutely coherent treatise, guided by the principles of a rigid, logical pattern of thought. The Spaniard, on the other side, will seem, if not incoherent, at least diffuse and erratic. Valdés follows the reason of the heart; Calvin follows the reason of the brain. Valdés is more akin to Pascal and Unamuno. Calvin is more akin to Thomas Aquinas.

As I understand, the first man lost this image and likeness of God by disobedience to God, and so he became passible and mortal—he became malevolent, cruel, impious, faithless, and mendacious.

After I understood this by reflection, desiring to compare it with Holy Scripture, I find that it coincides admirably with what Saint Paul says in Eph. 4:22–24, Col. 3:5–9; and thus I am so much the more confirmed in my conclusion.

And proceeding still further, I understand that this image of God was in the person of Christ, as far as his *soul* was involved, before his death, whence he was benign, merciful, just, faithful, and true; and with reference to soul and body, after his resurrection, inasmuch as he now possesses, in addition to benignity, mercy, justice, faithfulness, and truth, both immortality and impassibility.

Moreover,[3] I understand that they who, being called and drawn by God to the grace of the gospel, make Christ's righteousness their own, and are incorporated into Christ, recover partly in this present life that portion of the image of God which relates to the *soul*, and in eternal life recover also that part which relates to the body; and thus we shall all, through Christ, come to be like God, as Christ is; each one in his degree—Christ as the Head, and we as the members.

And it will truly be the greatest felicity to see in men goodness, mercy, justice, faithfulness, and truth; and to see them likewise impassible and immortal—to see them very like Christ, and to see them very like God: and to see that the glory of God increases with this happiness of man, and that the glory of the Son of God is thereby promoted also, through whom we shall all confess that we have attained our happiness, all recognizing as our Head the self-same Jesus Christ our Lord.

Consideration II

THAT THE HAPPINESS OF MAN CONSISTS IN KNOWING GOD, AND THAT WE CANNOT KNOW GOD UNLESS WE FIRST KNOW CHRIST

Many have labored much, desiring to understand in what

---

3 This is a striking example of how difficult it is to keep, in a translation, the semantic overtones of the original. "Moreover" is an acceptable translation of "e allende de esto," yet not completely adequate. It means, rather "if you have a farther perspective," "if you look on the farther side of the question," etc.

man's happiness properly consists; and, having striven to do so as men, by human prudence they have all erred in their imaginations, as they are wont to err in almost everything, the knowledge of which is sought through the same way. That which I say so many have labored anxiously to understand, our Lord Jesus Christ teaches in these words: *Haec est vita aeterna ut cognoscant te verum Deum solum et quem misisti Jesus Christum* (John 17:3). "This is life eternal, to know thee the only true God, and Jesus Christ whom thou hast sent": as if he had said, men's happiness consists in this, that they know God and Christ. But though Christ teaches this, they alone understand it who cease to be men—that is to say, who lay aside the image of Adam and put on the image of Christ—because these alone know Christ, and only in Christ and through Christ do they know God.

Truly, men attain, whilst but men, to a certain knowledge of God, by contemplation of the created things, but they do not obtain happiness by this knowledge; for in truth happiness is not involved in it, but consists only in that knowledge of God which they alone acquire who have ceased to be (mere) men and, being incorporated into Christ, know God by first knowing Christ. And I understand that the reading of Holy Scripture and the contemplation of the creatures serve to increase and augment in them that knowledge of God which involves happiness and eternal life.

The knowledge which they acquire of God, who know him through the creatures, I conceive to be similar to that knowledge which an inferior artist acquires of a consummate painter by looking at his paintings; and the knowledge which they acquire of God who know him through the Holy Scriptures, I conceive to be similar to that which an idiot, or an unlettered man, acquires of a highly celebrated author by reading his works. And the knowledge which they who know Christ, and are incorporated into Christ, have of God, I conceive to be similar to the knowledge which I have of the Emperor through the sight of his portrait, and through an exceedingly minute account of all his habits, by the report of individuals who are· upon very intimate terms with the Emperor. I conceive that they who know God after this fashion, in reading the Scriptures, know him as a learned man knows a great author—by reading his works. And I conceive that these very same individuals, in contemplating the creatures, know God as a good painter knows a perfect artist—by studying his paintings.

Having apprehended thus much, I understand in what man's happiness consists, and I find myself happy, and I understand much better than I ever previously did the great obligation under which men are to God, and to the Son of God, Jesus Christ our Lord.

Consideration III

OF THAT WHEREIN THE SONS OF GOD DIFFER FROM THE SONS OF ADAM

We are sons of God just so far as we let ourselves to be ruled and governed by God. Thus Saint Paul says: *Qui spiritu Dei aguntur, ii sunt filii Dei* (Rom. 8:14)—"They who are led by the Spirit of God, they are the sons of God." And hence it is certain that he who is a son of God, lets himself to be ruled and governed by God; and that he who is ruled and governed by God is a son of God; and, on the other hand, they who are ruled and governed by human wisdom are sons of Adam; and the sons of Adam are guided and governed by human wisdom, because they neither know, nor are conscious of, any other rule or control. I understand this rule and control as exerting an influence on the body as well as on the soul.

The sons of Adam, guided and governed by human prudence, have certain medical laws to preserve and maintain health, and they have others to regain health when sick; having, as they have, herbs, roots, and many other things of which they avail themselves to do so. But the difficulty is for them to know the time and season when to employ these things, which is almost impossible.

These same sons of Adam, in order to preserve their souls in purity and simplicity, have the laws of God and the doctrine of Christ and his apostles. But the difficulty is for them to understand these laws and this doctrine, and to understand their application, which I hold to be still more impossible. But were either one or the other possible, I might perchance admit that, as they know how to apply those drugs in the preservation and maintenance of bodily health, so likewise they, by knowing how to apply Holy Scripture, might preserve and maintain moral health. But holding both to be impossible, I hold it to be equally impossible for a son of Adam to maintain either bodily health or spiritual health.

The sons of God, as they inwardly mortify their human

wisdom, so do they equally renounce the utility of medicine, together with all things appertaining and belonging to it, accepting God alone as their physician, who is their Father, by whom they are immediately governed, and kept in bodily health, of which, if they have not as much as they desire, they have at least as much as suffices to promote their spiritual health, which is with them the principal thing. God permits them to fall sick, but it is at one time to mortify them, at another to try them, and again that they may know him to be their Father and Lord; and when they are sick, he frequently restores them, without the use of the medicines which the sons of Adam employ. These same sons of God, in their drawing near to him, resemble those Samaritans who said to the woman: *Non propter tuam loquelam* (John 4:42)—"Now we believe, not because of thy saying"; and applying the words to the sacred Scriptures, they say likewise, *Non propter tuam loquelam.* We have another law and another doctrine, which keeps and preserves us in holiness and righteousness; this is the Spirit of God, who dwells in us, who so guides and governs us that we have no need of any other rule or control as long as we will not forsake our Heavenly Father. And as it is possible that an individual may be a son of God, and yield himself up to be guided and governed by God; so it is possible that a son of God may preserve and keep himself in bodily and spiritual health.

The sons of God indeed employ physicians and medicines to preserve bodily health, as they also employ Scripture to preserve spiritual health; but they do so without placing confidence in either one or the other, because all their confidence is placed in God. Moreover, they observe time and place with reference to the preservation of their bodily health, just as they observe certain ceremonies for the preservation of their spiritual health. This they do, rather in external conformity with the sons of Adam than from any conscious necessity of such observances. Nevertheless, these, being governed by God only, obey the will of God and depend solely upon it. They understand these truths, for they experience them; but others find them exceedingly intricate, because *animalis homo non percipit ea quae sunt spiritus Dei* (I Cor. 2:14)—"The natural man discerneth not the things of the Spirit"; and for this reason he ever censures and condemns them.

In order to be better understood I offer this example. Two men would like to swim across a great river. A man well acquainted with the river comes up to them, and says, "If you will pass over, you have but to go down into it here, and then you have to regulate yourselves thus and thus; but if you wish me to take you over, follow me, and be not afraid." One of these two men, trusting in his own knowledge, and in what he had been told, begins to ford the waters alone; I take this man to represent the sons of Adam. The other, trusting himself to the man acquainted with the river, follows him; this one I take to represent the sons of God.

And as I hold it certain that the folly, presumption, and error of the sons of Adam is much greater than that of him who, when he might cross the river with a guide, and safely, ventures to cross it alone; so, again, I certainly hold the prudence and discretion of the sons of God, who submit to be ruled and governed by the Spirit of Christ, to be much greater than that of the man who wishes to cross the river with a guide rather than alone.

And it is to be understood that we are to that extent the sons of God, in which we are incorporated into Jesus Christ our Lord.

Consideration V

Upon the Difficulty There Is of Entering Into the Kingdom of God; the Mode of Entry, and in What It Consists

Man by nature does not trust in his fellow man, unless it be in reference to what he cannot do himself; neither does he trust in God, unless in reference to what he knows and sees he cannot attain by means of any creature. Such is the wickedness of the human mind. And hence, the more a man is favored by the creatures, the more difficult is it for him to be brought to confide in God.

And that such is the fact we may learn from the sick, of whom those only are brought to resign themselves to the will of God who are destitute of means to pay for physicians and medicine, and those likewise who, though they have the means, are at last brought to despair of help from either one or the other.

Hence I am led to reflect upon man's perverseness and to meditate further upon the goodness of God, inasmuch as he still helps and favors those who, through their inability to resist further, submit themselves to his will; and disregarding, as for that matter, how far we have been pious or impious, he is simply intent to keep his word, by which he has engaged himself to help those who submit themselves to him.

That this is true we have constant proofs, not only in what I have stated about sickness, but likewise in everything occurring to man in this present life. Precisely that which we have seen experimentally in external things, I feel assured we shall be able to see in those which are internal; for man is never brought to commit his justification, his resurrection, or his eternal life to God, until he knows and sees them to be unattainable through the creatures.

Now, reflecting that the rich man has, as he thinks, the means of availing himself of the creatures, both for external as well as for internal things, without submitting himself to the will of God, that he may dispose of him as he pleases, I understand the reason why Christ says, in Matt. 19:23, "that it is difficult for a rich man to enter into the kingdom of heaven"—that is, that he be brought to resign himself to the will of God, and to allow himself to be guided and governed by God, renouncing the guidance and governance of human wisdom, and renouncing the assistance of the creatures.

Whence I gather that God first opens the eyes of any man—be he rich or be he poor—whom He purposes to introduce into his Kingdom, so that man may know his own impotence, and how impossible it is for the creatures to give God that which He aims at and desires. And I consider the difference between the pious and the wicked, when commending themselves to God, to consist in this, that the wicked submits to God when he can no longer resist; and the good man submits to God whilst he might still further use and avail himself of the creatures, and this both as to external things and internal things. And I think that a man may know when he has inward confidence in God, by what he discovers of his outward reliance upon God.

Those who are in the Kingdom of God in the way I have described, are the poor in spirit, whom Christ commends. David felt himself such when, in Ps. 40:17, he called himself poor and needy. And I consider that such have partly attained what is sought in the prayer, *Adveniat regnum tuum*—"Thy kingdom come." And contemplating the happiness that results from being and remaining in this Kingdom, I understand the motive why John began his preaching with announcing this Kingdom, and the reason why Christ began his with the same, and the reason why he sent forth the apostles for the very same purpose. Whence I gather that the beginning, middle, and end of Christian preaching should be to preach the Kingdom of God, and to constrain men to enter into it, renouncing the kingdom of the world, and all that belongs to it.

The men who are, as it were, the natives of this Kingdom I look upon as being planted in God, as a tree is planted in the earth; and, as the tree subsists and produces flowers and fruits by the virtue communicated to it by the earth, so he who is planted in the Kingdom of God subsists and produces flowers and fruits by the Spirit of God, which guides and governs him. And such a one is a son of God, is just, and will rise glorious, and have eternal life, because he is conformed to Jesus Christ, the Son of God; and, in addition—Matt., ch. 6—he enjoys this world's goods little or much, as best comports with the glory of God.

Between that which those persons know and understand of this Kingdom of God, by what they read and what they hear, who are outside it, and that which those know and understand of the same Kingdom, by what they feel and by what they experience, who are within it, I recognize a much greater difference than between what those persons know and understand of the rule and government of a most perfect king, by reading and hearsay, who are outside it, from what those know and understand of the same rule and government, from sight and experience, who are within it.

I will add what is in my judgment apposite: that precisely as diverse plants in the same meadow imbibe the virtues of the soil in different proportions, according to their respective qualities—the one more, the other less; one after this fashion, and another after that—so, according to the diverse constitutions of those who are in God's Kingdom, God communicates his Spirit to them in different degrees—to one more, to another less; and to one after this fashion, and to another after that. And all are in the same Kingdom, and all participate of the same Spirit; as all the plants that are in the same meadow, all participate of the same virtues of the soil. As all the plants, were they endowed with the faculty, would affirm the truth of what has been said of them; so they who belong to the Kingdom of God, because they have the Spirit, declare that to be true which has been said of them, recognizing everything as proceeding from the favor of God, through Jesus Christ our Lord,

Consideration VI

DEPRAVITY IN MAN IS OF TWO KINDS—THE ONE NATURAL, AND THE OTHER ACQUIRED

In all men not quickened by the Holy Spirit I consider two modes of depravity—the one natural, and the other acquired. I understand the natural one to be expressed in that passage in Job 14:4, *Neque infans unius diei*—"They go astray from the womb"; and in that in Ps. 51:5, *In iniquitatibus conceptus sum*—"In sin did my mother conceive me"; and in that of Saint Paul, Eph. 2:3, *Eramus natura filii irae*—"We were by nature children of wrath"; and similarly in all those places of Holy Scripture in which our human nature is condemned. I understand the acquired one to be set forth in Gen. 6:12, *Omnis caro corruperat viam suam*—"All flesh had corrupted his way"; and in that passage of Saint Paul in Rom. 7:9, *Ego autem vivebam sine lege quondam*—"For I was alive without the law once"; and generally in all those passages of Holy Scripture which speak of the corruption of our flesh. The acquired proceeds from the natural, and the natural is inflamed by the acquired.

Of these two kinds of depravity, I apprehend that the natural one cannot be rectified save by grace; and thus I apprehend that those persons only are freed from it who by faith enter into the Kingdom of God, and become children of God by the Holy Spirit which dwells in them. So that, in those who know Christ by revelation, and accept the covenant which he established between God and man, believe and because they believe are baptized, their natural depravity is corrected, and they retain only that which is acquired. From this they gradually free themselves, receiving for that end the help of God's Spirit. And whilst they are thus freeing themselves from it, their offences are not imputed to them as sin, because they are incorporated into Christ Jesus, and on that account, as Saint Paul says, Rom. 8:1, "Nothing now brings them under condemnation."

I apprehend that just as the acquired depravity which incites the natural is acquired by habit, so it may be laid aside by habit. And to accomplish this, I understand that they are helped by the laws and precepts which human prudence devises, so that a man may by himself free himself from acquired depravity and from inflaming natural depravity, as we read that many have freed themselves. But man will never free himself from natural depravity by himself, because, as I have said, we are freed from this by the grace of Jesus Christ our Lord.

Consideration VII

IT IS GOD'S WILL THAT WE COMMIT TO HIM THE EXECUTION OF ALL OUR DESIRES

True indeed it is, that we know many things by experience which we never should have understood by science only. Having frequently purposed to do many things, each more pious, more holy, and more Christian than the other, and having observed that my purposes almost always issued contrarily to what I had designed, and that many pious, holy, and Christian things in connection with myself have succeeded without my ever having exerted any previous thought or deliberation respecting them, I found myself as it were perplexed, not understanding wherein the secret lay.

I did not marvel that things upon which I, as a man, had resolved, should issue contrarily to what I wished; but I did marvel that the same should occur to me with reference to things upon which I, as a Christian, had resolved: and finding myself in this perplexity, it happened that I read that declaration of Saint Peter, in Mark 14:31, *Si oportuerit*—"Though I should have to die with thee, yet will I not deny thee." And reflecting that, although the resolution was pious, holy, and Christian, the issue was the reverse of what he had resolved; I understood the reason why my resolutions proved wholly in vain. It was because I resolved without taking into consideration my inability to carry into effect what I had resolved. Moreover, I learned that though God chastised my thoughtlessness by not permitting me to succeed in what I desired; yet, on the other hand, he satisfied my desire by permitting me to succeed in what I had never striven after, never hoped for, nor aimed at. Whence I have gathered that it is the will of God that I am so dependent on him, that I never resolve or propose anything without having him present in my mind, without laying before him my good purpose, and without leaving to him its execution; and that not only in things which relate to outward and bodily life, but likewise in those relating to inward and spiritual life. This the divine will so checks me that, although I know what I have said to be what he demands of me, yet I do not dare to resolve, saying, "I will do so and so"; because I know my inability to carry it out. And not daring to make resolution, I venture to desire to be ever conformed to this will of God, and to leave the execution of it with God; and I am assured that God in his mercy will favor me in this my good purpose; and I am convinced that I ought to regulate myself in all things after this manner. Fresh desire to confide in God in all things will come upon me, and I shall commit myself to him, in order that he may carry this my purpose into execution. Thus I desire to be ruled by love, hope, and self-denial; in a word, by all that may conduce to make me like Christ and like God, and in all that may result in bodily and spiritual advantage to my neighbors; so that whilst the purpose remains lively and entire in me, its execution is left to the goodness of God. I entreat every Christian thus to regulate himself, or, more properly speaking, thus to submit himself to be ruled by God, assuring him that God will not only fulfill his desires, but will satisfy him in many other things which will be done to the glory of God, to his own edification and to that of his neighbors, without his ever thinking of them, hoping or desiring them; God will do this through Jesus Christ our Lord.

In proof of what has been stated, I hold that a man naturally resolves only to do, or not to do, what he believes himself capable of doing; no man resolves to bring about either wet or fine weather. Whence I gather that our resolutions will never be free from arrogance and presumption if we think that to be in our power which is not more in it than to bring about wet or fine weather. Hence it is not our province to make resolutions, but to desire and to leave the execution of what we desire with God. And, keeping the same end in view, I hold that we ought, in our Christian resolutions, ever to reflect whether that which we resolve upon be pleasing to God or not; because it is a mark of great ignorance to resolve to do something to the honor of God of which we are not certain that it is pleasing to God. And thus I feel assured that our resolutions will then be good and wise, when they are conformable to God's will concerning us and conformable to our ability, seeing that it is folly to promise another what we are not able to perform. And this being the truth, it has been well said that resolution consists in desiring, leaving the execution of our desires with God, being assured that he favors us in them, through Jesus Christ our Lord.

Consideration VIII

THE COVENANTS WHICH OUR LORD JESUS CHRIST
ESTABLISHED BETWEEN GOD AND MEN

All men, in gratitude to God for the creation of our being, are born under obligation to love God, to depend on him, and to submit ourselves to be ruled and governed by him. This obligation, thwarted by our depravity and evil inclination, draws us in the contrary direction. We may call this obligation a law of nature, and we may say that the law which God gave the Hebrews, by the hands of Moses, came to discover our obligation and depravity (Rom. 3:30). For, "by law is the knowledge of sin." And so powerful is this evil inclination in the minds of men that, however much they may strive, they never succeed in the full discharge of their obligation. God, knowing this, sent his only-begotten Son, made man, into the world, and willed that his justice should be executed upon him for that wherein all men had failed, and should thereafter fail, in the obligation incident to their birth. So that this is the covenant between God and man: that they believe and hold that that justice which was executed upon Christ, the Son of God, frees and exempts them from the punishment which they deserved, in having failed in the obligation under which they were born; and that God justifies them, and accepts them as his adopted children, and as such rules and governs them during this life, and afterward raises them up and will give them eternal life. Human prudence is incapable of admitting this covenant; because, in the first place, looking upon Christ as an ordinary man, it does not apprehend that he is the Son of God; besides, it does not see on what basis the truth of this covenant is laid, so as to believe it, to hold it undoubtingly, and to rely on it. To attain this, a particular and peculiar revelation from God is needed, which may cast down all the arguments of human prudence; so that holding it as assured and settled that Christ is the Son of God, and that the justice which was executed upon him exempts us from responsibility in having failed in our obligation, we oblige God to justify us, according to the covenant which he has entered into with us. And being justified, we are incorporated into Christ and grafted into him. Precisely as a plant is sustained by the virtue of the earth where it springs up, or is planted, so we are sustained by Christ's virtue, in which we are planted in order that we may persevere in the covenant.

Two other covenants depend upon this covenant. The one is, that we believe that Christ rose from the dead glorified, and that faith in this gives us fellowship in Christ's resurrection, so that we rise again even as he rose, and that God will accomplish in us what he wrought in Christ. Human prudence finds no grounds to warrant belief in this resurrection, and does not believe it; but the man who has accepted the first covenant easily accepts this second. The other covenant is, that we believe that Christ lives evermore with God, in the highest exaltation; and that this faith gives us eternal life, and that by this faith God works in us what he wrought and still works in Christ. Human wisdom finds no grounds to warrant the hope of eternal life; but the man who has accepted the first covenant, through revelation, and through the first has accepted the second, easily accepts this third. So that, we, being assured that Christ is the Son of God, accept the covenant of justification by faith, which gives us fellowship in Christ's death; we accept the covenant of Christ's resurrection, which gives us fellowship in the resurrection; and we accept the covenant of eternal life, which gives us fellowship in the eternal life wherein Christ lives.

We believe four things, and God works four things in us. We believe that Christ is the Son of God, that he died, and rose again, and that he lives; and God makes us his children, justifies us, raises us again, and gives us eternal life. We enjoy the two first in this life, and they bring it to pass that we love God, that we depend on him, according to the obligation with which we are born, having in a great measure overcome our evil inclination; we shall enjoy the two others in a future state. And experiencing in this life, in the two first things, the truth there is in the covenant which Christ established between God and us, we are assured of the truth when it pleases the divine Majesty for us to do so; in the meanwhile, let us wait and persevere in the covenant and covenants which have been made with us by Jesus Christ our Lord.

Consideration IX

ONE EXCELLENT PRIVILEGE OF PIETY

All the good works to which we are excited in this life could be attributed either to our human nature or to our piety. The fact that we are men leads us to sympathize with, and help, each other; that is to say, in all things that belong to the comfort of life. Piety leads us to confide in God, to love him, to depend upon him: leads us to confide in Christ, to love him, and to preach him: leads us to mortify our fleshly affections and lusts: and leads us to condemn all that the world prizes, such as honors, status, and wealth. There shall be a person wholly alien to piety who, led by his humanity, will exercise himself not only in all offices that stand related to it, but, beyond these, will discharge those that stand peculiarly related to piety—striving to fulfill the one, and partly performing the other; and there shall be another decidedly pious, who not only will exercise himself in duties peculiar to piety, but moreover in those which are peculiar to humanity, ever discharging them when an opportunity presents itself. And as the alien to piety, exercising himself in duties peculiar to piety, does not exercise himself in piety, but in the duties which stand related to humanity, because his principal design is his own peculiar interest, which is incident to his being human; so, on the other hand, the person who is decidedly pious, exercising himself in the practice of duties incident to humanity, practices himself in piety, because his principal design is the glory of God, which is the characteristic of piety. And it will come to pass that an alien to piety will preach Christ, yet will not exercise himself in piety, because his principal design will be his own glory and his own private interest; and, on the other hand, it will come to pass that a pious man will do good to one that is without piety, and will practice himself in piety, because his principal design is the glory of God; and although he was not moved to that by Christian charity, but by human pity, nevertheless he exercised himself in piety. Whence I gather, how very great are the advantages which they enjoy who have piety wrought in them by the Holy Spirit, and communicated to the faithful through Jesus Christ our Lord.

Let me add, that he who is a stranger to piety is not only precluded from the perception of this difference between the works of the two classes of persons which is here laid down, but likewise precluded from knowing that he never practices piety himself; whilst the pious man perfectly well understands when he exercises himself in matters peculiar to humanity, and when he exercises himself in matters peculiar to piety: and this he does by reflecting for an instant, or, more properly speaking, by not forgetting himself. But, indeed, it is true that these privileges of piety are as books, as Isaiah says, "which God hath prepared for those who love him"; that is to say, for those who come to know and love him, being justified by faith in Jesus Christ our Lord.

Consideration X

IN WHAT RESPECT THE STATE OF THAT CHRISTIAN WHO BELIEVES WITH DIFFICULTY IS BETTER THAN THAT OF ANOTHER WHO BELIEVES WITH FACILITY

Amongst those who bear the Christian name, I note two classes of men: the one, to whom it is extremely easy to believe all that is said to them in matters of religion; and the other, to whom it is extremely difficult. And it appears to me that the facility of belief in the one springs from superstition, and slight consideration; whilst the difficulty in the other springs from excessive consideration. The former never take counsel of human prudence upon any subject whatever; whilst the latter call in its aid upon every occasion, and are brought with difficulty to believe in anything which human prudence does not approve. The former believe many things that are false, along with some that are true; and it does so happen that they give much greater credit to the many things that are false than they do to the few that are true: the latter do not believe the false, and hesitate to accept the true. Pondering the matter more deeply, I find that the former are assured as to the true things they believe in by the Spirit of God, when he is communicated to them, and by this attestation they are by degrees disabused as to the false, which they thus gradually abandon. Again, I find that the latter have it certified to them by the same Spirit of God, when he is communicated to them, what things are true; and by his attestation they are strengthened in the belief of things which are true, and in the disbelief of those which are false. So that the Holy Spirit, by its entrance into two individuals—the one of whom is very easy of belief, and the other very difficult—places them in this condition, that the one struggles with himself, laboring to dispel from his mind those untruths which he so easily accepted; whilst the other struggles with himself, laboring to attain conviction of those truths which, when delivered by men, he was unable to believe.

Both these men have to strive; but I hold the position of the man who found it difficult to believe better than that of the man who found it easy to believe: and this for three principal reasons. The first, because the man who is aided by the Holy

Spirit, and has many other subsidiary helps, finds it more easy to believe the truth than to disbelieve falsehood; the difficulty in doing which is owing to superstition and various other things. The second, because the man who believes easily may readily be deceived; whilst he to whom it is hard to believe is with difficulty misled. And the third, because the person who is ready to believe remains for a long time under various delusions, as did those in the primitive church who were converted from Judaism to Christianity; and he who is slow to believe remains free from every error, since he only believes what the Holy Spirit teaches him.

Hence I conclude that the position in which the Holy Spirit places the person who believes with difficulty, when He begins to teach him, is beyond all comparison better than that in which He places the man who believes easily. Again, I am clearly of opinion that he who believes, without having been taught by the Spirit of God, relies more upon opinion than upon faith, and is ever involved in error and false conceits. Whence it should be understood that, when a man believes alike in all the statements made to him, he is without the Spirit of God; he believes upon report, by human suasion, and by received opinion, and not by revelation, nor by inspiration. And it being true that the Christian's happiness does not consist in believing merely, but in believing through revelation and not by report, we are to conclude that the Christian's faith is not what is based upon report, but that the Christian's faith is by revelation alone: and this is what makes us happy; it is what brings with it love and hope, and is what purifies the heart, and it is also what is in every respect pleasing to God.[4] May we be enriched with it by God himself, through Jesus Christ our Lord!

[4] All thinkers presuppose, even before the start of all reflection, a universal criterion of truth. Valdés seems to express here, in a very unphilosophical way, his criterion. It may be considered an adequate answer to Pilate's famous question, "And what is truth?"

III

The Christian Alphabet
Which Teaches the True Way
to Acquire the Light of the Holy Spirit

INTRODUCTION

THE ORIGIN OF THIS DIALOGUE IS TOLD BY JUAN de Valdés himself in the short *envoi* which precedes it. Valdés has given us his own estimate of his work. It is intended only as a guide in the way of Christian perfection. When the way is known the guide is not needed any more.

The *Dialogue* was translated by Marco Antonio Magno for Giulia Gonzaga. His words seem to imply that Giulia herself trusted Marco Antonio with the Spanish manuscript.

The first edition of this work was printed in Venice in 1545. Four years later it was included in the Index of Prohibited Books.[1]

For the present selection, we have followed the Italian text, edited by B. Croce in 1938, the English version edited by Benjamin B. Wiffen in 1861, and the Spanish version edited by B. Foster Stockwell in 1948.

EDITIONS OF "THE CHRISTIAN ALPHABET"

Alphabeto Christiano, che insegna la vera via d'acquistare il lume dello Spirito Santo.—Con privilegio della Ill. Signoría di Vinegia che per X anni futuri non si possa stampare questa opera sotto 'l suo Dominio MDXLV.—(Colophon.) Stampato in Vinegia per Nicolo Boscarino, ad instantia di M. Marco Antonio Magno. (Found in the National Library of Naples by Eugenio Mele.)

Anonimo. *Alphabeto Christiano*, che insegna la vera via d'acquistare il lume dello Spirito Santo.—In che maniera il

[1] Fr. H. Reusch, *Die Indices Librorum Prohibitorum* des sechszehnten Jahrhunderts, Tübingen, 1886, p. 142.

christiano ha da studiare nel suo propio libro, et che frutto
hà da trahere dello studio, et come la santa scrittura gli
serve per interprete e commentario. (Venezia) s.t., stampata
con gratia l'anno MDXLVI.
Alfabeto christiano scritto in lingua spagnuola per Giovanni di
Valdés. E dallo stesso manoscritto autografo recato nell'
italiano per Marco Antonio Magno. Ora ristampata
fedelmente la versione italiana pagina per pagina, con
l'aggiunta di duc traduzioni, l'una in castigliano, l'altra in
inglese.—Valdesio hispanus scriptore superbi at orbis
Londra, l'anno MDCCCLX. (Reformistas Antinguos
Españoles, T. XV.)
Alfabeto Cristiano, by Juan de Valdés, which teaches the true way
to acquire the light of the Holy Spirit. From the Italian of
1546, with a notice on Juan de Valdés and Giulia Gonzaga.
By Benjamin B. Wiffen.—"Valdessio Hispanus Scriptore
Superbiat Orbis." D. Rogers. London, Bosworth and
Harrison, 1861. (Only one hundred copies printed for publi-
cation.)
Giovanni di Valdés. *Alfabeto Cristiano*. Dialogo con Giulia
Gonzaga. Introduzione note e appendici di B. Croce.
Ritratto della Gonzaga conforme all 'originale di Sebastiano
del Piombo, con la serie degli altri ritratti. Bari, Gius.
Laterza e figli, 1938.
Juan de Valdés, *Alfabeto Cristiano*. Que enseña el verdadero
camino de adquirir la luz del Espíritu Santo. Con notas
biográficas y críticas sobre el autor, por B. Foster Stockwell,
y sobre Julia Gonzaga, por Benjamin B. Wiffen. Editorial
"La Aurora," Buenos Aires, 1948.

The Christian Alphabet

INTRODUCTORY NOTE BY MARCO ANTONIO MAGNO

Marco Antonio Magno to the most illustrious lady the Signora
Donna Giulia Gonzaga his patroness

II

Having read the dialogue in the Spanish language, entitled
Alphabeto Christiano, written by a person who truly did not seek
honor to his name, yet who has indeed acquired it, because this
work inspires in the reader Christian piety more than any
other book that I have read, and considering that it will
excite me more to pursue the true way of Christ, that it teaches
us, I decided to translate it into our Italian language as closely
as my knowledge would permit. And not being solicitous to
write Tuscan dialect in other respects than so as to make it well
understood, I use almost the same words that the author
himself employed. And thus I send to your most illustrious
ladyship the effigy of yourself, that you may see whether I have
been able to make it discourse as persuasively in your language,
as the author of the work has made it inspire, by such divine
arguments, to the love of the Holy Spirit, in his own language.

The Christian Alphabet

INTRODUCTION BY JUAN DE VALDÉS

Juan de Valdés to the most illustrious lady, Signora Donna Giulia Gonzaga

Constrained by the commands of your most illustrious ladyship, disregarding my own opinion, I have written in form of dialogue all that religious conversation in which we were so deeply interested the other day when returning from the sermon[1] that only the night made it necessary for us to break it off. If I rightly remember, no point which we then discussed is here omitted, nor is any subject we then touched upon left unexamined. Read it when you have leisure; and if anything be wanting, or is superfluous, or if anything afresh occurs to you in reply to what is here stated, inform me of it; because by erasing the one and inserting the other, the dialogue will at length be left perfectly conformable to your wishes; for my purpose in writing it has solely been to please and satisfy your ladyship.

This reason may serve at the same time as an answer to such persons who, on reading this dialogue, may think it much too strict and rigid, and as a reply to others to whom it may appear as much too free and bold: they not reflecting that I did not discuss it with them, nor write it for them, but I did it with your ladyship, and write it for your ladyship, including, however, all such persons who, in your name, and as an affair entirely your own, may incline to make use and avail themselves of it.

In return for the labor I have for several days employed in writing this treatise, I desire from your ladyship only two things.

[1] The Preacher was Fr. Bernardino Occhino, whose sermons delivered in the church of S. Giovanni Maggiore were admired by the emperor himself. B. Croce says this dialogue took place during the Lenten season, 1536. (Cf. *Alfabeto Cristiano*, Introduzione, p. VII.)

One is that you may give to that which you will here read no trust or belief further than as it appears and is made clear to you that it has foundation in the Scriptures, and invites and leads you forward to that perfect Christian charity which is the mark by which Christ desires that his followers should be distinguished from all other persons. The other thing is: that you make use of this dialogue as children use a grammar when they learn Latin, in the manner of a Christian alphabet, in which you may learn the rudiments of Christian perfection, making it your aim, the elements being attained, to leave the alphabet and apply your soul to things more important, more excellent, more divine. It is convenient that your ladyship do as I say, as much for your own advantage as for my safety. Because if you do so, I shall not then fall into the error of those persons who sell their own writings and imaginations at the same price for which they sell Holy Scripture, nor will your ladyship fall into the mistake, far more hurtful than beneficial, into which those persons fall, who with a pious simplicity apply themselves to the mere writings of men, without looking for something far beyond them. It frequently happens to such persons, that finding in those writings the milk of the doctrine of rudiments, they make so much relish of it, that persuading themselves they can gain from it the higher consolations that belong to Christian perfection, they are not careful to go onward, seeking the food of the perfect Christian, which is to be found in the sacred Scriptures alone. Because those only in some measure accommodate themselves to the capacity of them that read, who at the first give the milk of the word and afterward present the stronger food to the more proficient for their nourishment. Hence it arises that such persons, depending upon men and always reading their writings, remain imperfect, and yet frequently judge of and satisfy themselves that they are most perfect. Now desiring that your ladyship may never judge nor satisfy yourself that you are perfect, but that you may be so in truth, both in view of God and the world, I wish you not to read this composition, not to hold it in greater estimation than ought to be given to the writings of one who, desirous to gratify you in this Christian object, only points out to you the way by which you may arrive at Christ himself and become united with him.

And I desire that your Christian intention may be to make Christ the peaceful possessor of your heart, in such a manner that he may absolutely and without contradiction rule and regulate all your purposes. And when your ladyship shall have done this, believe me that you will not feel the want of anything whatsoever in this present life that can give you entire contentment and repose. Because Christ himself will provide the most pleasant banquets for you, even the knowledge of his divinity, in which in quietness and confidence you shall lie down and rest. And when I shall know and see that your ladyship is in this glorious state, assured and certain of your spiritual progress, I shall not hesitate to believe that my intention in this work has been altogether a Christian one, and that your ladyship has perused it with a mind pure, humble, and discreet.

May God, our Lord, make it suitable for your most illustrious ladyship's need, and for the object which I, as your most affectionate servant, perpetually desire.

The Christian Alphabet

THE TEXT

Giulia Gonzaga   Juan de Valdés

Giula: I trust so much in our friendship, that it seems to me that I could freely communicate to you even those things that we scarcely reveal to the confessor. Therefore, wishing now to impart to you some things dearer to me than life itself, I entreat you, if you have not more important business elsewhere, to listen attentively to what I wish to say to you. And notice, if you think you cannot attend closely to me now, through having your thoughts engaged elsewhere, tell me with all freedom; for, if so, I can defer it to another day.

Valdés: On the contrary, *signora,* I gain a favor by whatever you command me; and you know already that I have no business which can hinder me, especially in what relates to your service.

G: Now, setting aside all vain rhetoric and useless ceremony, which between us are quite superfluous, I wish you to know that I live almost continually so dissatisfied with myself, and in like manner with everything in the world, and so disappointed with them, that if you saw my heart, I am sure you would pity me; for in it you would find nothing but confusion, uneasiness, and perplexity. And of these I have now more, now less, according to the nature of the circumstances that present themselves. But I never feel so much calmness of mind that, wishing to settle it, I can conclusively understand what it is that I would wish for, or what thing would satisfy it, or with what it would rest contented. Hence, I cannot conceive what can not be offered to me, sufficient to remove this, my confusion of mind, appease my uneasiness, and resolve this perplexity. Many years have I lived in the manner I describe, and during this time, as you know, various circumstances have happened to me sufficient to disturb a tranquil spirit, much more a soul so disquieted and confused as mine. Besides this, you know that at the first sermons I heard from our Preacher he persuaded me by his words that, by means of his doctrine, I should be able to calm myself and bring peace to my mind; but now, at last, I find it altogether the reverse of what I thought. And although I attribute this more to my own imperfections than to any defect in him, yet altogether it gives me pain to perceive that my hopes have not succeeded. This disappointment might be tolerable, yet it is the worse that, instead of being cured of one infirmity, I have entered into another, without being released from the former. This is a most heavy and cruel conflict, so bothersome and disgusting that tears frequently come into my eyes through not knowing what to do myself, or what to lean upon. The sermons of the Preacher have produced this conflict in my mind. Through them I see myself violently assailed, on the one side by the fear of hell and the love of paradise, and on the other by the dread of people's tongues and the love of the world's honor. In this manner two kinds of fears and two kinds of love, or to speak more correctly, two affections of fear and two different ones of love, are what fight within me, and have kept me such as I am for some days. If you could feel what I now feel, you might truly wonder how I can pass it off and conceal it as I do. This is what I find within me, and in this state (which I have described well or awkwardly, as I have been able) my concerns still remain. Since you have shown so much affection and good will to aid me in my outward affairs, I entreat you to be ready to assist and counsel me in these interior things, because I very well know that, if you are willing, you have more skill to assist me in these than in the others.

V: Say freely, *signora*, all that you wish to ask of me, and you may be assured that I will always expend in your service all that I know and am able to do.

G: In such confidence I have entered into this conversation with you, and in the first place, I wish you may tell me from what cause you believe the confusion, doubt, and perplexity spring, which for so long a time I have felt in my mind, and whether you think they can be bettered, and what means can be used for the purpose. This said, you will tell me concerning the contradictions that have arisen in me after I heard these sermons, whether it would be possible by any way to quiet my mind, either by assent, or really by resistance, because this tempest of affections and appetites, of imaginations and diversities of will, cannot endure much longer; and I wish you not to lose time with excusing yourself by the usual, not to say feigned, humility which in such a case people frequently use.

V: On the contrary, without any delay, I will at once make a beginning. Yet, I wish you first to make me one promise.

G: What promise?

V: It is this, that, if I make you truly comprehend from what cause your confusion, uneasiness, and contradictions proceed, and show you the way by which you can be freed from them, you will give me your assurance and word that you will walk in it.

G: If I might be so certain that you would do what you say, as I am certain that in such case I would do what you ask of me, I should already begin to quiet myself.

V: Now then, I hope, not so much from any skill or sufficiency of my own, as in the affection and willingness I have to serve you, and likewise in your lively understanding and lucid judgment, and above all in the grace of God, that before I leave this place you shall not only learn what you wish, but you shall know and understand the way by which you can free yourself from your former infirmity and from the subsequent consequences. Be very attentive, *signora*, because upon every single thing which I shall say to you, you can reply to me what may occur to you.

G: I will do so.

V: Then, in order to understand, *signora*, whence proceed the travail and confusion which you say you have felt for so many years, I wish you would bring to mind how that *man is made in the image and likeness of God.*

MAN, THE IMAGE OF GOD

G: Let me understand what this *image and likeness of God* is.

V: I wish rather that Saint Paul may explain it to you, and thus you will understand it by what he says to the Colossians, where, admonishing them to speak the truth one to another, he counsels them to put off the old man with his deeds, and to put on the new man, who is renewed in knowledge conformable to the *image and likeness* of Him who created him.[2] And you will also understand it by what Saint Paul again says to those of Ephesus, reminding them that by becoming Christians they have learned to put off the old man and to be renewed in the

2 Col. 3: 9–10.

spirit and clothed with the new man, who is created in the *image and likeness* of God.[3] From this it appears that in such a degree as man possesses and retains in himself the *image and likeness* of God, in the same measure he sees and knows, understands and relishes, spiritual things in a spiritual life and conversation. This truly known, and examining well the objects you set before your mind, you will understand clearly how all the uneasiness, all the travail, all the confusion you feel, arises; because your soul desires you to procure its restitution to the *image* of God to which it was created, and of which it appears you have deprived it. Submitting to your appetites, and persisting in obliterating this image, you have put before it things earthly and transitory, not by any means worthy of that excellence for which it was created. For this reason it cannot be satisfied or contented with any of these things. It seems to you that it knows not what it wishes for, and hence you know not how to set before it that which it would desire. This state of mind that happens to you, ever befalls worldly persons who having attained to a reflective intellect and clear judgment, knowing truly that their souls find not, nor ever can find, entire satisfaction in outward things, turn themselves to seek for it in things relating to the mind. Yet as the supernatural Light, by which alone truth is discovered, seen, and known, is wanting to them, they go wandering in a labyrinth of appearances and opinions. And thus some seek happiness in one thing, some in another. I think it not worth-while to refer here to examples, because this is not the point of your proposition. It is enough that you know this, that all these persons deceive themselves and could never imagine, not to say know, with certainty the things in which true happiness consists; who, if they had had a little of the light of faith, would most easily, and with the grace of God, have acquired it, and thus they would have quieted and pacified their souls. Have you now understood the cause whence your uneasiness, confusion, and labor proceed?

G: Yes, very well.

V: Now, then, you should know that it may surely be remedied, and that the remedy is in your own hands.

G: In my hands?

V: Yes! in your hands. Because whenever you determine yourself to do what I tell you, and what Saint Paul tells you, respecting the renewing and restoring within you of the *image*

[3] Eph. 4:12–24.

and likeness of God, you will find peace, quiet, and repose of spirit.

MAN'S HAPPINESS

G: And how must I do this?

V: By withdrawing your mind from things fallen and transitory, and by applying it to those that are fixed and eternal; not wishing or endeavoring to feed it with things corporal, but spiritual, not nourishing it with things worldly, but with things celestial. And in this manner your spirit, finding its proper alignment, and seeing itself clothed with the new man in the *image and likeness* of which it was created, will always live content and cheerful; and here in this present life it will begin to taste of that happiness which it expects to enjoy forever in the life eternal, being thus that the happiness of man consists in his knowledge of God and of Christ shown by the light of faith, and in the union of the soul with God through faith, hope, and charity. To this happiness only the true Christian can arrive.

G: I should well believe this you say, because indeed it appears founded in reason, but as I know many persons who have as much, and perhaps more, canceled the *image of God* than I have done, and who do not present to their minds things more spiritual than I present to mine, yet they live in pleasure, finding contentment and satisfaction in the things of this world; so that I know not what to believe.

V: Such persons' minds dwell in a low and vulgar state, and therefore low and mean objects give them satisfaction. But a spirit generous and refined like yours, cannot calm itself and take repose, except in that greatness for which it was created. Hence, I repeat, if you are disgusted and live with your mind in confusion, it is because you do not turn it to things spiritual and divine, and because you continually fix its consideration upon these low and transitory concerns. You will better understand it by this comparison.

Two persons set out from this place to go to Spain. One of them is so careless and forgetful of his purpose that, whenever anything amusing or delightful occurs on the way, he not only partakes of it and enjoys it, but quite forgets his principal journey, and gratifies his body and mind, stopping on the road. The other, on the contrary, is so solicitous and punctual that, with all the entertainments and feasts that are offered to him, he will not taste or enjoy any, because he knows and is sure that he is not to remain there; nay, they are frequently displeasing and distasteful to him, and he considers them as hindrances and interruptions of his journey. And such a person, even now, has a want of satisfaction in these things whenever his principal journey becomes more impressed on his remembrance, and although at times he may forget himself and lose sight of his object, there remains impressed upon his memory altogether a something, I know not what, which causes him to find no true enjoyment in anything that the journey presents to him.

Such are we in this life. We are all born and created to know God, to believe God, to love God, and after this state of existence to enjoy God. And, yet, there are some who feed on the pleasures of this world, not only delighting and giving themselves up to rest in them, but who are wholly forgetful of that other life for which they were created. There are also others who, being offered the same delights and pleasures, enjoy them not, nor take relish in them; nay, they are often insipid and distasteful, keeping always in view that other life for which God created them. And although for a time these forget themselves, losing the remembrance of the other life, yet because God stands ever at the door and calls them, it will be impossible that they should find relish and enjoyment in things of this world; and if they expect or endeavor to find them here, they will live in confusion, disgust, and inquietude, as you are living, *signora*. In the same manner, then—like him who knows how to taste of the things of this world, yet does not enjoy them as things suitable to his better nature, or that will be lasting, but who looks at them as the curious beholder views them, turning away from the recreations and banquets offered to him by the way—I wish, *signora*, you to do the same. Turn within yourself, open the ears of your soul, so that you may hear the voice of God, and think as a true Christian that in this life you can have no other real contentment and rest than what will come to you by means of the knowledge of God, through the faith and love of God. Settle your mind on this consideration, most earnestly putting aside all those things that are transitory and cannot endure. Doing this, I promise that you will occupy a much shorter time in quieting, soothing, and giving peace to your mind, than you have spent in disturbing it. And if you do not thus overcome it, I am content that you should never give credit to anything I may say to you.

G: Truly I believe that you have found the source whence my infirmity proceeds, without erring in a single point. O God, do thou assist me! How blindly do we worldly persons go on!

Even now I am sure that you have found truly how to give me the medicine by which I shall be healed of my weakness. It only remains that I put my trust in God and take it. I have no doubt that it will heal me, so much the more having such a physician as you on my side.

V: The true physician of the soul is Christ crucified. Put all your confidence in him alone, and you will discover the remedy.

G: From what you have said, one doubt has come to my recollection, on which I am often accustomed to think; I entreat you to tell me how it appears to you.

V: Ask it freely.

G: I wish to know from you how it comes to pass that people fall into such blindness, and go on lost in the things that gratify the senses, forgetful chiefly of those which they ought continually to care for?

V: These are remains of original sin.

ORIGINAL SIN. BAPTISM

G: This is what I do not understand. They say God pardons original sin in baptism. Since it is thus he pardons us, how is it that there remains with us these evil inclinations and this blindness, being so prejudicial to our salvation?

V: Signora, you must understand it in this manner. In original sin two things are to be considered, one the guilt, the other the inclination to evil, which is that of which you speak. And it is thus in baptism through faith, God pardons us the guilt of sin, and as to the inclination to evil he goes on medicating and curing it by his grace, little by little, in such a manner that a person may, by the grace and favor of God, so much perfect himself as almost to come to lose all evil inclinations, all unrestrained appetites, and all inordinate affections that reign in us through original sin. Conformable to this is that saying of Saint Augustine, that the Spirit of God restores and renews in us the *image and likeness of God* to which we were created. But you will understand it better by this example.

A great nobleman has a servant whom he loves and to whom he shows much grace and favor. This servant commits a serious offence against his lord, for which he not only deprives him of all favor and grace, but with just indignation sentences him to death. It happens at the time, that a person in high favor with the nobleman entreats for that servant, to whom, in consideration for such person, he graciously gives pardon of his life, and although he does not admit him to the same place in his favor as before he had sinned, he gives him the entry of his palace and chamber, so that he may in time return to occupy the station in which he stood at first.

G: By this example I completely understand it, and am so well satisfied that I remain tranquil, and am without any scruple as to this point. So you may believe that you have accomplished not a little.

V: If I were conversing with a person of a low, gross, and unpolished understanding, I might well think I had already done something; but, addressing whom I do, I have need of only a little diligence to make you capable of receiving the truth in a manner that leaves me with nothing to pride myself except the credit you give to my words.

G: Come now, no more of this. Let us come to the subject, and tell me your opinion about the mental contradiction that I feel.

V: I say, *signora*, that as I pity and regret that you are living under the confusion of mind, of which we have just now spoken, so also I am pleased and satisfied that you feel the contradiction of which you speak.

G: Why so?

V: I will tell you. I regret confusion, because it proceeds from your fault, as we have said, and tends to your injury, as you yourself experience; and I am pleased at the contradiction of mind, because I know that it proceeds from this: that the preaching of the gospel produces its first effect in you.

THE PREACHING OF THE GOSPEL

G: Why do you call this contradiction the first effect of preaching the gospel?

V: Because the first thing that light does when entering into a dark room is to disperse the darkness, and to discover and show what is not seen in the obscurity; so, in the same manner, when the light of evangelical truth begins to shine in the soul of a worldly person, dispersing in some degree the darkness and obscurity, as well of the senses as of human reason, it shows and brings to light what before was hidden; and then when such a person turns within himself he begins to feel that what he before regarded as good is evil; what he judged to be true is false; and that which seemed to him sweet is bitter. And because of our incapacity and fragility, the light of this evangelical truth shines not so much at first in our souls as would suffice to scatter from them at once all the obscurity, so that they could clearly and manifestly know the nature and existence of these things. It then happens that, the darkness contending with the light, and human reason with the Christian spirit, these contests cause them to feel those earthquakes of inward contradiction that you, *signora*, now feel. We have so many instances of this, as well in the history of Christ which the Evangelists wrote as in what Saint Luke wrote of the acts of the apostles, and also in the Epistles of Saint Paul, that if I wished to quote all the passages one by one, I should spend all our time in doing this; and not to spend the time in doing so, I will leave them for you, since you have the New Testament in Italian, to read them there yourself, I pointing them out to you. I only wish to tell you this: that you should consider these contradictions of mind which you feel as a gift and blessing from God, and you should make use of them as such, giving place to the Light as it shines more and more in your soul. In this manner you will become freed from the contradiction, and will put yourself into a capacity to receive the other gifts of God, which will be sweet and well flavored. May God preserve you, *signora*, from not feeling this contradiction, because not to feel it is a sign of hardness and obstinacy.

G: At last, this is my conclusion: that I cannot understand either of you. All the Preacher's theme is to say that the preaching of the gospel soothes and pacifies the conscience, and now you say quite the contrary. I know not what to say, except that I do not understand you.

V: Then I will make you understand us, and, comprehending it, you will know that we both speak rightly, and that there is no contradiction in our language. And it is thus: The Preacher says very truly that the preaching of the gospel soothes and pacifies the conscience. Yet you must understand that it produces this effect in all those persons who receive and embrace Christ through faith, in a way that by means of preaching the gospel, which announces remission and pardon of sin by Christ, faith soothes and pacifies the conscience, yet only of those persons who have living and entire faith. So, also, I speak truly that the same preaching begets contradiction, terror, and dismay, yet it is in those persons who hear the preaching, although they do not thereon determine to embrace the truth through faith, nor keep it, except as it may be merely for a rule of moral doctrine. Finding that it is opposed to their affections and appetites, and desiring to make it conform to them, at one time they desire one thing, and at another time they wish another, and, not concluding to determine themselves, they truly feel one of the effects of the gospel preaching, but do not enjoy the fruition of it. Have you understood it?

G: Yes, very well. But I do not understand why you are pleased to see me in this state of contradiction.

V: Because it is a sign that you hear the doctrine; and although the evangelical preaching does not exercise in you its chief office, which is that described by the Preacher, I may be glad that at least it executes the office of the law, which is what I describe to you, and I hope, in the grace of God, that after the preaching has performed in you the office of the law, it will then exercise the service of the gospel.

G: I imagine that I can nearly understand what you wish to explain, but I shall have pleasure in learning a little more particularly what is the office of the law, and what the office of the gospel.

THE LAW AND THE GOSPEL

V: Indeed it is most proper, *signora*, that you should understand both of them. Know then that the law is the rule of conscience, and it is thus that conscience is no other than the law understood; whose office is to evidence sin, and also to increase it. Saint Paul understood both by experience and, as he truly had experienced it, he writes to the Romans, in that his most excellent Epistle, and says himself that the law works wrath, because persons become resentful, angry, and excited when restricted by the law. (Rom., ch. 8.) He says more, that the law is spiritual, for it is not observed in its integrity, nor rightly understood, unless the person is a spiritual person. The prophets call the law a heavy yoke, a rigorous scepter, and other names of this kind, which signify severity. And when God gave the law to Moses, the people of Israel, who stood at the foot of the mountain, saw great lightnings and thunderings, so that all trembled with fear and dismay. All say that these things signify the terror, alarm, and conflict of the affections which the law generates in those minds to whom it is given. But with all this, you, *signora*, ought to know that the law is very needful to us, for if we had not the law, we would not have conscience, and if without conscience, sin would not be known, and if sin were not known, we should not humble ourselves, and if we did not humble ourselves, we should not obtain grace, if we did not obtain grace, we should not be justified, and not being justified, our souls would not be saved. And this I believe Saint Paul wishes to be understood where he says that the law is as a schoolmaster or governor who leads and conducts us to Christ, although by means of faith we are justified.[4] Here you perceive the office of the law. The gospel executes the same office in those persons who receive it only as law; but in them who receive it as an ambassador or messenger of grace, its own office is to heal the wounds made by the law, and to preach grace, peace, and remission of sins; to calm and pacify the conscience; to give strength to accomplish what the law shows us to be the will of God, and by which the enemies of the soul are warred with, and by which they are overcome and beaten down to the ground. And thus Christ comes to them compassionate, humble, pacific, and full of love and charity, and not terrible and alarming like the law. In this manner the law teaches us what we have to do; the gospel gives us spirit by which we are enabled to fulfill it. The law makes the wound; the gospel heals it; and finally, the law slays; the gospel gives life. I do not care to go on confirming this with the authority of the sacred Scriptures, not to occupy the time.

G: You have done very well. Do not trouble yourself if you do not quote your authorities; when you shall say anything that appears difficult to me, I will ask you to prove it to me by some authority from Scripture.

V: Let it be so. And since you have already understood the office of the law and of the gospel, by this too you will more clearly discover the source whence springs the contradiction that you feel; it will be as well that we go forward.

G: I wish first that you would tell me a little more about this subject.

V: I know not what more to tell you, if I do not go into particulars.

G: Now this is what I wish.

PARADISE AND HELL

V: The Preacher, *signora,* by his sermons, has awakened in your remembrance what you already had conceived of heaven and hell, and has known so well how to picture it to you that the fear of hell makes you love heaven, and the love of heaven

---

[4] Gal. 3:24.

makes you dread hell. And in connection with showing you this, he tells you that you cannot fly from hell except through the observance and keeping of the law and the doctrine of Christ. And as he declares this to you in a manner it seems to you that you cannot perform without hazard of being whispered about, disesteemed, undervalued, and considered as little by people of the world, the forecast for the future life conflicting within you on one side, and on the other an unwillingness to bear the troubles of this, so the contradiction you feel is generated. All this is born of the self-esteem[5] with which you love yourself. You fear hell for your own interest; you love heaven for your own interest; you fear the confusion of the world for your own interest; you love the glory and the honor of the world for your own interest. Thus in everything you fear and love, if strictly noticed, you will discover yourself there.

G: Then whom do you wish that I should find in my own things if not myself?

V: I wish that you should again find God, and not yourself, if you wish to be free from contradiction, confusion, inquietude, discontent, and a thousand other discomforts beside, from which you can never become freed; but when you find God, you will find peace, serenity, quietness, content, cheerfulness, and courage, and such an infinitude of spiritual blessings that you will not know how to gather them. Now if you wish to slight him, and if you are willing to deprive yourself of heaven and blind yourself to hell through unwillingness to go a little out of yourself and enter into God, why, see you do it. For myself, I assure you that there is nothing in the world that could give me equal satisfaction and content than to see you walk in this Christian path; because I know your mind so well inclined, I hold it certain that if you begin to enamor yourself with God, you will surpass in holiness many of those saints who stand in heaven.

G: Indeed I desire no other thing; God knows my wishes.

V: Then why do you not take what you desire?

---

5 In this case, we have translated the Spanish idiom "amor propio" by "self-esteem" and not by "self-love." There is not an exact English equivalent for this phrase. Valdés' own context is the best explanation of what the Spanish "amor propio" means. It is semantically related to the Spanish "point of honor" or "pundonor." In other places Valdés contrasts the human "point of honor" with the honor due to God and the honor of God in himself, offended by man's disobedience. There is a striking similarity between Valdés' ideas concerning God's honor and Anselm's theology of atonement as expressed in *Cur Deus Homo?*

G: Because I do not know how to do so.

V: Effort, effort, *signora*, is the only means the gospel concerned demands. And so Christ said: "From the days of John the Baptist until now, the Kingdom of Heaven suffereth violence, and the violent take it by force."[6] Thus if you wish to take the Kingdom of Heaven, do violence to yourself, and so you will fear nothing, because, as a Spanish lady of high rank said, although I think not upon this subject, "Quien a sí vence, á nadie teme" ("He who conquers himself fears no one").

G: Let us leave mere words; the fact is, that I indeed believe all my confusion, my inquietude, and my contradiction of mind would cease by entering upon the way of God, and for this reason I would resolve to enter upon it immediately, but it seems to me so difficult to find that I dare not set myself to seek it.

V: What do you see that makes it so troublesome to find?

G: I see few who walk by that road.

FIVE CLASSES OF PERSONS

V: In this you are so far right, that few walk in it. But you should know that this does not arise so much from the difficulty of the way as from our own evil nature and imperfection. And because I desire to confirm you in this truth, I wish you to know that in the present life you will discover five kinds of persons. Some there are who know not the way of God, neither wish to know it, because they foresee that by walking in that way they must deprive themselves of their amusements and pleasures. And these persons, although they do not speak it with the lips, yet from the heart they use the language that Job utters when noticing the wickedness of the impious: "Depart from us, for we desire not the knowledge of thy ways."[7] The same says David: "The fool hath said in his heart there is no God." You will find other persons who know the way of God, but overcome by their affections and appetites they do not conclusively determine to walk in it. Christ says of such: "The servant who knew his lord's will and did it not shall be beaten with many stripes." And truly it is so also in this world. Such persons feel a continual remorse of conscience which keeps them discontented and without enjoyment.

You will find another kind of persons who desire and have the will to learn and know the way of God, but being bound by

6 Matt. 11:12.   7 Job 21:14.

the love of the things of this present life, and taking supreme delight in them, they are not willing to give them up, and so they do not dispose themselves in a manner that God should teach and show them his way. Satan directly sets before such persons certain masked passages, which he gives them to understand are the right paths, and they, blind with love of themselves, willingly yield themselves to be deceived and injured by supposing that God carries them whilst it is the devil who is leading them. Hence are born superfluous ceremonies; hence arise pernicious superstitions; hence come false worships. God says of such persons by Isaiah: "They seek me daily, wishing to learn and know my ways like people who have lived righteously, and have not abandoned the justice and judgment of the Lord their God."[8]

You will find another kind of persons who are willing to know the way of God and dispose themselves toward it. These, hearing in their souls the voice of Christ which says: "Come to yourselves, ye who go wandering; that is not the right path in which you are walking for you cannot go by that to the Kingdom of Heaven," these come to themselves and, perceiving that they are lost, leave the road they are pursuing, and before they take any other course pray unto God that he would show them the true way. And the disposal is this. Such persons are presently sensible of Christ who says to them: "Whoever will walk by the true and certain way, let him deny himself, take up his cross and follow me, imitating me in what he can";[9] and they are sensible that in another place of Scripture he declares this to them: "Learn of me, for I am meek and lowly of heart, and ye shall find rest unto your souls."[10] And thus they immediately enter by the way of patience and true humility.

You will find some other persons who know the way of God and walk by it, some with more and greater fervency than others, yet in a manner that neither one nor the other go out of their way or forsake it. They go on well, and these in truth are but few, as you say, *signora*, although they are not so few as you think, because their path being spiritual, they cannot be seen but by spiritual sight, nor are they possibly known except by persons who walk by the same road. These live in continual care not to offend God; and if at times they fall into any mortal sin through weakness, overcome by temptation, they turn

[8] Isa. 58:2.   [9] Matt. 16:24; Mark 8:34; Luke 9:23.
[10] Matt. 11:29.

immediately to God, confess their offense, and have no need of many preparations for their confession, for as David says, speaking of himself, their sin is ever before their eyes. These very persons have some negligences and defects which are signs that their minds stand not entirely mortified. Indeed their defects and negligences are often the cause of their improvement, because they repent and humble themselves, and thus learn to mistrust themselves and to confide in God. For this reason Saint Paul says that all things work together for good to them that love God, and hence he says in another place that there is nothing to bring condemnation to them who, having entered upon this road, stand united to Christ Jesus by faith and love.[11]

The first persons are the wicked; the second, the blind; the third, the unsteady; the fourth, the prudent; the fifth, the holy. In this manner you can see that if few persons walk by the Christian way, it is more through their impiety, blindness, and fickleness than through its difficulty; and knowing this, you should have no fear of finding it. And since you, *signora*, as I think, are one of the fourth sort of persons, set yourself to listen to the voice of Christ, for he will put you forward by the true way; and consider it certain that as soon as you shall have entered upon it, you will feel no more confusion, inquietude, travail, or perplexity; in short, you will not feel any of those conflicts of mind, but, on the contrary, you will experience great peace, cheerfulness, satisfaction, and supreme content.

G: All that you have said satisfies me. And since I absolutely wish to enter upon this way, it remains for you to lead me by the hand, instructing me in those footsteps by which I believe you have walked.

V: I know not what more you wish to learn from me of that which the Preacher tells you every day.

G: I am weak, and cannot make such resistance to my inclination as the Preacher speaks of.

V: I already, in good part, understand you, *signora*. What need have you to go by the branches? I know well what you would wish.

G: How annoying! Since you know it, why do you not mention it?

V: Because I wait that you should ask it with your own lips.

G: Please say it, since you know it; and I will admit the truth if you tell it to me in all its different aspects.

11 Rom. 8:28 and 8:1.

A ROYAL ROAD

V: I am agreeable to this. You, *signora,* wish to be freed from the troublesome things that come and go through your imagination and, being convinced that this is the true way to free you from them, you wish me to show you some royal and ladylike road by which you may be able to get to God without turning away from the world, and by which you can attain the interior humility without showing it outwardly; possess the virtue of patience without the occurrence to you of what would exercise it; despise the world, but in a manner that the world may not condemn you; clothe your soul with Christian virtues without despoiling the body of its accustomed ornaments; nourish your soul with spiritual viands without depriving the body of its usual banquets; you wish to appear good in the sight of God without appearing ill in the eyes of the world; and in short by this path you wish to be able to lead your religious life, but in a mode that no person of the world, even with the great familiarity and intercourse he might have with you, could discover in your life more than he at present knows. Am I right?

G: Very nearly; or at least if you are not completely right, you can say that you have almost hit the mark.

V: This suffices me to be able to tell you that, as I understand it, you would free yourself from the conflict you feel rather by compromise than by verdict.

G: Don't you always tell me that a bad compromise is better than a good verdict?

V: Yes, I say so, but not in this case in which the compromise is very dangerous and terribly hurtful. Know you not that Christ says that we cannot serve God and the world; either we must serve the world and despise God, or we must love God and despise the world. And have you not understood that Job says that the life of man, here in this world, is but a constant warfare? But know that the warfare is between the flesh and the spirit, when the flesh draws us towards the world, and the spirit draws us towards God. And woe to those who do not feel this warfare!

G: Now, then, I well understand and experience both, and I wish that without more delaying you would decidedly tell me whether your mind is sufficient to put me into a way which leads somewhat to that which you have described, although it be not so loose, for I am not so subjected to my appetites as you must think, according to what you have expressed by your words.

V: If I knew, *signora*, anything in your manner of life and outward conversation disgraceful or base, or that you had any relic, or any show or appearance of evil, I would freely tell you, that my mind is not sufficient for me to satisfy you in what you desire, because it being necessary in such a case that you should depart from all that might be evil, it would be necessary that there should be seen in you a different person from her whom we now see and know. But knowing your way of life and conversation to be so decorous, your manners as regular as can be wished for in such a lady, and seeing that all the reformation necessary to you in order to conquer and obtain the end you desire consists in the affection and appetites of the soul, which corrected and reformed, it would be an easy thing to reform the exterior in what appears to have need of reformation, I am bold to tell you, my mind is equal to set you in the way you desire, without worldly persons perceiving it in you, in such a manner that if you engage yourself to it, with the grace of God, before many days have passed, you will begin to feel the peace of conscience and the other benefits which spiritual persons enjoy.

G: If you do this, I shall remain forever obliged to you.

V: With the grace of God I will do this; and I only wish that you should remain obliged to God himself, from whom I wish you to acknowledge every good that comes.

G: I will endeavor to do what you say. Now do that which belongs to you to do.

V: I am agreeable to it. But first, tell me whether you have ever crossed any stream by a ford.

G: Yes, I have, many times.

V: And have you considered how that, by looking upon the water, it seemed as though your head swam, so that if you have not assisted yourself, either by closing your eyes, or by fixing them on the opposite shore, you would have fallen into the water in great danger of drowning?

G: Yes, I have noticed it.

V: And have you seen how by keeping always for your object the view of the land that lies on the other side, you have not felt the swimming of the head, and so have suffered no danger of drowning?

G: I have noticed this too.

V: Then, if you, *signora*, wish to cross the running flood of things of this world, do so in the same manner. Look not upon them with your affections, so that such danger may not happen to you as befalls them who, gazing on the stream, fall into it and are drowned. And endeavor to keep the view of your soul, fixed and nailed with Christ, on the cross. And if at any time, through want of care, you set your eyes upon the things of the world, in such a manner that you feel your heart incline to them, turn back upon yourself, and return to fix your view upon Christ crucified, and in this way your course will go on well. And, therefore, I wish you, *signora* to take above all things, for your principal purpose, to enamor yourself with Christ, regulating all your works, all your words, all your thoughts by that divine command which says: "Thou shalt love the Lord thy God with all thy heart, with all thy mind, and with all thy strength, and thy neighbor as thyself."[12] And I say, hold fast this command as your principal rule, for Christian perfection consists in loving God above all things and your neighbor as yourself.

CHRISTIAN PERFECTION

G: I marvel at what you say, because I have all my life been told that friars and nuns are in the rule of perfection by the vows that they make, if they observe them.

V: Let them say so, *signora*, and give credit to me that, whether friars or nonfriars, they possess so much of Christian perfection as they have of faith and love of God, and not a grain more.

G: It would much please me if you could enable me to understand this.

SELF-LOVE AND LOVE OF GOD

V: I will do it very willingly. You must know, *signora*, that the human heart is naturally inclined to love; in such a way, it must either love God and all things for God, or it must love itself and all things for itself. That which loves itself does all things for itself. I mean to say that it is so far moved to them as its own self-interest invites it, and thus if it love anything beyond itself, it loves it for itself and for its own interest, and if it have any love toward God, it has it for its own interest and in no other respect. Such a one, friar or nonfriar, because he has his affection in a state of disorder, having placed it in himself,

12 Mark 12:30–31.

never knows how, or in what manner, he ought to love created things. Rather when he desires to dispose himself to love God, because he does not conceive how to go out of himself, he never discovers the way, and therefore goes continually wandering in mere appearances, and thus being always confused and variable in his affections, bad or good, he lives far away from the life of Christian perfection; and so much the more will he live farther from it as the more he becomes enamored of himself, although he may be very perfect in outward observances; because God requires the heart.

He who loves God performs everything he does for him. I would say that he is moved to this by the love he bears to God, and this he does with as much warmth and earnestness as the degree of affection moves or incites him. And thus if he love anything besides God, he loves it for the sake of God, and because God wills it so, and he likewise loves himself, because he knows that God wills that he be loved. Such a one, friar or nonfriar, because he has his love ordered in God, takes hence the mode and manner how he should love all created things and is most regulated and ordered in his love, and loves nothing inordinately. And now his good works please and are grateful before God, because he is moved to work by the impulse of love, because as God is love, so no work is grateful to him that is not done by love. Agreeable to this is what Saint Augustine says: "Good works follow them who are already justified, and do not go before in him who has to be justified."[13] I mean to say that works are good when done by a person already justified, and none can be justified unless he stand in love and charity with God and his neighbor.[14] In such a manner a person will be more perfect, the more he continues fervent in this love. You can confirm this truth yourself by considering how you estimate what a person does in your affairs when you know that he is not moved to do it by the affection he bears toward you, but by

---

13 For the Augustinian position with respect to the relation of justification and works, see Etienne Gilson's *Introduction a l'Etude de Saint Augustine*, J. Vrin, Paris, 1949, pp. 200 ff. and W. J. Oates, *Basic Writings of Saint Augustine*, Random House, 1948, V. I, "On Nature and Grace," p. 540; "On the Grace of Christ," p. 602; "Enchiridion," p. 675; "On Grace and Free Will," p. 743.

14 The influence of Saint Augustine is obvious in all Valdés' works. On the importance of Christian love (agape) in Valdés' thought, see my Introduction. For the same theme in Augustine, see the above-quoted volume of his *Basic Writings*, "Enchiridion," pp. 719, 727, and "On Grace and Free Will," p. 763.

some other design of his own. But since you wish one not born under the obligation to love you, to serve you for love, as all of us are born to love God, think whether God would at least require from us the same that you wish; how much more from those persons who are regenerate and born again in Christ, by the new, spiritual regeneration through faith and baptism; because such of us have a fresh obligation to love God. Speak I of one obligation? Rather should I say infinite obligations, since we see that he loved us infinitely, and Christ loves us, and by infinite modes and ways he sought, and still seeks to bring us to himself and to unite us with himself through grace and love. Reflecting on this, I am sure you will make yourself capable of this truth, that Christian perfection consists in loving God, and that each one will be so much more perfect as he shall so much the more love God, whether he make monastic vows, or whether he make them not, provided only that he keep the vow that he made in baptism by which we are Christians.

G: I rest satisfied now with what you have said of perfection, in such a degree that I already know from your argument what I had not known until now. And since you wish me to take for my chief purpose the love of God and of my neighbor in order to become a perfect Christian, and I determine to do so, it will be well, if you please, to mention some rules by which I may know and understand what it is I ought to do, and how I must conduct myself not to swerve from the love of God and of my neighbor; because I wish absolutely to give myself up to be enamored with God, so much so as may deprive of God's favor, not only you, but a hundred others like you.

V: Be deprived of favor! No! Learn rather, *signora*, that in this divine love there is no jealousy because it is communicable from itself. And it is thus, that so much the more you love God, so much more you will rejoice that God loves others of us, and that God should be loved by others of us. But leaving this, until you learn it in time by experience, I say, *signora*, that there are no better rules for this that you ask than those God has given to us in his most perfect law, which we understand not like the Jews, but as Christians, in the form and manner in which Christ declared it. It teaches us what we ought to do in order not to swerve from the love of God and of our neighbor.

THE TEN COMMANDMENTS

G: If it be not troublesome to you, since you say that the rules of the law of God are right for what I desire, it will be well that you should briefly describe the way in which you understand them.

V: I will do so very willingly because I know this is the door that leads and conducts you in the way I have pointed out. But as I desire that my words should not generate scruples in your conscience, I wish to advise you first of this, that I will explain to you the law of God, not in a manner that you are obliged to observe it under pain of mortal sin, but in the way that all those persons should understand it who desire to become so much masters of their own affections and appetites as that they may in all things be obedient to the Spirit. For, as he is in danger of poison who carries a viper or scorpion in his bosom, so he goes in danger of mortal sin who bears about his affections and appetites active and entire.

G: You have found out the scruples. Take no further care, but begin to tell me, for I shall remain so attentive that perhaps I shall not lose a single word.

Thou Shalt Love Thy God

V: You ought to do so. You will take for the *first rule* to make God in such a manner absolute lord of your heart that you do not hope or confide in any created thing, nor love or fear, except God alone. In a manner that then you may be able to count that you keep your heart ordered conformably to this rule, when, despoiled of all mere human affections, you shall feel within you that neither prosperity will elevate you, nor adversity depress you, honors will not make you proud, nor injuries abase you, and with all this, you shall continue to believe in Christ, hope in Christ, love Christ, and live safely and contentedly with Christ, embracing the cross of Christ, and taking it as sweet to suffer with Christ, having in abhorrence the glory of the world, and holding the pleasures of the world as bitter.

And since it is not enough that the heart be kept in this manner if the lips do not conform to it, it is proper that you take as a rein to them the *second rule*, and this will be that you continually praise, magnify, invoke, and bless the name of God, slighting and holding in little consideration your own name and glory, in such manner that all your words go always directed. And because the divine Majesty is much offended by our oaths, we should ever hold in remembrance those words of

Christ, where, after he has reminded us that we should by no means swear at all, he says: "Let your communication be yea, yea; nay, nay,"[15] meaning to say that when we would affirm a thing, we should assert it with a simple yes; and when we would deny a thing, we should deny it by the like simple no. Because when more than this is said, it is a sign that the heart is not well ordered.

Again, since God is not satisfied without being absolute lord of our hearts and of our lips, but wishes to govern our actions, take for the *third rule* to make an offering to God of your whole will, referring it in all and for all to his divine Majesty, in such mode that he may regulate it and govern it without your putting into your concerns anything of your own. And this remitting of yourself to the divine will, you should know, *signora*, is the celebrating of the Christian Sabbath, for by bodily rest is understood the spiritual rest, and by servile labors are understood the works of sin. Saint Paul entreats us to make this offering, saying: "I beseech you therefore, brethren, by the mercies of God, that ye present your bodies a living sacrifice, holy, acceptable unto God,"[16] in a manner that you entirely offer to him all your will, all your understanding, all your memory. And I entreat you also, that you do not conform your conduct to the conduct of persons of the world, and that you be transformed by the renewing of your mind, that you may know and understand the will of God.[17]

See here, *signora*, three rules according to the three commandments of the law of God, which are so spiritual that while you observe them, you may be certain that you truly love God in the manner he desires to be loved. And consider that you will be so much nearer, or farther from this love, as you feel your affections and appetites remain nearer, or farther from conformity with these three rules, which I entreat you to print on your memory. And though it will indeed be, that while you live in conformity with these rules, living with love to God you will live in love to your neighbor, it may therefore seem in a manner superfluous to give you any rule for this yet considering that God, to assist our weakness, has also given us rules by which we may live in love toward our neighbor, I am willing to repeat them. And so you will take those already given, as well as these now mentioned, as rules of God and not mine.

The *first rule* will be, such being the will of God, that with

15 Matt. 5:33–37.   16 Rom. 12:1.   17 Rom. 12:2.

inward obedience you obey and be submissive to your parents, to your seniors, to your superiors in whatever pre-eminence or authority they may be, not opposing them, nor murmuring at them. And observe, *signora*, that you do not think to satisfy yourself with exterior observance, because God is not satisfied that his commands be kept only in appearance, but he chiefly desires the heart.

And because the worldly things most corrupting to Christian charity are strifes, hatred, and enmities, from which proceed homicides, I wish you to take for the *second rule*, that you make your mind patient, quiet, pacific, humane, compassionate, all feelings of hatred, anger, and retaliation being eradicated and banished. Doing this, you will live conformably to that doctrine of Jesus Christ which in short says that we should not be angry against our neighbor, nor scorn him by outward signs, nor revile him with injurious words. And consider, that you cannot do this, unless you have first composed your mind in the manner I have told you. And that you may conceive the great importance of this, consider what Saint John says: "Whosoever hateth his brother is a murderer."[18]

So that in order not to be homicidal, you must allow to die in you all feelings of wrath, retaliation, rancor, and ill-will. Begin, then, *signora*, henceforward to make this self-denial, for the sooner you begin it, the sooner you will come out of it, and pass on to the *third rule*. This will be, that you endeavor, as much as possible, to hold all your outward senses subjected, in such manner, that nothing rude or disreputable may ever pass through them to your mind. For God desires that your actions, your words, and your thoughts may be chaste and modest. And in order to be able to fulfill this, it is proper that you keep your feelings so subdued as I have said. It is proper also that you be temperate in eating, in drinking, and sleeping, in intercourse with worldly persons, and, in short, in all those things that can generate in your mind any unlawful desire. Know surely that as well to preserve your mind pure and spotless as also not to offend Christian charity, it is necessary that all the sensual appetites, from which spring many hindrances to the love of our neighbor, should die out. Therefore, Christ, closing the entrance of such thoughts to us, says: "Whosoever looketh on a woman to lust after her hath committed adultery with her already in his heart."[19] So that he who wishes not to sin

18 I John 3:15.   19 Matt. 5:28

desires the affections and appetites toward sinful things within him to die out.

Another rule is, because this *mine* and *thine* are mortal enemies of Christian charity, God provides us a healthy, wise and necessary doctrine, which you may take for the *fourth rule*. This is, that you subdue in your heart all desire and appetite for those things which people of the world call good, in such degree that, not putting any happiness in them, you do not even wish for what you have not; and that you possess those things you have, not as owner, but as a trustee, so that if you were wronged, you would not be so disturbed as that you should come to feel ill-will toward the person, or those persons, who took them from you. Then, having your mind so well ordered, you will willingly do what Christ says, whether as to leaving the cloak to him who would bring you into litigation for the gown, or as to giving up your property to them who demand it.[20] This is Christian liberality, and this is the true poverty so much praised and commended in the Holy Scriptures. And I certainly believe that David for this calls them poor who so serve and obey God. And hold for certain that this is the true way to root out and expel cursed avarice, which is so intimate an evil that they are little aware of it who are most addicted to it. But ask Saint Paul the inconveniences that follow from it, and he will tell you that covetousness is idolatry.[21]

Thus, as God wishes us not to offend divine love by the lips he lays down the second rule, which I have mentioned, speaking of the care you ought to take for the love of God, so also for the care of the love of our neighbor he lays down a rule over the tongue, and this will be the *fifth rule*. This is, that you keep the tongue well ruled and governed, and use it only for the glory of God, and for the religious or physical good of your neighbor and your own, taking away and removing from you every occasion that may lead or induce you to let anything escape from your lips that offends, or may offend, the most lowly or abject individual of all who are found in the world. And that you may see how important this is, I wish you to know that Saint James says: "If any man offend not in word, the same is a perfect man."[22] And notice, *signora*, that I do not tell you that in order to keep the commandment of love toward his neighbor perfectly, a person must do all these things precisely, for I do not say so; but that a person who wishes to be perfect must

---

[20] Matt. 5:40–42.   [21] Col. 3:5.   [22] James 3:2.

keep all his affections so obedient and well regulated that when it may be needful for the honor of God to do so, he will not find in himself a repugnance to them.

In conclusion, I may say that you ought to compose your mind in conformity with these five rules which you have heard, if you wish to attain to the love of your neighbor perfectly, and maintain yourself in it, which Christ comprises in a *single rule* saying: "Do unto others what you wish others should do unto you."[23] And it is so, that there is no person in the world who is not pleased by being obeyed by them who ought to obey him; nor is there an individual who is not pleased to preserve his life, or not to have ill-will or hatred from another; nor any who are not pleased that people entertain no ill thought of their wife, children, sisters, or relatives, especially as to disreputable deeds; nor is there anyone who is not pleased to be assisted and succored in his necessities, and who, if he have property, does not endeavor not to be wronged, or encroached upon; and finally, there is no one who is not pleased when everybody speaks well of him, and who is not grieved by the contrary. So that doing to our neighbor all that would please us that he should do toward us, we should accomplish the law of God, since we keep ourselves in accordance with them in love and charity. And on this, as Christ says, hang all the law and the prophets.[24] To this you can resolve all that is written in the sacred Scriptures.

G: You have kept me so much surprised after you began to enter into these rules, considering what perfection is necessary in order to live in conformity with them, that I have been unwilling to reply to anything that you have said. But now that you have finished, I wish you to tell me whether all those persons are condemned who do not live with the purity, sincerity, and care that you have described in these rules.

COMFORT IN SAINT JOHN

V: Saint John, in one of his epistles, says: "My little children, these things I write unto you, that ye sin not. And if any man sin, we have an advocate with the Father, Jesus Christ the righteous. And he is the propitiation for our sins."[25] This same I say unto you, *signora*, that I set before you this perfection, in order that laboring and attaining to live conformably to it, you may never sin. But should you commit sin, I wish you to

[23] Matt. 7:12.   [24] Matt. 22:40.   [25] I John 2:1-2.

remember that Jesus Christ is your advocate before his eternal Father, who satisfied for our sins and for the sins of the whole world. So you may not think that the persons will therefore be condemned, who have not so mortified their appetites as I say that I wish you to hold yours, according to these rules that I have shown you. Yet I wish you to know, that those persons who, not arriving at this perfection, but having opened their eyes, and known their evil way and discovered the way which Christ teaches, according to what I have here told you, if they would be saved, endeavor and strive to walk in this path, truly, as far as human weakness allows, mortifying the old man, and renewing the new, whilst they do not arrive at perfection, they confess in the sorrow of their soul that they are not what God would wish them to be. Having this lively conviction, they use most affectingly the expression of the Lord's Prayer: "Forgive us our debts," and those of David: "Create in me a clean heart, O God! and blot out my transgressions; therefore I acknowledge my iniquity, and my sin is ever before me."[26] If all who walk by the Christian way would always thus perfectly live as we have said, Saint John would not have said that if we say we have no sin, we deceive ourselves, and the truth is not in us,[27] and a just man falleth seven times and riseth up again.[28] And know, *signora*, that he is a just man because he goes by the way of justification, which is that which Christ taught us. He who falls through weakness, and turns to arise again through the faith and trust that he has in Jesus Christ, will be forgiven; and these are the infirmities which Saint Paul means, when, speaking of Christ, he says that we have a high priest who can have compassion on our infirmities, having been himself clothed with the garment of humanity.[29] The whole affair consists of leaving at once the way of the world and entering into the way of God; and after having entered upon it, falling and rising, stumbling and not falling, everything goes well for us. Hence fear not the purity of this Christian perfection. And so I entreat you rather that you may enamor yourself of it, for I warrant you, that you would never have understood it, if God had not first internally taught it to you. And because he gives you to understand it, proper it is that you should dispose yourself to experience it.

G: I would wish this, that you would let me comprehend, for what purpose God sets before us a rule so painful to observe

26 Ps. 51:3–10.   27 I John 1:8.   28 Prov. 24:16.
29 Heb. 4:15.

that we have always to confess ourselves his debtors; for it has in appearance an odor, I know not how, of tyranny.

On the Difficulty of Observing the Law

V: Rather know, *signora*, that God has shown the love he bears toward us as well in this as in all the rest he has done for us, for so arrogant is the human mind that unless it were acknowledged debtor to fulfill the whole law, it would not consider itself as a sinner and unless it considered itself a sinner, it would not fear the judgment of God; and unless it were humbled it would not gain the grace of God and without his grace it could not become justified before him, and if not justified, then not saved. Now think whether this singular blessing of God may not be as good as all the others! And know, *signora*, that so much as a person in this present life will be more perfect, and will stand more united to God in love and charity, so much the more will he humble himself before God, as knowing more his imperfection and the necessity he has that God would continually pardon him his faults, and purify and accept his actions. Therefore David calls, not those persons who never sinned, blessed, for all have sinned, but he calls them blessed to whom God pardons the sins they commit.[30] Do you rest satisfied with this explanation?

G: Yes, I rest satisfied; you can now proceed further.

The Three Ways of Sin

V: I wish you now to consider that in this present life we sin in three ways: through evil design, through ignorance, and through weakness. They sin by evil design who neither know the way of God nor wish to know it. According to Saint Paul, the sin of these is punished by blindness and obstinacy in sin.[31] God pronounces a similar sentence by Jeremiah. These with difficulty raise themselves, as Jeremiah says. Through ignorance they sin who, not caring to discover the way of the Lord, depart from him.[32] He is ready to pardon these, according to Saint Paul, for so he says that because he sinned through ignorance in persecuting the Christians, God had mercy on him. They sin through weakness who, having entered upon the way of God, wish in no manner to offend his divine Majesty, but at times

---

[30] Ps. 32:2.   [31] Rom. 1:28.   [32] Jer. 5:4.

fall, overcome by temptation. David was one of these, and one of such was Peter, when he denied Christ. The sin of such as these God pardons more readily than any others, because as soon as they know it, they speedily humble themselves and thus quickly regain the grace of God. It even frequently happens that, humbled by the sin, they walk more resolutely on the Christian way. Thus David shows it occurred so with him, saying: "Good for me was it that thou humblest me, that so I might learn thy forgiveness."[33] I have wished to tell you this because you raise in your conscience all sorts of scruples, which are commonly born of self-love, and slight knowledge of God, being certain that walking by this Christian way you will not sin, except through weakness. God will quickly forgive you for this in which you so offend, by the humility with which you will ask his pardon, and through the faith and trust that you will maintain in Jesus Christ.

G: You have entirely given me life by this, for you had kept me greatly terrified.

V: If you wish to banish all fear from your soul, love Christ, *signora*, for no fear can ever dwell in the soul which sets its view with a lively and efficacious sentiment on Christ crucified, considering with entire faith that Christ made atonement and payment for it. Now I say, *signora*, in conclusion, that these rules will lead you to the love of God and of your neighbor, and will preserve you in both. And then you will know by experience the fruits of charity, according as Saint Paul describes them, saying: "Charity suffereth long, and is kind; charity envieth not; charity vaunteth not itself, is not puffed up, doth not behave itself unseemly, seeketh not her own, is not easily provoked, thinketh no evil, rejoiceth not in iniquity, but rejoiceth in the truth; beareth all things, believeth all things, hopeth all things, endureth all things."[34] You will also know, that which Saint John says that perfect love casteth out all fear from the conscience.[35] For they who truly love have no fear.

G: I am already satisfied with what refers to charity. May it please God to make me feel and relish it in my soul as well as you have made it penetrate my understanding. But because at times I have heard you say that charity is the fruit of faith, I wish you to tell me something relating to faith.

[33] Ps. 119:71.   [34] I Cor. 13:4–7.   [35] I John 4:18.

CHARITY AS THE FRUIT OF FAITH

V: It is true, as you say, that I have told you that charity is the fruit of faith. And do you know why I said so? Because I am sure that where there is a living faith, there is charity. And know, *signora*, that, as fire cannot fail to warm, so a living faith cannot fail to work deeds of charity, and you must imagine that faith is like a tree; as the tree when it is dried up yields no fruit, so faith wanting in the heart of a person, there is no charity. And notice, *signora*, that when I speak of faith, I do not understand by faith a mere historical belief in the history of Christ, for this can well exist without charity, and therefore Saint James calls the faith bad Christians have a dead faith, such as the evil spirits of hell have.[36] But understand that when I say faith I mean to speak of that faith which is alive in the soul, acquired not by industry, nor human contrivance, but by means of the grace of God communicated with supernatural light. This faith gives credit to all the words of God, as well to his threatenings as to his promises, so that when it hears said what Christ said, that he who will believe and is baptized shall be saved, and that he who will not believe shall be condemned,[36] giving such credit to these words as holding them for a certainty, it has not the least doubt of salvation.

G: In this we so well agree, both you and I, because in believing, no one shall be before me.

V: Do not presume, *signora*, that you believe, for very spiritual must he be who would have a faith so lively as to be fit to be justified by it. Rather know that you are weak in the faith, and call upon Christ with the apostles: "Lord, increase my faith!" and say with the lunatic's father: "Lord, I believe, help thou mine unbelief!"[37] And in this manner you will gain more than by persuading yourself that you believe. It is a great thing, *signora*, to obtain from our souls that they entirely confide in God. You will see it by this: that if you are asked whether you believe the articles of faith, one by one, you will answer yes; but if inadvertently, on your coming to confession, they should ask you whether you believe that God has pardoned all your sins, you will say you think so, but that you are not certain. Now know that this uncertainty arises from want of faith, because if you entirely relied upon the words of Christ, who says to the priests[38] that whatsoever they shall bind on earth shall be bound in heaven; and whatsoever they shall loose

36 James 2:17–19.   37 Mark 9:24.   38 Matt. 18:18; John 20:23.

on earth shall be loosed in heaven; and if you shall truly believe that which you confess in the Creed when you say that you believe the remission of sins, you will not hesitate to say with a full voice, feeling grief in your soul for the offense done to God, and having confessed it, that you hold it certain that God has pardoned all your sins. Do you wish to see clearly and manifestly how you do not entirely confide in God? Tell me with what thing you would rest most without care and be most at ease with, and in what you most confide to assure yourself that you have this year wherewith to live upon; whether with a good sum of money that you have in a bank, or in that which Christ promises to them who seek the Kingdom of God, when he says to them: "Take no thought, saying what shall we eat, or what shall we drink, or wherewithal shall we be clothed? Since God takes thought for you, seek first the Kingdom of God, and God himself will provide for you all these things."[39]

G: There is no doubt but that I should have most confidence in the money in the bank. But if I knew myself so perfect as to merit that God should take thought of me, perhaps I should then trust more in the words of Christ.

V: Rather it is the contrary. The more perfect you might be, so much the want of merit would you find in yourself. And it is thus, that he who stands nearest to the grace of God stands farthest from thinking that he merits it. And for this reason Saint Paul said that by the grace of God he was what he was; not attributing anything to his own merit.[40] So that, *signora,* if you have little confidence in the words of Christ, it is not because of what you say, but through not giving credence to them; and this is the greatest injury you can do toward God.

G: You are too sharp with me. You will soon make me to believe that I have no faith.

V: I do not wish you to believe that you have it not, but I wish you to think that what you have is a dead faith; and I wish you to pray very urgently to God, that he would quicken it and make you strong in that faith, for according to Saint Paul, without faith no one can please God;[41] and if you are willing to notice this, you will find that in nothing can your friend offend you so much as by not giving credence to your word; and on the contrary, nothing can do you greater service, or give you more pleasure, than by his giving entire faith to whatever you shall say to him.

[39] Matt. 6:31–33.   [40] I Cor. 15:10.   [41] Heb. 11:6.

G: In this you so rightly speak the truth, that it extremely grieves me when I am not believed, and I am greatly pleased when others give me credence.

V: Since you know this of yourself, you ought at least to think the same of God. And thinking so, you should labor to confine and subject your intellect to the obedience of faith; thus you would learn to confide in God and to give entire faith to his words, as much so when he threatens as when he promises. Not to dwell much upon this, I may say that if we put all our confidence entirely in Christ, giving entire faith to all his promises, we shall not depend upon, nor be so bound to, created things, in which we put more confidence than we do in Christ, since we are carnal and we judge of things only so far as the outward sense represents them to us, and so we make no count of the interior. I could well tell marvelous things if I wished to begin to praise faith to you, but this is enough to know, that you will be so far a Christian as you shall know that you confide in Christ; it being thus—that to be a Christian person is to be justified; and no one can be justified except by faith, because the just live by faith.[42]

Faith and Hope

G: Never have I been able to understand fully what difference there is between faith and hope; and it would gratify me to know from you in what manner you distinguish between them.

V: I do not wonder that you do not understand this, because the same thing occurs to many learned persons. Know then that faith is exercised in the things of the present life, hope in those of the life eternal. This you should understand in this way. You wish to go from the pier to the Isle of Capri, but you do not know how. I come to you and say, "Trust yourself to me, *signora*; for I will lead you on foot by the hand without your being drowned in the passage, and when crossed over, I will place you in that spot of the island where you desire to be." You, although it appears to you a thing beyond all reason, give credence to my words, and, trusting in them, you take my hand and walk through the water. See here, faith carries you, and you are at the same time borne up by the expectation of enjoying the satisfaction you have said you should feel when you

[42] Rom. 1:17.

should find yourself upon the island. Do you now comprehend the difference?

G: Yes, very well.

A GUIDE TO CHRISTIAN PERFECTION

V: Now, turning to our subject, I wish, *signora*, that you set before the view of your soul the idea of Christian perfection, according to what we have discoursed, and that you set yourself to be enamored of it, and when enamored of it, you will not satisfy yourself until you have reached very near to it; and consider that you will then be near it when you shall know in truth that your heart is not inclined to love anything out of God, nor your tongue taste sweetness in naming any other name than that of God, and this only when naming it for his glory. And when you shall feel that you are not inclined to perform anything that may not be conformable to the will of God; and when you shall find your mind most obedient and submissive to your superiors, and far removed from all ire and all revenge and rancor, filled with peace and humility; and as far removed from all sensual vice that you will not find in it a thought that is not chaste; and so poor in spirit, that you would incline your desire to nothing more than to preserve what it has; and so fervent in love toward your neighbor that you not only never speak to his prejudice, but if you hear others speak so, you excuse and exculpate him as much as possible; by all this I wish to say, that when you shall feel yourself as dead to the outward affections and appetites as to the interior, that neither the estimation of the world exalts you nor its dishonor abases you, that neither anger overrules you nor envy molests, nor less the flesh disturbs you—then well and truly may you believe that you are indeed near to Christian perfection. I say not that you should imagine you are not in a good state, when you are not so much advanced in Christian perfection as I have said; but I say that until you feel and know this perfection within, such as I have depicted it, you should not fail to entreat God continually that he would increase it in you, although you should come to perform miracles; and on the other side, until you should feel yourself very strong and firm in this Christian perfection, I would not wish that you should think you had gained anything. This is the perfection to which Christ invites us when he says: "Be ye perfect, even as your Father in heaven is perfect."[43] Saint Paul invites us to the same, saying to us: "Be ye therefore followers of God as dear children";[44] and in another place saying: "Follow me as I have followed Christ."[45] To the same perfection I invite you, and to the same I desire you to ask me to come by words and by works.

G: O my God, what would I pay to see a Christian so perfect as the one you have here pictured! I think it would be worth that I should strip myself of all that I have.

V: And would it not be still better to see yourself as perfect a Christian as I have here described?

G: Yes, but this is impossible!

V: How impossible? Do you not know what Christ says, that all things are possible to him who attains,[46] as it were naturally, to put his whole confidence in God?

G: I have indeed heard say so, but I am weak.

V: And yet so much the more you are weak so much greater will be the grace of God which will make you strong; if then you confess in sincerity that you are weak, and trust in Christ, he will strengthen you. Do you not know what the gospel says, that the things that are impossible with men are possible with God?[47]

G: I desire it so much that I dare not expect it.

V: Now if you wish it, ask it of God, and entreating him for it, as Saint James says, confidently, he will give it you,[48] and I promise you that it will not be wanting to you. A grand thing this is, that persons wish to be believed in their promises, being naturally fickle and, as David calls them, liars, and that they are not willing to give credence, nor trust themselves to the promises of God! I truly believe that this may be the greatest injury that a person can do to the divine Majesty, as to believe and trust in his promises is also the most grateful sacrifice that can be made to him.

G: Do not care to detain longer upon this point, but begin to guide me in this way of Christian perfection; since you have already enamored me so much of it, that it seems as though I could not live content until I attain it, if not entirely, at least in such a degree as may be needful to me, that my concerns may become accepted in the sight of God. But it is understood that you always have regard to lead me so privately that no person be sensible of me, because, if I can avoid it, I wish not to give occasion for talk among the people.

[43] Matt. 5:48. [44] Eph. 5:1. [45] I Cor. 11:1.
[46] Mark 9:23. [47] Luke 18:27. [48] James 1:5.

V: I will do what you say; but notice, *signora,* that again I wish you to promise me to govern yourself by what I shall say to you, because I shall not be willing to have lost my time, and that you should remain the same individual as before.

G: Trust me; and I promise you that, with the grace of God, before many days you will see the effect of your words upon me.

BIBLIOGRAPHY

I

WORKS BY JUAN DE VALDÉS NOT INCLUDED IN THE SELECTIONS

Cartas Inéditas de Juan de Valdés al Cardenal Gonzaga. Introduction and Notes by José F. Montesinos, Madrid, Revista de Filología Española, 1931.
Commentary on the Gospel of St. Matthew, translated by John T. Betts, London, Trübner and Co., 1882.
Commentary on St. Paul's Epistle to the Romans, translated by John T. Betts, London, Trübner and Co., 1883.
Comentario a los Salmos. Escrito por Juan de Valdés en el siglo XVI y ahora impreso por primera vez. (Editado por Manuel Carrasco.) Madrid, Librería Nacional y Extranjera, 1885.
Diálogo de la Lengua, edición de J. Moreno Villa, Madrid, Saturnino Calleja, 1919.
Diálogo de la Lengua, Introducción y notas por José F. Montesinos, Madrid, La Lectura, 1928.
Instruzione Cristiana e Comparazioni, Firenze, Tip. Claudiana, 1884.
In qual maniera si doverebbono instituire i figliuoli dei christiani (?) 154. . . . (Prohibited in the Index for 1549.)
Qual maniera si dovrebbe tenere a informare insino da fanciullezza i figliuoli dei christiani delle cose della religione. S. n.t.
Lacte spirituale col quale si debbono nutrire et allevare i figliuoli dei christiani in gloria di Dio. *Proverb.* I. Accio che a piccioli sia data prudentia, et a giovinetti scientia et intelletto. De tali è il regno di Dio. *Luc.* XVIII. Pavia, Francesco Moscheno, 1550.
Illustri atque optimae spei puero D. Eberhardo, Illustrissimi Principis et Domini Christophori Ducis Wirtembergensis & c. filio primogenito munusculum Vergerii exulis Jesu Christi. s.1.4.6., MDLIIII.
Lac spirituale, pro alendis ac educandis christianorum pueris ad gloriam Dei. Munusculum Vergerii. Illustrissimo Domino Nicolao, illustrissimi Principis D. Nicolai Radivili Ducis Olicae ac Nesuvisi, Palatini Vilnensis &c., primogenito. A diecta sunt: Varia aliorum authorum. (155?.)

Ein Edel Schrifftlich Kleinath und verehrung des Ehrwürdigen Herrn Petri Pauli Vergerii, An des Durchleüchtigen Hochgebornen Fürsten und Herrn, Herrn Christoffs Hertzogen zu Würtemberg. u. erstgebornen Son, Herrn Eberhartum, lateinisch geschriben: Dieser Zeit aber zu nutz und wolfarth aller Christlichen lieben Jugendt ins Teüsch gebracht. 2 *Timoth*. 3. Weil du von Kind auff die heilige Schrifft weissest, kan dich die selbig underweisen zur seligkeit durch den Glauben an Christum Jesum. Tübingen, Anno DMLV (sic.).

Upominek. Ktory Vergerius Jasnemu panu, Mikolaiowi. Oswieconego Pana: Mikalaia Radzivila, Kxiazecia W. Olice y Wnieswiezu Woiewody Wilenskiego c. Synowi pierwssemu Poslal. *II Timo. III.* Chciei statecnie, stac, y zostac przy tym czegos sie nauczyl, y coc iest zwierzono, wiedzac od kogos sie nauczyl. A izes iesscze wneth, proczawssy od dziecinnych lath, swiete pismo umial, ktorecie moze dobrze wycwiczyz y wyprawic kuzbawienu ktore iest w Christusie Jesusie. Wycisnal, Alexander Augezdecky, w Krolewcu Pruskym Rohu pañskiego. 1556. (The only known copy of this version is found in the University Library of Koenisberg.)

Lac Spirituale. Institutio puerorum christianorum Vergeriana. Edidit F. Koldewey. Brunsvigae, sumptibus Alfredi Bruhn, MDVVVLXIV.

Lac Spirituale. Johannis de Valdés institutio puerorum christiana edidit Fredericus Koldewey. Accedit epistola Eduardi Boehmer ad editorem dat libri scriptore. Editio altera. Halis, sumptibus G. Aemilii Barthel, MDCCCLXXI.

Geistliche Milch fur Christenkinder, um sie damit zur Ehre Gottes zu nähren und aufzuziehen. Von Juan de Valdés. Aus dem Lateinischen des P. R. Vergerio von Ludwig de Marées. In *Christliches Volksblatt*, VI (21 Juli, 1872), n. 30, pp. 273–279.

Juan de Valdés. *Spiritual Milk*, or Christian instruction for children. Translated from the Italian, edited and published by J. T. Betts. (With the lives of Juan and Alfonso Valdés by E. Boehmer, with introduction by the editor.) London, Trübner and Co., 1882.

Giovanni Valdés. *La Instruzione Cristiana per li Fanciulli.* (Con lettera introductiva di E. Boehmer.) In *Revista Cristiana*, Firenze, X, 1882, pp. 3–15.

Juan de Valdés. *Leche Espiritual.* (Re-traducción española de E. Boehmer.) In *Revista Cristiana*, Madrid, III, 1882, pp. 44–46, 58–62.

Joya cristian del siglo XVI. Manera que se debería observar para informar desde la niñez a los cristianos en las cosas de la religion, por Juan de Valdés. Madrid, Librería Nacional y Extranjera, 1882. (This edition was reprinted in 1884.)

Juan de Valdés. *Instrucción cristiana para los niños. En ocho lenguas.* (Octaglot) *Christliche Kinderlehre.* Die ubersetzungen des sechzehnten Jahrhunderts ins Italienische, Lateinische, Polnische, und neue aus den Italienischen ins Deutsche, Englische, Französische, Engandinische, nebst Rückübersetzung ins Spanische. Bonn, Webers Verlag, 1883. (With an Introduction by Edward Boehmer.)

II

GENERAL WORKS

Amabile, Luigi, *Il Santo Officio della Inquistione in Napoli*, Citta di Castello S. Lapi, 1892.

Amante, Bruto, *Giulia Gonzaga, Contesa di Fondi e il movimiento religioso femenino sul secolo XVI*, Bologna, N. Namichelli, 1896.

Bertrand Barraud, Daniel, *Les Idées Philosophiques de Bernardin Ochin de Sienne*, Paris, F. Vrin, 1924.

Bochmer, Eduard, *Alfonsi Valdessii Litteras XL Ineditas*, in *Homenaje a Menéndez y Pelayo*, Madrid, Victoriano Suárez, v. I, pp. 385–412.

Boehmer, Eduard, *Spanish Reformers of Two Centuries*, Strassburg, Karl Trübner, 1874, 2 vols.

Brown, G. K., *Italy and the Reformation to 1550*, Oxford, B. Blackwell, 1933, pp. 224–235.

Caballero, Fermín, *Conquenses Ilustres, Alfonso y Juan de Valdés*, Madrid, Oficini Tip. del Hospicio, 1873.

Carrasco, Manuel, *Alonso et Juan de Valdés, leur vie et leur écrits religieux*, Génève, Imp. Ch. Schuchardt, 1890.

Cione, Edmondo, *Juan de Valdés, la sua vita e il suo pensiero religioso, con una completa bibliografia delle opere del Valdés e degli scriti in torno a lui*. Bari, Gius Laterza e Figli, 1938.

González Blanco, A. *Juan de Valdés, el gran heresiarca español*, Estudio III, 1919, pp. 353–405.

Hare, Cristopher, *Men and Women of the Italian Reformation*, London, Stanley Paul and Co., 1914, pp. 219–240.

Heep, Jacob, *Juan de Valdés, seine Religion—sein Werden—seine Bedeutung*, Leipzig, Verlag von M. Heinsius Nachfolger, 1909.

Jones, Rufus M., *Spiritual Reformers in the Sixteenth and Seventeenth Centuries*, London, Macmillan & Co., 1914, pp. 235–238.

Linhorff, Lisclotte, *Spanische Protestanten und England*, Emsdetten, H. & F. Lechte, 1934.

Longhurst, John E., *Erasmus and the Spanish Inquisition: the Case of Juan de Valdés*, Albuquerque, The University of New Mexico Press, 1950.

Longhurst, John E., "The Alumbrados of Toledo: Juan del Castillo and the Lucenas," in *Archiv für Reformationgeschichte*, Berlin, C. Bertelsmann Verlag, 1954, pp. 233–253.

Menéndez y Pelayo Marcelino., *Historia de los Heterodoxos Españoles*, Buenos Aires, Librería Perlado, 1945.

Morpurgo, Giuseppe, *Un umanista martire*. Aonio Paleario e la riforma teórica italiana nel secolo XVI. Citta di Castello S. Lapi, 1912, pp. 324–326.

Paladino, Giuseppe, *Giulia Gonzaga el il movimento valdesiano*, Napoli, Tip. Sangiovanni, 1909, pp. 31–56 and 69–74.

Schlatter, Wilhelm, *Die Brüder Alonso und Juan de Valdés*, Zwei Lebensbilder aus der Geschichte der Reformation in Spanisch und Italien, Basel, R. Reich, 1901.

Stern, Eugène, *Alonso et Juan de Valdés*. Thèse à la Faculte de Théologie protestante de Strassbourgh. G. Silbermann, 1869.

Tacchi-Venturi, Pietro, *Stato della religione in Italia alla metà del secolo XVI*, Roma, Milano, Abrighi et Segati, 1909.

Valdés, Alfonso de, *Diálago de Mercurio y Carón*, Introducción y notas por José F. Montesinos, Madrid, La Lectura, 1928.

Valdés, Alfonso de, *Diálogo de las Cosas Ocurridas en Roma*, entre Lactancio y un Arcediano. Introducción y notas por José F. Montesinos, Madrid, La Lectura, 1928.

Webster, W., *Gleanings in Church History*, chiefly in Spain and France, London, S.P.C.K., 1902, pp. 136–157.

INDEXES

Topical and Analytical Index

395

INDEX OF MODERN AUTHORS

BIBLICAL REFERENCES